Difference and Orientation

Series editor: Peter Uwe Hohendahl, Cornell University

Signale|TRANSFER provides a unique channel for the transmission of critical German-language texts, newly translated into English, through to current debates on theory, philosophy, and social and cultural criticism. *Signale|TRANSFER* is a component of the series *Signale: Modern German Letters, Culture, and Thought*, which publishes books in literary studies, cultural criticism, and intellectual history. *Signale* books are published under the joint imprint of Cornell University Press and Cornell University Library. Please see http://signale.cornell.edu/.

DIFFERENCE AND ORIENTATION

An Alexander Kluge Reader

BY ALEXANDER KLUGE
EDITED BY RICHARD LANGSTON

A Signale Book

CORNELL UNIVERSITY PRESS AND CORNELL UNIVERSITY LIBRARY
ITHACA AND LONDON

Cornell University Press and Cornell University Library gratefully acknowledge the College of Arts & Sciences, Cornell University, for support of the Signale series.

Original German-language pieces Copyright © Alexander Kluge.

Introduction and all translations in this volume Copyright © 2019 Cornell University, with the exception of the following previously published translations, which are reproduced here by permission:

Edgar Rietz, Alexander Kluge, and Wilfried Reinke, "Word and Film," translated by Miriam Hansen, *October* 46 (1988): 83–95.

Alexander Kluge, "Kluge on Opera, Film, and Feelings," edited by Miriam Hansen and translated by Sara S. Poor and Miriam Hansen, *New German Critique* 49 (1990): 89–138.

All rights reserved. Except for brief quotations in a review, this book, or parts thereof, must not be reproduced in any form without permission in writing from the publisher. For information, address Cornell University Press, Sage House, 512 East State Street, Ithaca, New York 14850.

First published 2019 by Cornell University Press and Cornell University Library

Library of Congress Control Number: 2019944779

ISBN 978-1-5017-3920-0 (cloth)
ISBN 978-1-5017-3921-7 (pbk.)
ISBN 978-1-5017-3922-4 (pdf)
ISBN 978-1-5017-3923-1 (epub/mobi)

Contents

Translator Information — ix

List of Illustrations — xi

Acknowledgments — xiii

Part I Introduction — 1

The Guardian of Difference: The Essayist Alexander Kluge *by Richard Langston* — 3

Part II Literature — 23

1. The Difference: Heinrich von Kleist (1985) — 25
2. Storytelling Is the Representation of Differences (2001) — 43
3. The Peacemaker (2003) — 71
4. Companions in Now-Time (2007) — 84
5. Storytelling Means Dissolving Relations (2008) — 88

6. Theory of Storytelling: Lecture One (2013) 100

7. What Is a Metaphor? (2016) 111

Part III Film 121

8. Word and Film (1965) *by Edgar Reitz, Alexander Kluge, and Wilfried Reinke* 123

9. Bits of Conversation (1966) 142

10. The Realistic Method and the "Filmic" (1975) 155

11. Film: A Utopia (1983) 166

12. A Plan with the Force of a Battleship (2008) 208

13. No Farewell to Yesterday: New German Cinema from 1962 to 1981 as Seen from 2011 (2012) 218

Part IV From Classical to New Media: Opera, Television, Internet 227

14. An Answer to Two Opera Quotations (1983/84) 229

15. On the Expressions "Media" and "New Media": A Selection of Keywords (1984) 249

16. Medialization—Musealization (1990) 293

17. The Opera Machine (2001) 305

18. Primitive Diversity (2002) 318

19. Planting Gardens in the Data Tsunami (2010) 331

Part V Theory 337

20. The Role of Fantasy (1974) 339

21. The Function of the Distorted Angle in the Destructive Intention (1989) 353

22. The Political without Its Despair: On the Concept of "Populism" (1992) 378

23. War (2001)	392
24. The Art of Drawing Distinctions (2003)	407
25. Critique, Up Close and Personal (2007)	434
26. The Actuality of Adorno (2009)	450
27. Inventory of a Century: On Walter Benjamin's *Arcades Project* (2013)	462
28. An Instance of Internet Telephony over the Himalayas (2016)	484
Index	513

Translator Information

The essays and dialogues comprising this book were translated by a team of international scholars under the coordination of Richard Langston. Their contributions are greatly appreciated. They are

Rory Bradley
Martin Brady
Andreas Freytag Hill
Miriam Hansen
Helen Hughes
Steffen Kaupp
Taylor Kent
Richard Lambert
Richard Langston
Samantha Lankford
Sandra Niethardt
Sara S. Poor
Nathan Wagner
Emma Woelk

Illustrations

1. "The battle over film" — 171
2. "Locomotion" — 174
3. "A film like an earthquake, a man like a volcano" — 177
4. Writing conventions for the orders of magnitude — 191
5. People — 192
6. *Easy* — 192
7. The Paramount-Palace on Broadway — 193
8. A media corporation — 194
9. The Etruscan shrew — 198
10. The bumblebee bat — 199
11. Instructions for the transferral of a dead person — 233
12. The pale man — 238
13. Senta — 241
14. *Volksempfänger* on Christmas Eve in 1942 — 258
15. The ENIAC computer in 1946 — 259

16. A microcomputer in 1980 — 260
17. The human nervous system — 261
18. *Paranthropus boisei* and *Paranthropus robustus* — 262
19. Electronics function directly — 263
20. "A powerful servant," formerly a slave — 288
21. Old territory — 289
22. The trust that binds them can be called love — 426

Acknowledgments

I traveled to Munich in the summer of 2010 with the intention of paying Alexander Kluge a visit and floating the idea of an English-language reader of newly translated essays. *Difference and Orientation* is just one of many collaborations and projects that resulted from that initial conversation. Foremost among these were my involvement as principal translator of Kluge and his longtime collaborator Oskar Negt's magnum opus, *History and Obstinacy* (Zone Books, 2014); my editorial oversight of the second volume of the Alexander Kluge-Jahrbuch entitled *Glass Shards* (Vandenhoeck & Ruprecht, 2015); and my forthcoming monograph, *Dark Matter: A Guide to Alexander Kluge and Oskar Negt* (Verso, 2020). The last of these projects to come to fruition, *Difference and Orientation* profited from a wealth of experience and acquired knowledge initially made possible by a research leave supported by the Alexander von Humboldt Foundation. Like everything before it, this anthology would have been impossible without Kluge's long-standing support, for which I am endlessly grateful. Beate Wiggen and Gülsen Döhr at Kluge's DCTP offices in Düsseldorf have also been invaluable interlocutors. Initial work on the translations contained in these pages began in the fall of 2011 and concluded in the fall of 2017. Of the many translators involved in rendering Kluge's thought into English, the esteemed British team Martin Brady and Helen Hughes as well as Samantha Lankford deserve special recognition for joining the original team after the project set sail and making their work available. Responsible for the lion's share of these translations, Emma Woelk was a key collaborator who constantly went beyond the call of duty. Bethany Wasik of Cornell University Press was instrumental, especially in securing rights to reproduce the only two previously published translations included in *Difference and Orientation*. I am indebted to Miriam Hansen's estate for allowing me and Cornell University Press to include her and Sally Poor's seminal translations. Kizer Walker of Cornell University Library and the Signale series was a crucial advocate early on; without his enthusiasm and support, this anthology would have never gotten off the ground. Similarly, the editor in chief at Cornell University Press, Mahinder Kingra, championed the idea for this anthology and generously accommodated its considerable scope. Marian Rogers's meticulous editorial work conferred on the manuscript spit and polish, for which I am most appreciative. Above all, *Difference and Orientation* would have simply never materialized without Leslie Adelson's support. Her advocacy, expertise, advice, and feedback have been the linchpin that ensured that the many essays and dialogues assembled here reach the wide English-language readership they rightfully deserve.

Richard Langston
Durham, North Carolina

Difference and Orientation

Part I

Introduction

THE GUARDIAN OF DIFFERENCE

The Essayist Alexander Kluge

Richard Langston

Born in 1932 in the central German city of Halberstadt, the German polymath Alexander Kluge is certainly known both at home and abroad for wearing many hats. Above all, his career as one of New German Cinema's most cerebral filmmakers still commands international acclaim, even though he officially bid adieu to celluloid with his last feature, *Miscellaneous News* (1986). First and foremost a writer of stories before he ever shot *Brutality in Stone*, his first short made together with Peter Schamoni in 1960, Kluge returned to writing in earnest in 2000 with his massive *Chronik der Gefühle* [Chronicle of Feelings] and has generated since then an astonishing complex corpus of storybooks that has grown more than twice the size of what he published during his first robust literary phase, which was framed by his literary debut, *Attendance List for a Funeral* (first published in German in 1962 and later republished as *Case Studies*), and the extensively revised fifth German edition (1978) of his second book, *The Battle* (the first edition of which was published in

1964). Far less accessible to English-language audiences when inaugurated in the second half of the 1980s, three "cultural windows" were broadcast weekly on late-night German cable television by Kluge's television production company, Development Company for Television Program, at its peak, and have continued uninterrupted into the present, making him a singular phenomenon in the history of the medium. Few if any can lay equal claim to his long-standing status as television auteur with unobstructed authority as both executive producer and director. A wave of recent translations in English (not to mention Chinese and most European languages) and affordable reproduction technologies have increased the worldwide accessibility to not only Kluge's television programs but also his films and literature. A filmmaker, author, and television producer, Kluge is, however, more than just the sum of this triumvirate. He is also recognized as a trained musician and lawyer, an accomplished theorist with roots in the Frankfurt School, a savvy media activist and entrepreneur, and a celebrated public intellectual of the highest stature. The translated texts assembled in *Difference and Orientation* bear witness to yet another long-standing preoccupation, one enmeshed in virtually all of his other spheres of activity. Kluge is also arguably one of Germany's great essayists of the late twentieth- and twenty-first centuries. Collected in the present volume are twenty-eight examples of Kluge's essayistic thinking that attest to his long-standing commitment to what his friend and mentor Theodor W. Adorno once called the essay's affinity to "intellectual freedom."[1]

Calling Kluge an essayist may initially strike readers of this anthology as a strange proposition, especially given how a quick scan confirms that roughly half of the texts contained in the following pages look less like what we formally expect of essays and more like run-of-the-mill dialogues. Sorting Kluge's massive canon according to medium and then genre would appear to substantiate such doubts. Even though occasional essays by Kluge have appeared in German literary and theory journals (like *Merkur*, *Kursbuch*, and *Ästhetik und Kommunikation*) as well as in miscellaneous anthologies since the sixties, he has published so few stand-alone volumes of collected essays throughout his sixty-year career that they can be counted on just a few fingers. When thought of in these terms, Kluge the essayist appears to pale in comparison to other more prolific German essayists like his contemporaries Hans Magnus Enzensberger and Karl Heinz Bohrer, or Michael Rutschky and Botho Strauß from the next younger generation, or even elders, mentors, and idols like Adorno, Walter Benjamin, Heinrich Böll, Siegfried Kracauer, Thomas Mann, and Robert Musil. What counts as the first formal anthology of Kluge's essays—*Gelegenheitsarbeit einer Sklavin: Zur realistischen Methode* [Part-Time Work of a Female Slave: On the Realistic Method, 1975]—was written in response to Helke Sander's scathing feminist critique of his film of the same name released in 1973.[2] Other volumes, like his *Theodor Fontane, Heinrich von Kleist und Anna Wilde: Zur Grammatik der Zeit* [Theodor Fontane, Heinrich von Kleist, and Anna Wilde: On the Grammar of Time, 1987] and *Personen und Reden* [People and Speeches, 2012], complicate matters further given the fact that most of what looks like essays therein were originally speeches. Apart from these exceptional instances curated by Kluge himself, the few remaining compendia of Kluge's essays have been compiled by others and usually limit their scope to cinema.[3] How then is it possible to call Kluge an essayist when so much of what we might designate as his own bona fide essayistic output is the result of a defensive strategy or a concession to institutional rituals? Does the essay really belong to Kluge's core register of expression? What, for that matter, is to be gained by calling Kluge's speeches and dialogues essays? Are his essays limited to just his printed work, or does the term also apply to his films and videos? In other words, where exactly does the essay reside in Kluge's oeuvre, and what relationship does it assume to the rest of his work?

What may look dubious from one perspective appears quite obvious from another. Overlooking the status of these aforementioned essay collections entirely, film scholars have had few if any qualms calling Kluge the filmmaker an essayist, especially given how both his celluloid films (1960–86) and his recent video films, like the nearly ten-hour *News from Ideological Antiquity: Marx-Eisenstein-"Capital"* (2008), all conveniently fall under the aegis of the "essay film."[4] Indeed, Kluge once availed himself of this designation when reflecting on the seemingly ambitious objectives for his penultimate 1985 film, *The Assault of the Present on the Rest of Time* (also known as *The Blind Director*). In an essay on his film's ambitions, he writes: "In cases where experience, or, rather, its translation is blocked, we need to resort to the format of the essay film. I know of no other possibility for conveying such an abundance of material so quickly."[5] Yet this admission is actually one exceptional instance of Kluge making explicit mention of this subgenre; more often than not, he writes and speaks of just films, stories, or broadcasts without any further qualification. Certainly not limited to just film studies, scholarly appeals to genre employed in an effort to pin down Kluge's idiosyncratic works invariably give rise to narrow classifications and artificial hierarchies that reflect little on just how the essayistic infiltrates all of Kluge's works regardless of medium. Some of his greatest films (like *The Patriot* [1979] and *The Power of Emotion* [1983]) accompanied film books that contain not just screenplays, but also essays and stories that together must be recognized as robust instantiations of a sustained indexical practice crisscrossing, to and fro, different mediums without concern for adhering to the rules of genre. "Regardless of whether one is dealing with a documentary or a feature film," Kluge writes in the essay "The Realistic Method and the 'Filmic'" included here, "the most intensive observation or most probable plot is predicated on the schema of its genre that excludes real contexts."[6] The logic of genre with its categories, rules, and divisions is, in other words, an anathema to Kluge's longstanding, core interest in forging otherwise indiscernible connections by transcending the "artificial opposition[s]" that such conventions generate.[7] The key to Kluge's realistic method, and by extension his essayism, has always been the principle of montage he robustly theorized in the context of his filmmaking as both a theory of and attendant praxis for forging cognitive relationships that no camera can record and no films can ever show.[8] Hardly limited to just his films, the contrasts and gaps typical of montage are also present, albeit in transposed form, in Kluge's literature, television programs, streaming video, and video films. With the explicit inclusion of indexes in his recent books, films on DVD, and online streaming videos, Kluge has in fact upped the ante, insofar as readers and viewers are encouraged now more than ever before to think about relationships that exceed the boundaries of genre and flow across his multiple media.

Difference and Orientation

To call Kluge an essayist is therefore not to speak of a distinct subgenre in his multimedia oeuvre, but rather of a peculiar way his work thinks critically about the "real contexts" of contemporary life. In his seminal essay "The Essay as Form," published three years after he serendipitously met the twenty-four-year old Kluge at a classics lecture held at the Goethe University Frankfurt, Adorno extolled the essay as a hybrid form when most postwar West German academics frowned upon it as something trivial and relativistic. For Adorno, the essay's reliance on play and luck, its aversion to methods and systems, as well as its open, fragmentary character, are just some of the many features that made it for him "the critical form par excellence."[9] The essay's unique claim to truth—or more accurately its repudiation of culture's untruths by penetrating "what hides behind the façade under the name of objectivity"—is also a function of its ability to stand in relation to other spheres of experience and knowledge without ever replicating them; neither a pure and tidy philosophy nor an "aconceptual intuitive" art, the essay nevertheless "has something *like* aesthetic autonomy," Adorno insists, and aspires to its own conceptual thought while behaving "cautiously toward theory."[10] In this respect, the aforementioned "abundance of material" typical of many of Kluge's essays is not merely a function of their formal features; the essay's aloof propinquity to the concerns of theory and art is also what facilitates Kluge's wild mixture of narration, illustration, commentary, and abstraction without ever fully occupying or conflating them. "What I do," Kluge explains in an interview with literary critics Ulrich Greiner and Iris Radisch included in the following pages, "is below the threshold of literature."[11] And in his first 2012 lecture on poetics held at the Goethe University Frankfurt, where he had met Adorno nearly sixty years earlier, he confessed from the outset, "I am . . . the court poet of the great philosophers. I myself am no philosopher."[12] There is indeed much more in Adorno's essay on the essay (like, for example, the role of the object, interpretation, its incorporation of truths and untruths, and happiness in the essay) that resonates with Kluge's own hybrid, fragmentary forms, regardless of whether they are cinematic (film, video, streaming video) or literary (stories, speeches, dialogues, essays) in nature. Arguably, the most important point is, however, Adorno's elucidation of *how* the essay thinks.

It is not the essayist who thinks but rather the essay itself—Adorno calls it "an arena for intellectual experience"—and it does so idiosyncratically and in opposition to dominant modes of thought predicated on scientific and philosophical notions of truth.[13] To this end, the essay negates, says Adorno, the "compulsion of identity" and instead "allows for the consciousness of nonidentity."[14] In other words, it traffics in difference, the very ingredient that Adorno and Max Horkheimer said instrumental reason was dead set on expelling from the world.[15] "Differentiatedness," he goes on to underscore, is the essay's "medium."[16] It is, in other words, the hallmark of dialectics. If there is one recurrent theme throughout all of Kluge's thought collected in these pages, then it is that of difference. "We writers," he proclaims in his acceptance speech for the Kleist Prize that begins this volume, "are the guardians of the last leftover bits from the grammar of time, a difference between present time, the future, and the past."[17] To the rhetorical question "Can film attain the same expressive effects as highly differentiated language?" Kluge and his coauthors, Edgar Reitz and Wilfried Reinke, provide a resounding yes.[18] In order to grasp the productive possibilities of television, it is not enough, he says, to comprehend how film and new media *"are aligned under different stars"*; one must also acknowledge how television stands as a hybrid between them.[19] To understand the full potential of critique, what Kluge identifies as an elusive human "capacity to differentiate practically at the crucial moment," we must recognize *res extensa*'s ability to interrupt *res cogitans*.[20] In spite of the considerable weight Kluge's thought consistently places on the production of difference, be it temporal, expressive, medial, or critical, it would surely be an oversight to equate his sense of difference with that of Adorno's. Whereas the latter operates exclusively according to the "principle of contradiction," the former identifies dialectics as just one of several possibilities.[21] "Dialectics is a category of relationality [*Zusammenhangs*]," Kluge recently explained, "but multidimensionality is also a category of relationality. It can be dialectical, but it does not have to be so."[22]

Both of these manifestations of relationality—dialectical and multidimensional difference—are equally important for Kluge's essayistic thinking. The first evokes Adorno's account of the essay as a "critique of system," but in Kluge's hands the locus of this critique shifts in part from the thinking mind to the sensing body.[23] Suspicious of the eye's (and, by extension, the mind's) weakness for immanence (like Adorno before him), Kluge writes of an embodied critique in the form of the allergic reactions of the skin, the keen and especially trustworthy ear, the hardened soles of the feet, the unruly diaphragm, just to name a few.[24] As he first articulated it in his aforementioned 1975 essay collection, *Gelegenheitsarbeit einer Sklavin*, Kluge groups these decentered protests under a dialectical theory of realism not in terms of any aesthetic method, but rather as the human capacity he calls the "antirealism of feeling."[25] In his Frankfurt lectures on poetics held in June 2012, he uses broad anthropological strokes to sketch the origins of this feeling in the art of survival: "In the course of the evolutionary process, only those humans survived who were capable of repudiating those conditions of reality that did not mean them well. They did this not only on a large scale through uprisings and revolts, but also imperceptibly by taking everything they perceived in reality and deflecting it slightly through illusion."[26] What both social revolt and storytelling's illusions have in common is a shared antipathy to what Sigmund Freud once called the reality principle, yet this negative reaction is only a first step. The critical, says Kluge, must also eventually turn "positive and practical," and to this end his essayistic thinking seeks out reality's multidimensionality.[27] The prison of reality resides on the surface of present experience, yet reality also burrows into "catacombs, wells, and abysses," a polyphony of underestimated temporalities that can be articulated using grammatical moods like the subjunctive and optative, tenses like the present perfect and *futur antérieur*, and time spans evolutionary and planetary, if not cosmic, in dimension.[28] Asked in the same interview with Greiner and Radisch whether his rummaging through time serves a utopian-like principle of hope, Kluge replied: "No, I am looking for the principle of ways out."[29]

Looking for ways out of the prison house of reality requires guarding temporal differences that industrialized consciousness, manifest for Kluge in commercial cinema and television, otherwise threatens to demolish. It involves distinguishing not just past, present, and future, but also fortuitous *kairos* (the time of good fortune), from the forward march of *chronos* (mechanical time) toward future disaster. Seeking out such opportunities entails employing facts and fiction in equal measure just as it avails itself of ambiguity and metaphor, narrative and image, and solitary monologue as well as collaborative dialogue. It means delineating a provisional space akin to a garden where more time and experience can be cultivated beyond the mayhem brought on by the Internet's flood of information and data. All of this counterproduction, Kluge underscores in his poetics lecture, ultimately boils down to a matter of orientation. Taking Immanuel Kant's reflections on orientation as his model, Kluge points out in his poetics lecture two basic forms of orientation available to experience:

> When I talk about orienting oneself, I mean it in the sense of lighthouses, of which there are two kinds. Using lanterns, wreckers based on the shores of the North Sea would lure ships into running aground so that they could be looted. All of Sylt is comprised of such loot assembled there in the island's church. The second sort of orientation is the orientation toward objects we humans can neither reach nor touch, objects that cannot be displaced. One example of such objects is stars in the firmament. Stars are a means of navigation for ships at sea and wanderers in the desert alike.[30]

Orientation is, in other words, achieved through either direct or indirect experience; in each instance, the conditions conducive to differentiation are what matters. Yet as Kluge's illustrations of wreckers and wanderers suggest, neither immediate nor mediated experience is inherently more advantageous for a successful outcome, even though we humans tend to orient ourselves "according to the criteria of *direct* life experience."[31] Unable to discern a wrecker's lanterns from legitimate lighthouses, seafarers directly learn only too late that the light source informing their plotted course was motivated by deception and doom. Conversely, wanderers lost in a desert can never judge firsthand the source of light radiating down from the starry firmament, but their safe passage is all but guaranteed, assuming they weather their journey back home. Essential is not only maintaining a balance between these two very different types of experience but also ensuring their relevance for orienting oneself. Yet this capacity also entails an additional faculty, one responsible for assigning trust to orientation that differentiation can provide. As the range of Kluge's engagements with the history of media included in this anthology shows, the historical vicissitudes of trust are closely tied to the increasingly mediated nature of social experience—the rapidly metamorphosing postclassical public spheres of today—and their attendant challenges to our powers of differentiation. This critical negotiation of difference, orientation, and, by extension, trust comprises the core of all of Kluge's essayistic thinking. While some readers may care to enlist the texts assembled in this volume as "hermetically privileged entry points" into the elusive meanings of Kluge's notoriously perplexing books, films, and broadcasts, others may care to recognize in concentrated form an opportunity for studying this very search for difference and orientation operative in all of Kluge's essayistic thinking.[32]

Notes on Text Selection

At first glance, the divisions in *Difference and Orientation* may give readers the impression that Kluge is quite simply a multimedia artist at home in not just one or two but four, if not five, *métiers*. With its four ensuing sections on literature, film, media, and social theory, it would appear that the "doctrine of medium specificity," along with its attendant essentialisms, is also operative in Kluge's shifts from one medium to another.[33] Yet the very word "media" fails to capture the core of Kluge's project. In a brief position statement on media published in 1979, he opined, "People talk of 'film producers' and 'screenwriters.' Accordingly, television, video companies, radio, and film all regard themselves individually as mediums when, in fact, they are actually forms, conditions under which a medium emerges. It is never specialists but rather real people who are the real medium of experience [*Erfahrung*], wishes, fantasies, and even an appreciation of art."[34] While Kluge does write of individual media—in his essay "Film: A Utopia," he offers, for example, a typology of the happy endings "organized according to media"—readers will surely notice that in every section of this anthology focused on one medium Kluge invariably addresses others and therewith implies a larger medial array at work in his aesthetic politics, one in which all his many forms are connected and communicate with one another.[35] This does not, however, imply that Kluge's literature, for example, is film by another means. What Kluge achieves in one form is indeed predicated on a difference with respect to others, but this difference is never ontologically fixed.

Difference and Orientation provides English-speaking readers with a broad, exemplary spectrum of Kluge's essayistic thinking spanning the entirety of his career. While some texts included are essential (like "Film: A Utopia," of which there exist three different versions), others were chosen for their ability to either represent Kluge's thinking at crucial historical junctures or address his engagement with particular themes and problems. Given the sheer enormity and sprawl of Kluge's writings and dialogues, a certain degree of arbitrariness was unavoidable, and yet the regularity with which Kluge recycles and revises his ideas ensures that practically every niche of his thought, including many of the topics from his theoretical collaborations penned together with social philosopher Oskar Negt, can be found here. As the overwhelming majority of texts appear here in English translation for the first time, the objective for this volume has also been to ensure complementarity with the readily available translations published largely in academic journals. In only two cases have previously published translations of essential works been reproduced in the present volume: Miriam Hansen's "Word and Film," originally published in *October* in 1988; and excerpts from Sara Poor and Hansen's co-translation of Kluge's seminal thinking on opera, originally published in *New German Critique* in 1990.

The remaining selection of texts took cues from Christian Schulte's exhaustive, German-language collection of Kluge's cinematic writings *In Gefahr und größter Not bringt der Mittelweg den Tod*, originally published in 1999. The four essays in Schulte's reader included here in translation compliment the eleven Kluge texts included in Tara Forrest's English-language anthology, *Alexander Kluge: Raw Materials for the Imagination* (2012).

Difference and Orientation begins with that aesthetic form—namely, literature—with which Kluge embarked on his career. It was 1958 when Kluge, disenchanted with the legal profession, left his legal mentor Hellmut Becker for West Berlin and, at Adorno's recommendation, worked as luminary filmmaker Fritz Lang's intern on the set of *The Tiger of Eschnapur* (1959), a studio production that stripped Lang of his authority.[36] When not mediating Lang's opposition to the film's meddling producer, Kluge spent his time in the canteen writing stories he had already started as a lawyer.[37] Both of Kluge's breakthroughs, his storybook *Attendance List for a Funeral* (1962) and his feature *Yesterday Girl* (1966) based on the story "Anita G." included in his literary debut, can be traced back to these early days of writing. Whereas neither writing nor filmmaking took precedence in the sixties and seventies, both would eventually take a backseat over the course of the eighties as a result of the grueling demands of producing television. In the nearly two decades since 2000 when Kluge suddenly returned to literature like never before, the number of English translations of his storybooks has increased by 80 percent (there are thirteen discrete titles available to date), yet English readers have at their disposal virtually none of Kluge's many recent reflections on storytelling. Instead of reaching back to his literary beginnings around 1958, the first chapter in part 2 of *Difference and Orientation* begins with Kluge's 1985 acceptance speech on the occasion of receiving the Kleist Prize, which had been revived after a half-century hiatus. Chapters 2, 3, and 5 then jump to three subsequent dialogues that capture Kluge's thinking at the time of his first three book publications in the new millennium: *Chronik der Gefühle* (2000), *Die Lücke, die der Teufel läßt* [The Devil's Blind Spot: Tales from the New Century, 2004], and *Tür an Tür mit einem anderen Leben* [Next Door to Another Life, 2006]. An oblique meditation on books and collecting, chapter 4 echoes Benjamin's reflections on the topic in his 1931 essay "Unpacking My Library." Chapter 6 includes the first of four lectures Kluge gave in 2012 in conjunction with the acclaimed series Frankfurt Lectures on Poetics. Chapter 7, the final chapter in part 2, finds Kluge joining the fray that has engaged a great many intellectuals who have deliberated on the power and importance of metaphor.

Well aware of the wealth of Kluge's cinematic essays already available in translation, *Difference and Orientation* includes in part 3 texts intended to round out these existent resources. It begins, in chapter 8, with the aforementioned reprint of the coauthored 1965 essay "Word and Film" by Kluge, Reitz, and Reinke, originally published when all three taught at the Ulm School of Design's trailblazing film department.[38] An interview between Kluge and Enno Patalas and his wife, Frieda Grafe, published in the film journal *Filmkritik* shortly after Kluge received the Special Jury Prize at the 1966 Venice Film Festival then follows in chapter 9 and provides insights into the making of his first feature, *Yesterday Girl* (1966). Chapter 10 provides readers access to one of the last remaining, untranslated portions from Kluge's aforementioned essay collection of 1975 on antagonistic realism, *Gelegenheitsarbeit einer Sklavin*. The crux of part 3, the seminal essay "Film: A Utopia" that constitutes chapter 11, finds Kluge reflecting on the radical potential of auteur cinema at precisely that moment at the dawn of commercial television when cinema's livelihood was in the balance. The final two chapters, 12 and 13, document Kluge's far more recent retrospective evaluations of Soviet avant-garde cinema practices (which inspired his own *News from Ideological Antiquity* [2008]) and the organizational politics that gave rise to New German Cinema as seen through the uncertainty of cinema's future in the new millennium.

Part 4 zooms out from Kluge's engagement with cinema to what might be best called his long-standing genealogical interest in pre-cinematic forms of the classical public sphere. Before cinema emerged at the end of the nineteenth century, public life in Europe was captivated by the emotional economy of opera and, before it, the dramaturgy of the circus. To each of these forms,

Kluge has dedicated a feature film: *Artists under the Big Top: Perplexed* (1968) is his circus film; *Power of Emotion* (1983) is the culmination of his interest in opera; and his penultimate film, *The Assault of the Present on the Rest of Time* (1985), like the aforementioned essay "Film: A Utopia," tarries on cinema itself on the eve before turning his energies full-time to smuggling the principle of auteurism into television, beginning a year later. Much more than an academic interest in cinema's precursors, Kluge's films and the attendant essays included in this section ultimately grow out of his and Negt's conviction that a transformation in the public sphere never obliterates its previous instantiations. What Negt and Kluge call the "pseudo-public spheres" orchestrated by today's "consciousness and programming industry" merely sit on top of classical forms of the public sphere, of which the circus and the opera are but two among many examples.[39] The viability of authentic social experience in the postclassical age of public spheres of production thus boils down to the possibility of counterpublics emerging at the seams and fractures between all the many coexistent spheres of publicity.[40] Seen from this vantage point, the essays included in part 4 of *Difference and Orientation* testify to Kluge's expansive engagement with the public sphere. Whereas the essay in chapter 14 engages with opera on its own terms, the dialogue in chapter 17 queries opera's historical relationship to film. The dialogue in chapter 18 ruminates on Kluge's indebtedness to the cinema of attraction. Chapter 15 finds Kluge reckoning with the distinctions between classical media and new media, the advent of which Kluge ties to the advance of digital technologies, attendant reductive forms of programming, the acceleration of experience, and the acquisition of new forms of private property located in viewers' heads. In chapters 16 and 19, he turns to old and new forums (the museum and the Internet) that have become especially important in his most recent collaborations.

Keeping in mind Adorno's caveat that essays do not rigorously deduce themselves from theory, readers should recognize that the contributions in the fifth and final part of *Difference and Orientation*, entitled "Theory," constitute neither in part nor in whole a discrete theoretical corpus either detached from the rest of Kluge's aesthetic work or the exclusive property of his collaborations with social philosopher Oskar Negt. On the contrary, these nine works attest to both the indebtedness to and distance from theory Kluge's essayistic thinking maintains. Chapter 20 on fantasy reaches back to Kluge's days as an honorary professor lecturing on film and television at Goethe University Frankfurt in 1973, a year after his first collaboration with Negt, *Public Sphere and Experience*, appeared. Chapters 21, 26, and 27 demonstrate not only Adorno's and Benjamin's strong influence on Kluge's theoretical orientation, but also Kluge's points of departure from his mentors' work. Chapter 22 on populism and passivity makes available for the first time in English one of four essays Kluge penned alone for his third collaboration with Negt, *Maßverhältnisse des Politischen* [Measured Relations of the Political, 1992]. As Kluge was a student of the history of war like his father, his encyclopedia entry on war in chapter 23 harks back to both his controversial book on the Battle of Stalingrad, *The Battle* (1964), and those portions of the third book of *History and Obstinacy* (1981) coauthored with Negt on war as a special case of the public sphere of production. Kluge's dialogue in chapter 24 and his thought-images in chapter 25 illustrate the origins and consequences of his theory of feeling for critique. Closing the anthology is Kluge's Skype conversation with renowned Chinese literary scholar Wang Hui, recorded in the spring of 2012. A testimony to Kluge's desire to think beyond Europe's geographic and intellectual boundaries, the interview, which was held following a public screening of *News from Ideological Antiquity* subtitled in Chinese, engages the viability of Marxist thinking in the age of globalization and testifies to the centrality of cooperation and collaboration in the form of dialogue for Kluge's essayism.

On Reading and Translating Kluge: Word, Text, Image

Kluge's essayistic thinking assumes myriad guises. How he writes a formal essay is vastly different from how he delivers a prepared speech to an audience, and this, in turn, is quite different from how he dialogues with another person face-to-face. Unlike his speeches and dialogues, Kluge's essays written for readers are especially vexing. When reading such essays, readers piece together parts of a puzzle, get their bearings, and then cautiously move forward, only to encounter another roadblock not far down the road. This is at least what Kluge's translators encounter when rendering his essays into another language. In its most condensed form, Kluge's essayistic thought is always jumping, shifting, jerking, and spinning. He regularly traffics in repetition and rephrasing as well as commentary and digression such that distinctions between parataxis and hypotaxis make readers pause. Frequently, long strings of concatenated clauses bury subjects at the end of sentences. His word choices are occasionally antiquated or highly technical, but never arbitrary. His punctuation is unorthodox; readers regularly encounter, for example, extensive semicolon-laced lists, colons and equal signs that stand in for copular verbs, and singular em dashes that substitute for adverbs. Italics, capitalization, and bold typeface are frequently used for emphasis. Sentence fragments, digressions, commentaries, and excurses frequently interrupt the flow of thought. Seemingly unnatural tenses (like his guru Walter Benjamin, Kluge often writes in the present tense about past events), the incorporation of unattributed quotations, and the unexpected shift in voice are equally disorientating. Similarly, Kluge occasionally slips in and out of first-person singular voices that are often not his own. All of these features make for a sometimes dense and difficult read. For the translator of Kluge, all of these idiosyncrasies boil down to the fundamental question as to whether to preserve the German original's character at the expense of immediate intelligibility or to mold the originals in an effort to maximize the reader's access to Kluge's thought. As was the case with the translation of *History and Obstinacy*, the translations included in *Difference and Orientation* have sought out a middle ground that preserves as much of Kluge's form as possible while nevertheless ensuring that English-language readers hear both his voices and their messages. This means that the translators made difficult decisions regarding such matters as punctuation, sentence fragments, long concatenated clauses, the passive voice, the frequent inversion of subject and object, and the frequent use of the impersonal "one" (*man* in German) modeled after Robert Musil's writing, just to name a few.

Customary in many translators' introductions to theoretical texts are glossaries that identify and define concepts from the original language especially difficult to render into English, concepts that merit qualification for newcomers unfamiliar with the semantics of the original in order for the fullness of their meaning and significance to fully resonate. No such glossary is included in *Difference and Orientation* and with good reason. Readers will certainly notice throughout the entirety of *Difference and Orientation* that Kluge's essayistic thinking does avail itself of a recurring set of concepts, the meanings of which are not always self-evident. Concepts like the cumbersome "relationality" (derived from *Zusammenhang*, which is also sometimes rendered as "context") or the deceptively simple yet remarkably complex "reality" (which Kluge captures as *Wirklichkeit* and *Realität*) are just two among many that he has glossed in the appendix to the second volume of social philosophy that he coauthored with Oskar Negt, *History and Obstinacy*.[41] Readers should at the very least keep in mind this extensive glossary penned especially for foreigners when working through Kluge's many ideas contained in the following pages. Another layer of concepts operative throughout *Difference and Orientation* are those that Kluge has acquired from his Frankfurt School mentors. Arguably the two most important for Kluge's (and Negt's) thinking about the public sphere are *Erfahrung* and *Erlebnis*, both of which mean "experience" in English but have radically different meanings in German according to the philosophical writings of Adorno and Benjamin. Novices unfamiliar with these distinctions, not to mention the many other conceptual trappings of the German tradition of Critical Theory woven into Kluge's essays, would profit enormously from the insightful introductions to Kluge and Negt's translated collaborations.[42] What readers will not find in these indispensable resources is an annotated catalogue of concepts exclusive to Kluge's aesthetic theory and its attendant practices that are scattered throughout the essays and dialogues contained in *Difference and Orientation*. Quite often such concepts not sufficiently explicated in one essay resurface in a later work in this volume with ample clarity. Accordingly, the volume's index should prove especially helpful for readers unclear about Kluge's language. In exceptional instances, the editor and translators provide in the endnotes brief glosses of peculiar concepts, unfamiliar historical events, and forgotten people. Also included in the endnotes are not only Kluge's many commentaries and citations, which appeared in the original more often than not in the form of footnotes, but also many of those citations omitted in the original that the editor and translators successfully identified in the course of the translation process.

Kluge has avidly incorporated images since the seventies into not only his stories but also his essays and dialogues. One third of the works included in *Difference and Orientation* included images in the German original. Given structural limitations for the following volume, only four of these ten texts are reproduced with some, if not all, of their accompanying illustrations. In these cases, the substantive intratextual dialogue between word and image required their inclusion. Often designated as "figures" in the German originals, Kluge's images do not conform to readerly expectations of illustrations. Rarely do his images just illustrate an essay's content in subordinate fashion. What they show is rarely what is seen. The relation to and significance of images for the content of Kluge's illustrated essays are anything but self-evident. Kluge's images operate within a web of intertextual references, some of them linguistic and others visual. Captions seldom explain what is shown, but rather index thought beyond the frame. Often organized in clusters, Kluge's images are themselves dialogical and thus require viewers to read them against one another for the differences and the orientation they provide.

Notes

1. Theodor W. Adorno, "The Essay as Form," in *Notes on Literature*, trans. Shierry Weber Nicholsen (New York: Columbia University Press, 1991), 1:3.

2. See, for example, Helke Sander, "'You Can't Always Get What You Want': The Films of Alexander Kluge," trans. Regina Cornwell, *New German Critique* 49 (Winter 1990): 59–68. See also Heide Schlüpmann's essay "Femininity as Productive Force: Kluge and Critical Theory" in the same volume; and Jan Dawson, ed., *Alexander Kluge and "The Occasional Work of a Female Slave"* (New York: Zoetrope, 1977).

3. The best example is Alexander Kluge, *In Gefahr und grösster Not bringt der Mittelweg den Tod: Texte zu Kino, Film, Politik*, ed. Christian Schulte (Berlin: Vorwerk 8, 1999). For English readers, Tara Forrest's anthology casts a wider thematic net with its selection of scholarly essays and eleven Kluge texts, including television conversations, interviews, excerpted literary texts, and essays. See Tara Forrest, ed., *Alexander Kluge: Raw Materials for the Imagination* (Amsterdam: Amsterdam University Press, 2012).

4. For example, Timothy Corrigan writes: "For me and others, Kluge is one of the most important theoreticians and filmmakers associated with the essay film." See Timothy Corrigan, *The Essay Film: From Montaigne, after Marker* (New York: Oxford University Press, 2011), 207n15. Similarly, Christian Schulte designates the essay film as the supraordinate concept that guided his first coproduced short from 1960, *Brutality in Stone*, from which all of Kluge's other subordinate working concepts (e.g., image, archive, critique, the temporality of *kairos*) follow. See Christian Schulte, "Kritik und Kairos: Essayismus zwischen den Medien bei Alexander Kluge," in *Inszenierung und Gedächtnis: Soziokulturelle und ästhetische Praxis*, ed. Hermann Blume et al. (Bielefeld: transcript, 2014), 243–60.

5. Alexander Kluge, "The Assault of the Present on the Rest of Time," trans. Tamara Evans and Stuart Liebman, *New German Critique* 49 (Winter 1990): 13. Translation slightly modified to accord with the original: Alexander Kluge, *Der Angriff der Gegenwart auf die übrige Zeit: Das Drehbuch zum Film* (Frankfurt am Main: Syndikat, 1985), 12.

6. Alexander Kluge, "The Realistic Method and the 'Filmic,'" 156 in this volume.

7. Alexander Kluge, "On Film and the Public Sphere," trans. Thomas Y. Levin and Miriam B. Hansen, in Forrest, *Alexander Kluge*, 33.

8. Kluge, "On Film and the Public Sphere," 46.

9. Adorno, "The Essay as Form," 18.

10. Adorno, "The Essay as Form," 4, 7, 8, 5, 18 (emphasis mine).

11. Alexander Kluge, "The Peacemaker," 73 in this volume.

12. Alexander Kluge, "Theory of Storytelling: Lecture One," 100–101 in this volume.

13. Adorno, "The Essay as Form," 13, 11.

14. Adorno, 17, 9.

15. Max Horkheimer and Theodor W. Adorno, *The Dialectic of Enlightenment: Philosophical Fragments*, ed. Gunzelin Schmid Noerr, trans. Edmund Jephcott (Stanford, CA: Stanford University Press, 2002), 5.

16. Adorno, "The Essay as Form," 15.

17. Alexander Kluge, "The Difference," 41 in this volume.

18. Edgar Reitz, Alexander Kluge, and Wilfried Reinke, "Word and Film," 125–26 in this volume.

19. Alexander Kluge, "On the Expressions 'Media' and 'New Media,'" 256 in this volume.
20. Alexander Kluge, "Critique, Up Close and Personal," 434 in this volume.
21. Theodor W. Adorno, *Negative Dialectics*, trans. E. B. Ashton (New York: Continuum, 1983), 5.
22. Richard Langston, "'Das ist die umgekehrte Flaschenpost': Ein montiertes Interview mit Oskar Negt und Alexander Kluge," *Alexander Kluge-Jahrbuch* 2 (2015): 64.
23. Adorno, "The Essay as Form," 9.
24. On Adorno's distrust of images, see Alexander Kluge, "The Function of the Distorted Angle in the Destructive Intention," 360–62; on the skin and ear, Kluge, "Critique, Up Close and Personal," 446–47; on the passion of the feet and the resistance of the diaphragm, Kluge, "The Art of Drawing Distinctions," 412–13—all in this volume.
25. Kluge, "Theory of Storytelling: Lecture One," 103 in this volume. The original essay in which this theory of antirealism first emerges is Alexander Kluge, "The Sharpest Ideology: That Reality Appeals to Its Realistic Character," trans. David Roberts, in Forrest, *Alexander Kluge*, 191–96.
26. Kluge, "Theory of Storytelling: Lecture One," 103 in this volume.
27. Kluge, "Critique, Up Close and Personal," 441 in this volume.
28. Kluge, "Theory of Storytelling: Lecture One," 103 in this volume.
29. Kluge, "The Peacemaker," 76 in this volume.
30. Kluge, "Theory of Storytelling: Lecture One," 101 in this volume.
31. Kluge, "On the Expressions 'Media' and 'New Media,'" 266 in this volume.
32. Georg Stanitzek, *Essay—BRD* (Berlin: Vorwerk 8, 2011), 14.
33. Noël Carroll, *Theorizing the Moving Image* (Cambridge: Cambridge University Press, 1996), 2.
34. Alexander Kluge, "Die Medien stehen auf dem Kopf," in *Die Patriotin: Texte/Bilder 1–6* (Frankfurt am Main: Zweitausendeins, 1979), 294.
35. Alexander Kluge, "Film: A Utopia," 182–83 in this volume.
36. Alexander Kluge, "Bits of Conversation," 151 in this volume.
37. Thomas Combrink, "Die Stunde Null als 'Zeitmaß der sich überstürzenden Ereignisse,'" in *Doppelleben: Literarische Szenen aus Nachkriegsdeutschland; Materialien zur Ausstellung*, ed. Bernd Busch and Thomas Combrink (Göttingen: Wallstein, 2009), 300. See also in this volume Alexander Kluge, "Companions in Now Time," 85.
38. In addition to Forrest's aforementioned anthology, which reprints English-language translations of a few of Kluge's seminal film essays, there are also special issues of *October* (Fall 1988) and *New German Critique* (Winter 1990) that are dedicated to Kluge and include important writings on film. Additionally, Eric Rentschler's *West German Filmmakers on Film: Visions and Voices* (New York: Holmes & Meier, 1988) contains six shorter essays spanning Kluge's engagement with film and new media.
39. Oskar Negt and Alexander Kluge, *Public Sphere and Experience: Toward an Analysis of the Bourgeois and Proletarian Public Sphere*, trans. Peter Labanyi, Jamie Owen Daniel, and Assenka Oksiloff (Minneapolis: University of Minnesota Press, 1993), xlvi.

40. On the contemporary conditions for counterpublics, see Miriam Hansen, foreword to Negt and Kluge, *Public Sphere and Experience*, xxxix–xli.

41. Alexander Kluge and Oskar Negt, *History and Obstinacy*, ed. Devin Fore, trans. Richard Langston et al. (New York: Zone Book, 2014), 389–440.

42. See both Hansen's aforementioned foreword (ix–xli) and Devin Fore's introduction to Kluge and Negt, *History and* Obstinacy (15–67). On the distinction between *Erfahrung* and *Erlebnis* as it relates to Negt and Kluge's social philosophy, see Hansen, xvi–xx. See also Richard Langston, "Oskar Negt and Alexander Kluge: From the Underestimated Subject to the Political Constitution of Commonwealth," in *The SAGE Handbook of Frankfurt School Critical Theory*, ed. Werner Bonefeld et al. (London: Sage Publications, 2018), 1:317–34.

Part II

Literature

1

The Difference

Heinrich von Kleist

The inquest and autopsy take place on the afternoon of November 22, 1811. In the evening hours, the two coffins for Frau Vogel and Heinrich von Kleist are laid to rest. Their deaths have a hermetic effect. Something closes itself off. It was once written, "A man who dies at the age of thirty-five . . . is at every point in his life a man who dies at the age of thirty-five."[1] So much for literary quotes. Kleist was thirty-four when he died. It seems wrong to me now, on this occasion of receiving a literary prize that bears Heinrich von Kleist's name, to try and approach the chimera of Heinrich von Kleist. He would fend off any such attempt, even were I to venture it by interpreting just one of his texts. If there is anyone in the German literary tradition who insists on the importance of difference then it is Heinrich von Kleist.

The long interruption, during which the Kleist Prize was not awarded, lasted a total of fifty-two years.[2] Maybe this period of time is, in fact, *a* relationality. The list of prize recipients leaves considerably large shoes for the somewhat smaller literary feet of our own time to fill. I feel *touched*, as you may well understand, that Robert Musil is, for example, among the award's many recipients. My work acquires meaning only if it can seize on one or another thread that Musil left behind. Please therefore allow me to call on the prizewinner Robert Musil as a relay station, if you will, in my efforts today to approach Heinrich von Kleist in a way free of chimera. In so doing, I shall edge closer to Kleist in a manner that is real to me.

The Horizon of Two Centuries

While residing in a cabin in the spring of 1942 during his Genevan exile, Robert Musil makes desperate attempts at editing once and for all the mass of text he compiled to be the continuation of his novel *The Man without Qualities*. He dies in April while doing this. Outside, far away from Swiss soil, the force of history is afoot. Confrontations manifest in industrialized war are rebuilding Europe at exactly that moment. Musil seems not to have troubled himself very much with these current events. He deals almost exclusively with just two decades that capture his attention. He justifies his focus because what developed between 1890 and 1910 has the tendency to devour the entire reality of the twentieth century. These two decades tend, in other words, to comport themselves cannibalistically toward the future, thereby creating an imaginary century. He describes the forces that lead to World War I, forces that incidentally prevent him again and again from finishing his literary work. It could be said that his huge fragmentary novel—2,036 pages in length—actually describes nothing more than the preparation for World War I and does so from the perspective of a group of people not instrumental in making decisions. This group represents, therefore, something extremely hard to grasp, namely, a particularity within a general development: humans who see themselves as secondary characters. He does not master this task he assigns himself, a scrupulous task I regard to be the highest of virtues. He does not allow himself to be distracted by the many events and experiences that occur between 1939 and 1942.

In the meantime, we now have a mere fifteen years left till that point in time when we bid the twentieth century adieu. We have a fin de siècle once again. Robert Musil depicts the last fin de siècle from the nineteenth to the twentieth century, and we are already chroniclers of the turn from the twentieth to the twenty-first century. This century appears to have produced little authentic work. One could even say that the twentieth century needs to be *detained*. It is a continuation of the nineteenth century using other means. It copies the last century. If one reads both centuries as a *single* text of real relations, it becomes an inordinately long period of stagnant time.

There is something else I must underscore further for your consideration, something important in my own quest for connections to Heinrich von Kleist, something I consider to be part of my own self-understanding. I am of the opinion that when we write we authors do not reside on secluded islands like Robinson Crusoe. Of course, we work alone and individually, but it is precisely writing itself that allows for connections to those who worked in the past. For this reason, I cite Robert Musil in order to suggest that when we sit with pencil in hand before a sheet of paper we live in an imaginary laboratory full of other people who take writing seriously.

It is not *I* who writes texts, but rather I write texts when I can disregard the fact that I am an *ego*. Connecting my feelings inherited from my parents and forefathers, the external world, and words, which have their own intractability, is an extremely objective activity. As Kleist says, "For it is not *we* who know things but pre-eminently a certain *condition* of ours which knows."[3] He says this in his essay "On the Gradual Production of Thoughts whilst Speaking." This is, however, not a solitary endeavor, for it links up with past authors. I can only *notice* that they are speaking through me. In this respect, literary texts are similar to music. Past composers speak through contemporary composers.

When I try to explore the phenomena of the fin de siècle using my childhood from the 1930s along with my emotions firmly anchored in that era—my actual parents are sitting there in 1936 and they supply me with a motive—then my navigation relies on other authors, first on Robert Musil and then, if you will, Heinrich von Kleist, as is the case this evening. For me, the matter at hand concerns the cipher of our double century comprised of the nineteenth and twentieth, which will end only calendrically on December 31, 1999.

"But thou wilt scarce demand that I should see things only with thine eyes"[4]

I was born and grew up in Halberstadt located in Germany's Harz region. Permit me now to explore additional connections. Three years after Musil's death in April 1945, a brigade of bombers reaches Halberstadt. The brigade took off from airfields in South England. None of the crew members have any conceivable relationship to the city beneath their warplanes. They are actually on a mission to bomb the city of Stendal, but amid clear skies they report "three-quarters cloud cover," meaning low visibility. They then turn their colossal, flying industrial formation toward Halberstadt and unload their cargo over the city. Herr Frischmeyer, the curator of the Gleim House, where the memory of Enlightenment poet Johann Wilhelm Ludwig Gleim is preserved, survives the attack. But he then notices that the ensuing fire is creeping from the castle steps along a street called Hoher Weg. The educated and bespectacled man convinces three firemen not from the area to help him save the Gleim House. "But why should we save these few oil paintings and wobbly tables in the middle of the firestorm that has blown up our friends and leaders and taken them from us? What is so important about them?" Curator Frischmeyer answers: "Gleim's memory." Therein lies something that amazes me again and again: Where does the motive for excessive, voluntary action come from? The three men knew nothing of Gleim. They did not like Frischmeyer. He was stingy and did not even offer them something to eat. Museums in Halberstadt do not have such things. And still they applied themselves and saved the Gleim House.

There are places in the Gleim House where Heinrich von Kleist set foot. As far as we know, he visited Gleim. One must read, however, the works of Arno Schmidt in order to get a sense of the world in which Gleim counts as the doyen of German literature. The building where this can be experienced, including its wood floors, was saved by the efforts of three irresponsible firemen and is maintained by the cleaning ladies of East Germany's publicly owned Cleaning and Care Service. Kleist began his trip in April 1801, and, beginning on May 18, used his own horses to travel through Halle, Halberstadt, Wernigerode, Brockenbesteigung, and Goslar until he reached Paris with his sister. I recount this connection between bomber squadrons, firemen, museum attendants, wood floors of the twentieth century, and Heinrich von Kleist's trip in 1801 only to emphasize *distance*. The same difference would arise if we were to look at Kleist's visit to Christoph Martin Wieland in the village of Oßmannstedt, where he fell in love with the latter's daughter. We forget all too easily that Kleist lived for twenty-three years in the eighteenth century and only eleven years in the nineteenth century.

This is the first point of my talk. I consider Heinrich von Kleist a part of the eighteenth century for the simple reason that his texts on philosophical language lean in that direction. Thoughts and feelings are for Kleist not two separate spheres. I would like to dwell therefore for a moment on the seam between the eighteenth and nineteenth centuries that also obviously disrupts parts of Kleist's development.

The Seam between the Nineteenth and Twentieth Centuries

A seam between two centuries is a period of thirty years. On New Year's Eve 1918, one could say, I know what this century holds for us human beings. I do not know this information in the year 1900. Between all centuries—but increasingly so between the eighteenth and nineteenth and between the nineteenth and twentieth—these zones of uncertainty are full of new possibilities and blockages.

The eighteenth century is considered the century of the Enlightenment. In 1781, the first edition of Immanuel Kant's *Critique of Pure Reason* appears. In 1789, the news of the French Revolution spreads across Europe. However, this Revolution quickly turns away from the Enlightenment. Processes are set in motion that influenced the nineteenth century about which one could say: Only after 1815 can one see how reactions to the western orientation of Prussian politics, the Holy Alliance, and the shifting of borders in accordance with the Congress of Vienna fully developed.

We are sitting here today in the State Library of the Prussian Cultural Heritage Foundation. This is a completely different building from the one that was originally the Prussian State Library. When you read how the Prussian minister of culture Karl vom Stein zum Altenstein describes after 1815 his intentions for books dating back to the eighteenth century, you realize what is new about the nineteenth century. He says: These books must all be destroyed. Because this cannot be done with the people's approval, they must instead be kept hidden. The library will be divided such that these books are kept in stacks for which visitors will need a small slip of paper to access. They are thus to be institutionally isolated like a prison or a closed hospital ward. He says this within the context of the Holy Alliance, in which members were compliant with the will of confederation. I mention this because a century is about to begin that is characterized by obvious breaks. Thoughts and feelings are separated. The world of social practice and the world of novels are being torn apart. The world of commonwealth and the world of goodwill are falling apart. Times and temporalities are also coming undone. A fictional realism found only in novels is underway that creates order by unifying different times into a single strand. I was, I am, I will be: that is a unity for every one of us. I cannot feel sensations without reawakening in myself the child I was and the parents who influenced that child. Without hope, I cannot even speak. I would be paralyzed. I cannot do without this *one* moment in which there still seems to be something to be decided: this is what we call the present. In this sense, the three grammatical times—I have named only the simple ones here—are present in every moment, thought, memory, thing forgotten, and job done. There is not *one* time, as the novels and new poetry of the nineteenth century would have us believe. Kleist's work makes clear just how broken the old concept of time is.

I spoke of the seam between these centuries, a seam where especially open forms developed. We find them in not only Kleist's but also Friedrich Hölderlin's work. At this seam spanning more than three decades bridging these two antagonistic centuries, three new developments arise while individual forces struggle against one another: *popular war, industrialization,* and the codification of a *new tenderness*. In our own time at the end of the twentieth century, it is important to recognize the changed guises these three elementary processes have assumed, processes that begin in earnest in the early nineteenth century but whose roots go back to the eighteenth century: we find it in the grasping for the stars, which industrialized war does; in the departure from classical industry; and in this chimeric turn toward a new subjectivity reminiscent of the one characteristic of the 1950s. Subjectivity in the 1950s was, however, completely different. Since the beginning of this turn, this new inwardness is really just a turn to an imaginary 1950s. Political change is one of the trappings of this process.

Revolution in Another Country

It is very difficult for us to imagine a revolution taking place in France while the Germans, who, by the way, are still separated into many states, are *observers*. In general, Prussian and Bavarian patriots are observers of an event essentially closed off to them. Regardless of whether it pertains to the freedom of trade in England or the revolution in France, they remain observers. They sit in their box seats. They have time for sensations but no opportunity to do anything.

I could point out all of this in Kleist's tragedy *Schroffenstein*, in the variant ending of his comedy *The Broken Jug*, in the story "The Duel," and in his novella "Michael Kohlhaas." I could also discuss how this relates to Kleist's influences and to the *surplus* of meaning contained in his language. When he writes in *The Broken*

Jug: "Last night conceals some other wrongdoing / than merely the ruination of my jug," we have a new word in the expression "the violence done to my jug" (*Krugverwüstung*), which sounds like *Landesvertreibung* (the expulsion from one's country).[5] And in the phrase "last night" (*die Nacht von gestern*) you actually have a title, a shadow that goes far beyond saying *gestern Nacht*. It is not without reason that these words are metaphorically loaded, because they essentially reveal more than is present within the scene.

We know that in 1801 Kleist was looking for a fresh start in Switzerland. He, for one, did not want to remain solely a spectator. He intends on interesting his bride in a lifestyle change. He wanted to buy a farm in the Swiss countryside. At this point in time, he was motivated by the belief that it would be critical for Europe if the French revolutionaries once and for all schooled themselves and the new human characteristics both commercial and technical in nature that arose out of the Revolution by reading Kant. This could also be seen as a variation on partisanship, a new patriotism, that aims to *connect* the interests of the Prussian patriots with those in new France. Try and imagine that moment: what kind of *craftsmanly* Europe it would be, had manual and intellectual labor been introduced into the spirit of patriotism! Allow me now to briefly describe the following scene.

Fleeing from Russia in the winter of 1812, the pontoniers of Napoleon's defeated army together with their general, Jean Baptiste Eblé, are standing up to their necks in the freezing water of the Berezina River. A bridge is built for the grotesque purpose of evacuating the few surviving units from the Grande Armée. All of these pontoniers died of exhaustion in the following days. "For if your own life you are not willing to stake / That life will never be yours to make."[6] This line, this attitude—but not the language of the usurper Bonaparte's communiqué—are what the young people of Prussia and southern Germany could understand. Additionally, there is concrete cooperation in the Westphalian Kingdom in the streets and poplar-lined roads. But this cooperation was split off from emotional communication and patriotic spirit. These roads are developed thanks to cooperation between French engineers and the German workforce, just like the later railroad tracks designed by Prussian engineers that run in the opposite direction and whose automatism was programmed for the transport of troops in August 1914. It seems to me that there is a central motif in Kleist's work that supports the idea of goodwill. As illustrated in *Schroffenstein*, this motif suggests that these separations are unnecessary and unreal, even when they are compulsory and real in the realm of facts.

The possibility of a cooperative relationality on the Continent, assuming such a possibility ever existed, was decided negatively in the Battle of Waterloo. It was the London Stock Exchange and not the pulse of united craftsmen that decided the fate of the European continent and all the others on our planet for the ensuing two centuries. After losing its Eurocentric orientation, this programmed world that resembled Babylonia now drifts away toward the Pacific Rim, the "Antipodes" as Kleist would say, the Californians. This is convenient for dramaturgically inclined presidents, Hollywood, and all the new suits ready to make comprehensive decisions, mistakes, and divisions anew, as if the task at hand were to bundle two forgetful centuries together.

Kleist's newspaper *Berliner Abendblätter* is another relevant connection. As you know, this is what Kleist planned to live off of. He promised himself to become a journalist and publish a tabloid, a more or less new medium at the time. Neither Mr. Manfred Lahnstein, a modern media entrepreneur for Bertelsmann, nor a director of one of the public broadcasting corporations has ever or would ever produce a television program by themselves. In Kleist's vision for the *Berliner Abendblätter*, he is the entrepreneur, the director, the author, the creator of stories, and the investigator for the daily police reports. He is, to use the language of the Conference of Ministers-President, an "independent producer of programming for the German-speaking world."[7]

At this time, the Prussian public sphere is watched over by suspicious French agents and governed practically like a closed institution. Starting a new entrepreneurship is far too premature. After publishing the 153rd edition of this fascinating newspaper, the enterprise falls apart. We owe *Berliner Abendblätter* thanks for its

Kleistian brevity, not to mention the short prose form itself, and its combination of news, editorials, and fiction. None of our newspapers continues this practice today. Works such as "The Puppet Theater" and the unfinished "On the Gradual Production of Thoughts whilst Speaking," written a few years prior, would have fit in well in its pages. Berlin's messenger boys handed out the paper in the evening for ten pfennigs (I am not exactly sure of the type of currency). These papers were delivered all around Berlin, distributed widely, and Kleist sits there like an innkeeper, excited about every individual customer. He counts the cards, the number of sold copies. Even though this work was never continued, it desperately should be.

"The Duel"; "In martial panoply"[8]

Like Carl von Clausewitz, Kleist uses the metaphor of war as a duel. "Upon my life, I'll force a path," he writes.[9] This proceeds from a *concrete* image of war. I can apprehend my enemy; he is concrete, I can wrestle him to the ground. "In a delirious strange confusion of . . . senses," this type of war carries over into relationships and passions.[10] One recurring form of proof of love and trust between lovers is when one lover drinks from a vial supposedly filled with poison. They accept the poison from their loved one.

In the second volume of *The Man without Qualities*, the following note appears: "Ulrich-Agathe is really an attempt at anarchy in love. Which ends negatively even there. That's the deeper link between the love story and the war."[11] At the time when Kleist penned the words "martial panoply" in *Penthesilea*, we have the beginnings of industrialized war. Newly divided into departments and divisions and grouped together according to tools like hammers, anvils, and pliers, the mass of war machinery—humans and weapons—represents the beginning of instrumentalized battle. What corresponds to this within the Biedermeier home are its taste and emotional characteristics, but tenderness and warmth are doled out according to the division of labor. Coldheartedness is for the sons who are sent out into the winter campaign. Coldheartness is also for the daughters who are forced into bleak marriages with businessmen. Warmheartedness is for every newborn child. Emotional life of the nineteenth century says: Inside is warm, whereas outside is cold. Georg Wilhelm Friedrich Hegel talks about the selective heat and coldness at the heart of this so-called *feeling's* transmission from generation to generation. Industry, popular war, and a new tenderness all have the same embryonic kernel. Tenderness is about nothing more than war. Now if I look here in Berlin at this kernel not from the vantage point of November 22, 1811, but rather from December 31, 1918—a time when I can see where the twentieth century is heading—then I can say that the signs pointing to Verdun must already be in place in their earliest stages. Kleist must have noticed them.

I would now like to bring New Year's Eve 1918 to your attention for a moment: this is a point in time after the end of four years of World War I and the November Revolution, a moment when there was no controlling the government here in Berlin. We have, on the one hand, a socialist government, the Spartacists, and, on the other, the 4th Guard Cavalry Rifle Division. It is total confusion. Wilmersdorf is politically on the right, the eastern part of Berlin is on the left, whatever that means. You have to imagine that the western areas of Berlin were celebrating like crazy. In the *Vossische Zeitung* on New Year's Eve 1918—it was a Tuesday—you can read in the classifieds about everything being offered as a means to forget about the war. And meanwhile, not far from here, at Leipziger Straße 3, in the Prussian Landtag, the so-called House of Lords, where Bismarck held his speech, the Sparticists knew the concierge. That was how they could get in at night. In the middle of the night between New Year's Eve and New Year's Day, they founded the Communist Party. Rosa Luxemburg speaks for the party leadership and gives her speech "Proletarians in Uniform" about soldiers. Nineteen days later she is dead. If you pick up the *Rote Fahne* and look in the classifieds, you see that Ernst Lubitsch, the great director of comedies, is producing *Carmen* as the film industry's response to the First World War. And that he is doing it as a crazy, over-the-top story with Pola Negri. If you take this *Carmen* and think about the fact that we have been captivated by seven versions of the opera *Carmen*, then you see how intensely the progress of human consciousness is carried out in our century.

Back to Kleist: "In the cruel war in which he himself was quite rejuvenated," he says.[12] But he also says, "Go away, my senses will not hold."[13] Of a man who has committed fratricide, Kleist writes that he responds, "concealing the moral harm done to his soul."[14] "Had I been able," it is written at another point, "to look into your eyes . . ., even were everything else about you black, I would have drunk from a poisoned chalice with you."[15] War and love relationships are the two metaphors of emergency. This is what Clausewitz refers to when he says that the worst mistakes are those made with good intentions. The opponent falls into the void of my mistake. These are movements for which neither the will of one nor the will of another is decisive in the real result, because each will is broken by the other. One would have to look at the *results*. That is what any physicist would do. But the way humans develop subjectively, in accordance with the canon of the nineteenth century, makes us look at only our own will and that of our enemy, rather than at the movements of both. Self-consciousness, autonomy, and human dignity cannot be predicated on war or the ability to love. This has been true for the last 200 years, even since the beginning of time. This is Kleist's constant theme. It is *our* unresolved problem.

I will describe for you now a scene that will be accompanied by images from Henri-Georges Clouzot's 1953 film *The Wages of Fear*. Imagine two trucks encounter each other on a lonely stretch of mountain road. There is a sharp descent to the right. It is drizzling or snowing. One of the drivers vaguely sees the other in his cab for a few seconds. If one of the wheels of one of the vehicles touches the wheels of the other, they will both fall into the chasm. How intently both of these professional drivers work their equipment, the steering wheel, the pedals! How respectfully they continue to think of each other for only a few minutes after they have passed each other! They could have seen each other only for a few seconds. How different and disdainful their feelings would have been had the other made a mistake! I call this an *objectified encounter with danger*. This is the only humane development that has ever been brought about by industry and its attendant discipline that is devoid of any ambivalent interference.

How carelessly both drivers presumably treat their wives when they come home, even though this kind of carelessness is just as dangerous as the mountain drive! Our society does not possess an ideal objectivity, neither in times of war nor in those leading up to it, nor in tender relationships. I contend, however, that the curiosity we inherited from Kleist is to be applied here. Robert Musil formulated this as follows: "The difficulty, then, cannot be anything other than a skewed relationship, an abiding miscommunication between the intellect and the soul. We do not have too much intellect and too little soul, but too little intellect in matters of the soul."[16]

I am always asked: "Can't you make it a little cheaper? Can't you make it somehow easier on the viewer? Then you'd sell more tickets at the theater." I cannot do it that way. We filmmakers get just as few discounts as reputable physicists. I once saw an ad on CBS, in which a child says with a fake child's voice (children do not really sound like that) how comfortable he feels in his little bed in his little house. Then he points out the window at a rainbow. This rainbow turns out to be the celestial dome to which a *celestial dome defense* is affixed: and there are the bouncing rockets.[17] The enemy's rockets then arrive and explode. They cannot destroy the house or the child's little bed. This is a commercial for SDI, Star Wars.[18] This is the manner in which you can persuade people and win them over when you do not think very highly of them. Think for a second about what kind of need or childhood desire lurks behind this Ptolemaic worldview: if I could live in a world like a shell again, with my little bed and my little house below the firmament and its little stars! I can even slip through this curtain while on Intourist trips to the Soviet Union. Then I will see distant lands and surprises. The entertainment industry now rejects the Copernican system by way of popular vote, because it relativizes and suddenly jettisons us from the center of the universe. This happens even though we are far removed from the Copernican worldview and modern physicists seriously believe in Einstein.

Take notice of the difference. Under this type of guidance, the soul remains at a standstill while physics marches forward. I would like to align myself with societal relations, with good physics, with objectivity, *precisely because I have feelings* [*Empfindungen*]. The direct combat that plays this role out in Kleist—the personal side of poisoning or seducing—takes us far back in time from our vantage point at the end of the twentieth century. I do not just mean that a combatant in a submarine will never see his opponent in wartime, or that I will not be able to decide if I am brave or cowardly in the thirteen seconds between the time I realize a rocket is approaching and the time it hits HMS *Sheffield*.[19] In that short period of time, it would be entirely pointless. Here we have the end of the battle—a de-objectification of war—that turns war into an accident.

There is another issue here. Humans have practically no influence over decisions declaring war or peace, decisions that determine sovereignty and the freedom of a people as these terms are classically understood. In lieu of wonderfully confused senses, a conspiracy takes hold affecting things, circumstances, completed groundwork, forced alliances, and every coincidence. As Kleist writes, "All a man needs for slipping up is feet."[20] Countless feet have marched back and forth throughout Europe so much, that this no longer holds true. Or, one could say: All the feet that ever were have together rotted into something that has become uncontrollable and that can effectively do only one thing: stumble! We act as if we were helpers standing by.

Significant changes of this kind involving de-subjectification make the act of writing, which still occurs individually and is subject to the fixed editions typical of publishing books, into a luxurious activity. We are writing messages in bottles. I would not underestimate, however, this activity, for within it lies a great deal of continuity.

"His feelings were too soft spoken"[21]

"His feelings were too soft spoken." Kleist writes this in his story "The Duel" about a defense lawyer representing a wrongly accused woman. He relied on going on the defensive in his duel with Count

Jacob, just like the bear does with the fencer in Kleist's essay "The Puppet Theater" and just like General Kutusov does with Bonaparte when he invades Russia. He does this by placing trust in winter. But now the righteous fighter hears grumbling from the audience. Rather than God, he sees the audience of the duel, which includes the Kaiser, as the arbitrator of this divine judgment. He attacks and is injured. Before he makes his fateful decision, which his feelings did not support, Kleist writes of this fighter, "His feelings were too soft spoken."

These soft-spoken feelings sometimes carry messages and instructions over four to five generations. They can be heard only individually, even when they alone are bound to the collective flow. There are connections in the form of an intergenerational contract. It can be said that these connections establish majorities among humans over decades and centuries. A few human characteristics remain bound together throughout time. These are, in fact, the characteristics upon which a person would rely in an emergency; they are present in 1945, but not during luxurious New Year's festivities. These are quite different majorities than those that make up the 76 percent of daily television viewership watching series like "The Black Forest Clinic."[22] Today these soft-spoken feelings emigrate from images that television endows with noisy sounds. The economies of sound scatter these soft voices and relegate them to a diaspora. Herein lies the task of the text, which no use of force will ever be able to replace. The subcutaneous structure of music found in quiet sounds avoids dramatic intensification because it essentially comprises considerably shorter-lived bursts of energy in the moment and considerably longer-term flows of time typical of decades, life spans, and centuries. This is the real relation. Loudness reproduces unreal relations that tear open wounds.

"We or our descendants, my brothers!"[23]

It is ultimately a matter of choosing sides. There is a tradition of storytelling that uses a egalitarian-poetic form of literature in order to shepherd everything in the world into a unitary form. There is also an infatuation with the repetition compulsions of experiences typical of tragic theater; spurned women afflicted by pulmonary disease decorated with camellias who could be cured today with penicillin; the murderous confusion of Don José; and Carmen's resolve amid extreme indecisiveness. She actually does not know what she wants. I have become involved with this musical tradition's messages on account of my parents, my own love for opera, and many other factors. Precisely for this reason, I take a biased stance in favor of analytical work that attempts not only to record and take stock of two fateful centuries as they come to a close, but also to mothball them.

"All real beauty is analytic," says Edgar Allan Poe. My relay stations—the lonely Musil, on the one hand, and Heinrich von Kleist from a completely different time in history—write in this analytic way. That means writing commentaries on the words "beauty," "real," "all," "analytic," and "is."

"Analytic" does not mean nonnaturalistic, nonnarrative, or nonrealistic. Allow me to quote a few passages by Kleist: "about four miles from here, near the Gull Pond, in the forest bordering on it from the mountains."[24] This description is so *inexact* that it could be anywhere. It is a sentence that can be put together using a Latin template and a line of poetry. "A play of quite extraordinary grace about her lips and about the long lashes showing over her downcast eyes."[25] "She leapt behind the curtains of the window, taking care to keep out of the moonlight that might have given her away."[26] "Taking care to keep out . . ."[27] This is a matter-of-fact attitude that presupposes ample time for deliberation. Even if it was only a few fractions of a second, her capacity for love was enough to separate out this small amount of time for deliberation from the hurry and confusion. While she leaps "behind the window curtains," the emotional impulse is not disrupted.[28] All the while, the moon—dangerous only from certain angles—radiates. There are three different emotional temporalities in this sentence that coexist. They are tolerant of each other. This is polyphonic and antithetical to any unifying realism. This is what I find both in Kleist and in the eighteenth century.

In the age of new media, I am not afraid of what this media can accomplish, but rather of its incompetence and destructive power to fill people's heads. In this age, we writers are the guardians of the last leftover bits from the grammar of time, a difference between present time, the future, and the past. We are the guardians of difference. You may notice now that in my preceding attempt to get closer to Heinrich von Kleist I have not gone considerably far beyond his visit to Halberstadt. Long since covered over by the cleaning ladies of Halberstadt, these footprints are no longer visible, but they remain the real connection I follow. How good it was that those three firemen were there. I will make an effort.

Translated by Emma Woelk

Notes

This speech, given in 1985 on the occasion of receiving the newly rehabilitated Kleist Prize, was originally published in German as Alexander Kluge, "Die Differenz: Heinrich von Kleist," in *Theodor Fontane, Heinrich von Kleist und Anna Wilde: Zur Grammatik der Zeit* (Berlin: Klaus Wagenbach, 1987), 73–89.

The recording of both Kluge's original speech and Helmut Heißenbüttel's *laudatio* can be heard at https://www.kluge-alexander.de/fileadmin/kluge/xyzaudio35/Kleist-Preis%201985.mp3.

The three images included in the German original are not reproduced in the present translation.

1. [Translator's citation: Walter Benjamin, "The Storyteller: Observations on the Works of Nikolai Leskov," trans. Harry Zohn, in *Selected Writings,* ed. Howard Eiland and Michael W. Jennings (Cambridge, MA: Harvard University Press, 2002), 156.]

2. [Translator's note: Kluge received the Kleist Prize in 1985, the first year the reconstituted Heinrich von Kleist Society bestowed the award after it was discontinued in 1933 because of National Socialism's rise to power in Germany. Awarded to luminaries like Bertolt Brecht (1922) and Robert Musil (1923), two of Kluge's most important influences, the Kleist Prize was the most coveted of cultural recognitions during the Weimar Republic.]

3. [Translator's citation: Heinrich von Kleist, "On the Gradual Production of Thoughts whilst Speaking," in *Selected Writings,* ed. and trans. David Constantine (Indianapolis: Hackett, 1997), 408.]

4. [Translator's citation: Heinrich von Kleist, *The Feud of the Schroffensteins,* trans. Mary J. Price and Lawrence Marsden Price (Boston: R.G. Badger, 1916), 515.]

5. [Translator's citation: Heinrich von Kleist, "The Broken Jug," in Constantine, *Selected Writings,* 43.]

6. [Translator's citation: Friedrich Schiller, "Wallenstein," in *The Robbers and Wallenstein,* trans. F. J. Lamport (New York: Penguin Books, 1993), 214.]

7. [Translator's note: The Conference of Ministers-President is a committee comprised of all sixteen states of the Federal Republic of Germany responsible for

coordinating policy that falls within the jurisdiction of each member. In addition to regulating equalization payments between the federal government and the individual states, it is responsible for the Interstate Broadcasting Agreement that licenses radio and television within each state.]

8. [Translator's citation: Heinrich von Kleist, *Penthesilea*, trans. Joel Agee (New York: Harper Collins, 1998), 7.]

9. [Translator's citation: Kleist, *The Feud of the Schroffensteins*, 557.]

10. [Translator's citation: Heinrich von Kleist, "Betrothal in San Domingo," in Constantine, *Selected Writings*, 333.]

11. Robert Musil, *The Man without Qualities*, trans. Sophie Wilkins (New York: Knopf, 1995), 2:1752.

12. [Translator's citation: Kleist, "Betrothal in San Domingo," 325.]

13. [Translator's citation: Heinrich von Kleist, "The Duel," in Constantine, *Selected Writings*, 393.]

14. [Translator's citation: Kleist, "The Duel," 380.]

15. [Translator's citation: Kleist, "Betrothal in San Domingo," 330.]

16. [Translator's citation: Robert Musil, "Helpless Europe: A Digressive Journey," trans. Philip H. Beard, in *Precision and Soul: Essays and Addresses*, ed. and trans. Burton Pike and David S. Luft (Chicago: University of Chicago Press, 1990), 131.]

17. [Translator's note: Kluge shifts here to English in the original, but does so using a stilted formulation. The translation smooths Kluge's English to improve readability.]

18. [Translator's note: Kluge is referring here to President Ronald Reagan's proposed Strategic Defense Initiative (SDI), otherwise known as "Star Wars."]

19. [Translator's note: The HMS *Sheffield* was a guided missile destroyer sunk by Argentine forces during the Falklands War of 1982.]

20. [Translator's citation: Kleist, "The Broken Jug," 4.]

21. [Translator's note: The English here is an original translation that parts ways with Constantine's. The original German reads: "Herr Friedrich, obschon sein Verfahren auf guten Gründen beruhen mochte, fühlte dennoch zu leise, als daß er es nicht sogleich gegen die Forderung derer, die in diesem Augenblick über seine Ehre entschieden, hätte aufopfern sollen." Constantine's translation erases any mention of feeling, which for Kluge is of central importance. See Kleist, "The Duel," 389.]

22. [Translator's note: "Die Schwarzwaldklinik," or The Black Forest Clinic in English, was one of the most popular television dramas aired on West Germany's second, public-service television station (ZDF) between 1985 and 1989.]

23. [Translator's note: Heinrich von Kleist, *The Battle of Hermann*, trans. Rachel MagShamhrain (Würzburg: Königshausen & Neumann, 2008), 122.]

24. [Translator's citation: Kleist, "Betrothal in San Domingo," 327.]

25. [Translator's citation: Kleist, "Betrothal in San Domingo," 333.]

26. [Translator's citation: Kleist, "Betrothal in San Domingo," 342.]

27. [Translator's citation: Kleist, "Betrothal in San Domingo," 342.]

28. [Translator's citation: Kleist, "Betrothal in San Domingo," 342.]

2

Storytelling Is the Representation of Differences

JOCHEN RACK: *Your* Chronik der Gefühle [Chronicle of Feelings] *could be considered your literary crowning achievement. It is 2,000 pages long, 800 of which were published in the last few decades:* Case Histories, Learning Processes with a Deadly Outcome, The Battle, *and* Die Unheimlichkeit der Zeit [The Uncanniness of Time]. *What question holds this magnum opus together?*[1]

ALEXANDER KLUGE: Everybody knows what a chronicle is. The year 1945, the "Spiegel Crisis" in 1962, the student protest movement, the possibility of a World War III in the early eighties, and the year 1989 paired with the year 1991 when the Russian empire collapses.[2] All these moments changed the contours of the world and happened within my lifetime. Those are collective novels that tell the story of our century. They include terrible novels

	like World War I, World War II, and Auschwitz. And now we are confronted with something like an opening balance sheet for the twenty-first century, and we ask ourselves: What actually happened? The purpose of a chronicle is to allow us to remind ourselves, for example: Where was I when Kennedy died? We have the choice between an objective chronicle, a chronicle of events, or a chronicle of feelings, which describes what happened subjectively. It seems to me that this subjectivity has more staying power. It is the more materialist of the two elements. On the one hand, feelings are highly adaptable, and are quite resilient against distress and suffering. At the same time, however, they are more obstinate and more like concrete than anything else I can think of, because they do not fundamentally change over the course of 2,000 years.
JR:	*So you understand those historical events as expressions of emotional states? Are feelings the root causes of what has happened historically?*
AK:	Exactly. There is the saying, "The Celts are everywhere, we just do not see them." The Romans used this phrase. It is exactly the same with feelings. They are everywhere, even in unexpected places. For example, they live in institutions, which only become solid and have staying power when they are filled with feelings. This is equally true for Thomas Mann's novel *Buddenbrooks* as it is for an insurance company or the German Reich. At the same time, feelings are also present in the form of errors, blunders, and silence. It is not as easy as it may seem to discover a feeling or to describe how it behaves. Feelings are too rich and complex for the mind to comprehend. The philosopher Blaise Pascal says the heart has a mind, but that the mind itself cannot understand. This could also be the guiding theme for my *Chronik der Gefühle*. This is not an argument for or against feelings.

Rather, it is an attempt to direct our attention. The things that move humans from within are indeed significantly stronger and more powerful than anything that happens on the outside.

JR: *Do you think that historical interpretation has thus far ignored feelings? Do you see your own work as an attempt at correcting a, let us say, positivistic or objective conception of history?*

AK: Feelings definitely do not play a significant enough role in the way history is currently told. As such, historians are astonished when all of a sudden feelings pave the way for National Socialism. Ignored feelings that drive mass migrations are dangerous. It is not that I celebrate feelings. I just want people to recognize their existence. Also, it is not about inner worlds, but rather about the feelings that can be recognized in physical structures and not just in monuments set in stone. The houses we live in are feelings converted into space.

JR: *With his book from the 1930s,* The Heritage of Our Times, *Ernst Bloch tried to return to buried and forgotten feelings in order to explain how those feelings, which once may have been orientated toward an original solidarity, made their way into fascism. Do you consider your own work in line with this project?*

AK: You can be sure of that. However, this lineage can be drawn in another way, one that accounts for the gap between Ernst Bloch and Theodor W. Adorno. I see myself more in accordance with Adorno's line of thinking. He would never publish a book entitled *The Principle of Hope*. He would nevertheless admit that we cannot live without hope, even if we have to produce hope at the expense of truth. The most wonderful fallacy that has generally allowed creatures to continue to live on this planet is basic trust. Every life-form gets its share of this basic trust at birth. Even animals have it. Evolution teaches us those life-forms that survive are those that begin their existence believing that the world has their interests at heart. Looking at our century, this assumption is revealed to be a fundamental fallacy. The world has neither the intentions of those who died at Verdun at heart nor does it have the interests of Holocaust victims at heart. We can therefore objectively say: this is ideology, a wonderful fallacy that nonetheless sustains us and gives us strength. Adorno would agree on this point. It is for this reason that the last chapter in *Chronik der Gefühle* is called "The Long March of Basic Trust."

JR: *It sounds like those basic feelings are anthropologically fixed within human beings. Where does the idea of this "fallacious belief"—the idea that basic trust is so deeply anchored in every human being—come from?*

AK: In order to answer this question, I would have to refer to a personal, biographical experience. My father was a doctor and a midwife. Many births took place in our home. It is clear that a basic trust exists in both human beings and animals. But there is still no reason to have much hope. The aforementioned chapter, "The Long March of Basic Trust," in particular, brings to light horrendous things. Basic trust exists only in trace amounts. And such trace elements stray, much like in an exodus. They form dispersed herds. Yet they manifest themselves in the invariant ability of human beings to change. *Case Histories* is made up of metamorphoses, they bear witness to the fact that people can almost completely transform themselves. Morally steadfast people are capable of changing just as much as opportunists are. This has always fascinated me.

JR: *How do these changes in feelings, these metamorphoses, take place? Does your desire to enlighten manifest itself in the description of the circumstances in which feelings are reorganized?*

AK: I see myself as someone compiling a collection of different kinds of fallacies and revolving feelings after the end of civil and religious wars. This is a collection that can be connected to the collections of others, like Montaigne's or Michel Foucault's, for example. It is my goal to make containers, boxes, tubes, and ampules available in an archive in which people can store and test experiences. My book offers historical snapshots, a gigantic warehouse of examples and didactic plays.

JR: *Dialectic of Enlightenment*—*you mentioned Adorno already*—*presents the position that, throughout the course of history, the abstraction of instrumental reason has resulted in the demise of feelings. Max Horkheimer and Adorno use Homer's* Odyssey *to prove this thesis, claiming that Odysseus has to kill his feelings in order to emancipate himself from the forces of myth. Is this too pessimistic?*

AK: No. You are describing precisely the cave in which I find myself: *Dialectic of Enlightenment* is the foundational book to which I have committed myself. Suppression of the self is required if you want to sail between Scylla and Charybdis and make it home. And this suppression correlates with the enslavement of others and your own inner self. Odysseus's comrades who have to row in the boat are essentially slaves, certainly not knights. Applied to our own country, we have to add that our forefathers on the medieval farmsteads in the time before the Peasants' Wars did not have the option of escaping the Cyclops by boat. They were landlocked. Thus, for us the fairy tale "The Wolf and the Seven Young Kids" is what the *Odyssey* is for the seafaring Greeks.[3] This fairy tale poses fundamental questions: Whom may I let in, and whom should I not let in under any circumstance? Who has to be locked out of the house? This is the mistake the little kids make initially. They let the wolf in, just as we let in Hitler in 1933. And then, on the other hand, the little kids miraculously manage to get out of the wolf's belly safe and sound. These are continental variants of the same attempt to create security: "How can I protect myself? What must I be afraid of? What holds voluntary actions together? What can I put my trust in?" I can put my trust in the mother's hands. You can make a forgery of her hands, however, by dusting a wolf's paws with flour. These are fundamental problems treated differently in this fairy tale than in the *Odyssey*. Nevertheless, it is the same struggle. Feelings allow themselves to be dominated by myth until reason emancipates feelings by suppressing them. We have to find a way out of this dialectic.

JR: *Are your stories meant to reflect the way in which feelings are produced? Are you arguing that more well-trained feelings would not fall prey to this tragic cycle?*

AK: That gets to the core, and still it is not really all that different than the *Dialectic of Enlightenment*. If you go searching for traces of feelings and use the methods of poetry to observe carefully, you will find that these feelings are quite diverse. They are subject to the kind of metamorphoses described by Ovid. As such, they far exceed moral character, reason, or society. If a creature cannot bear something any longer, it transforms itself. This means that feelings have many ways out. They have, in fact, always been partisans with respect to myth, and they also behave like partisans with respect to reason, which seeks to overcome myth. They are, therefore, capable of resistance. Homer and Adorno pay close attention to the scene that describes the execution of the maidens following Odysseus's victory: one maiden's feet are still twitching. I have written at least twenty stories inspired by this story. My story "Clumsiness with a Deadly Result," for example, describes how a German army officer is told while fighting on the eastern front that Jews were killed, but their children were spared.[4] They are lost, sitting in basements and starving. The officer then has a change of heart and wants to protect and provide for the children. He tries to negotiate with his superiors and the *Einsatzgruppe*, but he breaks the military's code of conduct and fails in his attempt to rescue the children. This is a repetition of Homer's story. The upsetting knowledge of the murdered maidens lingers. It is memories like these that make up the group of partisans, an emotional army, that lives on within us in small traces.

JR: *This would then be the anthropological hope that the plebeian swarm of feelings never fully subjects itself to the logistics of reason.*

AK: It never does, even though those feelings condemned to express themselves individually a majority of the time repeatedly lose their battles against the collective's organized reason. When a feeling is organized from on high, by a medium, a party, or a nation, it is no longer an emancipatory matter, but instead becomes the most oppressive force possible. Every war lives off the strength of such organized feelings. The feelings of a woman in a basement, who practices what I call a "strategy from below," stand in contradistinction to the flying factory of real feelings embedded within the squadrons of bombers. The men flying the planes probably are either indifferent to the bombing or find it uncanny. However, in order to invent gunpowder, flying, or industrial discipline in the first place, you need a certain amount of emotional energy that is built into the bombing squad. Even though the squadrons may seem quite powerful at first, the bitter experience of a bombing raid can, in the long run, be a strong force in the search for a way out. The glorification of Bomber Harris will not necessarily continue.[5] The bombing of cities could be banned one day. These are very complex movements. In Richard Wagner's writings, we read: "Ah! All is hopeless, that I know, yet hope revives and longs to grow."[6] In *Chronik der Gefühle*, one story is titled "He Who Hopes Dies Singing."[7] Thus, you have to apply a dialectical movement, as articulated by Horkheimer and Adorno, to the notion of hope. You do not escape disaster just because you are hopeful.

JR: *But hope would be a function of the remembrance of victims and thus consistently produced.*

AK: Hope is a horizon that human beings can permanently fabricate. In his short story "A Report to an Academy," Franz Kafka, another exemplary witness, describes a maelstrom emanating from the horizon that catches up with a monkey. This convinces the monkey that there is something outside himself on which he can base his egocentrism.

JR: *In one of the stories in* Chronik der Gefühle, *a caretaker is supposed to give the child she has been taking care of to its adoptive parents.*[8] *However, as a move is currently underway, the woman of the house does not take the time to listen to caretaker. She then leaves the house without handing over the child.*

AK: This is called taking pride in your work. You can find more stories like this in my book. The parents are killed in an accident, the child is given to a caretaker, the caretaker feels responsible for the child, and she successfully raises the child. The life of such a child consists of sleeping habits, food preferences, and so on. A caretaker's raising of the child is one of the most attentive jobs there is. This starts with the midwife and continues with the nanny. The fact that the child is going to legal guardians who do not have time for it hurts her pride, and thus she takes the child with her. She does not pass her job along to someone who cannot do it properly. Work has its own set of feelings associated with it. We always pretend that feelings in relationships matter the most, especially since they are what consumes figures in novels and are retold in literature over and over again. In the sphere of labor, a Chinese and a German worker can easily communicate about the finesse it takes to tighten a screw. The story of the caretaker is exactly about this kind of precise feeling that resides in one's fingertips. This is the mimetic and artisanal side of feelings, the ability of feelings. A surgeon exhibits this, too. A halted destructiveness manifests itself as finesse. I am mostly interested in feelings like these. The romantic feelings that populate operas and novels are only one type of feeling rare throughout everyday life, whereas the labor process relates to a multitude of feelings that make up both ability and self-confidence. This is exactly the reason why someone who wants to be an author refuses to let a publisher correct his novels. There is something slavish about poetic work when it is just a service for advertisers.

JR: *This feeling in our fingertips is an enlightening, reasonable, useful, and guiding feeling. There are also stories in your book, however, that deal with what cannot be elucidated. They deal with the blind spots of feelings inside human beings. "Qualification for Judicial Office" tells the story of a woman who shot a man, apparently without any intention to do so.[9] However, her criminal act is not just a coincidence or accident. Throughout the legal proceedings, the court tries unsuccessfully to shed light on the woman's motives, and yet the aporia remains unsolved. This case reminded me of Robert*

	Musil's story of Moosbrugger, the murderer in The Man without Qualities, *whose motive is as obscure as this woman's. The judge would like to prove Moosbrugger's guilt, and therefore assumes that he is dealing with a concise subject with free will who can thus be declared guilty. Meanwhile, Moosbrugger perceives his crimes as "a series of completely separate incidents."*[10] *He perceives them outside himself that then find him. Apparently, every attempt to render motivations and emotional states transparent has its limits.*
AK:	Based on language and the perceptions of others. For the human being, those birds flying by—the mix of coincidence and response one lives with—are something you can understand, but perhaps not convey verbally under certain circumstances. As a lawyer, the enormous discrepancy between the concrete facts of a case and the failed attempts at relating these facts verbally has always struck me during court proceedings.
JR:	*It also shows that feelings are not attached to the center of a single ego. Instead, they develop a life of their own, perhaps similarly to what you find in Homer's writing from antiquity. Take Achilles, for example: the decentralized power located in his knee governs his actions. This results in puzzling stories and dark spots in behavior.*
AK:	Writers have always been concerned with this. You can find it in Ovid, just as you can find it in Robert Musil or Heinrich von Kleist. There are stories that could be printed next to each other like cousins. Within these stories, there are two groups—one analytical and the other observant—that pay attention to the difference in values and tell us: Hope is not dependent on the existence of famous personalities like Goethe's Wilhelm Meister, but rather on the confusion of feelings, on the fact that feelings well up and exist.

The kaleidoscopic nature of human beings gives rise to Police Battalion 102, but it can also lead to the rescue of others.[11] Based on a misunderstanding, for example, an order gets lost. Bertolt Brecht's example: bombs were thrown sloppily and landed in a field.[12] In this case, attributes like inertness, aberrance, egotism, and laziness come into effect. It is an examination of these feelings, organized into distinct categories based on moral reflections, for their diverse potentials that tries to find out how emancipatory potential can be culled unintentionally.

JR: *What is it then that human hope can rely on so that these emotions are guided toward emancipatory ends? Do your stories not also evince a certain skepticism toward overly noble projects of individual self-definition?*

AK: You cannot "guide" feelings. Being able to "train" an individual feeling hides the fact that the willfulness of feelings is grounded in their diversity and interconnectivity. This is what makes them all together unruly and autonomous.

JR: *You tell the story from which your seventh chapter from volume 1 takes part of its name, "How Can I Protect Myself? What Holds Voluntary Actions Together?," using pictures.[13] This story seems to suggest that there is something like an automation of human action that exists below the rational surface and has no recourse to morals, consciousness, or will, and to which we are oblivious.*

AK: Absentmindedness and devotion seem to be rooted deep within humans. They usually come to the fore when I do not intentionally fall back on them. No ruler can bring this about. When parents jump in front of a tractor to save a child from being run over, or when a mother lifts a four-ton car for just a moment to free her child, this is evidence of forces that are older than any one life span, evidence of forces that probably stem from earlier times and that merely pass through us. These forces are peculiarly helpful, good-natured, enthusiastic, and just devoted. This does not happen only out of love. When it comes to love, egoism—for example, in *Tristan and Isolde*—is a lot stronger than usual. That is not the case in the following example from my book: "'And if you do not risk your life, then you will never make anything of it . . .': Sigrid Berger, risking her life, saved a 50-centimeter-long dog at the corner of Gneisenaustraße. 'Why,' Ms. Schaffner asks, 'did you risk your life?' Frau Berger did it 'without thinking' about it. A living creature was whimpering. That is when she lost her head."[14] You could almost accuse this woman of lacking all common sense. But clearly her actions stem from some sort of undercurrent that flows through us humans.

JR: *Someone falls into the water and the rescuer immediately, without thinking, jumps in as well and rescues the person.*

AK: The air raid on Halberstadt plays an important role in my work and that is why I chose those examples, but I could just as easily use examples from any other life-and-death situation. Only in these situations does this internal spontaneity, the self-organization of feelings, become verifiable. Take the firefighter, for example, whom I talk about: he drives by his own house and sees that it has been destroyed. But he does not stop to go in to save his family. Instead, he joins his team extinguishing a fire. Only afterward does he go home and find that—thank God—his family is not dead. Here, the reserve of feelings, which cannot be activated in everyday life, is part of the organization itself. It is found in the loyalty of one person to another. I cannot suddenly get out of the car and let others drive on. I do not act privately.

JR:	*You give another example with regard to this topic: a group of Soviet firefighters in Kiev leaves the burning city conquered by the Germans, only then to return, going behind German lines, in order to put out the fire.*[15]
AK:	This awareness is important to me. Before, when they were putting out the fires, they were focusing on the details, but now they are outside the city limits. This group of firefighters, a brigade that is only qualified to put out large fires, can now look out over the totality of the burning city. And this then triggers a feeling: we will not let this city burn down. So, they drive back through the German lines, into a trap, so to speak. But the technical equipment guides them, their know-how guides them, that is how they learned it. It is a moral force that guides this brigade.
JR:	*Is this some sort of a moral automatism that lies in the logic of technical equipment?*
AK:	That is it exactly. Just like the medieval pirate Klaus Störtebecker who rescues some of his companions after his head had been chopped off; the companions he runs past are granted reprieve. You could see that there is a reserve of feelings at play contained here: an automatism, if you like. That is actually human. I am interested in the humor that arises when those involved afterward, right when they are being honored as role models for others, say: "We were not like that at all, we did not think about it, we just took action."
JR:	*But there is a story in your book, it seems to me, that contradicts what we see in the stories just discussed. It is the story entitled "Undoing a Crime through Cooperation."*[16] *This is also a portrayal of a moment of crisis. A prostitute finds a man who apparently was beaten to death in her apartment, and she and her pimp try to drag the corpse out of her apartment without*

	calling the police. They do so out of calculated self-interest; this is not a spontaneous act, but rather a very deliberate and clever one. In the end, the seemingly dead man actually recovers and survives.
AK:	These are completely separate, coincidental incidents. They ensure that the prostitute's finesse, the feeling in her fingertips, brings a dead man back to life. This led to an ideal outcome for both sides. In this regard, this celebration of cooperation is a celebration of rational actions and the rational protection of self-interests. God rewards, so to speak, the removal of the dead body, just as is the case with Baucis and Philemon. In this sense, I do believe in gods. I think that our actions contain within them rewards from the past. Just as we can find reserves of reason, devotion, faithfulness, and so on deep within humans, we can also find these feelings in a person's most advanced actions. This means of course the very opposite of automatism. I do not care where a particular feeling is located, but if it contributes to our emancipation, to the volitional way we construct ourselves, then I will find and label it.
JR:	*Whether or not feelings can make their mark also depends on the situation. In your book* The Battle, *you attribute the Germans' failure on the eastern front to the contradiction between the soldiers' feelings and their forlornness in the vast Russian landscape. You pick this theme up again in* Chronik der Gefühle *in the chapter "Heidegger in Crimea," and you show how feelings get lost.*
AK:	In that story, one leg returns home while the other moves forward in the direction of the enemy.[17] This is due to the fact that feelings do not see any reason to settle in the conquered land. If you had promised everyone with a Knight's Cross some land on Crimea, and every

ethnic German living abroad the chance to relocate to a promised land, then maybe such a raid would have been appealing just like the great migrations brought about when the Goths conquered northern Italy and everybody was offered the chance to own a manor.

JR: *But the German privates did not really want that, just as the French soldiers under Napoleon in the parallel story did not want to take the vastness of East Prussia or Russia into their possession.*

AK: That is where feelings are never wrong. Whenever something unwanted is promised, no propaganda in the world can move them.

JR: *However, rulers do err.*

AK: Rulers err and, when translated into concrete terms, the systems of command meant that any individual could save his home and his family in the Allgäu only after marching around in southern Russia and doing something absurd. Such a deployment or straining of emotions endures only as long as the enemy does not threaten to destroy this connection. As soon as that happens, the individual no longer obeys, and no command will force him to attention. The implosion of the Wehrmacht's Sixth Army in Stalingrad really moved me when my parents told me about it, despite the fact that it was unsettling for me as a child. Indeed, there are not many more Russians in the snowy landscape than there are Germans in the Stalingrad cauldron. As a matter of fact, we cannot really speak of a Russian advantage. But the Germans are in a place without hope. They first lose hope, then the battle, and then finally their lives.

JR: *In addition to military logistics, there is also emotional logistics, and leaders who do not pay attention to these logistics are doomed to fail.*

AK: They lose the loyalty of their underlings. This is the case in the *Song of Roland*. It is the case in

JR: Stalingrad. And it was also the case for the last Roman legions at the Danube.

The examples that we have been discussing clearly show that there are different, conflicting layers of emotions. You capture this along with all these contradictions in the stories that you tell. This leads me to the question about the structure and form of Chronik der Gefühle. *Referring to Adorno, you once described your poetics in an earlier book with the title "Stories without a Metaphoric Concept."*[18] *Is the decision to narrate in such an incoherent form basic in the tradition of Critical Theory?*

AK: Absolutely. There are different derivations. On the one hand, there is all the oral communication, the things discussed in bars in Oberhausen or Halberstadt. Those are circular or spherical conversations that always come back to similar things, but never to the same point. But they are not linear narratives describing a progression or digression. Imagine a narrator at the center of a sphere who describes everything around him as if he were at the center of the earth describing a starry sky. You also have to imagine that everything is in motion, the horizons change, the sphere does not keep its shape, the narrator wanders, and is not always the same. The narrative is more complex, dynamic, and chaotic. The Talmud is constructed in a similar fashion: in the middle you have the Holy Scripture, which is the narrator and is immutable. Built around that you have the Gemara, which are the approved interpretations, the indisputable statements of the great rabbis. And all around this, the commentaries branch out in all directions. Once you reach the outer margins, you are at the center and on the surface at the same time. At its peak moment, the Internet will function in the same way. This narrative structure also serves as the foundation of Critical Theory. Adorno's style of writing is fragmentary. However, ellipsis is also, simply put, a narrative form I love. It is a fundamental form of the epic. I have enough role models: Ovid's *Metamorphoses* or Homer's narrative style in the *Iliad*. All great narratives have this structure. The linear story is an exception and an idea of the nineteenth century. By carefully moving the narrative from A to B, along a common thread, it does away with every side issue. It is a strategy for main streets and highways. On the other hand, walking on trails and garden paths, which involves sensing, guessing, wandering, and strolling, functions according to other rules.

JR: *This, of course, requires a lot of initiative on the readers' part. Reading such a story entails traversing it and wandering through it. Readers have to find their own common thread.*

AK: It requires a certain amount of trust in advance. Storytelling is the representation of differences.

JR: *There is the horizontal succession of stories within one temporal level, but also a vertical relationship between stories belonging to different times. For example, if you tell stories about the present-day era of German reunification, these stories always reference others from the past. As such, interferences and patterns emerge within a single temporal level and they overlap over time as well. Can we see this as a parallel to Walter Benjamin, who, in his philosophical theses on history, developed the idea that every moment in time calls up other moments in time, for example, that the French Revolution may cite Roman antiquity?*

AK: It is not that the French Revolution randomly calls Romans to mind by reenacting Cato the Elder. What this actually demonstrates is that the French Revolution is pursuing something different than it claims. It claims to advance the emancipation of humankind, but in reality it creates a nation with Paris at its center, a tool of violence that subjugates Europe. It creates freedom of trade in the name of fraternity, liberty, and equality. And it masks the difference between idolatry and political action by alluding to the Romans. That is what Marx and Benjamin are talking about.

JR: *Reading your book, the leitmotifs are fairly obvious, among them the opera stories. In one of the stories, one character defines opera like this: "The fundamental structure of the opera is based on passion overwhelming reason, and reason killing passion."*[19] *This reminds me of the passage in* Dialectic of Enlightenment *that comments on Odysseus passing the Sirens. Odysseus allows himself to be chained to the mast—but not before taming his passion through reason—in order not to fall for the Sirens' music. The Sirens sit among the bleached bones of those who followed their calling: you die if you surrender to passion. Why does opera play such an important role in your book as an engine of feelings?*

AK: First of all, something that was declared the highest form of art for more than a century—from Mozart to Richard Wagner to Alban Berg—has to be taken seriously. It is not a coincidence that humans long for a new altar, a nonreligious altar. I have studied operas all my life because my father was an opera fanatic. It baffled me that operas never made use of ways out, that an emergency can never just be turned into a moment of luck. There are some attempts to do this. In *Iphigenie*, for example, opera tries to create a happy reversal. In *The Meistersinger*, too, a lot of brute force is used to turn the outcome into something positive.

JR: *In* Fidelio *as well . . .*

AK: With a lot of brute force. But the ending is actually happy. The Stuttgart Opera's recent

Chapter 2

	interpretation has a rather modern twist, as the adaption has a fatal ending. In the moment of liberation—contrary to what we experienced in 1989—there is shooting. My objective with opera stories is to find the blind spot where the disaster could be disrupted.
JR:	*Where can we find this blind spot?*
AK:	With Scylla and Charybdis, you have to pay close attention to the bones. You have to reconstruct the stories of these deaths in order to find out at what point they could have chosen a different path. Odysseus proceeds rather carefully. He shows us how an emancipated man must act if he is to return home. He disguises himself and arrives home as a defenseless old man. With each step, he convinces himself that Agamemnon is not being slaughtered, that his son is no traitor, and only then does he kill the suitors. The path home is long.
JR:	*What significance does enlightenment have over the power of emotions provided by opera?*
AK:	It offers pseudo-enlightenment, a concentration of false assumptions about the automatism of evil, an incorrect opinion on human nature. I cannot correct this opinion by saying, "That is not what it is like." I have to factor in the passion that it creates in order to destroy this pessimistic machinery of lamentation called opera. I, too, can be taken in by operas. The music provides constant comfort while something horrible happens. Using irony and cynicism, the horror could be concentrated even further. Thus, operas dissipate the horror, they "distract" in the same way that the music performs the work of mourning.
JR:	*Let us come back to the question about the powers of emotions that are at play in your stories. Gorbachev is one of the central figures in the stories that deal with the "Outward Signs of Power's Decline," reunification, and the collapse*

	of the Soviet Union.[20] Here, you tell the story of how Gorbachev's vigor seemed to be paralyzed at the Madrid Conference's most decisive moment, and you try to connect this weakening of vigor, which is also addressed in connection with other figures, to a theory of the gods. How seriously do you take the stories in which gods appear at the decisive moment?
AK:	Completely seriously. I see no difference between what was considered in 2500 B.C.E. from a subjective, narrative point of view to be a trustworthy text and the things that can be considered trustworthy today. This is what I consider consistency. I can also imagine that we live in multiple universes simultaneously without even noticing it. Just as quantum physics describes conditions that make sense only if you assume that a second reality permeates our reality. This does not contradict my own observations. Only when all realities, ten or twelve aggregate states, are taken together do they build real relations. In that case, I think that gods permeate us like a paralysis. What Hitler called destiny is mentally plausible. When Napoleon all of a sudden loses his strength as if it were being sucked away by the Russian land, then I can interpret this as a sign that either he never had any reason to go there; or that the indigenous Russians, who started to hate him, drained all of his strength; or that the gods have forsaken him, as they say. Or the gods sharpened and blinded him. I think it is true that we can be blinded by strengths we carry inside ourselves and that these strengths are indifferent to human beings.
JR:	Your film company is called Kairos. Kairos is the god of the right moment, the one that must be seized. If so, you can do things that become impossible the very next moment. To illustrate this, you include the story of one of Hitler's

adjutants who is told in 1941 to come up with a plan of attack.[21] *However, the* Führer *gives him only five minutes to do so. The adjutant drank the night before though, and his skills are not as well honed as usual. And so he misses the decisive moment.*

AK: History is made up of cases like this. The belief that wars are necessary is one of the strongest, most prevalent myths there is. It begins as early as 1914. The German Reich chancellor marches around on his country estate along the Oder River and says: "The Russians are going to come down this road." This road still exists today, but the Russians never walked down it. However, this idea led him to declare the war inevitable. For this reason, no alternative plan exists on the day before the outbreak of the war. That is why there is no escape. This one-dimensional world first emerges from this inner, almost faith-like tendency to disaster. I have not determined yet what inner force is at play in situations like this, a death drive or something similar. So I think that this accumulation of new coincidences and previous coincidences and previous actions and mistakes is something worth fighting against.

JR: *A close consideration of circumstances often makes the rationality of our actions appear questionable. You describe, for example, how Hans-Dietrich Genscher decided during a trip to the Balkans to diplomatically recognize Slovenia and Croatia.*[22] *People say that Genscher was influenced by a mood brought on by a grueling wait.*

AK: The American ambassador Richard Holbrooke, who later became a key player in the Dayton Accords, describes the waiting period in which Genscher finds himself outside of his comfort zone, separated from the Federal Foreign Office.

The sensory deprivation he experiences causes him to act. His actions are sparked by privation. It is a kind of torture for an active person to be stuck in a foreign, poorly organized country, unable to make use of his many skills. He thus makes use of them to the wrong end. Nietzsche says, "Man still prefers to *will nothingness,* than *not* to will."[23]

JR: *Even the first story in your book programmatically starts with the description of the weather conditions, and you also refer to the weather in other stories. In your attempt to reconstruct the Reykjavik Summit of 1985, you ask in one of your TV shows both Gorbachev and the former national security advisor to Reagan about the weather during the summit. Apparently the weather was cold and drizzly. Are these circumstances, which we consider to be of peripheral significance for rational political decisions, historical actors in your opinion?*

AK: Especially low-pressure weather systems. A storm resulting from this type of system in Helgoland directly influences Willy Brandt's resignation. When the sun beats down, an aggressive high-pressure system can also constitute dangerous weather conditions for the mind. We are not really built for either of them. We are built for mixed weather conditions with a slight tension and change. The uniformity of a storm front is something dangerous; it threatens life and reminds us of life's fragility. If you consider that *The Man without Qualities* starts out with a detailed description of the weather, then you will see that these insights are not new. From Homer to Robert Musil, weather is used as a metaphor. For me, it is a basic feeling. The cold blowing from Astrakhan to Stalingrad is a real thing, just like the dust over a city after an air raid, when the glare of the sun pours over it, and the corpses smell. These are moments when weather is not

JR: just weather anymore. I believe that our dispositions will always be dependent on the weather. *I would like to talk about the turning point from 1989 to 1990. This represents not only a transition between the 1980s and the 1990s, but also a complete paradigm shift. The historical depression that lasted until the end of the Cold War, and which Don DeLillo's novel* Underworld *dealt with, disappeared like a ghost. The Wall came down, and communism, as a real existing alternative to capitalism, disappeared from everyday life. How would you describe this state of mind and this paradigm shift?*

AK: The majority of my stories are case studies that evolve around the year 1989. The fall of the Wall and the implosion of the Soviet Union signify the end of a superpower. This is the beginning of a disinhibition of the world. At the same time, this disinhibition, this process of the world becoming more brutal, also leads to an expanded horizon. Everybody can now catch up on a little bit of the nineteenth century that was not possible in the twentieth century. This leads to a liberation of our fantasy. You could now put on stage Brecht's *Baal* or *Mahogany* again, everything that was once deemed too wild and brutal during the twentieth century: world conquest, inward colonialism. And oddly enough, there is something exciting about this, just as peculiar as the outbreak of the war in 1914. With this, a new century begins. I, too, can perceive this as liberating, even though my analysis reveals it to be similar to the outbreak of war, a disinhibition that brings with it new brutalities. We agree on the fact that in the year 1989 a new century begins euphorically. The life spans that evolve around it reflect a new feeling of being alive.

JR: *On the other hand, there was a workers' movement in the late nineteenth century, as well as*

	the hope that anticapitalist protest could be organized. Marxism was a strong force. Do you think that the critique of capitalism has any material basis today?
AK:	You cannot look at the euphoria at the end of the nineteenth century solely from a European perspective, but instead must consider the perspective from New York, during the founding of America. There, you do not have any basis for a critique of capitalism. Instead, you have the unification of many immigrant peoples establishing for themselves a land of open horizons, even though they achieve this by exterminating both the buffalo and native Indians. This scenario is repeated in Europe. The idea of the Wild West and open horizons arrives here belatedly, briefly in 1949, and then again in 1989. We are basically continuing the process of monetary reform, and the founding of the Republic is taking place once again. And at the same time, there is a Europe developing that has its own horizons, where I can live with all of the selfish and altruistic forces that are hidden inside me, and with a little bit of utopianism. Utopia takes root in a different way. That is why a new temporality emerges in this case, one that is based on other values and coalitions of feelings.
JR:	*However, there were also those who, like Cassandra, warned against this happy legitimation of the new capitalism. Heiner Müller, for example, who appears in many stories in your book. In his text "Mommsen's Block," he talks about the "zombies of capital."[24] How do you see this solemn objection?*
AK:	In Heiner Müller's work there is an exciting engagement with the abysses of the West after the collapse of the GDR. He does it in a Shakespearean way. Triumph rarely lasts. Now we have the

JR: outright triumph of the stock market and finance capitalism. However, judging by all rules of collapse, this will very likely come to an end. *You see yourself as a chronicler. Is the* Chronik der Gefühle *your legacy? A 2,000-page letter in a bottle?*

AK: Well, writing happens compulsively. As Heiner Mueller says, This is my way of life. After writing something like *Chronik der Gefühle*, I think about other authors who might continue a project like this. Because I think that you would need about 400 authors, a Balzacian collective, to describe the footprint of our experience. All of my stories are really novels in disguise. Under the growing pressure of our intensified reality, a novel like *Buddenbrooks* gets compressed into fourteen pages. You have to be brief. Hemingway's short stories are not relevant because ads have to be squeezed between them in the newspaper, but because this is our fundamental form of communication. I prefer to work in this short form: short stories that contain small differences just like an insect caught in amber. I can remember and recognize them. Flaubert once planned to summarize all mistakes and bad expressions in two compendia so that these could later be recognized. To me, every error we make is valuable, every insight, every virtue along with its metamorphosis into negative virtue, every oscillation between good and bad is so important that it has to be captured and made visible in this form, so that communication substantially accelerates. At the moment, it accelerates at the substance's expense. This can be changed. This is, you could say, literary horticulture. I am thinking of an auteur literature analogous to the auteur cinema. It would be nice if more writers collaborated on this: Durs Grünbein, Christoph Schlingensief, myself, Peter Weiss, Max Frisch, if

68   *Difference and Orientation*

they were alive, and others, too. Then we could slip into Musil's clothes, for example, and finish *The Man without Qualities* or create forgeries of Marcel Proust's *Recherche* and write paralipomena. Now that would be literature.

Translated by Steffen Kaupp

Notes

This dialogue was originally published in German as "Erzählen ist die Darstellung von Differenzen: Alexander Kluge im Gespräch mit Jochen Rack," *Neue Rundschau* 2 (2001): 73–91.

1. [Translator's note: Rack first refers here to Alexander Kluge, *Chronik der Gefühle*, 2 vols. (Frankfurt am Main: Suhrkamp, 2000), an omnibus of Kluge's prose written since his literary debut in 1962. More than 50 percent of the work contains whole chapters of new stories written since his last proper literary publication in 1977: *Neue Geschichten: Hefte 1–18, Unheimlichkeit der Zeit*. Although *Chronik der Gefühle* has yet to be translated into English in its entirety, many of the earlier titles included therein are available in translation. They include the 1996 translation *Attendance List for a Funeral* (the later 1988 edition is entitled *Case Histories*) of *Lebensläufe*, which was originally published in 1962; *The Battle*, a 1967 translation of *Schlachtbeschreibung*, originally published in 1964; *Learning Processes with a Deadly Outcome*, a partial translation from 1996 of the 1973 collection of stories *Lernprozesse mit tödlichem Ausgang*; and *Air Raid* of 2014, a partial translation of the aforementioned *Neue Geschichten*.]

2. [Translator's note: Generally called the Spiegel Affair, this refers to the West German government's storming of *Der Spiegel* magazine's headquarters in Hamburg and the accusation of several journalists employed there of sabotage. Protests against the government's actions led to the collapse of the Adenauer government and to the resignation of Defense Minister Franz Josef Strauss.]

3. [Translator's citation: For an extensive discussion of this fairy tale in conjunction with the "capacity for differentiation," see Alexander Kluge and Oskar Negt, *History and Obstinacy*, trans. Richard Langston et al. (New York: Zone Books, 2014), 284–86.]

4. [Translator's citation: See the four-part story in book 4 entitled "Heidegger in Crimea" contained in volume 1 of *Chronik der Gefühle*: Alexander Kluge, "Ungeschick mit Todesfolge: Inwiefern gehört Geschicklichkeit zur moralischen Leistung?," in *Chronik der Gefühle*, vol. 1, *Basisgeschichten* (Frankfurt am Main: Suhrkamp, 2000), 444–52.]

5. [Translator's note: Sir Arthur Harris, Marshal of the Royal Air Force, played an active role in carrying out the RAF's bombing campaigns on German cities in World War II and figures as well in Kluge's seminal story "The Air Raid on Halberstadt on 8 April 1945." Alexander Kluge, *Air Raid*, trans. Martin Chalmers (London: Seagull Press, 2014), 44.]

6. [Translator's citation: Richard Wagner, *Der fliegende Holländer = The Flying Dutchman*, trans. David Pountney (New York: Riverrun Press, 1982), 55.]

7. [Translator's citation: Alexander Kluge, "Wer immer hofft, stirbt singend," in *Chronik der Gefühle*, vol. 2, *Lebensläufe* (Frankfurt am Main: Suhrkamp, 2000), 928–29.]

8. [Translator's citation: Alexander Kluge, "Übergabe des Kindes," in *Chronik der Gefühle*, 1:321–26. See also the concluding scenes 32–40 in Kluge's 1985 film *The Assault of the Present on the Rest of Time*, entitled "Übergabe des Kindes" [Handing Over the Child]. Cf. Alexander Kluge, *Der Angriff der Gegenwart auf die übrige Zeit: Das Drehbuch zum Film* (Frankfurt am Main: Syndikat, 1985), 91–104.]

9. [Translator's citation: Alexander Kluge, "Befähigung zum Richteramt: Immer wenn der Richter eine Frage stellte, entglitt der Tatbestand," in *Chronik der Gefühle*, 1:327–35. See also the second sequence (scenes 12–15), entitled "Der Schuss" [The Shot] based on a treatment entitled "Die Befähigung zum Richteramt" in Kluge's 1983 feature *The Power of Emotion*. Cf. Alexander Kluge, *Die Macht der Gefühle* (Frankfurt am Main: Zweitausendeins, 1984), 82–92, 34–44.]

10. [Translator's citation: Robert Musil, *The Man without Qualities*, trans Sophie Wilkins, (New York: Knopf Books, 1995), 1:75.]

11. [Translator's note and citation: Kluge is referring here to the second of three Nazi paramilitary formations deployed from Hamburg that are primarily responsible for the Holocaust in occupied Poland. The most notorious was Battalion 101, featured in Christopher R. Browning, *Ordinary Men: Reserve Police Battalion 101 and the Final Solution in Poland* (New York: HarperCollins, 1992).]

12. [Translator's citation: Kluge likely makes reference here to Brecht's collection of soldier folk songs contained in Bertolt Brecht, *Journals, 1945–1955*, ed. John Willett, trans. Hugh Rorrison (London: Bloomsbury, 2016), 301: "Oh, the pilots all drink / The airplanes stink / And the navvies don't know where they are / The bombardiers couldn't hit / A target when lit. / Oh, Colonel, we've been here too long."]

13. [Translator's citation: Alexander Kluge, "Was hält freiwillige Taten zusammen?," *Chronik der Gefühle*, 1:921–27.]

14. [Translator's citation: The core of Kluge's picture story originally appeared in Kluge, *Die Macht der Gefühle*, 45–47. A variant English translation of the entire story included in *Chronik der Gefühle* can be found in Kluge, *Air Raid*, 99–105.]

15. [Translator's citation: Alexander Kluge, "Die näheren Umstände der moralischen Kraft: Erfahrungen einer sowjetischen Feuerlöschbrigade aus Kiew im Jahre 1941," in *Chronik der Gefühle*, 1:434–40.]

16. [Translator's citation: Alexander Kluge, "Abbau eines Verbrechens durch Kooperation," in *Chronik der Gefühle*, 2:930–37. A precursor of the story can be found in the eleventh sequence (scenes 119–65) from Kluge's film *The Power of Emotion*. Cf. Kluge, *Die Macht der Gefühle*, 140–61.]

17. [Translator's citation: Alexander Kluge, "Heidegger auf der Krim," in *Chronik der Gefühle*, 1:417–34.]

18. [Translator's citation: Kluge, *Neue Geschichten*, 9.]

19. [Translator's citation: Alexander Kluge, "Das veruntreute Front-Theater," in *Chronik der Gefühle*, 1:813.]

20. [Translator's note: "Outward Signs of Power's Decline" is the title of chapter 2 in volume 1 of *Chronik der Gefühle*. See Kluge, *Chronik der Gefühle*, 1:147–305.]

21. [Translator's citation: Alexander Kluge, "Historische Sekunde," in *Chronik der Gefühle*, 1:231–32.]

22. [Translator's citation: Alexander Kluge, "Gefangen im Nirgendwo," in *Chronik der Gefühle*, 1:227–31.]

23. [Translator's citation: Friedrich Nietzsche, *"On the Genealogy of Morals" and Other Writings*, ed. Keith Ansell-Pearson, trans. Carole Diethe (New York: Cambridge University Press, 1994), 128.]

24. [Translator's citation: Heiner Müller, "Mommsen's Block," in *A Heiner Müller Reader*, ed. Carl Weber (Baltimore: Johns Hopkins University Press, 2006), 128.]

3

THE PEACEMAKER

DIE ZEIT: *Your major new work is called* The Devil's Blind Spot [Die Lücke, die der Teufel läßt].¹ *Who is the devil?*

ALEXANDER KLUGE: I know no better than you do.

DZ: *Could the book also be called* God's Blind Spot?

AK: If the devil is God's observer, then one could say that. The emphasis is on the gap, the blind spot. People live in the gap. The book is not about the devil, but about the process of enlightenment. If we take our own present-day experience as a basis, then the historical enlightenment of the eighteenth century is no longer sufficient. It is too indifferent toward plan economies, too rhetorical, and emotional. One hundred years ago, there was a completely different conception of property and emancipation. A self-conscious man around 1600 would say: My property centers around the time span of my life, my feelings, and my bonds. Only after this, do my business dealings and the money I earn come into play. This is the "new man."

DZ: *Your huge collections of stories know something about the blind spot ripped open by modernity. Are your stories there to fill this hole, to recreate the lost relationality?*

AK: I cannot do that. But to tell stories about it is a different matter. Storytelling is something like asking questions. A bat projects sounds against a wall. From this echo it hears a space. This is what storytelling can do.

DZ: *What is astounding about your books is that the narrator disappears in them in a certain way.*

AK: Egoless diversity! One of my chapters is called "Man without a Head."[2] I have a lot of respect for emotions and their antirealism. When a person comes across something they cannot tolerate, they get a rash. They are allergic to bad fortune. This antirealism in people has to be recognized. The ego reacts to this allergy like a bugaboo.

DZ: *Your stories want to be more than simple retellings, more than chronicles. They are meant to prove something.*

AK: There are two types of stories. One type points to absolutely nothing. They are monads. The others are maps. When stories are laid on top of each other like maps *cross-mapping* occurs. A Dadaist line commands: "Wander through the Harz region of Germany while blindly following the directions of a map of London."[3] This is productive when you become keenly aware of falling into an abyss. You can experience a lot with an incorrect map. We can never say exactly which maps are correct.

DZ: *The results of laying maps on top of one another are baffling. Suddenly, it seems as if there were time and again many more related stories from across the centuries.*

Chapter 3   73

AK: You could imagine Brecht telling stories like this. Then some moral would rear its head. With my stories, a narrative space emerges. There are experiential tremors much like earthquakes. These tremors alter a story's linearity. I measure this like a devil.

DZ: *Allegorical stories are bound together by the book's title, the blind spot. Is this blind spot good fortune?*

AK: Occurrences like Chernobyl, September 11, Auschwitz, Verdun, chemical warfare, and other writings on the wall from this and previous centuries are unbearable to me. I try to tell just as many stories about salvation in improbable circumstances.

DZ: *Like a kind of literary catastrophe prevention? Can narrating catastrophes ward off the next one?*

AK: No. Your questions are framed too radically. You are imagining normal literature. What I do is below the threshold of literature. It is antiliterature. If literature is not capable of doing anything against fascism, then, says Theodor W. Adorno, we have to make literature richer. We have to go back to its *raw materials*. Staying closer to the raw materials, we need to work on building roads under simpler conditions.

DZ: *In other words, documentary literature?*

AK: I am not responsible for these terms. But instead of catastrophe prevention I would say perspective. Storytelling means that I am responsible for perspectivity. In my book about Stalingrad, *The Battle* [*Schlachtbeschreibung*], I tried to express my respect for the dead by working exclusively with documentary material. Then I noticed that something was not right. *The Battle* is the book I have rewritten the most.[4] In *Chronik der Gefühle* [Chronicle of Feelings], I again added eighty pages and tore many others out. It is no longer documentary.

DZ: *What are the advantages of antiliterature when compared to literature?*

AK: The word "antiliterature" is polemical. Of course, I follow trustworthy authors. Philology is holy to me, because books are storehouses of experience. There is something lacking in literature today and there is too much of something else. I want to go back to what people discussed among themselves when experiencing something and learning from it. I want to go back to discussions between mother and child as well as those about relationship issues. These are stories about wanderers. Simple diversity. *Primitive diversity.* You find something similar in Walter Benjamin's *Arcades Project*.

DZ: *Benjamin had a sense of utopia. He believed that if he brought his material into constellations, it would begin to speak. Then something would come into being that is more than the sum of the stories told.*

AK: Adorno calls this "dialectical kitsch." I share Benjamin's interest, but I am much more skeptical, more careful than he is.

DZ: *You have no utopia?*

AK: I do. If we succeed in reuniting poetry and science once again, then we need to reconstruct intellectual self-consciousness, and we need the intellectual capacity of the bourgeois individual. I believe that our self-consciousness developed incorrectly at the beginning of our modern era, much like Siamese twins. On the one hand, Galileo has no respect for what he does not understand, and at the same time he is self-conscious. How can I separate the false feeling of omnipotence—the Western fundamentalist perspective that does not appear religious but is nevertheless completely religious—from its good side: the ability to displace horizons? How can I separate these two characteristics again? Proceeding similarly to the way Singapore operates will not work. I want to tell stories about spaces in which this question can be dealt with. I can hope that this self-consciousness creates different coalitions of emotions, intelligence, and sociability. Immanuel Kant once said that we are builders and want to build houses for our experiences. We then went down a wrong path and built a tower. In doing so, we split in two and linguistic confusion emerged. So we have to return to the basic construction materials. This is what I do.

DZ: *Where is your ego? Does it not make any decisions, do you not give your stories direction?*

AK: Of course. At least half of my stories have a happy ending. Against all odds. A woman throws herself from the cathedral in Milan.[5] She falls onto a poorly constructed car. Its flexible metal cushions her such that she is saved. You cannot create any causality out of this.

DZ: *At one point you write, "The causal chains march separately but attack in unison."*[6]

AK: This is what I find so awful. There are causal chains from Verdun that have not stopped having an effect today. They can kill people, while on the other hand people are closed off from one another and live their lives from a worm's-eye view.

DZ: *Can causal chains also have positive effects?*

AK: In one story, an American pilot flies toward a bunker somewhere in Asia where terrorists supposedly lie in wait.[7] In reality, it is a wedding party celebrating. His head is of no help here. But in this very moment, his bowels spasm and he soils his flight suit. He gets confused and redirects the plane. There you have one of my favorite theses: your gut can be smarter than your head.

DZ: *Is there a relationality between events across time that is invisible to the naked eye?*

AK: I do not think so. For me, pathos lies in the subjunctive and optative moods. The wish form does not change reality. You can still die holding onto the wish that things could be different. There are cases of luck hidden in the past that were not used; this is the *futur antérieur*. In *Die Unheimlichkeit der Zeit* [The Uncanniness of Time], I turn myself into a female teacher with three children who experience the same things I did when bombs rained down around me. She does not know whether she might possibly get confused if she starts praying and then gets hit by a bomb, or, if she does not pray, whether she has neglected something. This is impossible to solve. Now I think to myself: Where in this prison of reality, where we humans find no escape, is the last way out? This *last exit* is nothing other than narrative space that can be examined for its trustworthiness. Like money inside a cash register, it rattles around in me till I know the conditions for a way out of a hopeless situation. In 1928, a teacher would have had the chance to band together with other teachers so that there would never be a year like 1933, 1936, or 1945. I provide nothing more than the conditions for a happy ending. I call this my favorite thesis.

DZ: *Since you do not know if there is a God, do you ever think retrospectively what God would have had to do in order to save a person?*

AK: It could also be that I do think there is a God who does not look after us.

DZ: *What do you lean toward?*

AK: The latter. He is not meaningfully involved in our lives.

DZ: *Yet you rifle through history looking for the principle of hope.*

AK: No, I am looking for the principle of ways out. A way out means I am still on the move and searching even though both action and inaction can be mistakes.

DZ: *In order to save the past?*

AK: My parents got divorced in 1942. I was only a ten-year-old kid. I could never internally

	differentiate whether this was the end of my parental home or the year 1945, when it burned down. I still confuse the two. I was always conspiring to get my parents back together.
DZ:	*Successfully?*
AK:	I never succeeded. But I have retained the perspective that I would like to change this outcome in retrospect. That is why I became a lawyer. I can be a peacemaker. I can achieve this both politically and literarily. I do not believe there is a meaningful context to the world. Conversely, I believe that no one will ever be able to convince me that such a meaningful context cannot fundamentally exist.
DZ:	*You are designing good fortune.*
AK:	On the contrary. I firmly believe in Brecht when he wrote, "Aye, make yourself a plan. . . . Happiness comes in last."[8] In *The Devil's Blind Spot*, I show, for example, how a planned economy and Chernobyl correlate with one another.[9] There is no planned economy in love. A basic feeling I inherited from my mother tells me that enlightenment cannot be financed with insight, but rather with the expectation of good fortune. To this end, I construct metaphors that slow down the description of real relations to such an extent that emotions can come into contact with the issue at hand. Think about the story of the married couple on their way to get divorced who then get stopped by wildfires in the Lüneburg Heath. In the end, they do not get a divorce.[10] The fire is a coincidence, but it correlates to something hidden inside both of them. People have many voices. They are a score and an orchestra. Space has to be made for this.
DZ:	*You spoke about the reconciliation of poetry and science. Where is poetry in your work?*
AK:	Poetry is concentrated emotion. It can either tell a story or contain thoughts. As a lawyer, I use my reason; as a storyteller I rely on the powers

	of my emotions. They have set relationships. Here is my mother, there is my father, here is my wife, there are my two children, and this keeps on going, as if they were fields.
DZ:	*The characters in your stories rarely have more than a page to rely on the powers of their emotions. Why do the thousands of stories you have written up to now hardly ever play out in the interiority of human beings?*
AK:	Think of *Anna Karenina*. When all the time and effort in Leo Tolstoy's admirable novel, which I really do love, only leads to her death in the end, then I say to myself that Count Vronsky's emotions as well as Anna Karenina's are unnecessary for a happy ending. I am only interested in the happy ending.
DZ:	*Literature does not inquire into the utility of emotions.*
AK:	But a child does. Think of Anna Karenina's ten-year-old child, in whom I project my ego and the whole of my observational gifts. This child does not want his mother to perish under the train. Intelligence should not be demonized in this way. It has it bad enough already. It hardly exists anymore.
DZ:	*Despite all your intelligence, you are just a writer.*
AK:	Adorno always told me that it is unnecessary for me to write stories. "You cannot be better than Proust. Literature is really Noah's ark at full capacity." I am of a different mind. I think that all stories must be told again from under the pull of now time. I describe people's emotional flashpoints perspectively with the help of novels that have already described the fundamentals. I do not have to repeat all that.
DZ:	*You are result-oriented.*
AK:	I would be bored to death if I had to tell a story that indulged in relations to other stories that also needed to be told. It is about the relations of

Chapter 3   79

DZ:	proportionality. I find it cumbersome to repeat the traditional attentiveness of pre-1914 societies again and again at a time when we need to reappraise our observational abilities in literature. *So Adorno was right then. What Proust already did should not be done again. This is obvious, but also terrible. Your children have the right to start anew. They are also allowed to write novels.*
AK:	My children neither read novels nor do they write any for that matter. Proust wrote the definitive account of twentieth-century human relationships. We do not need to repeat his work again. The principle of modernity is equivalent to a new building without relationality. It, too, must be created. I am trying this out like a bat that flies toward various walls. One story has a tonality that influences another like notes in a score.
DZ:	*There are many pitches and timbres to your stories. Yet readers can pick up on a root in the distance.*
AK:	I owe my characters precision and a part of precision is . . .
DZ:	*Antisentimentality?*
AK:	Yes. If I were, for example, to strike up a dirge in my story about Maxwell, who commits suicide, this would be farce.[11] Even great operas like Zimmermann's *Soldaten* or Berg's *Wozzek* are essentially abbreviations. What lasts fifteen minutes in Wagner lasts seven seconds in these. The material of reality has changed; it has become concentrated. My question is always: Where is the way out? I am not looking for intensive description.
DZ:	*You are never pulled toward grand storytelling?*
AK:	The stories that appeal to me the most are the shortest ones.
DZ:	*Are there no words for the most important things?*

AK: Of course, but you cannot babble on.
DZ: *Art is when you refrain from babbling?*
AK: Art is abbreviation. Not everyone can do this. I am antirhetorical. In my opinion, rhetorical gestures are of the devil. When things get serious, people need to talk and then phrases are forbidden. They stop. Compression is a virtue. My writing aspires to the short parts at the end of a story. People do not speak in life's most serious moments.
DZ: *Do you also see this worn-out, rhetorical language in contemporary literature?*
AK: I am not a critic, but I often feel this way. Take Georg Büchner's last sentence in *Lenz*, "Thus he lived for the rest of his days."[12] This is condensation. What already exists does not need to be duplicated. There are a lot of people whom I would trust who lived in the seventeenth century. Not because I am at home there. But because they still have an open mind about how rich our interests actually are. That love stories and balance sheets are not opposites. That tulip fields and politics belong together. They can still make discoveries.
DZ: *So the misfortune of German literature began with Romanticism.*
AK: In a certain sense, yes. You could insert me into *Elective Affinities* as a porter. I would read French texts. The master would find me quite nice. The captain would greet me. But I would be completely on the side of the boy who jumps into the river after the thing he loves the most and then gets married. I like this better than when Goethe's Ottilie lets Charlotte's child fall into the water, and the lovers are only able to meet in the afterlife.
DZ: *The golden age of literature . . .*
AK: More publications appeared that year than in 1928. The intervening years are deserts. I find it

unsettling that if you look you will find a great many construction sites from the seventeenth century that we could continue writing in the twenty-first century. In 1989, I thought we were heading toward a fortuitous era. Now I see that things have become atavistic since 2001. Civil rights are disappearing again. Insights such as Bismarck's "Politics is the art of the possible" are being transformed into "A superpower cannot be contained by the possible." When I hear things like this, something stirs within me. Schools of thought from 1914 are now re-emerging in completely different parts of the world. This irritates me. I want to bring this to storytelling just as much as the question: How can I make divorce impossible? Poetics is the task of collectors.

DZ: *Who are your accomplices in this poetic endeavor?*

AK: Tacitus, Ovid, Montaigne, Caesarius of Heisterbach from the Middle Ages. This is where I come from.

DZ: *You are quite lonely among the living.*

AK: Heiner Müller and Einar Schleef are still alive in spirit. I love speaking with Durs Grünbein, but Gottfried Benn would be closer to me. I can quote you Proust verbatim. Flaubert, Tolstoy, and Thomas Mann mean a lot to me. I actually wanted to write like Thomas Mann, but nothing came of it. This type of ornamental embellishment does not really interest me at all. I am not a storyteller who recounts things to others in their downtime. I am a nervous person who realizes that complete perspectives and horizons are changing to a ruinous extent. I need to get at this. In a single image. In a single sentence. Most stories I write come down to a single sentence.

DZ: *Who is the most important person in your life?*

AK: My emotional attitudes come from my mother. They turn everything in the world toward peacemaking. My mother once told me she witnessed an accident while driving and stopped immediately so that the disaster would not be repeated. I do not know whether this is correct or incorrect, but it is certainly worth trying. This is how I think.

Translated by Emma Woelk

Notes

This dialogue was originally published in German as Ulrich Greiner and Iris Radisch, "Der Friedensstifter," *Die Zeit*, October 23, 2003, 44.

1. [Translator's citation: Alexander Kluge, *The Devil's Blind Spot: Tales from the New Century*, trans. Martin Chalmers and Michael Hulse (New York: New Directions, 2004). The German original is Alexander Kluge, *Die Lücke, die der Teufel läßt: Im Umfeld des neuen Jahrhunderts* (Frankfurt am Main: Suhrkamp, 2003.)]

2. [Translator's citation: Kluge, *The Devil's Blind Spot*, 257–77.]

3. [Translator's note and citation: Kluge has regularly attributed this directive to the Dadaists, when in fact it was the then Letterist Guy Debord who first penned it in the postsurrealist journal *Les lèvres nues* based in Belgium. See Guy Debord, "Introduction to a Critique of Urban Geography," in *Situationist International Anthology*, ed. and trans. Ken Knabb (Berkeley, CA: Bureau of Public Secrets, 2006), 6: "A friend recently told me that he had just wandered through the Harz region of Germany while blindly following the directions of a map of London. This sort of game is obviously only a feeble beginning in comparison to the complete creation of architecture and urbanism that will someday be within the power of everyone." Translation slightly modified to fix Kluge's syntax.]

4. [Translator's note and citation: There exist a total of seven editions of *Schlachtbeschreibung*, which was originally published in hardcover in 1964. A revised paperback appeared in 1968; two editions with different titles in 1969; a significantly revised version in 1978; a reprint with a slight title change in 1983; and most recently the revised version that appeared in 2000 in *Chronik der Gefühle*. In English, see Alexander Kluge, *The Battle*, trans. Leila Vennewitz (New York: McGraw-Hill, 1967).]

5. [Translator's citation: Kluge, "The Luck of the Devil," in *The Devil's Blind Spot*, 3.]

6. [Translator's citation: Alexander Kluge, "Aufklärung in Indien," in *Die Lücke, die der Teufel läßt* (Frankfurt: Suhrkamp, 2003), 537–38.]

7. [Translator's citation: Alexander Kluge, "Unintentional Stroke of Luck," in *The Devil's Blind Spot*, 38–39.]

8. [Translator's citation: Bertolt Brecht, *The Threepenny Opera*, trans. Ralph Manhein and John Willett (New York: Bloomsburg, 2000), 62.]

9. [Translator's note: See the stories in chapter 2, entitled "Kann ein Gemeinwesen ICH sagen? / Tschernobyl," in *Die Lücke, die der Teufel läßt*, 105–93. See also the translated stories "A Steel Casing for Chernobyl," "Burnt Souls," and "From the Standpoint of the Skin," in *The Devil's Blind Spot*, 22–24, 211–23.]

10. [Translator's citation: Alexander Kluge, "Die mißglückte Scheidung," in *Die Lücke, die der Teufel läßt*, 503–4.]

11. [Translator's citation: Alexander Kluge, "Maxwells Tod," in *Die Lücke, die der Teufel läßt*, 598–600.]

12. [Translator's citation: Georg Büchner, *Complete Plays, Lenz, and Other Writings*, trans. John Reddick (New York: Penguin, 1993), 164.]

4

Companions in Now-Time

Dear Mr. B.,

You want to know something about either my library or my relation to books in just two pages. You are presumably expecting something different than what I am able to deliver.

I have always considered books to be like the food we eat. This does not mean, however, that they form a "library." In almost all of the spaces I live and work, there are piles of books. When arranged vertically and horizontally next to each other in bookshelves, they are no more orderly than when they just lie around. They nevertheless create a relationality when they lie or stand next to each other in confounding rows. I find them quickly. I could not find them at all if a friendly hand were to organize them.

* * *

Books have a will of their own. They find each other on their own accord. That is the principle guiding their rows, stacks, and piles.

Were you to make the effort, you could reconstruct a few completed projects I worked on from the way my books were stored like geological strata. This is not the case for every phase of my career. There is no single book that bears witness to my first publication, the story collection *Case Histories* [*Lebensläufe*]. I wrote this book in courtrooms, on the train, in cafés, and during my time as a lawyer. You cannot bring books with you into these places. I also need no documentation for my stories. My stories emerge from the tip of my pencil. In other words, from my head or my ears.

Theoretical texts are a completely different matter. They require a particular effort. The book I wrote with my friend Oskar Negt, *Public Sphere and Experience*, brought together a wide selection of books just like *History and Obstinacy* did years later. These books have stayed together as a group right where we left them after our collaboration. Packed in boxes, they have survived many a move.

I do not wish to destroy a "garden" like this one that has grown over time. I also refrain from doing so, because I enjoying thinking back on the time we collaborated so intensively. These unorganized books, which no chance could have ever assembled together the way we did, are something like a memory turned inside out, one I carry around with me in my head entirely independent of the books we wrote together.

Another grouping seemingly devoid of organization is my images. I store them in large laundry baskets. The tradition dates back to about 1972. I introduced this storage method because the images get scattered very quickly. Their unruly formats can only be accommodated in bags, boxes, or large folders. These baskets store my images for a long time. Some of these baskets have forfeited their contents to boxes kept in my basement. They are all grouped by year. There are periods when I made films or prepared collections of stories like *Die Unheimlichkeit der Zeit* [The Uncanniness of Time] by working through collections of images.

For me, these "collections" are distinctive, because I certainly do not seek out the same images at a later date. Similarly, coral reefs thought to be the same are never identical. The search for images changes with the material, but the fact that I use images like texts and texts like images—an idiosyncrasy of mine—creates the impression that I use similar images time and time again. This is just as untrue for me as it is for W. G. Sebald. The utility of these baskets (that I could compare to fish ponds) becomes apparent when great book designers like Franz Greno and Martin Weinmann show up and read the images against the grain for the layout of a book.

I do not own the books I most admire. I live with them. Books connect centuries. This is what I find trustworthy about them. No other medium connects authors over 2,000 years so reliably as the book. It moved me that while he was in California Heiner Müller, already suffering from cancer, bought a used copy of Ovid's *Metamorposes* translated into English and cast in verse. An unconventional reproduction of the original text by the great master. He told me about this. He carried the book with him when he was brought to the intensive care unit on the day he died. I am more connected to Ovid on account of this oral and personal relation. I would not store Ovid, this companion of my now-time (who, like Heiner Müller, is not dead for me), on a shelf in the form of a book.

* * *

How I treat my beloved books cannot be compared to the nurturing of a library. In my parents' house, books were kept in an orderly fashion in the so-called gentlemen's study: a luxury edition of *Die Befreiungskriege* in three volumes; Shakespeare's complete works in red leather (brought into the marriage by my mother, but read by neither of my parents); lots of biographies; and many novels. You could also find indecent works, were you to reach behind them. This room was not for reading, but rather was especially meant for playing bridge. In one corner, the men would have their nightly round of drinks. This order was brought to a definitive end with the destruction of the house by the air raid on Halberstadt on April 8, 1945. I have never recreated it in my own life. The writing on the wall and sign of the times must be read carefully. They are final. They are also books. They just do not look like a library.

With warmest greetings,

Alexander Kluge

Translated by Emma Woelk

Note

This text was originally published in German as Alexander Kluge, "Gefährten der Jetztzeit," *Neue Zürcher Zeitung*, December 1, 2007, 74.

5

STORYTELLING MEANS DISSOLVING RELATIONS

PIERO SALABÈ: *You write that your stories change, but the questions remain the same. Which questions interest you?*

ALEXANDER KLUGE: If real relations do not respect a person, then he will in turn deny these nonhuman relations. This is the antirealism of feeling. People are not objective in this respect, but rather human and subjective. This makes the topic of "reality" volatile because a person's subjective reality is just as real as the objective relations, the wall we run into headfirst. As long as I make films and write, I will pursue this discrepancy between the subjective and the objective, which always appear together and are two fundamentally different texts.

PS: *Could you give an example of this discrepancy?*
AK: The first industrialized war takes place between 1914 and 1918. It involves a horrible clash of

stockpiled munitions made from the labor of countless workers and engineers. Also involved are miners from both the Ruhr region and French coal mining regions who each dug tunnels into a hill outside of Verdun that were to be detonated. This is highly specialized labor power at work that will soon become dead labor. Marx applied the concept of the collective worker [*Gesamtarbeiter*] to this labor power; employed by two competing companies, the collective worker withdraws himself from the economic possibilities of both. The collective worker is tragic because he could develop a self-consciousness about his labor power, but instead he works against his own interests. Disconnected, objective, and subjective realities diverge. In contrast, capitalism, united by stock markets, knows quite well how to collaborate because it is only a matter of commodity exchange. Because everything comes down to the exchange of commodities, nothing matters all that much and nothing is psychically difficult, whereas labor is something quite valuable that people cling to and pin their own identity to. If the object of this labor involves people, as is the case with the teacher Gabi Teichert in my film *The Patriot*, then this exchange is hardly possible. This is the tragic element in subjective texts.

PS: *If feelings have an antirealistic tendency, does this also apply to sadness?*

AK: There are always two aspects to sadness: it isolates, but it can also bring people in contact with one another. Sadness and crying are capable of dissolving hardened relations. If I am sad, then I am receptive to solace. This second form of sadness can be answered and leads not to unhappiness. It is instead a dowry, the most valuable element of a culture.

PS: *This sadness that results from the tension between feelings and reality does not necessarily culminate in historical pessimism?*

AK: I am neither a pessimist nor an optimist and do not encourage others to consign themselves to one or the other. How one understands melancholy depends on the capacity for differentiation: as a feeling, it either remains social or it turns away from society—as it does with Philoctetes—as a sadness that can lead to anger or resentment. There are always two completely different developments. When people are, for example, driven out of their hometowns and into industrial metropolises—the most collective form of suffering known as "primitive accumulation"—new skills develop, on the one hand, and negative phenomena such as alienation and anomie emerge, on the other. There is never just loss or gain. If instead of pursuing my interest in the question "What is real?" I ask: "How do we understand progress" or "What is enlightenment about?" then the answer is the capacity for differentiation: to explore how human characteristics largely develop autonomously in society.

PS: *Do you believe in progress? Do you consider the project of enlightenment incomplete?*

AK: I do not believe in linear progress because for me the past is always coming at us from the future. Instead, I believe in circular movements like those in whirlpools. The concept of enlightenment must begin with the real phenomenon that time does not actually pass. The past, the future, the subjunctive case all belong to the present. I do not imagine there to be any realities, but rather two components, the subjective and the objective, that are always recreating these realities. This is just one human process of production where I can discern whether people are involved or excluded. If we really grapple with this, then a new field of action for enlightenment emerges akin to a new encyclopedia. We must continue to tell stories about problems in the world, and with storytelling we must also push back against these problems that people fail to respect. Storytelling means dissolving in the literal sense of "analyzing."[1] It does not mean that I oppose real relations with the point of my thoughts, but rather that I first mollify and then dissolve them by telling stories and thus make them receptive. This is the great, unfinished project of enlightenment that I sincerely believe in.

PS: *But feeling can also impair our capacity for differentiation and cloud our view of objective relations. Brecht criticizes the principle of empathy.*

AK: Empathy is one of our greatest assets and at the same time it is worthless when it comes off sentimental. Feelings possess a capacity for differentiation like human skin, which is very good at saying who it likes and does not like or if it is hot or cold. The way in which each individual organ of differentiation functions proves that we humans are equipped with a complete score of culturally and biologically determined feelings. It is important to assemble them into clusters that are not solely sentimental. If sentimental narration leads to Anna Karenina's death at the end of Tolstoy's novel, then there is something in my identity as an author that pushes back. It is important to me to continue writing until I find the gap in this inescapable fate and thereby save this woman, for example. In my story, she would survive. This is art. Tightrope walking is a form of artistry whereby I test real relations, as Brecht suggests, and simultaneously I accept that in doing so my motivation—the search for happiness—coincides with the motivation of many other people who have evolved into seekers of happiness. Brecht would not object to this principle of empathy.

PS: *When you test "real relations," do you approach this from a theoretical background?*

AK: It is the same critical background as Brecht's: classical economists, who were also storytellers, incidentally. My stories are based on observation and are ultimately not accountable to any theory. There are certainly sworn witnesses like Walter Benjamin and many other confidants like Karl Korsch, Adorno, Horkheimer, and also Montaigne, who happily cohabitate in my texts. I do not feel conflicted when, for example, Horkheimer writes a decisive critique of Montaigne's skeptical tradition. Horkheimer is right to criticize Montaigne's indifference, but Montaigne is also right in that he wants to prevent civil war. One has to be more generous than twentieth-century theoreticians believed was necessary. In the twenty-first century, we need an entirely new amalgam of thinking and storytelling.

PS: *Does the coexistence in your work of heterogeneous stories, which have as much to do with the circus as they do with revolution, represent such an amalgam?*

AK: New figurations emerge that do not fit together by correlating different texts like maps superimposed on top of each other. When I also write about the circus and trains alongside very serious stories about Iraq or Germany in the month of December 1941 in my book *Tür an Tür mit einem anderen Leben* [Next Door to Another Life], I want to confound my readers and provoke them to think. I do this in following the chapter about the time required for revolutions because there exists a metaphor for revolutions as trains of world history that I find incorrect. With the circus, I am fascinated by the idea that people's fantasy can do everything. By assuming the form of a circus, the revolution competes with the illusion of the guillotine. One could breed the *citoyen* with a blade. My actual literary form is that of the commentary. Commentaries tend to create constellations and never

Chapter 5

	grasp stories in isolation but rather always in relationship to others. One story full of strong emotional vehemence goes in one direction, and the next goes in another. If we look at the cosmos, we realize this is the most obvious way something moves.
PS:	*The correlative method of storytelling is radically different from linear narrative forms. Is traditional* belles lettres *a genre of the past?*
AK:	When I write, I write antirhetorically. Poetry and rhetoric are two different disciplines. Adorno talks about the subcutaneous structure that makes up poetry and remains even when ornamentation and syntax are left out. As an observer, I cannot narrate in the first person that was so customary in the eighteenth and nineteenth centuries, nor can I do so according to the rules of street traffic and railroads from that era. Nothing of this *belles lettres* remains. This finely wrought tragedy only slows things down. I am not so sure how much of it we need. Of course, it is a good thing, insofar as it differentiates the soul, but you can read good novels and still carry out a massacre, as was the case in World War II. Educated people can do this. From its beginnings until today, the form of the novel is insufficient for understanding and navigating our world. One needs clearer, more rigorous instruments.
PS:	*There is also an autobiographical element in your correlation of texts. How do you explain this if you see yourself as an observer of real relations?*
AK:	I have always written and made films subjectively, even when the author's person plays no leading role. If an air raid affects me, it is my job as author first to understand and describe the phenomenon of an air raid, rather than what I think as a boy. With age you begin to notice that the experiences of the six-year-old person

you once were are present. I believe that the political is an intensive form of everyday experience. This raw material is commonplace. When I make observations about my relation to my parents, then it is also exploring the human need for warmth, as is the case in the chapter "We Fortunate Children of the First Globalization" in my book *Tür an Tür mit einem anderen Leben*.[2] I previously had not written any stories that begin 550 million years before Christ when the world was made of ice. I was interested in the question regarding the origins of our internal need for warmth at 98.6 degrees as well as the warmheartedness of feeling and the empathy that enables one person to understand another. Karl Marx writes that one man is another's mirror and this is the basic form of empathy. Freed from any intent to espouse a particular political opinion, I really delve into the private sphere and even more forcefully into the sphere of labor. Of course, my capacity for differentiation is partisan, but partisanship in the limited sense from the 1930s is of no use to us in the twenty-first century. The ability to observe must direct itself much more toward trivial matters and leave the determination of what the main issue is to the relations themselves.

PS: *From Napoleon to the animal tamers from the Russian state circus, from Hitler's favorite operetta to the Croatian immigration to Chile—your observations are historically diverse and well grounded in documentary evidence. Where do you see the border between your writing of stories and the writing of history?*

AK: I create constellations between stories in motion. A writer of history, on the other hand, would have to fill in the gaps and pin down the stories. Benjamin cites an image by J. J. Grandville in which an interplanetary bridge made of iron extends to Saturn. This is characteristic of the way in which people attempted to create relationships constructively at the beginning of the twentieth century. Even Brecht and the Bauhaus adhered to this constructivism. Without giving up an interest in this construction, one can accept that the planets will never align themselves according to this bridge and would instead completely rip it apart. I therefore think that one can add in different forms of storytelling. In this respect, I am partisan and not a writer of history.

PS: *Do you not fear that arbitrariness could arise in the creation of these constellations? What holds your stories together?*

AK: A reader can do very little with finished buildings. He is better off when he builds his own house, but not arbitrarily. All 350 stories in my book *Tür an Tür mit einem anderen Leben* have a single core, just as there is a core at the center of the earth from which gravitational relations emerge. This gravitational thinking holds things on the sphere's surface together, but also the sphere itself, and this corresponds with other spheres that zip around in space like planets. They are autonomously formulated stories that come into contact with others also formulated autonomously. They are like Leibniz's monads and communicate quite well even though they are blind.

PS: *Is it left to the reader to find a common thread?*

AK: I do not believe this is hidden. Readers have this subtext within themselves. Take three stories on the topic of divorce: The first is that of a married couple who, on their way to divorce court, come across an impassable forest fire, return home, and thus leave the divorce judge waiting.[3] Then think about Anna Karenina's divorce, which, according to Tolstoy, separates this woman from her young son and eventually kills her.[4] And finally consider *The Princess of Cleves* by Madame de La Fayette, a woman who forbids herself to get a divorce.[5] Despite her love for the duke, she remains true to her wedding vows. When she tells her husband this, he dies. She kills him in a certain sense. Now both lovers could come together, as the entire courtly society wishes, but instead she decides to join a cloister in order to avoid facing the pain she caused her husband. The ideal of celibacy appears to be the only paradoxical way to preserve feelings and to simultaneously resist their inescapability. These three stories have a single internal core, are three parts of a constellation, and revolve around the discrepancy between subjective and objective reality. I could tell more stories like those that end with my parents' divorce, which I never condoned, which is the real motive for my writing. As I write in one story, "All research into parallel worlds or the concession of a second life revolves around the possibility of recreating this 'alliance.'"[6] This is my partisanship. It can establish neither a national party nor a new social class, but with this type of orientation all conflicts in the world can be divided into those that lead to people or those that lead to isolation.

PS: *Is this form of the constellation that you also use in your films particularly well suited to investigate our time?*

AK: It is not a "new form." Many great works from literary history are constructed according to this principle. Take Ovid's *Metamorphoses*, for example. Poems operate with variations, with chains of constellations, but variational novels—just think of François Rabelais—also piece together autonomous elements. This can happen horizontally and vertically. In times of upheaval, these forms are particularly sought after and Rabelais wrote in one such time. James Joyce is a great collector of these self-contained, heterogeneous elements in which the universe is reflected. And Proust's novels can also be cut into

	with scissors and reassembled without falsifying them. I believe this method is necessary for the twenty-first century. I learned it in 1945 when the relations were too turbulent to be considered linearly.
PS:	*You have always dealt with the history of National Socialism in Germany in an engaged and critical manner. What do you think of the current tendency in film and other media such as comics to treat the Third Reich with humor? This supposedly promotes a more relaxed relationship to the past among younger generations.*
AK:	Jokes from the period of the Third Reich are a reflection of oppression. I believe that they are better, more apt than today's malapropisms, which, for example, would say that Hitler protected the last of Germany's unemployed because he always held his hands in front of his genitals during events. History itself develops something against tyrants and to observe this, Jacques Derrida would say, is better than making jokes after the fact. Instead of making the Third Reich ridiculous, I prefer to put its ridiculousness on display. In my collection *Cinema Stories*, there is a text, "The Final Film Screening in the Reich Chancellery," which is based on a real episode.[7] Because the top of the hall of the Reich Chancellery has already been destroyed, the surviving leaders of the Third Reich are sitting under an open roof, with small lights because of the risk of bombs. They watch the movie *Opfergang* based on Rudolf Binding's novella and directed by Veit Harlan. It is the absurd story of a former colonial officer who returns home, is torn between two women, and dies in an epidemic. Dressed in his clothes, his wife rides past the home of his dying mistress so she can die in peace. This convoluted story has comic potential and makes one think. I am interested in describing why it was shown as the

PS:

AK:

last screening in the already destroyed Reich Chancellery in 1945.
You have not been making longer films for a while now. Instead, you have been making shorts or writing books that provide solace because they "look back on a much longer stratum."[8] What does the future of film look like? Will "longer strata" be created that we can look back on?
I think so, but the mediums will be different. I do not see any classical films in multiplex cinemas anymore. But film museums are turning into production centers and there are editions of classical films on DVD. I believe that the old foundations will reappear beyond the Internet. It was for this reason that together with cameraman Michael Ballhaus I presented my *Minute Films*, which were filmed in 65mm instead of 35mm, at one of the last film exhibitions in Venice.[9] We wanted to lay claim with these films to a visual quality that stands in opposition to the digital quality of YouTube, and that paradoxically leads back to the Lumière brothers' shorts. When film is revived, it is possible that we will not recognize it immediately, but it will still be film.

Translated by Emma Woelk

Notes

This dialogue was originally published in German as "Erzählen heißt auflösen: Piero Salabé im Gespräch mit Alexander Kluge," *Neue Rundschau* 119 (2008): 72–80.

1. [Translator's note: Kluge says in the German original, "Erzählen heißt auflösen, im wörtlichen Sinne von 'analytisch.'" In order to maintain a parallelism between "storytelling" and "dissolving," the translation renders the adjective as the present participle of its verbal form: "analyzing." The etymology that Kluge invokes is the related compound noun's two principal parts: (1) the Greek prefix *ana* [ἀνά] for "up," "back," or "again" and 2) the Greek verb *luein* [λύειν] for "to loosen." While the English "unloosening" is the direct translation of "analysis," the primary

meanings of the German word "auflösen" are "to dissolve," "to disperse," and "to turn into." The first is clearly what Kluge means given the ensuing context.]

2. [Translator's citation: Alexander Kluge, *Tür an Tür mit einem anderen Leben* (Frankfurt am Main: Suhrkamp, 2006), 9–55.]

3. [Translator's citation: Alexander Kluge, "Die mißglückte Scheidung," in *Die Lücke, die der Teufel läßt* (Frankfurt: Suhrkamp, 2002), 503–4.]

4. [Translator's citation: Alexander Kluge, "Generosität," in *Tür an Tür mit einem anderen Leben*, 516–18.]

5. [Translator's citation: Alexander Kluge, "Kommentar zu Princesse de Clèves," in *Chronik der Gefühle*, vol. 1, *Basisgeschichten* (Frankfurt am Main: Suhrkamp, 2000), 939–43.]

6. [Translator's citation: Alexander Kluge, "Mein wahres Motiv," in *Tür an Tür mit einem anderen Leben*, 595.]

7. [Translator's citation: Alexander Kluge, "Die letzte Filmvorstellung in der Reichskanzlei," in *Geschichten vom Kino* (Frankfurt am Main: Suhrkamp, 2007), 233–37. See also Alexander Kluge, "The Final Film Screening in the Reich Chancellery," in *Cinema Stories*, trans. Martin Brady and Helen Hughes (New York: New Directions, 2007), 61–66.]

8. [Translator's note: Although the source of Salabè's quotation proves elusive, Kluge has repeatedly spoken about the solace books provide. See, for example, Alexander Kluge, "Die Geduld der Bücher: Alexander Kluge im Gespräch mit Claus Philipp," *Volltext: Magazin für Literatur* 6 (2006): 1, 28–30.]

9. [Translator's citation: Alexander Kluge, dir., "Minutenfilme im 65 Millimeterformat: Für die Mostra in Venedig," *Seen sind für Fische Inseln* (Frankfurt am Main: Zweitausendeins, 2009), DVD 13, track 8.]

6

THEORY OF STORYTELLING

Lecture One

Rumblings of the Swallowed World—
Life Spans and the Real

I have entitled my Frankfurt lectures "Theory of Storytelling."[1] I somewhat carelessly borrowed my title from Helmut Heißenbüttel, who once lectured here on poetics.[2] What I did not know, and what I have noticed only after thorough examination is that this is an extremely difficult topic. To be clear, a praxis of poetics and narrative can be explained. A collection of every practical experience is also a task none too difficult. But a theory, that is indeed something very difficult. Since I made a promise, I wish all the same to give an account of narrative theory in four lectures starting with narrative and then moving to the subject matter of both theory and narrative, namely, the real—in other words, reality—and its abysses.

I use the term "theory" in the sense of Critical Theory. I am, so to speak, the court poet of the great philosophers. I myself am no philosopher. But as a storyteller I continue with all my heart what Theodor W. Adorno, Max Horkheimer, Paul Tillich, and others already prepared: a rich trove of tools each furnished with fundamental, oppositional attitudes. Theory in the sense of Critical Theory is always nourished on interests that are simultaneously practical, political, and vital. It does not theorize in any old manner, but rather serves as an orientation for essential questions. Immanuel Kant already formulated this proposition brilliantly in the eighteenth century: What does it mean to orient oneself in thinking?[3] He begins by noting how the sun rises in the East and how, through the cardinal directions, one can find its zenith. From this simple analogy, he draws the conclusion that humans will never permit the proscription of their own emancipation. This capacity for orientation thus goes far beyond matters of cardinal directions. Kant's stance—bound to both Critical Theory and the experiences of the twentieth century—is the topic at hand. And, as I have said, this is more of a stance or attitude, more of an ability to orient oneself, than a way of looking at Aristotelian ideas or the second order of reality attributed to the actuality of theory.[4]

When I talk about orienting oneself, I mean it in the sense of lighthouses, of which there are two kinds. Using lanterns, wreckers based on the shores of the North Sea would lure ships into running aground so that they could be looted. All of Sylt is comprised of such loot assembled there in the island's church. The second sort of orientation is the orientation toward objects we humans can neither reach nor touch, objects that cannot be displaced. One example of such objects is stars in the firmament. Stars are a means of navigation for ships at sea and wanderers in the desert alike. There is a great metaphor, an image, for this: there was an architect of the French Revolution, Jean-Jacques Lequeu, who envisioned in Paris a lighthouse for travelers gone astray in the desert.[5] I have not been able to ascertain whether it was ever erected in a desert somewhere or whether it saved anyone. But the very idea that someone could do such a thing, that is the solitary merit of theory. The exchange we are about to engage in here should be just as solitary as Lequeu's experiment was. . . .

It is thoroughly interesting to note that cooperation also belongs to what I earlier called "theory" and "narrative." This cooperation, which transpires alongside reality, lasts only a heterotopian moment. That the likes of Jürgen Habermas, Adorno, Hans-Jürgen Krahl, and a stream of students in training could have formed a collective and worked together with Niklas Luhmann, that would have been as wonderful as if the Augsburg Concordat had been ratified and the schism in the church had never occurred.[6] That would have been cooperation. That would have been Frankfurt at its full potential. Frankfurt could have been able to achieve that. I have always wished that Systems Theory, which is so practical in its orientation and offers such clear definitions, might work together with Critical Theory. There was a brief moment in time at the Max Planck Institute on the Preconditions of Human Life in the Modern World when Habermas and Luhmann made this a reality before ultimately having a falling-out with one another.[7] I find this painful. I deeply regret that my parents divorced, that the Peasants' War failed to bring about a cantonal constitution, and that in Frankfurt no such workshop for theory was assembled out of the unification of the minds that once resided here. I am quite willing to work, promote, and write texts in order to bring this about. The attitude of narration is to tell stories with happy endings that do not lie. This is a rare event. . . .

My first book, published in 1962, is called *Lebensläufe* [Case Histories], in English literally "Life Spans."[8] Writing now in the twenty-first century, I have a pressing need to write *Lebensläufe* anew. This need began to express itself quite differently after 1989 than I imagined it would prior to the demise of the Cold War. This is because the narration of life spans changes over time. Furthermore, it is very important to note that the narrative space in which we humans narrate and experience—together they constitute life spans—is first and foremost a vessel of time between birth and death. Within this receptacle, three generations together create an intelligible narrative space insofar as they directly engage one another in the act of storytelling.

There is another aspect to this—namely, that we also look outward from within our many concurrent life spans. For example, that six-year-old boy I once was is watching you right now because I am now curious and the kind of curiosity I had as a child is not something you can easily unlearn. At the same time, my thirty-year-old self that played the organ is also active. This, too, is present, but not at every moment of my life. As is the case with a Russian grandmother, sixteen if not eighty eyes peer out of a single adult human being upon the world, and the world looks back at them. And other people look back as well. These are, in toto, the unified life spans of experience, something that is an abiding theme for me, one that belongs to storytelling.

Over against these life spans stands a reality that purports to be something real. One need not always believe this claim. At first glance, reality is characterized by an extreme rigidity. An inmate who runs headfirst into the wall of his jail cell realizes instantly how objective the real conditions around him are. Conversely, these conditions are also brittle. This form—at times capricious and capable of metamorphosing like spirits and at other times hardened matter—is what we must understand when we say that Critical Theory works with an antagonistic concept of reality. The reality contained within this concept is real in the sense that, for example, an accident has cost someone his life or wars break out. Likewise, reality is a crude invention, a cocoon we fashion around ourselves so as to be able to withstand the real world. Reality, then, has many properties when it comes to narration. When it comes to enumeration, registration, or balancing accounts, reality is fairly straightforward. But once you begin to tell stories, you begin to notice that reality has catacombs, wells, and abysses. Below every linear narrative lie happiness and misfortune.

In addition to the objective inconsistencies of reality, which are neither smooth nor clear and thus constitute a kind of spirit world, there exists within us humans an antirealism of feeling. In the course of the evolutionary process, only those humans survived who were capable of repudiating those conditions of reality that did not mean them well. They did this not only on a large scale through uprisings and revolts, but also imperceptibly by taking everything they perceived in reality and deflecting it slightly through illusion. This is characteristic of the labor required for transcription. Monks did this with the Holy Scriptures, which changed over time under their hand. Humans do the same with their experiences. Accordingly, storytelling can be found everywhere like a game of telephone, wherein the process of telling and retelling slowly and successively changes what is being said. This happens when a person gives a monologue; they speak with themselves, and others speak in them. The first rule of thumb concerning narrative is that antagonism, a characteristic representative of all real relations, cannot be pinned to reality's brittleness.

The second rule of thumb is to show respect for subjective resistance in doubled forms of narration about the real, in which humans, instead of resigning themselves to reality, decide to change it. They do not wait until Judgment Day or a revolution. A permanent revolution in the sense of a nondogmatic Marxism would be storytelling in which humans voluntarily decide to alter their reality spontaneously and irrefutably. In this sense, the smallest social change would be, for example, moving from one apartment into another.

I have now come to the definition of narrative and must note here that narrative distinguishes itself from information quite clearly. Imagine there appeared a poetic text in the nightly news, which is, after all, nothing more than reporting on current events. The poem would have to be contained in quotation marks. Or imagine the news with a musical accompaniment. This idea would have been possible in Homer's era. The singer would begin with a report of Troy's downfall: "We are now defeated." In other words, this narration of current events remains indifferent to emotion. In the same way, storytelling is also topical. For instance, "I just saw an accident." Or, "we just came inside, it was light outside." We can tell one another everything.

But in the case of storytelling something extra spontaneously appears that includes, above all, all the residual times otherwise left out. A quotidian grammar of experience is just a present without its own past let alone all the other pasts, the future (which is hope), the sense of possibility (which is the subjunctive), and the optative (the Greek form for wishes). The Greeks had an entire grammar exclusive for the world of wishes, and this world is as real as the world of facts. In this way, narration is a pattern of behavior that simultaneously comprises and mixes well with all these aggregate states of experience. It is a very old form not equally possible in every society.

Imagine you are involved in a car accident. Doctors are in the process of evacuating the injured. It is all quite urgent. Right at this moment, a narrator—a particularly good one who can tell stories like Goethe—arrives on the scene and holds everything up. Or, imagine the same thing in the middle of stock market trading during the global financial crisis of 2008: at one o'clock, Lehman Brothers will be closed and the Tokyo Stock Exchange will open. Someone shows up all of the sudden and starts telling a story. We must be clear that narrative—ways out through which humans manage to keep themselves alive—is not practical in every circumstance. Servants can tell stories. Landscapes can tell stories. Nation-states can tell stories. History tells stories. But at the same time, there is something about all this that fascinates me in particular—namely, all of these tell stories simultaneously. They are choruses telling stories.

I wish to show this through means of a simple example. You see, my father was a great storyteller and came from a family that always told stories. For over 200 years, they would sit down to midday coffee and cake and begin by telling stories to one another. That is just how it happened in central Germany. My mother was also a storyteller, but she told stories differently through interjections and brief commentaries. Her company would work itself up at the bridge table while I, a young boy sitting in front of them, could not get enough of their talk even though they spoke too fast for me to understand a word. That hum remains something unrecoverable in my mind.

My mother did not tell stories like my father. Her method was disorderly but it was nevertheless accompanied by both a chorus and music, while his was orderly. Both of these forms of narrating have their respective abysses. Let us take, for example, my father when I visited him on the first of May in 1970 in what was then East Germany. I arrived with the eyes of a West German at a point in my life when I was working in Frankfurt. My father sat at the desk of his medical practice that contained a maternity ward; on the first floor lay a pregnant woman in labor. My father, always the focused doctor and obstetrician, took a pause before the onset of the woman's next set of contractions. Long preoccupied with the Battle of Marne of 1914, which he believed could have ended differently, he was reading a book about Napoleon's Russian campaign. Outside his window, the National People's Army drilled on Bismarck Square, replete with brass band, an official address, and a delegation of Communist Party officials. You are perhaps starting to see how disparate this reality is. I do not think that anyone on the square would have mentioned Napoleon in his speech; that would have been strange. Nor was the Battle of Marne topical for them. They experienced that May Day in the GDR along with all the cells in their bodies just like every other person equally equipped with billions of companions inside their bodies.

Now, my father was then called upstairs to the pregnant woman whose contractions started up again. He operated in four realities simultaneously. This is narrative. When I allow it to happen, I create multidimensionality, which, in the case of Bach, contains polyphony. I would hold it in high regard were that also the case with my stories. In fact, I can easily produce it through respect and observation. I do not have to make it, for reality is itself multifaceted. This is what I meant earlier when I said that there is the linear narrative perspective as well as a vertical structure made of comments, catacombs, and wells that fundamentally enrich storytelling. For this reason, there is no narrative without a subtext, without double meanings, without ambiguity, or without metaphors about which I will talk next time. They are a mechanism for intercourse between so many levels that comprise a nonacademic—emotional—mine. That is a human being. . . .

It is observable that nowhere does the same intense degree of cooperation exist—the penetration of one force into that of another—than in wars. An alien observing a war would consider it to be cooperation. This is painful. We call it cross-mapping when multiple maps are overlaid on top of one another. The difference here is that it is not cooperative; whole lives are extinguished.

This cannot be taken seriously enough. We can also call this a "fall from reality."[9] . . . The "rumblings of the swallowed world" is also suggestive of this. We do not know whether the "rumblings of the swallowed world" means we are in the belly of a fish and take it to be reality, or whether we humans have swallowed the world such that it lies in the belly of humanity just like the thousand stones that filled the wolf in the Grimms's fairy tale about the seven kids.[10]

I ask you now to try and imagine the image I am about to describe. I think everyone will recognize it from the news. The day after Osama bin Laden was shot, a picture of leading figures sitting together in the White House began to circulate. The American secretary of state held her hand in front of her face, very likely a cough reflex, though perhaps a reaction of shock. The president sat in a peculiar manner on the side, as if at a school desk, not wishing to occupy a prominent place in the scene. Presiding is a large general commanding the computer. Were he to sit off to the side of the photograph, only then would he be able to observe everything. He could compose a report. This is where the storyteller sits. There is nothing to see on the computer screen. Everything is erased.

Just how brittle is reality? How does one chance lead to another? Where are the breaks and abysses in reality possible? What if something had gone drastically wrong with the commando operation? And indeed it nearly did, since a helicopter went up in flames in the course of the raid. It was not guaranteed that Pakistan, uninformed about the clandestine operation, would interpret the operation as a Taliban attack and try and blow up the aircraft. Monitors in the White House would have showed all of this as it happened. The photograph of the group watching the events unfold would have been censored. The position at the margins of the image is a very complex concept that grows more important for narration only as the twenty-first century advances.

It is obvious for a filmmaker that composing an image always means looking outside the frame. Right next to the shot is where the most interesting action unfolds. Accordingly, the more I find the future averted, the stronger my interest grows in my ancestors: my parents, their parents, their great-grandparents, and so on. Everyone sitting here has eight great-grandparents. Given the thousand of us here in this room, that is a lot of people. All of your great-grandparents can in turn be potentiated once more. Everything that these people were, everything that they felt in their organs and spirit lives on within us. I look at my daughter and see a small commonwealth of combatants from an ancestral civil war assembled together in her body that no longer quarrel. The civil war is over. In other words, nature has an irrepressible tolerance that makes both it and family trustworthy narrators.

Walter Benjamin writes of Paul Klee's image of the angel of history who faces the past to witness something terrible while he is blown forward into the future by the winds of progress. This image can be interpreted in another way. It could also very well be the case that this angel is a guardian angel who originates from the untapped forces of humankind. These forces from every possible past have protected us up until now such that we are in fact smarter than our appeals to reason. We might in a certain sense host within us a balancing mechanism that enables us to continue our existence despite our frequent attempts, from Syria to the present, to eradicate our own species. That humankind may in fact be *homo compensator* instead of *homo sapiens* is admittedly a faint hope, though certainly more justified than merely entrusting the retelling of stories with the task of sustaining a straightforward, linear notion of hope for the future.[11]

Twenty-one thousand, five hundred eighty-six years before Christ. Imagine the place where we are gathered today as a steppe in the tundra, one entirely unfamiliar to us. For over 30,000 years, a steady wind blew in from the northeast. The weather report was always the same. Woolly mammoths freely roamed. Always on the move, our ancestors marched through extremes. They did not scamper. They had to hunt, and if they were not quick enough, they starved. I find it extremely rewarding to think about our distant ancestors who are directly related to us. These primates certainly possessed a few characteristics we no longer have. Likewise, it is equally rewarding to think how adversity gives rise to ingenuity.

Only then does one notice the sort of tenacity inherent within us and why the subjective factor—this is, after all, the entire point of my lecture—is just as hard, strong, and massive as everything objective put together. This will never change. . . .

Translated by Nathan Wagner

Notes

This video was originally published on DVD as Alexander Kluge. *Theorie des Erzählens: Frankfurter Poetikvorlesungen* (Berlin: Suhrkamp, 2013), DVD 1.
 Kluge's poetics lectures took place on four Tuesdays in June 2012. Included for translation here is only the first of these four lectures, which occurred on Tuesday, June 5, 2012. The ellipses included in the translation index screenings of Kluge's films and videos as well as readings from his then recently published story collection entitled *Das fünfte Buch*.
 1. [Translator's note: The original German title of Kluge's lectures is *Theorie der Erzählung*, which poses translational difficulties given the different contexts in which "Erzählung" is used. Also an allusion to Walter Benjamin's 1936 essay "The Storyteller: Reflections on the Works of Nikolai Leskov," Kluge's title refers not only to the concerns of narration, but also to narrators and the storytelling they perform. "Erzählung" is thus rendered henceforth as "narrative" when Kluge addresses more theoretical concerns, and as "storytelling" when he addresses what storytellers do.]
 2. [Translator's note and citation: Helmut Heißenbüttel held his own Frankfurt lectures entitled "Grundbegriffe einer Poetik im 20. Jahrhundert" [Basic Concepts for a Twentieth-Century Poetics] in the summer semester of 1963 and published them in *Über Literatur: Aufsätze und Frankfurter Vorlesungen* (Olten-Freiburg: Walter-Verlag, 1966), 123–205.]
 3. Cf. Immanuel Kant, "What Does It Mean to Orient Oneself in Thinking?," in *Religion within the Boundaries of Mere Reason: And Other Writings*, ed. and trans. Allen Wood and George di Giovanni (Cambridge: Cambridge University Press, 1998), 3–14.
 4. [Translator's note: Kluge uses in the first paragraph both "das Wirkliche" (the real) and "die Realität" (reality) within a larger semantic field that here is rendered as both "second-order reality" and "actuality" in order to convey literally the German original ("eine zweite Wirklichkeit") as well as theory's implied claim on reality.]
 5. [Translator's citation: Cf. Oskar Negt and Alexander Kluge's notes in "Utopias of Bourgeois, Political Architecture," in *Public Sphere and Experience: Toward an Analysis of the Bourgeois and Proletarian Public Sphere*, trans. Peter Labanyi, Jamie Owen Daniel, and Assenka Oksiloff (Minneapolis: University of Minnesota Press, 1993), 280–82.]
 6. [Translator's note and citation: Kluge is referring here to a collaboration that could have materialized in the winter semester of 1968–69 at the Goethe

University Frankfurt, when the Bielefeld-trained Niklas Luhmann briefly substituted for Adorno. Kluge recounts this opportunity passed up by Adorno's student Hans-Jürgen Krahl and others in the twelve-part story cycle entitled "The Kitchen of Good Fortune"; see Alexander Kluge, "Die Küche des Glücks," in *Das fünfte Buch: Neue Lebensläufe* (Berlin: Suhrkamp, 2012), 351–67. See also Kluge's brief account translated here in Alexander Kluge, "The Actuality of Adorno," 450–61 in this volume.]

7. [See Jürgen Habermas and Niklas Luhmann, *Theorie der Gesellschaft oder Sozialtechnologie: Was leistet die Systemforschung?* (Frankfurt am Main: Suhrkamp, 1971).]

8. [Translator's note: Leila Vennewitz's English translation of *Lebensläufe* was published under two different titles, neither of which conveys the meaning contained in the German original that has continued to operate as a central category in Kluge's thinking. They are *Attendance List for a Funeral* (1966) and *Case Histories* (1988).]

9. [Translator's note: Kluge borrows the expression "fall from reality" from a cycle of stories that begins chapter 5 of *Das fünfte Buch* entitled "Rumblings of the Swallowed World," which also serves as the title of his first of four Frankfurt poetic lectures. See Kluge, *Das fünfte Buch*, 369–543.]

10. [Translator's citation: See Alexander Kluge and Oskar Negt, *History and Obstinacy*, ed. Devin Fore, trans. Richard Langston et al. (New York: Zone Books, 2014), 280–87.]

11. [Translator's note: Kluge here is harking back to his previous allusion to the game of telephone he attributes to the storytelling characteristic of everyday social life.]

7

WHAT IS A METAPHOR?

RAINER STOLLMANN: *"Primitive accumulation" is a term from Marx. You call it a metaphor. Why?*

ALEXANDER KLUGE: "Accumulation" is a "pileup," as in a pile of earth one shovels. This is an image. We no longer realize this because it is a Latin word, so we see it only as a concept.

RS: *And "capital"?*

AK: It comes from the Latin *caput* for "head." Capital can also refer to a capital city or a main idea. It is a metaphor transferred from the human body and applied to external reality. You cannot clearly differentiate between a metaphor and a concept. A metaphor is the creation of a web of ideas. Ovid's spinner Arachne is a woman who paints stories onto clothes. She stands in competition with the goddess Athena who prefers concepts. Arachne can sew

	stories into a person's clothing like a second skin. She is later turned into a spider. Arachne is my trademark on the Internet. ARACHNE'S WEB is like a metaphor. Metaphors unify facts into a coral reef.
RS:	*Marx's description of primitive accumulation is one of these webs?*
AK:	Yes. That is why he let English history serve as his example, even though primitive accumulation assumes a different form in every country, which he also acknowledges. In Russia they ask questions after the revolution of 1917 like: Where is primitive accumulation here? Is an industry possible without primitive accumulation? They attempt to artificially and violently create it under Stalin. They thought that a bit of violence was needed in the same way one adds a pinch of pepper to soup. This does not take into account that a government is not a cook.
RS:	*On the other hand, you just said that what a camera unerringly sees can be distorted in the mind of the author through concepts or metaphors like "capital" or "primitive accumulation."*
AK:	We need to dissolve historically specific metaphors. The Russian example shows that metaphors must also be dissolvable. The creation of metaphors is not an end in itself. Their brevity lasts in the time immediately after they evolve. In later eras, they provide a foil or commentary. The narrative about the far-reaching effects of the stock market in Antwerp is a powerful metaphor. In the sixteenth century, wool is so valuable in Antwerp that no one working on English farms could produce anything that would be adequate. The farms therefore had to be free and clear of people. So the farmers were removed, the huts burned down, and the fields turned into pastures. Where people once were are now sheep. This is metaphor. It must be

translated for our current situation. Could we say, "Where people once were is now the digital?" This too has a certain force to it. It is certainly not the same as the "enclosures" from the sixteenth century. Metaphors do not reflect observations, but instead provoke questions.

If eight generations developed a Ruhr region in the way that four generations develop an industrial center in China but then the world market goes in another direction and the production of coal and iron is no longer profitable, then this leads to migration. This requires, however, new metaphors. They must describe the fact that this whole is something real, even though every portion of it seems unreal. They must also describe the fact that the suffering of today's generations is repeated within the interiority of their grandchildren, in their subjective republic of characteristics.[1] But how? Imagine a married woman and her two children. Her husband must leave their home in the Ruhr region or Bremen to look for work in Stuttgart on account of its booming new technology sector. The marriage gets stretched out over 500 kilometers and becomes a weekend marriage. Can she stand it? If she can, then it is a metaphor or an opera on par with Beethoven's *Fidelio*.

To convey this contemporaneously—because it is only real if it is contemporaneous—is to avail oneself of the Marxist method. This is Eisenstein's focus. By using my confidant Eisenstein as a relay station, I can come in contact with the very old Marx. Born in 1818, he could be my great-grandfather's grandfather. I cannot address him informally. I cannot film him, even though I believe his point of view, his analytical abilities, his sharp intellect, and his sensual powers of observation are characteristics present within us today. In this respect, he is no ghost when I try to let him tell me which cinematic form can be used to describe his thoughts. He is only effective when he gives me advice on how I should film, how not to film how the world functions economically as a large map. There is no way I can film that.

RS: *Primitive accumulation is occurring rapidly in China right now. In the incidences of primitive accumulation we know happening now in various countries, it is the case that the new country carrying it out must base it in a new branch of industry. Prussia cannot build up a wool industry that already exists in England. Instead, it concentrates on the iron and steel industries. Yet in China it appears at the moment that the Chinese are repeating the era of iron and steel.*

AK: The question you pose makes a key point. What is tragic, what is dangerous about primitive accumulation, comes about when a transfer is no longer possible. People are broken out of the primitive means of production not by a higher authority but by the market. In Silesia, the weavers' looms could not keep up with the mass production in the English Midlands where the British mechanical looms prevailed. With twelve men from a single family relieving each other, the Silesians could work all night and exhaust all their cooperative efforts and still be powerless against the competition. They go hungry or must emigrate. If they reach the United States, then they will prosper. If they can emigrate to the Ruhr region, then they will also prosper. In these cases, a quantum always arises. One could almost say that 50 percent are new characteristics. People become resourceful out of necessity. This is a true but bitter word, because 50 percent of what occurs is also destruction. Old characteristics—for example, "the house as community"—are abandoned as ways of life. Something is destroyed and something is created in people. This is progress. This fits completely with modernism's observations, incidentally. It cannot be said that Marx observed something that no longer exists.

I cannot keep redirecting myself if all this were to come to an end. I find no new refuge. I cannot emigrate because the planet has been globalized and we cannot get to Mars. I can get from Sinkiang to Shanghai, but they will not have me because they are already overcrowded. I am sent away like Mary and Joseph in Bethlehem. When there is no way out, then violence arises. This is the origin of a SOCIETY based on FORCED EXCHANGE, about which we have both spoken at length.² A forced exchange society is the ERUPTION of a human being who must produce both subjectively and objectively and who wants to have his place in the world; if he cannot have it, then he will occupy it violently. This can be a revolution or it can turn into fascism. It cannot be predicted in advance. This process cannot be stopped or administered. This means that today new, heterogeneous sources of danger emerge from the process of primitive accumulation. We must draw new conclusions from the history of primitive accumulation, rather than remarking on the suffering of those whom history expropriates. This alone is not the central point. When large masses of people are herded into mega-agglomerations like Lagos from their native tribal areas in Africa because they are no longer livable, then this is a social problem. Yet it is one that experts like Rem Koolhaas or Richard Sennett say people are better able to solve themselves than planners. Lagging behind such spontaneous developments and inventions, city planners and humanitarian organizations learn about modern urban renewal from those who have long been resourceful when all plans fail. There is still a solution. What is not solvable is when this way out does not exist, when you cannot get to the city or to Europe, where there is no continent left to emigrate to, when a society hits a wall.

RS: *As was the case in part with the Peasants' War when only a few made it to Switzerland.*

AK: As with the Peasants' War. We should study these relationalities as best we can for the good of our children and our children's children, for the good of our countries and our communities. If 1914 derailed the twentieth century, then our twenty-first century can be derailed for completely different reasons.

RS: *Your Marx-Eisenstein film* News from Ideological Antiquity *is simultaneously a document and a metaphor that Marx is not buried in the spot where all the pilgrims travel, but lies somewhere else entirely.*[3]

AK: You are surprised when you realize you found him.

RS: *The beautiful thing about it is this is really true. It does not even have to be made-up. Rather, your daughter obviously discovered the real grave by chance.*

AK: Exactly! I read, for example, the table of contents in the thick volumes of Marx, which are themselves too long to read, all the way through and see in the index "Antaeus." It is written there that he is a giant of antiquity who always had the strength to lift himself back up as long as no one else lifted him off the ground. Already I read the page cited in the index where Marx actually says that GROUNDEDNESS is the fundament of societies. Where I stand with my feet on the ground I can assert myself politically. If I lift myself off the ground and take a seat in the web of government as a peasant, then I have lost my groundedness and

	can wrangle my way to become the leader of the Agrarian Party.[4]
RS:	*Does not the monument to Marx also lack groundedness if Marx was actually buried somewhere else?*
AK:	He is somewhere else entirely and the public monument does not reflect his spirit.
RS:	*Then there is also the chapter "Liquification," in which two supposed Stasi agents are talking.[5] One of the women talks at the other quite obtrusively. She wants to convince her that everything is made of water. You watch her and internally shake your head at what is going on.*
AK:	That is right, and the relations in the GDR actually did become more fluid later. Things started to flow. Ossified relations became liquefied. This is nothing more than an expression, a metaphor from Marx. He not only said we must play the melodies of petrified things, but he also spoke about liquefaction, the change in the solid state of matter. What was stone begins to move over time.
RS:	*Did you record this before 1989?*
AK:	I recorded this in 1984. We wanted to film the year 1984 that appears as a year of transformation in George Orwell. That was sixteen years after the student movement and sixteen years before the year 2000, so we thought this was some kind of midpoint. Almost nothing surprising occurred that year in Europe, not only for the film. We offered the two women these Marx quotes to discuss. This is not montage. This is staging. You take an *abstractum,* something from theory like a sentence from Immanuel Kant, Marx, Confucius, or Mao Tse-tung and bring it face-to-face with the experience of the performers. One of them is an actress and the other is someone from the world of work. They spin this out. Expression develops in the confrontation between lived experience

RS: and theoretical writing. This is contained in the "hard rock" of humanity that Marx discusses.[6] Where they possess groundedness they are like cisterns.

RS: *The woman who speaks so forcefully, is she the actress?*

AK: The woman who speaks so forcefully and ideologically is a woman from Switzerland. She comes from the world of work.

Translated by Emma Woelk

Notes

This dialogue was originally published in German as Rainer Stollmann and Alexander Kluge, *Ferngespräche: Über Eisenstein, Marx, das Kapital, die Liebe und die Macht der zärtlichen Kraft* (Berlin: Vorwerk 8, 2016), 19–23.

The three images included in the German original are not reproduced in the present translation.

1. [Translator's note: Kluge says in the German original "subjektive Republik" and implies here an otherwise usual idea articulated most clearly in *History and Obstinacy*, coauthored with Oskar Negt. With respect to the nature of human characteristics and their involvement in the transformation of labor capacity into labor power, Kluge and Negt write of an internal "corporeal community" of innumerable, innate characteristics influenced by what Hegel calls "second nature." This community or "republic," as Kluge calls it here, is what may or may not prevent "me from really forming a collective community with others." See Alexander Kluge and Oskar Negt, *History and Obstinacy*, ed. Devin Fore, trans. Richard Langston et al. (New York: Zone Books, 2014), 141. "The internal community is another expression for the laboring physiology of the human being. In this respect, human producers carry the phylogenesis of their species around with them for the duration of their entire lives" (159).]

2. Cf. Rainer Sollmann, *Die Entstehung des Schönheitssinnes aus dem Eis: Gespräche über Geschichten mit Alexander Kluge* (Berlin: Kulturverlag Kadmos, 2005), 24. [Translator's note and citation: For an English discussion of the origins and meaning of the German term *Zwangstauschgesellschaft*, see Stuart Liebman and and Alexander Kluge, "On New German Cinema, Art, Enlightenment, and the Public Sphere: An Interview with Alexander Kluge," *October* 46 (Autumn 1988): 44–45.]

3. [Translator's citation: Alexander Kluge, dir., "Das Denkmal und das wahre Grab/Karl Marx in London," *Nachrichten aus der ideologischen Antike: Marx—Eisenstein—Das Kapital* (Frankfurt am Main: Suhrkamp), DVD 2, track 3. The track can also be viewed via Cornell University's online portal "Alexander

Kluge: Cultural History in Dialogue" at https://kluge.library.cornell.edu/films/ideological-antiquity/film/2103.]

4. [Translator's note: Kluge is making a distinction between professional politics and the political in everyday life that he and Negt outline in their third collaboration *Maßverhältnisse des Politischen* (Frankfurt am Main: S. Fischer, 1992). The Agrarian Party referenced here is a generic stand-in for numerous German political parties especially active during the Weimar Republic that represented farming interests.]

5. [Translator's citation: Alexander Kluge, dir., "Flüssigmachen," *Nachrichten aus der ideologischen Antike*, DVD 1, track 12. The track can also be viewed via Cornell University's online portal "Alexander Kluge: Cultural History in Dialogue" at https://kluge.library.cornell.edu/films/ideological-antiquity/film/2102.]

6. [Translator's citation: Karl Marx, "Speech at the Anniversary of *The People's Paper*," in Karl Marx and Friedrich Engels, *Collected Works*, vol. 14, *Marx and Engels, 1855–1856* (London: Lawrence and Wishart, 1980), 655.]

Part III

Film

Word and Film

Edgar Reitz, Alexander Kluge, and
Wilfried Reinke

I.

Experts and publicists have proposed a whole series of views on film and language. These views resemble and contradict each other.[1] A random selection of statements corresponding to various conceptions of film and evidently varying degrees of importance have one thing in common: they proceed from a fixed notion of film as well as an established, or presumably established, notion of language. The issue at hand, however, requires going beyond such general definitions. As trivial as it may sound, words can interact with film in a hundred different ways. Add to this the diversity of conceptions of film. For every one of these conceptions, for every kind of literary expression, the issue presents itself differently and demands a different answer. Walter Hagemann argues that film does not raise any new questions, "because it does not speak a new language; rather it conveys the old language through a new medium. This is the real reason for the backlash which the language of film suffered with the advent of sound."[2] We have to examine how the old language relates to the old film, how new forms of language available today relate to new concepts of film, and how the interplay of word and film may produce new, nonliterary forms of language. Given the essay format, we can only outline a set of problems, we cannot offer any solutions. The following speculations, therefore, are merely intended as examples.

II.

In the cultural history of the cinema, the transition to sound marks a radical break. In the beginning of the silent era, films often consisted of lengthy shots of theatrically staged scenes. This method proved problematic when making the transitions from one scene to the next. The principle of montage was the answer to this problem of transition, which could not have been solved otherwise. Montage, in turn, set free a whole range of forms of filmic expression. Without montage, neither the German, nor the Russian, nor the French cinema of the 1920s would have been conceivable. With the introduction of sound, however, film—or rather, commercial film—reverted to the naturalism toward which it had aspired in its early stages. Thus, the addition of sound actually entailed an impoverishment rather than the extraordinary opportunity that it could have been and should be today; this is why Chaplin, in his first sound films, used sound so sparingly, if at all.

As Walter Benjamin has shown, film works on the principle of attention without concentration; the viewer is distracted. This disposition permits film images to move along by association, which involves temporal gaps between shots as well as leaps of logic. The introduction of sound, then, makes it possible to create polyphonic effects that before could have been deployed only successively. François Truffaut, for instance, uses verbal effects like adjectives in conjunction with particular images; other films utilize various registers of sound and thus achieve an epic[3] multiplicity of layers. The current movement in filmmaking, which can be observed on an international level, points toward an emancipation of film sound, in particular of verbal language. These films make it difficult to determine whether speech is subordinated to action, image to speech, or action to theme, or vice versa. The films as they are elude this kind of hierarchical definition.

Why are such innovations so hard to accomplish in Germany? Why does the emancipation of film encounter such powerful obstacles? A major reason for this is the intellectual indifference of German film productions—they just have not contained an idea in years. Apart from the particular conditions in Germany, however, two other reasons have been important. (1) The pressures of naturalism: allegedly, audiences who are interested in nothing but "sitting and staring" do not wish to be disturbed by language they have not heard a hundred times before in the media and everyday life. (2) The demand for coherence and superficial continuity makes every film conform to the model of the novella. "Pure entertainment and what it implies," as Adorno and Horkheimer say, "the relaxed abandoning of the self to diverse associations and happy nonsense, is cut short by what is currently marketed as entertainment; it is impeded by the surrogate of a coherent meaning by means of which the culture industry insists on ennobling its products, while actually and admittedly misusing them as a pretext for the presentation of stars."[4] This procedure is typical of conventional commercial films, but it can also be found in films produced with artistic intentions. Cinema is hampered in this regard by modeling itself on the genre of the novella, which prevents cinema from developing its epic possibilities. Only in the epic ranges of film, however, could language fully unfold. As far as the construction of plots is concerned, even silent film, with its limited registers, could do better than the multilevel sound film.

III.

Let us compare film and literature as modes of expression, choosing two examples at random. Is film capable of condensation? Can film attain the same expressive effects as highly differentiated language? Can film be precise? Helmut Heißenbüttel recently quoted the following sentences from Barbey d'Aurevilly's *The She-Devils* (1874): "And to all this fury she replied like the woman of the species [*Frauenzimmer*], who no longer has any reason to care, who knows the man she lives with down to his bones, and who knows that at the bottom of this pigsty of a common household lies eternal warfare. She was not as coarse as he, but more atrocious, more insulting, and more cruel in her coldness than he was in his anger."[5] With prose of such a high degree of figuration, film cannot compete.

Film cannot form metaphoric concepts [*Oberbegriffe*] (pigsty of a common household, fits of fury) or clichés (the female of the species); it is not capable of antithetical discourse on such a level of abstraction; it can never condense in such a manner; finally, film does not have the means to imitate the internal movement of language—which is what distinguishes this text—unless the filmmaker decides to quote the text. It might be interesting to imagine ways in which the event described could be rendered in filmic terms. This would probably require a short film of about twenty minutes, which could be broken down into the following sequences:

- study of the argument between husband and wife;
- study of irritated, reactive behavior of this woman and of women in general;
- study of marital habits;
- study of the habit of loving someone "down to the bones";
- the helplessness of both in the course of a long marriage, largely on the part of the husband;
- the history of bourgeois marriage over the past 200 years;
- the condition of eternal warfare;
- the biological superiority of the woman, her coldness;
- visual analysis of the conflict by means of a montage sequence that alternates, over an extended period of time, between the facial expression of the woman and that of the man, thus conveying the disproportionate and a-synchronic nature of their struggle.

This filmic treatment would attempt, with great effort, to destroy the superficial sense of precision that film conveys on account of its excessive visual presence [*Anschauung*]; likewise, one would have to recover the degree of abstraction inherent in language by accumulating details. Only then would a film be capable of achieving any degree of conceptual precision.

As is well known, language has an advantage over film, owing to several thousand years of tradition. Modern Western languages derive from the differentiated languages of antiquity, which in turn are influenced by more archaic languages. If the cinema were to cultivate the narrative forms necessary to cope with the d'Aurevilly text over a longer period of history, at a later date a whole range of filmic metaphors would be available to filmmakers, allowing them to achieve the same economy of narration as is now available in the figurative and conceptual ranges of language. Even today we can discern developments in this direction. Louis Malle, for instance, alludes to individual films by Chaplin and thus evokes the aura of Chaplin's oeuvre as a whole. Another instance would be the conventions of a genre like the Western, which can be quoted and repeated with figurative brevity. Most of the more recent Westerns are animated by allusions to the old clichés of Western narratives. The stagecoach, the entry into the saloon, the beginning of the showdown, the new sheriff, the almost masochistic position of the drunk judge, the iconography of the Western hero, and the code of honor that binds all participants—through all these elements the accumulated aura of the genre is present in each individual Western. This opens up a space for ambiguity, polyphony, and variation, which, as is well known, has often made the Western a vehicle for political, social, and psychoanalytic messages; it might just as well encourage poetic modes of expression. Only when the cinema will have sufficiently enlarged its tradition of figuration will it be able to develop abstractions and differentiations comparable to those of literature. Because it already includes language anyway, film would actually have the capacity to articulate meanings that elude the grasp of verbal expression. Contemporary cinema, however, is not prepared for this project, since neither film production nor the spectator has as yet realized film's verbal and visual possibilities. The cinema, as we see it at this point, is not merely in the hands of the film authors (just as literature is not the product of writers alone), but is a form of expression that depends as much upon the receptivity of a social formation as on the imagination of its authors. A truly sophisticated film language requires a high level of filmic imagination on the part of spectators, exhibitors, and distributors alike.

Such a project, however, meets with almost total opposition from the cultural establishment, which regards the contamination of human minds by filmic images as a disastrous development. Instead, there is a tendency to impose upon the cinema the aesthetic ideals of the classical arts (which, in this context, could be said to include still photography). This creates a kind of visual "culture" that, in effect, robs film of its specific means of expression. The misleading ideal of the priority of image over word derives from a contemplative, purist position whose proponents dismiss filmic expression or content as merely secondary, a position that ultimately results in formalism. A cinema split between, on the one hand, the formalism of experimental film (whose experiments do not seek any new experience but rather aim to perpetuate a metaphysical "state of transition") and, on the other, the superficial naturalism of narrative film—this kind of cinema will never be able to compete with the great tradition of literary language.

Would a twenty-minute adaptation of the two sentences by d'Aurevilly have a substantially different, or even more complex, meaning than those two sentences? The film would have to use language, over and above the image track. Language in this case would not be literature, but an integrated part of the film. Compared to the literary source, the film would probably fall short of the precision achieved there; in terms of visual detail, however, it would be superior to the written text. At first sight, this would produce an effect similar to that which would have been produced if Marcel Proust had used the d'Aurevilly text to satisfy his own narrative proclivities for 50 to 300 pages. The film would still remain on the side of visual presence. Yet the analytic capability of the camera might afford additional perspectives on the subject matter, which would go beyond subjective experience. Thus we would have an accumulation of subjective and objective, of literary, auditory, and visual moments, which would preserve a certain tension in relation to each other. This tension would make itself felt, among other things, in the gaps that montage created between the disparate elements of filmic expression. In layering expressive forms in such a manner, the film would succeed in concentrating its subject matter in the spaces between the forms of expression. For the material condensation of expression does not happen in the film itself but in the spectator's head, in the gaps between the elements of filmic expression. This kind of film does not posit a passive viewer "who just wants to sit and stare." Obviously such a conception of cinema remains a utopian project, given the limited ambitions of both film producers and audiences today; in the future, however, cinema could surpass even the tradition of literature, at least in certain aspects. The combination of verbal, auditory, and visual forms and their integration through montage enable film to strive for a greater degree of complexity than any of these forms in isolation. At the same time, the multiplication of materials harbors all the dangers of the *Gesamtkunstwerk* (total work of art).[6]

The relatively greater precision available to literary language is not merely a blessing. Centuries of tradition have endowed language with such polish and refinement that it has become immune to large areas of reality. Every expression, according to Kant, oscillates between concept [*Begriff*] and sensuous perception [*Anschauung*]. "Perception without concept is blind; concept without perception remains empty." Throughout most of its metaphors and expressions, language has settled into a compromise between these two poles; it is neither concrete nor really abstract. Film, by contrast, combines the radical concreteness of its materials with the conceptual possibilities of montage; thus it offers a form of expression that is as capable of a dialectical relationship between concept and perception as is verbal language, without, however, stabilizing this relationship, as language is bound to do. This opens up particular opportunities for the insertion of literary language into film, especially because it might help rid that language of some of its literary constraints.

Let us raise the question from the reverse angle. Is film capable of controlling its degree of precision? Can film refract or deconstruct [*auflösen*] a given expression? How can it maintain a sufficient degree of indeterminacy? Does film have the option of remaining imprecise? Literary language can easily do so because it may use a conventional expression as a stylistic device. "When the secretary opened the door, a young lady, pretty as a picture and dressed to tease, entered the room"—such a phrase could not be reproduced in filmic terms. Film does not grant the variety of impressions that words like "pretty as a picture and dressed to tease" or "young lady" may provoke in the imagination of different readers; the image always refers to an individual instance. This could be counteracted somewhat by devices such as an extreme long shot or close-up, both of which introduce a high degree of indeterminacy. Likewise, iconic information can be reduced by means of shallow focus, high contrast, shots of extreme brevity or duration, transgressions of chronological order, multiple exposure, negation of the image track through sound or written text. All these, and other devices that one might use to achieve the effect of indeterminacy, are devices that interfere with reality and that question the apparent concreteness of iconic information. If a film were to give its viewers conceptual instructions as they are implied in phrases like "dressed to tease," for instance, or "pretty as a picture," it would have to resort to concrete clichés—which is what Hollywood films tend to do. We conclude, therefore, that film, insofar as it uses its resources legitimately, cannot convey any really precise mental images.

We cannot ignore the fact that producers of commercial films, like those of dime novels, have no intention whatsoever of disturbing the massive circulation of their products by anything that resembles precise description. The empty shells of literary commonplaces, such as those that abound in bad novels, are ideally suited for deploying narrative clichés. In the course of its history, conservative narrative cinema has succeeded in amalgamating the prefabricated forms of imagination with prefabricated vernacular language, so that people have come to expect this amalgam from any narrative film. If the pretty young lady above actually were to appear in a film, this event would be read in a way similar to its literary equivalent. Nonetheless, commercial cinema has to keep reestablishing the basis of these conventions. While literary commonplaces may have a certain degree of legitimacy, since they appeal to something in the reader's imagination, which is not yet totally absorbed by cliché, and while such commonplaces may even be stylistically necessary, as, for instance, in Madame de La Fayette's *Princess of Cleves* or in Brecht's plays, film inevitably distorts reality when it typifies. For film allows inference from the concrete only in the direction of a cliché, but is incapable of creating a general image of concrete multiplicity. The question remains whether or not individual films can escape this quandary through particular uses of language, for instance, by speaking about things on the soundtrack, which will not appear on the image track.

IV.

There are no rules for combining word and image in film. We can roughly distinguish between modes of dialogue, modes of commentary, and more independent combinations of word and image.

Dialogue

Narrative cinema promotes the fictitious ideal of realistic dialogue. This type of dialogue is supposed to accompany the image track in a "natural" manner. Dialogue is motivated by narrative action, or all too often substitutes for action. Such is the case not only in commercial films, but also in films that simply adopt stage conventions to the screen, for example, *Twelve Angry Men* (1957; directed by Sidney Lumet, based on a play by Reginald Rose), *Les jeux sont faits* (1947; based on a play by Sartre), *Zeit der Schuldlosen* (*The Time of Your Life*, 1948; based on a play by William Saroyan). In either case, both language and the image track are subject to the regime of narrative. Such a concept of dialogue hinges on the belief that narrative events relate to each other as an organic whole, that drama is still possible. Take a film like *The*

River Line (*Kennwort: Reiher*; directed by Rudolf Jugert, 1964), recently awarded the Federal Film Prize; consider, for instance, the moment at which the characters note, via dialogue, that they "have been waiting here for hours." Immediately following the accidental killing of a patriot, a man emerges from a completely different chain of dramatic events and happens to identify the dead "comrade," whom he had not seen in twenty years, and thus the enigma gets resolved. The entanglement comes about, in the first place, because the hero stumbles into the very center of the French Resistance, led by an old man who, on the basis of a parallel chain of events dating back to World War I, is bound to misunderstand the hero. Held to a strictly realistic standard, such dramaturgy (unlike that of Ibsen, who first invented this kind of dramaturgical incest) would collapse. At the same time, such films are defined by a grotesque effort to make the illusion appear realistic. Realism in this sense extends only to the detail; the film as a whole remains in the realm of fiction. It is a realism without enlightenment, a realism intended to cover up the fact that once more we have been cheated out of reality.

It has become apparent that, as a rule of thumb, dialogue is not a suitable means for advancing action. Moreover, dialogue is a specialized branch of film production, which is to say that the texts are written by specialists as mere supplements to the image track. As we see in the work of Antonioni, however, the function of dialogue can just as well be taken over by the image track, while spoken dialogue is carried along like a shell or fossil. Spoken dialogue in this case does not tell us anything about the actual inner movements of the film; dialogue loses its function as dialogue. "We have replaced dialogue with the communiqué," as Camus says. One might add that precisely because it no longer serves any narrative purpose, dialogue is now available as a medium of reflection. When the prostitutes in Jean-Luc Godard's *Vivre sa vie* (1962) quote Montaigne, when Zazie and the other characters in Louis Malle's film *Zazie dans le métro* (1960) spout argot, their speech no longer has anything in common with the dialogue of conventional narrative film. But neither has it anything to do with Ionesco or Samuel Beckett; on the contrary, moments like these, when dialogue is actually not needed, allow for the development of specifically cinematic forms of expression. Godard and other film authors realize this opportunity when they apply to dialogue the same principles of montage as to the image track.

Voice-Over Commentary

Voice-over commentary is usually reserved for documentary film. It has the reputation of being "uncinematic," not only because it seems to be tied to a particular subject matter, but also because it assumes a certain autonomy in coordinating text and image and because it is often merely superimposed over live sound. There seems to be a general injunction against using voice-over in a way that would merely duplicate the events on the image track. This injunction presumes that commentary and a sequence of images are identical if they refer to one and the same thing; as a rule, however, this is not the case. A documentary on industrial work processes, for instance, shows a worker taking a scoop of liquid metal from one container and pouring it into another; voice-over: "The worker removes a small amount of liquid alloy for testing purposes to ensure a consistent quality in the final product." Or, in another film, the voice-over explains: "The extract can be obtained from the abdominal cavity of the dead mouse without difficulty"; the image shows a dead animal laid out on a red surface and rubber-gloved hands manipulating a syringe in its belly.[7] In both instances, the image would remain illegible without the voice-over, and it would take a considerable amount of demonstration to produce the same meaning.

Voice-over commentary is not limited to documentary film; it may also be used in fictional genres—as, indeed, it has been—with interesting effects. Narrative events tend to come across in different ways, depending on whether they are enacted on the image track or narrated by a voice-over. A double-track description may stylize an event and produce a mutual distancing effect [*Verfremdungseffekt*], as it calls attention to the material difference of verbal and visual expression. The voice-over in this case may either be identifiable as that of a particular character within the diegesis—and thus associated with a particular narrative function—or the voice could be altogether foreign to the narrative.

A special case in this context is the insertion of written titles. This practice has a tradition of its own dating back to the silent era. Whereas at that time written titles were the only way of confronting image and language, their special effect today is one of muteness. The result is an overlay of filmic events with the inner voice of the reading spectator—the spectator has to assume a more active role. The language of written titles, which does not assume any particular voice and thus cannot really be attached to characters within the diegesis, is even further removed from the filmic events than any conceivable form of voice-over. This greater distance, however, gives it an affinity with literary language. The increased participation of the spectator, in turn, creates a peculiar identification of the meaning of this language with the visually concretized events of the film (a recent impressive example in this respect is Godard's *Vivre sa vie*). Written language may enter a film in a variety of shapes and combinations: e.g., text superimposed upon moving images, inserts of written text, or text superimposed upon background images [*Stehkader*]. Writing may even push images aside completely; whole passages of film could consist of writing; written and spoken texts could be interwoven in many different ways.

Language at Liberty

Under this rubric, we are dealing with language that, detached from narrative events, accompanies and colors the image track, language that is not motivated by any subjective or objective point of view as in the case of dialogue or commentary. Examples of such use of language can be found in *Hiroshima, mon amour* (1959) by Marguerite Duras and Alain Resnais, in *The Parallel Street* (*Parallelstrasse*, 1961) by Ferdinand Khittl, in *Moderato Cantabile* by Peter Brook (1960; text by Duras), and in other films. Its mode may be recitation, poetic meditation, or "nonsense language," as in *Zazie*. In the cinema, words may be used more freely than in their usual syntactic or grammatical configurations. Film permits the disruption of the linear sequence of scenes, as well as of individual shots. In the field of literature, an author like Hans G. Helms tries to liberate language from the conventions of grammar and existing vocabulary. Nonetheless, his writing depends upon elements of literary language. If he abandoned even those tenuous semantic links, he would lose the last means of conveying expression, an objective to which even a writer like Helms is still committed. We could imagine, however, an experimental film (albeit one of extreme artistic intensity) that forcefully utilizes the oscillation between literary, visual, and auditory elements as well as the gaps between these elements; such a film might succeed in producing clusters of expression that are not required to yield meaning down to the last detail, that can be understood without having to be prefabricated or historically reconstructed. In a world in which everyone else conforms to rational reason, someone at least could be unreasonable. Since the totalizing quest for meaning has itself become irrational, literary language should be shifted to areas in which it is not totally subjected to the imperative of meaning, as it is in its proper field. Language in film may be blind.

V.

We have been speaking of possibilities; let us now focus on actual instances and develop some criteria for the combination of language and film.

(1) Michelangelo Antonioni, *L'Avventura* (1960), scene 3: (Anna arrives at Sandro's apartment . . .).[8]

Commentary: What actually goes on between the two characters takes place on the image track. Detached from the image track, the text would not make sense. It does not consist of ordinary, "natural" speech, but a highly stylized form of language. This is even more evident at other points in the script. The difference between the inner movement of the filmic image and the movement of the dialogue paradoxically makes us aware of the sound of language. This device can also be found in films by Roman Polanski and Louis Malle.

(2) Alain Resnais, Marguerite Duras, *Hiroshima, mon amour* ("The streets of Hiroshima, more streets. . . . He laughs ecstatically, which has nothing to do with their words.")[9]

Commentary: Here we have a pure instance of parallelism between image and literary text. The image track does not settle on any particular scene; instead, moving shots of bridges and streets dissolve into each other and form a kind of impressionist tableau. This tableau-effect also emanates from the soundtrack. The visual texture colors the language; the spoken text modifies the meaning of the image track. Both resonate with associations of Hiroshima/Nevers—love, death, and so on. The method of composition is basically the same as in music by Richard Wagner or Richard Strauss. The film here taps emotional connotations, which exist in the social imaginary, in the spectator's head, rather than in the film itself. Without this point of reference, images and words would disintegrate, as would the Duras text, with its abrupt changes of mood. The immersion of language in image, the emergence of language from image, the mutual pursuit of verbal and visual texts, figures of parallelism and collision, polyphony—Resnais has developed a great variety of word/image constellations throughout his work, in other films as well. Even if one resents the pathos of the texts, one has to acknowledge Resnais's originality.

(3) Ferdinand Khittl, *The Parallel Street*.

Image track: A title card with the number 305. Documentary footage of Tahiti, an island in the Pacific: shots of a fishing expedition, of a girl named Roarai, of whaling, of a seaplane starting and landing in the lagoon between a coral reef and the beach. Then a series of shots from the burial site "at the big rock" near the capital of Madagascar, Tananarive: the ceremony of Famadhina, the so-called turning of the dead. A body that has been dead for three years is disinterred and given a new shroud, a "lamba." The corpse remains laid out for twenty-four hours, surrounded by dancing and celebrations; then it is returned to the burial chamber.

Soundtrack: "The plane is due at eight. If you have ever been in love, you know that the plane can come at any time. That it always comes at eight. The farewell without meaning recalls the spot behind the ear. The arc below the knee. To arrive only to say good-bye. Having never before thought of the warmth of this hair.

"Everyone listens to the dying odor of the old fish. The airplane comes at eight. Try not to think of it: the heart has already given up. A forgotten caress—your skin. A boat without wings, its sails smelling of hibiscus flowers. *Ia ora na*—welcome."[10]

Commentary: The text in this case confronts a rather stark, naive image track. The author of the images and the writer are two different individuals who evidently did not succeed in integrating their mutual intentions. The image track diverts attention to some degree from the bombastic quality of the text; but as a result, image and text move along in a rather disconnected manner. The effect at first is one of surprise, owing to the juxtaposition of unrelated elements; also, the fixed speed of the film tends to impair our literary judgment in a way that is not the case in the reading of a written text. Such surprise tactics, however, will not produce a cinematic integration of word and image. The words spill over the margins of the image. A film does not acquire a poetic quality through words alone. Nonetheless, *The Parallel Street* enjoyed a considerable success at various festivals, in particular with the leading French reviewers at Cannes in 1964. This once again confirms the impression that if one arbitrarily accumulates interesting ingredients and adds some sort of text, one ends up with an arbitrary product that may still reap success, since "he who gives generously, offers something to everyone."

(4) Orson Welles, *Citizen Kane* (1941): (a sequence from the "News on the March" section, beginning, "Its humble beginnings, a dying daily—"/shot of old *Inquirer* building).[11]

Commentary: This is an example of voice-over used in a fictional context. Of course, *Citizen Kane* also uses dialogue that differs little from conventional dramatic dialogue and obviously is not crucial to the textual and stylistic principles of the film. The voice-over commentary in this sequence more or less describes what we see on the image track. One could say that the image illustrates the text just as the text illustrates the image. When the voice-over speaks of "forests," the image track uses the rhetorical device of *pars pro toto* and shows a tree. When the text concerns the perspective of a whole continent, through a long shot so extreme as to suggest that the continent could not be captured in a single image, the voice-over implies this extensity by way of enumeration. When connotations like "humble, ramshackle, poor" dominate the commentary, three black people can be seen in one of the lower windows of the building. The mutual energizing of text and image is rather schematic, but at the same time incredibly robust. *Citizen Kane* is the kind of film in which neither sound nor image track, in themselves, have much artistic distinction, although together they constitute a work of art.

It would be interesting to explore further examples of the interaction of word and film, especially in the large realm of commercial film. The current use of language in film is likely to come across as highly dilettante. Often an especially badly written text serves to underscore the common remark "The camera work was excellent." On the map of the arts, film has always been placed next to photography. As a thorough inquiry into the history of cinematic forms would probably show, film has a much greater affinity with literature than with photography.

VI.

The cinema depends upon language not only within each film but also through all the stages of preparation and planning. Without highly differentiated skills of articulation, no filmmaker can approach the realization of his ideas. Author, cinematographer, and producer need to communicate with each other, a task for which the prevailing jargon of the industry is crudely inadequate. The unnecessary hierarchy that determines the production process of special features is just one aspect of this lack of verbal differentiation; another is the "speechlessness" that characterizes the studio sound of the ordinary commercial film. The organizational structure of film production in Germany only aggravates these problems, but these problems are not intrinsic to filmmaking, nor is the prevailing organization of production unalterable. According to a well-known nineteenth-century German thinker and political economist, all thought is mediated by language. Unlike the classical arts (and even television, which actually employs a considerable number of intellectuals), the cinema has to compensate for a lack of tradition. Therefore, the cinema is in a situation different from that of the classical arts, whose very purpose is to escape tradition. German cinema would benefit greatly from intellectual centers, which would have to be established independently of the commercial centers of production so as to exert influence upon the latter. Such intellectual centers, however, should above all foster an awareness of the immense lead that literary language still has over the expressive means of the mass media.

Cinema today stands at the crossroads of an important development. On the one hand, we can already envision a complexity of expression that film could achieve and the kind of intellectual institution that would encourage such complexity; on the other hand, we can just as well imagine an institutionalization of filmmaking that would merely canonize the inferior products of the status quo and make film into a specialized branch of the mass media, thus perpetuating the current ratio of 10 percent specials to 90 percent regular commercial features. Such films cheat not only the loyal patrons in whose name they pretend to be made, but also those who produce them, not to mention those who expect to see a work of art. It would be better if academies designed to teach that kind of filmmaking did not exist at all. The worst that could happen to film would be to be banished to its own domain.

Translated by Miriam Hansen

Notes

This essay was originally published in German as Edgar Reitz, Alexander Kluge, and Wilfried Reinke, "Wort und Film," *Sprache im technischen Zeitalter* 13 (1965): 1015–30. It was later published in English as Edgar Reitz, Alexander Kluge, and Wilfried Reinke, "Word and Film," trans. Miriam Hansen, *October* 46 (1988): 83–95.

The authors are identified as teachers at the Hochschule für Gestaltung at Ulm, where Kluge and Reitz had founded the Film Department the same year. In the following, unless otherwise noted, all notes are by the authors.

1. [Translator's note: The secondary texts that follow this first sentence from Reitz et al.'s essay quoted in the original German version of this text are omitted here. The sources of the quotes are Walter Hagemann, *Der Film: Wesen und Gestalt* (Heidelberg: K. Vowinckel, 1952), 46 (with reference to Gilbert Cohen-Séat, *Essai sur les principes d'une philosophie du cinema* [Paris: Presses universitaires de France, 1946], 41); Curt Hanno Gutbrod, "Von der Filmidee zum Drehbuch," in *Das Manuskript: Handbuch für Autoren,* ed. Otto Schumann (Wilhelmshaven: Hübner, 1954), 453; Béla Baláz, *Der Film: Werden und Wesen einer neuen Kunst* (Vienna: Globus, 1961); N. A. Lebedew, *Literatur und Film* (Leipzig: Urania, 1954), 8; Fedor Stepun, *Theater und Film* (Munich: Carl Hanser Verlag, 1953), 133; Erich Feldmann, Hermann M. Görgen, and Martin Keilhacker, eds., "Eigenart und Struktur des Filmbildes und der filmischen Aussage," *Beiträge zur Filmforschung* 6 (1961): 93; Rudolf Arheim, *Film als Kunst* (Berlin: Ernst Rowohlt Verlag, 1932), 240.]

2. Walter Hagemann, "Die Bestandteile der filmischen Aussageweise," *Beiträge zur Filmforschung* 1 (1955): 46.

3. [Translator's note: In addition to its conventional meaning, the term "epic" here invokes the particular connotations of Brecht's concept of epic theater.]

4. Max Horkheimer and Theodor W. Adorno, *Dialectic of Enlightenment* (Amsterdam: Querido, 1947), 169. [Editor's note: This is Hansen's own translation from the German original. See also Max Horkheimer and Theodor W. Adorno, *Dialectic of Enlightenment: Philosophical Fragments,* ed. Gunzelin Schmid Noerr, trans. Edmund Jephcott (Stanford, CA: Stanford University Press, 2002), 114: "Pure amusement indulged to the full, relaxed abandon to colorful associations and merry nonsense, is cut short by amusement in its marketable form: it is disrupted by the surrogate of a coherent meaning with which the culture industry insists on endowing its products while at the same time slyly misusing them as pretexts for bringing on the stars."]

5. [Translator's citation: Jules Amédée Barbey d'Aurevilly, "À un diner d'athées," *Les diaboliques: Les six premières* (Paris: Éditions Garnier Frères, 1963), 288; translated from both the French original and the German version cited in the original text.]

6. [Translator's note: Implied here is a critique of the *Gesamtkunstwerk* as developed in the context of the Frankfurt School. This critique focuses on the ideological trajectory linking Wagner's aesthetics with the total mobilization of effect in both the capitalist culture industry and fascist mass spectacles; cf. Walter Benjamin's preface to "The Work of Art in the Age of Its Technological Reproduction" (1935); Theodor W. Adorno's *In Search of Wagner* (1937–38); and the chapter on the culture industry in *Dialectic of Enlightenment.*]

7. These examples are taken at random from a medical and an industrial documentary. They may sound idiotic, but they highlight the interaction between commentary and images, which go beyond mere illustration.

8. Michelangelo Antonioni, *L'avventura* (New York: Orion Press, 1963), 99–100. [Editor's note: As with the beginning of her translation of this essay,

Hansen leaves out the quotations taken from film scripts for the following four examples. The citations here and below refer to these sequences briefly described in parentheses that serve as the basis for commentary.]

    9. Marguerite Duras and Alan Resnais, *Hiroshima, Mon Amour* (New York: Grove Press, 1961), 24–25.

    10. Ferdinand Khittl, *Parallelstrasse*; script in *Spectaculum: Texte moderner Filme* (Frankfurt: Suhrkamp, 1961), 346–47.

    11. Pauline Kael et al., *The Citizen Kane Book* (New York: Bantam, 1974), 142–43.

9

BITS OF CONVERSATION

ALEXANDER KLUGE: Anita is like a seismograph that goes through our society like a probe. I tried to register her fluctuations.[1]

The child of Jewish parents, Anita became acquainted with persecution during the Third Reich. It is a pervasive belief that a child who was eight years old in 1945 was not directly affected, but rather was only threatened and could therefore not actually be seriously defined by it. This is obviously not true. When I think about my own childhood, we may not have understood what was happening exactly, but we registered the power relations very clearly; we understood quite accurately the hierarchy, which was quite different from today's. As the child of Jewish parents in the Third Reich, Anita experienced her outside influences similarly. After the war, her parents were initially able to set up factories. Anita went to school in the German Democratic Republic for a few years, but then, as a "daughter of capitalists," she no longer felt safe and went to the West. I think she left because she no longer wanted to identify with what she perceived to be her parents' powerlessness. It is characteristic of her that she does not try to assert herself by gaining a foothold in her parents' reality—for example, by graduating high school and going on to the university in Leipzig, but instead by moving to the West to fulfill uncertain aspirations.

ENNO PATALAS: *According to what principle did you select the characters she encounters? Does this ensemble represent West German society?*

AK: No. It simply resulted from Anita's path. I did make a conscious decision in the cases of the district attorney Fritz Bauer and the manager at the Hotel Carlton because I thought that in a world made up of actors real people also needed to be shown. I wanted to make clear that not only Anita's utopian sensibility exists, but also people who understand, professionally as it were, something about this utopia. I would have liked to have shown more of this, for example, in the university. The other fictional characters simply result from Anita's path shown in the film. The judge, the parole officer, the boss, his wife, the landlady, etc. A minor character like the young man Anita meets remains relatively undefined; you will not be able to tell what my or Anita's opinion of him is or what he does for a living. The judge, on the other hand, is unmistakable. The *déformation professionelle* increases with the proximity to power. The distortion is therefore greater in the judge or Undersecretary Pichota than in the women who appear in the film. But this ensemble is not representative of the Federal Republic of Germany.

EP: *Conversely, to what extent are the characters Anita encounters specific to the Federal Republic?*

AK: Anita and her story are specific to the Federal Republic. Her story would be a different one if she lived in a different society. And it would also be a different one if Germany had a different history.

Anita learned from her parents that one always has to be an entrepreneur and this comes through again and again. This is also the point where she becomes corrupted. When, for example, she loves Undersecretary Pichota and also holds onto this love, there is an entrepreneurial perspective at play. Anita also has the tendency to go where authority or education reside, where a manager loves her, or where a boss helps her become especially successful. When she finds success, she wants to top it off by becoming her boss's lover, and then she buys herself another fur meant to protect her against the misunderstanding, if you will, that she is not rich. Someone might think she needs to make money. This imagined world has, of course, been passed down from her parents.

At the same time, this imagined world cannot be realized for lack of a motive. Anita's impulse is entirely independent from the circumstances that surround her. It is something like a normal virtue. In the film, it never becomes a real virtue. It is, however, a potential virtue that would be active if society could use it. There is no motive for Anita to fight for or against anything. Even though she was aware of how brutal history is—her grandparents were deported and her parents persecuted—this brutality was then hidden at the same time. The world does not exactly treat her with tenderness, but it does not go so far as to make Anita hate it. In the present, there are no storm troopers, but instead landladies she argues with who are not really dangerous. Anita has no set objective.

What is important is that society, on the one hand, does not give a person what he can demand but, on the other hand, is never aggressive enough to provoke a direct conflict. This society essentially demands a certain skeptical symmetry, but does not insist on any real will formation. Anita is constantly attempting to establish her will. In another context and with different challenges, Anita would be a social person and probably a first-class functionary. Because she never fully understands why people do certain things, for example, work, she remains on the outside.

I believe that an auteur should actually not arrange the image. He sets in motion his various probes, his sound team, his cameraman, his actors; he puts them in a situation and makes sure they really understand this situation. The crew has to unfurl the auteur's sensibility. The auteur is there to program the crew. The actors, the cameraman, and the sound team are his instruments as well his organizational leadership. When the auteur is sovereign, the planning process occurs before the shooting begins. Later on, he has more of an interpretive function. He is a midwife to a certain extent. Of course, you have to observe your coworkers closely. When the intensity subsides, you have to take a break. We required a lot of mobility from our crew because we filmed quickly at several locations and, most importantly, wanted a high degree of spontaneity.

I believe that the director does nothing other than create a contact. He sets a communication process in motion between the actors, the rest of the crew, and the cameraman. He stages the cameraman almost more than the actors. He must be observed above all else. There are two processes of compression: the actor acts and places himself in a situation. Only portions of the situation are photographed and recorded with sound, and of those only a smaller portion is retained for editing. Thus, two filtering processes occur that again compress what the director wants to express. My actress did not have to act any old way. She could do so as she imagined. She only had to place herself in the situation. In the prison, she fervently imagined that she was actually in prison. When she acts the scene where she falls into a fit of rage, she certainly had the feeling that something was up. It was not necessary to anger her or anything. The space also does a lot. Although the prison we filmed is perfectly run, it still made a devastating impression. This ability to place oneself in a situation fails in those moments that are strongly determined biologically. The actress can imagine going to prison, but having a child is something she cannot imagine because she has never had one. It would work against me if I tried to depict a pretend birth. Documentation must at the very least capture a person's fantasy. If you deviate from this, you automatically end up with a cliché.

EP: *But you also stage things. You use prepared material and provoke reality to get an image just as you also stage scenes and use actors who clearly impersonate.*

AK: I have two things to say to that. First, it is always made clear by the way the text is handled and the way they speak that these are actors who are not speaking as persons, but as someone playing a role. This comes at the cost of identification and it sometimes comes across as exaggeration. Full identification should not happen. Second, I also try to be responsive to my actors' interests so as to sniff out original points. For example, the actor who plays Pichota told me that he was interested in Hemingway. Then we interviewed him about Hemingway. In doing so, we discovered he was interested in Brecht, and we then let him read the story "If Mr. K Loved Someone" from the *Stories of Mr. Keuner*.[2] And from this, it came out completely on its own accord that the actress who plays Anita did not understand abstraction and believed that a sketch would practically have to be quite similar to the person. This is the opposite of Brecht's story. This is a typical misunderstanding.

EP: *This misunderstanding came about as you were recording the actors? It was not invented?*

AK: Exactly. We only recorded the scene because we wanted to portray Pichota, not Anita, but in doing so, it turned out that the relation between the two unfolded perfectly.

EP: *There is a whole spectrum of actors, from those who play themselves, like District Attorney Fritz Bauer, to those who bring their own experiences to their roles, to those who only embody roles, like Eva Maria Meineke.*[3]

AK: Exactly. The stronger a minor role is, the more it is splintered. We initially only wanted to ask the manager of the Hotel Carlton about how his hotel is organized. Then he told us his life story and later he came back and said that he had been in a concentration camp. At first, I did not intend on putting this into the film. I thought it would look too picturesque. But it later turned out to fit well with the other material.

This is an important part of our filming process: we do not work by dividing the script into shots and then filming each one in the most convenient order—for example, the ending first and then the middle and then the intercuts at the end. Instead, we prefer to work with two or three cameras and to let the action play out in one piece. In doing so, the crew also gets pulled into the situation. This leads, for example, to the fact that Anita was still in the room putting on makeup and chatting with the other maid when suddenly there was noise in the hotel hallway. Piano music started to play. The whole team ran out to film the girls playing the piano. I believe that such precision within a crew is possible only when you have this level of spontaneity, when in this case the crew has set out to capture the entire hotel. Using this method, I of course ended up with more material than could be used in the film. I could easily make another short out of the unused footage. Maybe I will do this at some point. It is nevertheless important that this level of spontaneity be reached. If this is the case, then the crew works with the reliability of a sleepwalker.

I believe this is the core: film assembles itself in the mind of the spectator. It is not a work of art that lives unto itself on the screen. Film must therefore work with associations activated in the spectator by the auteur to the extent they are both calculable and imaginable. I believe this is something that Jean-Luc Godard does as well. This demands an indirect method, whereby what is supposed to be imaged afterward in the spectator's head is never represented directly.

FRIEDA GRAFE: *Yet for the spectator it is very precise and vague at the same time such that he immediately draws a connection to his own ideas; the spectator is thereby both free and stimulated to complete what is shown.*

AK: To put it bluntly, the cuts not included in a film are just as important as the image. Adorno once said mockingly that what bothered him about film was really just the image. He meant that continuous reification kills off fantasy more than it encourages it, especially if there are no breaks where fantasy can affix itself. Film has to provide fantasy with a space where it can move, and nevertheless must convey something visually. What always thrilled me about silent films are their intertitles. Because intertitles are usually completely idiotic from a literary standpoint, completely uninformative, and also poorly placed, I asked myself why I liked them so much. I like them so much because my brain starts working at that moment and it has a bit of time to fantasize on its own. Afterward I am happy once again when the images return.

In this vein, I wish it were possible to make films in which the thought process involved in why one arrives at an idea is shown without portraying the crew.

FG: *But this comes through in the parts of your film where a complete lack of artificiality dominates.*

AK: One such example is when the manager at the Hotel Carlton asks: Are you bored? And the crew answers: No, we are interested in this. This is in the film. Or when the midwife in the prison says something dumb and the crew laughs. This is also in there. Another example: Anita laughs at the end of Mr. K.'s story and makes eye contact with the crew. We see this. She even looks beyond the frame. She laughs and repeats her line and then falls out of character. These are things I do not think are bad because they do not move beyond the film. We also filmed half a sequence in which the area around the main train station in Frankfurt was basically portrayed as a gold-mining town. This arose spontaneously out of our discussions. I could also have sent my crew in on their own and not gone with them, since this is what was planned. But this would have gone too far beyond the film. For this, I would have needed Frankfurt as my topic. What a great topic!

The music in the film functions as commentary. I also try to include the context in which the music exists. Music helps to make an aura present. With the hit song "Zwei blaue Augen," for example, everyone my age knows exactly what I mean from the instrumentation alone.[4] For younger generations, however, this music has something exotic about it just as the Third Reich does. This does not require the listener to be able to situate this hit.

FG: *The past is always automatically present in the image because the sounds from the thirties and forties linger in one's ears even without the music playing.*

EP: *Could music be used so extensively with other characters as a way of creating associations? Even apart from the historical dimension?*

AK: The music corresponds to the uncertainty in Anita's world of thoughts. Everything that she thinks and feels is both aggressive and, if you will, rebellious, but it is rebellious in an uncertain way. I do not believe that Anita loves ideas like she loves these sounds. It is, of course, also her parents' music, a musicality she learned from them. The world of her parent's home was still relatively intact. Even though she was externally threatened because her parents were Jews, she was also used to this domestic world. The attributes of this world included this music, tangos like "Hör mein Lied, Violetta." I did not seek out this music myself. I took the music from the Café Kranzler in Frankfurt, Anita's favorite haunt and the favorite of the actress who played her, too. That is exactly where you hear this kind of music. Anita daydreams to this music. She also likes other music—for example, the playful Spanish music at the end of the film, because she thought that the prison sequence should not end like this. She thought this cheap music was progressive.

EP: *But it fits exactly with Anita's attitude, the damage within, and the inexactitude of her protest. How did you start making films?*

AK: I originally studied law, and it really bored me. When I was done, I thought about what type of career I should pursue and primarily about how I could escape jurisprudence. Theater did not really interest me, and I did not believe I could write literature. Then a friend told me I should try film. Adorno advised me and sent a letter to Fritz Lang, who was then in Germany, saying he should let me be his assistant.[5] Of course, he did no such thing, but he did let me watch as an intern. This did not impress me all that much at the time. Fritz Lang practically stopped directing on the third day and limited himself to supervising the filming, because the producer Arthur Brauner basically took sides against him together with the lower-level crew members and set designers and refused to recognize Lang's qualities at all. In the meantime, I wrote stories in the cafeteria and from these came *Case Histories*. Then I came here, Munich, and wrote a synopsis for *Brutality in Stone* and sent it in to North Rhine-Westphalia. This became a film, and since then I have acquired a taste for it.

Today I know exactly why film interests me more than literature. Film always works with concrete forms of expression. You can do what you want, but the image always remains concrete. Yet with montage you can create concepts, the summation of concretizations. This drive toward a vividness [*Anschaulichkeit*] lacking in language appeals to me. If I believed a story were right, I would never notice that it was not. With film, a faulty conceptualization or a poorly imagined sequence in a screenplay negates itself during the shooting. I find it extremely interesting that ideas in a screenplay reverse themselves and change completely during filming simply because the reality portrayed resists it. In literature, I am dependent on the traditionally determined meanings embedded in words, whereas with images I am solely limited by what spectators are able to imagine. And I can then intensify that with provocative images. I have a lot of leeway here. Language is also innately much more rhetorical. When I say, "at the foot of the mountain," this is neither visible nor abstract, neither precise nor tangible. This is fundamentally different in film. When I bring an atmosphere and the crew into motion, I have a substance that is much stronger than anything I can invent.

I do not believe in a realism that depicts just anything. This always turns out to be just a formula and tends toward naturalism. The feature film as we know it in Germany after 1945 always had the tendency toward naturalism at precisely its best moments: the abdominal injury, the cries of pain, grimacing, etc., in Wicki's film were all going for external authenticity.[6] We have to try to overcome this realism such that the illusions such films depict of our society never arise. This illusion is right in neither documentary nor narrative film.

EP: *But, on the other hand, you do still try to bring in primary reality by quoting it more than in conventional realistic narrative films . . .*

AK: . . . because this is the substance. Just as I do not like to work with premasticated phrases in literature, I also seek to attain a point in film where the substance I narrate is original. It is not the case that using a piece of reality in cinematic narration creates a grander realism. An imaginary world could also be created purely out of real pieces of reality. On the one hand, the real world must enter into the work of art. On the other, an identity between reality and the work of art cannot be faked. Even if the work of art never really contains what is depicted and is not meant to arouse the pretense, it is still meant to show some of the substance.

Film is a general form of intelligence that works with concrete means of figuration and is otherwise no different from other forms of intelligence such as science or literature. If you think of film as a simple application of intelligence, you return to the model of the Lumière brothers, who simply stood in front of a train and filmed as it arrived into the station. Everything that exists in the world can be put together using pieces from this kind of mosaic. If you work with small building blocks, miniatures, the smallest dramaturgical elements and utterances, if you put these things together as a montage, then any statement can be made. In doing so, you do not assume that you have a style that is independent of the substance of the work—that object, style, and work are creative paths—but rather you strike out on a direct path that circumvents so-called style.

Translated by Emma Woelk

Notes

This dialogue was originally published in German as Enno Patalas and Frieda Grafe, "Gesprächsfetzen: Ein Interview mit Alexander Kluge," *Filmkritik* 10.9 (1966): 487–91.

1. [Translator's note and citation: For a detailed transcription of Kluge's debut *Yesterday Girl* (1966) executed by Enno Patalas, see Alexander Kluge, *Abschied von gestern: Protokoll* (Frankfurt am Main: Filmkritik, 1967).]

2. [Translator's citation: Bertolt Brecht, "If Mr. K. Loved Someone," in *Stories of Mr. Keuner*, trans. Martin Chalmers (San Francisco: City Light Books, 2001), 27.]

3. [Translator's note: Fritz Bauer [1903–68] was a prosecutor involved in the Auschwitz trials. The actress Eva Maria Meinecke [1923–] plays Mrs. Pichota, the wife of Undersecretary Pichota (Günter Mack).]

4. [Translator's note: Kluge refers here to Otto Stransky's hit song "Zwei blaue Augen und ein Tango" from 1931. Kluge uses various tangos in the film's

soundtrack, including Joe Rixner's "Blauer Himmel" and Othmar Klose's "Hör' mein Lied, Violetta," both from 1936. See Kluge, *Abschied von gestern*, 25.]

5. [Translator's citation: Cf. Theodor W. Adorno to Fritz Lang, June 19, 1958, in *Alexander-Kluge Jahrbuch* 2 (2015): 15–16.]

6. [Translator's note: Kluge refers here to Bernhard Wicki's 1959 film, *Die Brücke*, based on Gregor Dorfmeister's novel of the same name.]

10

THE REALISTIC METHOD AND THE "FILMIC"

People usually learn about the deductive method in our educational institutions. Starting with laws, rules, and values, we then descend to their application or illustrate them with examples. Reality is *represented*. The principle of illustration is that abstraction regulates concretion by destroying it.

Film seems to develop an oppositional program to this tendency. Its raw material is apparently made up of concrete depictions. According to its qualitative edict, it has little appreciation for thought. It lacks the polished and universal quality of a so-called trade language.[1] The majority of its products are oriented toward the direct imitation of reality.

The deductive method can, however, turn up in disguise. In such a case, it simply acts as though it were inductive. This is true, for example, of the natural scientific experiment understood in the eighteenth and nineteenth centuries as the prototype of inductive reasoning. Georg Lukács, *History and Class Consciousness,* trans. Rodney Livingstone (Cambridge, MA: MIT Press, 1971), 132: "In fact, scientific experiment is contemplation at its purest. The experimenter creates an artificial, abstract milieu in order to be able to *observe* undisturbed the untrammelled workings of the laws under examination, eliminating all irrational factors both of the subject and the object." See also Horst Kurnitzky, *Triebstruktur des Geldes: Ein Beitrag zur Theorie der Weiblichkeit* (Berlin: Klaus Wagenbach, 1974), 44ff. Here, a process of deductive demarcation actually precedes observation.

Something similar is true of cinema's direct access to reality, regardless of whether one is dealing with a documentary or a feature film. **The most intensive observation or most probable plot is predicated on the schema of its genre that excludes real contexts.**[2]

Film's basic procedural approach can be found in the beginning stages of film history with the Lumière brothers and Georges Méliès. The Lumières observe simple processes. Workers leave a factory or a train arrives at a station exactly how the camera captures the event. Méliès tells made-up stories. He photographs a reality prefabricated in an artist's atelier: the journey to the moon, stories by Jules Verne, etc.

From these two original cells—the recording of a documentary moment and a fictional one—the genres of the documentary and the feature film emerged. Current television and cinema mix documentation and fiction to such an extent that their functions are reversed: documentation becomes fictional, and fiction gives the impression of being documentary (as can be seen particularly clearly, for example, in National Socialist film, which simply could not have been "made-up"). Certain aspects like color, sound, and format have changed. Literature, theater, spectacle, radio, and journalism have been adapted. The basic elements of film are now highly specialized, but the basic principle has remained the same: small slices of reality, records of particular moments, are depicted and pieced together into a relationality.

The Basic Interest of Documentary Film

A documentary is filmed with three "cameras": (1) the camera in the technical sense, (2) the mind of the filmmaker, and (3) the genre's own awareness of the documentary based on the expectations that spectators train on a documentary. So it cannot be said that a documentary simply depicts facts. It photographs individual facts and then uses them to assemble a unified relationality of facts according to three schemata that run partially at cross-purposes. All other possible facts and relationalities of facts are excluded. Dealing with documentation naively thus provides a unique opportunity for telling fairy tales. In this way, a documentary is, in and of itself, no more realistic than a feature film. Günter Peter Straschek, *Handbuch wider das Kino* (Frankfurt am Main: Suhrkamp, 1975), 10: "Film is something made, assembled, artificial—epitomized by Josef von Sternberg's admission that the ideal film would be perfectly synthetic." What must ultimately be grasped is that the cinematographer's often-cited "documentary authenticity" is nothing other than the high stylization of opera. The fact that social reality does not necessarily appear through the mere process of filming the given world can be recognized in the light of prevalent misunderstandings, in recollection of Brecht's remarks: "The situation thereby becomes so complicated that a simple 'representation of reality' says something about reality less than ever before. A photograph of the Krupp Works or of A.E.G. yields nearly nothing about these institutions. Actual reality has slipped into the functional. The reification of human relationships, such as the factory, no longer produces the latter. So there is in fact 'something to build up,' something 'artificial,' 'contrived.'" All of that was a citation. The passage from Brecht that Straschek cites can be found in Bertolt Brecht, "From the Three Penny Trial: A Sociological Experiment," trans. Lance W. Garmer, in *German Essays on Film*, ed. Richard W. McCormick and Alison Guenther-Pal (New York: Continuum, 2004), 117.[3]

The tradition of documentary film has notably spawned a form of *critical* documentation. Among the many reasons for recording facts, the critical historical approach remains its principal motive. A knowledge-constitutive interest is needed, of course, in order to bring recordings of particular moments into relationality with each other. The majority of resultant products have a scientific, propagandistic, or critical interest, or a mix of several interests. They are seldom radical and usually command midlevel interest in trade.

This "critical" interest, which functions from the top down as a "natural" critique lacking any particular method, runs counter to what the camera is capable of as a technical instrument. Indeed, the camera is precisely noncritical (and in this way, radical) when it records. The contrast between the filmmaker's socially constructed cinematic eye (along with that of the genre) and the naturalistic camera eye of the instrument paralyzes the radicalization of observation reciprocally.

The message of the medium (the reception of the genre by the spectators) is likewise divided. The critical intention of the filmmaker and the genre work against each other. In documentary work, for example, a mass of critical reality has been collected that could incite protest in the spectator. At the same time, the intense pressure of reality is also documented: the superiority of the unchanged course of real events. The reduction to objectivity and simple facts actually has an altogether negative effect: bad reality proves its staying power. For example, if I watch a television documentary about South Africa, I not only register that the events are occurring. I also feel disheartened, because sitting there in front of the television screen, I cannot change them. By calling up this contradictory attitude, the genre produces inurement, regardless of whether the documentarian intends to.

It is no good to answer by celebrating film: "It gives us reality twenty-four times in one second!" A technical instrument that records twenty-four images per second makes no autonomous sense for truth. In the end, the camera documents the indolence of the human eye, which, when it sees only twenty-four images per second, no longer perceives the darkness, but produces the illusion of a continuous sequence of events.

The Basic Interest of Feature Film

In the human mind, facts and wishes are never separate from one another. In some ways, the wish is the form in which the fact is recorded.[4]

Wishes are by nature no less real than facts. They are rooted primarily in the fact that the entire libidinal experience is learned in childhood through contact with people, their primal objects. **The wish is to recognize these human relationships in the form of a dramatic plot, to disassemble the world into human relationships. This utopia is realistic.**

What happens is not actually determined by humans, but rather by the laws of commodity production and history. Human action—the "plot"—is, in certain auspicious instances, dragged along behind these objective movements. More often than not, it is dismantled and disrupted. In the early spring of 1939, a man starts to fall in love. Then he is called up to the battlefield in Poland and comes back one-legged in 1952. This love story is not determined by him.

But it is precisely these sorts of experiences that make the need for a permanent retelling of plots all the more urgent. Wishes cleave to this tension, to the unifying principle of narration, which sorts the real relationalities humanely and thereby limits the oppressive majority of all that can be told. This is similar to how meaning is forced in documentary—it must have a point—that cuts off observation. But the pressure of plot is far greater than the need for sensory connections or facticity can ever be in documentary film: it comes down to wishes. The schema of all feature film genres—prefabricated in the spectator before even seeing the film—lies in this transformation of all that is real into an exciting plot.

Even a reformed cinema cannot break through this schema. What, for example, do cinema's sensitive aesthetes do? They refine individual senses.[5] But this refinement is of no use in societal praxis. In order to deal with the chaos of a full-throated reality including the "immense accumulation of commodities" impressed upon the mind, a practical person has to shut down this refined sensibility.[6] Mere specialization of sensibility has a tendency to lead to disuse: reality might damage the instrument. Reality must be made to fit the sensitive instruments instead of forcing sensibility to learn to deal robustly with the relationalities of reality. For Wilhelm Meister, who spends his whole life educating himself and not working, the world is an experimental laboratory, something contemplative. As a subject, he stands at a distance to it. "I think, therefore I am," decreed Descartes. "The world did not exist before I created it," wrote Goethe in *Faust II*. One hundred years later: in Alfred Döblin's *Berlin Alexanderplatz*, violent steam hammers are pounding the objective associations of the surrounding world directly into Franz Biberkopf's head. He could not tell you any longer which things in his head were subjective and which were free-floating, objective particles. Individual personality is a myriad of isolated, prematurely forced, or ruined characteristics. It makes no sense for him to hone any *one* of these characteristics to a fine point.[7]

The Classical Description of the Realistic Method

"It would seem right to start with the real and concrete, with the actual presupposition, e.g. in political economy to start with the population, which forms that basis and the subject of the whole social act of production. Closer consideration shows, however, that this is wrong. Population is an abstraction if, for instance, one disregards the classes of which it is composed. These classes in turn remain an empty phrase if one does not know the elements on which they are based, e.g. wage labour, capital, etc. These presuppose exchange, division of labour, prices, etc. For example, capital is nothing without wage labour, without value, money, price, etc. If one were to start with population, it would be a chaotic conception of the whole, and through closer definition one would arrive analytically at increasingly simple concepts; from the imagined concrete, one would move to more and more tenuous abstractions until one arrived at the simplest determinations. From there it would be necessary to make a return journey until one finally arrived once more at population, which this time would be not a chaotic conception of a whole, but a rich totality of many determinations and relations. The first course is the one taken by political economy historically at its inception. . . . The latter is obviously the correct scientist method. The concrete is concrete because it is a synthesis of many determinations, thus a unity of the diverse."[8]

The so-called "filmic," whether in documentary or fictional films, begins with "the real and concrete, with the actual presupposition." This is the direct, manual access of the instrument: the way that documentary film records a particular moment; the typologically, dramaturgically, or psychologically *motivated* scene of narrative films or its opposite: the surprising, the atypical, the particular, all of which are based in the same realistic illusion. Straschek, *Handbuch wider das Kino*, 11: "Naturalism of the image, the theory of reflection. The hugely abstract content of film—'it is a grave error to attach it to the visual arts as though it were a subgenus of painting' [Galvano Della Volpe, *Critica del gusto* (Milan: Feltrinelli, 1966), 150]—is forever negated by cinema's provocative foregrounding of the image (which comes in part from naive conceptions of influence and propaganda)."

"Closer consideration shows, however, that this is wrong."[9] An ordering of the real arises that cannot grasp the chaos of the whole. In reality, this process is one of exploitation. As a "rich totality" of many determinations and relationships, film does not come about through unmediated access, but rather through the analytical method, which is not a matter of mental consciousness but rather the fundamental form of sensory experience.[10] This method is learned through the *resistance of the senses*.[11] Radical fiction and radically authentic observation: these are the *raw materials*. Montage, processing into relationalities, the translation of spectators' interests, the transformation of the medium's means of production: these are further applications of the analytic-sensuous method. It opens up social experience (and *simultaneously* the potential realized in them for entertainment, comedy, surprise, suspense, though none of these audience reactions remain as they once appeared historically). It is construction work, the same way one might build railroads, bridges, and cities, but in no way linear or square.[12]

It is not a question of any sort of closed system. We might look at it this way: for tens of thousands of years, there have been films in people's heads: streams of associations, daydreams, experiences, sensuousness, consciousness. The technological invention of cinema merely introduced the added element of reproducible images.

Technological mass media are therefore not the fundamental element. This is true of all forms of mass media. *For this reason, they cannot ever be truly complete.* The fundamental element—in other words, the comprehensive mass medium—is living labor, the irrepressible relation of production. Even though it has never been examined, it possesses an autonomous realism that has the potential to correct the mistakes and deficits of every realist construct.

In contrast, praxis is disappointing. In film work, a systematically realist approach typically results in "more tenuous abstractions."[13] One sees perhaps the evidence of construction work but not the realism. Here lies a difficult problem to solve: **the productive power of cinema can only be developed in conjunction with the spectator's perceptive powers; it is therefore not only a question regarding efforts on the part of filmmakers whether they stall somewhere on the path toward the "unity of the diverse."**[14] For as long as they do this, they will be caught in the middle. Their films do not have classical cinema's nevertheless plausible illusionary impact, and they are also not truly concrete. They are the attempts of a not-yet developed force of production whose emergence requires the transformation of the whole of cinematic reality. Such films feel broken. But if the path forward is not pursued, then film history itself will be a collection of primitive attempts.

Radical, authentic observation brings about a result that seems altogether foreign and "invisible" to run-of-the-mill realism. Radical fiction, which, for example, pulls together contradictions not typically confronted in everyday life (or only to a small degree), appears overwrought to a healthy human understanding. This is due to the fact that the perspectives of middling realism constitute an ideological amalgam, a reality of appearances wherein certain habituated ideas crystallize. These habituated ideas are programmatically identical with the labor of the consciousness apparatus learned in schools and that takes part in societal development in official bureaucracy and the domestic sphere.

Beneath the threshold of the dominant consciousness, there nevertheless exists living labor oppressed by the dominant system: a subdominant consciousness. Because of its repression, there was neither opportunity nor reason to domesticate it. It is a hallmark of this segment of our capacity of perception that it functions primarily as something self-regulated: it is by and large without the organizational standards of socially useful labor power. Nevertheless, it certainly has expressive needs interested in breaking through the punitive laws of so-called traditional consciousness (see also Dagmar von Doetichem and Klaus Hartung's work: *Zum Thema Gewalt im Superhelden-Comics* [Berlin: Basisverlag, 1974]).

Just as ideological realism, logic, the dramaturgy of meaning, and the apparatus of official consciousness connect with one another, so too can a corresponding countermovement develop, but only by way of an alliance between a radically analytical process and those characteristics of the spectator's perception that form a repressed class according to the consciousness, which child-rearing brings about.

Translated by Rory Bradley

Notes

This essay was originally published in German as Alexander Kluge, "Die realistische Methode und das sog. 'Filmische,'" in *Gelegenheitsarbeit einer Sklavin: Zur realistischen Methode* (Frankfurt am Main: Suhrkamp, 1975), 201–9.

The one image included in the German original is not reproduced in the present translation.

1. This is obviously in the language of business and bureaucracy. But it is also true for the metaphors in colloquial speech. I say, for example, "at the foot of a mountain." This does not contain an image, because the mountain does not have a foot. As a concept is it also imprecise, since I do not know, for example, where exactly this "foot" begins and where it ends. This is somewhere in between an abstraction and an intuition. Our need for such a trade language lies in the quick control of approximate determinations. When wanting to be more precise, for example, when using technical language, we distance ourselves from "language." Consider, for example, the two-page definition of the railroad according to the Imperial Court of Justice, or the language of the technical patents, etc.

Recorded film cannot imitate the midlevel abstraction of trade language. In the case of the mountain, it can either provide an actual, exact topography, or it fails and remains indeterminable. The difficulty of recorded film stems from the fact that it contains too much information, so much so that it has difficulty producing clearly defined abstractions.

2. For more on this and on what follows, see the introductory chapter in Günter Peter Straschek's *Handbuch wider das Kino* (Frankfurt am Main: Suhrkamp, 1975), 9.

3. [Translator's citation: Bertolt Brecht, "From the Three Penny Trial: A Sociological Experiment," trans. Lance W. Garmer, in *German Essays on Film*, ed. Richard W. McCormick and Alison Guenther-Pal (New York: Continuum, 2004), 117.]

4. It was initially in the mass media, the managers of human wishes and facts, where separate superstructures arise for the need for facts as well as the expression of wishes: divisions for television and film and a subdivision for documentation. These genres develop separate ideas.

5. This reductive claim, of course, does not pertain to films by Vlado Kristl, Jean-Marie Straub, Werner Herzog, etc. An inherent feature of schematism is that it will never encompass all forms of a medium.

6. [Translator's citation: Karl Marx, *Capital*, vol. 1, in Karl Marx and Friedrich Engels, *Collected Works*, vol. 35, *Marx* (London: Lawrence and Wishart, 1996), 45.]

7. Consistent sensitization appears to be the requirement for the subjective filmmaker who has time for this and keeps his head clear of noise, meaning he closes himself off to real experience. Yet it is doubtful whether this conservative requirement is not already primed, is not *radical subjectivity* (for which it claims to fight), but rather is a *result of dearth of experience* in the spirit of a new *jeunesse dorée*. Wim Wenders and Peter Handke openly problematize this in their film *Wrong Move*. Here, the writer Wilhelm Meister, who shuts himself off from the mixed experiences of German reality for the sake of the quality of his subjective writing style, looks out from the Zugspitze with his gaze set on nothing in particular. But do you really need to put so many professional tools of film and human sensitivity to work—and consume Goethe's work in the process—in order to develop a pseudo-problem? A writer who works consistently and subjectively like Arno Schmidt is actually a gigantic laborer: a rehabilitator of the associative method and a well-grounded concept of realism. In other words, he is a radical advocate for a conservative-subjective point of view, in the correct sense (which I would rigorously defend without differentiating the status between the needs of the reader or spectator); he is the complete opposite of the aspiring writer Wilhelm Meister. Why is our interest focused on this would-be Hamlet? Why is the film not told from Mignon's much more interesting perspective? This kind of displacement in narrative perspective would reverse the entire film. The film's landscapes (a yellow autumn foliage), the intensity of the scenes, the city lights would gain meaning from Mignon's thirst for experience, *her* dependence, and *her* sensuous curiosity. But the perceptions of film would probably be much too narrow for her. She is not primarily interested in what the camera can do without straining itself: abstract beauty that an intellectual can then reject. That the film does not seek out this kind of curiosity in its persons makes it a *Bildungsfilm*. So-called sensibility is intellectuality in the worst sense: a program of sensuous indifference that lowers itself so that it acts as if it were the meta-critique of this coldness. But you cannot create a meta-critique of something that has not been attempted. "Indeterminate negation."

8. Karl Marx, "Economic Manuscripts of 1857–58," in Karl Marx and Friedrich Engels, *Collected Works*, vol. 28, *Karl Marx: 1857–61* (1986), 37–38.

9. [Translator's citation: Marx, "Economic Manuscripts of 1857–58," 37.]

10. [Translator's citation: Marx, "Economic Manuscripts of 1857–58," 37.]

11. [Translator's note and citation: In the German original, Kluge cross-references his later essay contained in the same volume in which the present essay first appeared, *Gelegenheitsarbeit einer Sklavin: Zur realistischen Methode*. See Alexander Kluge, "The Sharpest Ideology: That Reality Appeals Is Its Realistic Character," trans. David Roberts, in *Alexander Kluge: Raw Materials for the Imagination*, ed. Tara Forrest (Amsterdam: Amsterdam University Press, 2012), 191–96.]

12. Helmut Färber's *Baukunst und Film: Etwas über die Geschichte des Gebrauchs von Bildern* will appear shortly with the publishing house Film-Kritiker-Kooperative in Munich. This work places film, architecture, art cinema, *Gesamtkunstwerk*, the world's fair, the world as a store window, and the illusion of the cinema in relationship with each other: "An important part of this home is now the world's fair itself, meaning the television . . . television has superseded architecture" (25). "Considering its relationalities to the past, the feature film has become its own area, much like the opera, together with Hollywood as Versailles. From *this* perspective, the history of cinema is an episode between architecture and television." (27) [Translator's note: Helmut Färber published his book himself in 1977 under the title *Baukunst und Film: Aus der Geschichte des Sehens*.]

13. [Translator's citation: Marx, "Economic Manuscripts of 1857–58," 37.]

14. [Translator's citation: Marx, "Economic Manuscripts of 1857–58," 38.]

11

FILM

A Utopia

> **Cinema Is Waiting**
> Utopia gets better and better while we wait for it.[1]

I.

"Rather than pass the time, one must invite it in. To pass the time (to kill time, expel it): the gambler. Time spills from his every pore.—To store time as a battery stores energy: the *flâneur*. Finally, the third type: he who waits. He takes in the time and renders it up in altered form—that of expectation."[2]

The **gambler**, the **flâneur**, and the **one who waits** have together built a **time machine**; their favorite toy is the **cinema**. The gambler sits there impatiently. His goal is to destroy time, to create suspense. He tries his luck at contracting time. For his companion the *flâneur*, the expansion of time is never drawn out enough. Where in the world are there **moments in time**, if not in a film? When everything in this world apart from our childhood is too short, the cinema reproduces **protracted time** [*eine lange Weile*] again, which itself makes moments possible in the first place. The one who waits, on the other hand, is not interested in all the many contemporaneities that captivate the *flâneur*. He waits for a better world, for something **beyond the cinematic image**. Cinema was created out of this threefold discord. It will be deconstructed and reconstructed again and again. If classical cinema perishes, then the disagreements among three time-honored figures will be the first to disappear: that of the soldier of fortune, that of the voyeur, and that of the one who waits. Without the poison of their hostile interests, however, no amount of movement can establish *cinema* on the basis of their respective attitudes.

Boredom [*Langweile*]

All great moments in film are strangely "boring" [*langweilig*]. They do not consist of an accumulation of images, but instead of a peculiar, momentary dilution of information. The spectator awakens from the daily flood of images and the usual sensory overload (a simultaneous narcoticization), and is attentive for a moment. What is described here is reconstructed in the movie theater. In reality, it is in moments like these that children discover what constitutes a happy time and what is actually interesting in the world.

One can assume in turn that three poisons of perception can trigger this **momentary standstill—otherwise known as attention—in the midst of stimulus**. I want to **participate** in the abbreviated tempo of adults. Yet, I am at the same time absentmindedly **immersed** in the time of my **game** that is poisonous for adults; this hybrid existence is important, because it **is waiting** for something:

> I must have poison;
> here it is sliding around;
> blissfully burrowing;
> it will slay me yet.[3]

"We are bored when we don't know what we are waiting for. That we do know, or think we know, is nearly always the expression of our superficiality or inattention. Boredom is the threshold to great deeds.—Now, it would be important to know: What is the dialectical antithesis to boredom [*Langeweile*]?"[4] This antipode could not be "suspense." If boredom is the threshold to great deeds, then absentmindedness (lack of time) is the threshold to little deeds.

> Suspense = "suspense that takes your breath away," "breathtaking." What does it mean theologically when my breath is taken from me? That the breath of another is introduced into me? What does it mean in child-rearing when I am lifted up by my feet, swung around, rocked, and set down again on my feet? The experience [*Erlebnis*] of suspense (and its concentration at the movies) contains an antipode in itself: the right moment.
>
> For this reason, an imaginary point of tranquility always emerges simultaneously. Expressed differently: moments of suspense do not merely pile up. They do not generate short-lived moments, but rather the exact opposite happens: long time arcs and prolonged patience. In this respect, so-called boredom also works by means of suspense in a range of classical works of art. As a relative tempo, suspense can be produced as much by a prior thinning out of experience (i.e., something adverse to the gauge of everyday life) as by condensing the chains of experience (as measured by everyday life). The difference rests on whether suspense leads to me and the slow tempos according to which a person can interact with themselves, or whether I am torn away from myself and thrust into a foreign, interesting tempo (as if I had just left a village and entered a city).
>
> Film history knows these sorts of movements that travel in a number of directions. They should be recalled here only because they can always be differentiated from "the principle of absentmindedness." **If I expropriate a person's own time and it proves impossible to capture that time with a foreign temporality, then a permanent back-and-forth—a search for time—will emerge out of this expulsion.** This search sidetracks every other form of attention until something akin to one's own inherent time [*Eigenzeit*] is regained. In this state (outwardly similar to hysteria but psychologically rooted differently), people find themselves neither in search of happiness (as with the gambler) nor observant (as with the *flâneur*) nor do they have the impression that something real

> is waiting for them (the one who waits). People are entirely unaware when they are in this state. This eradication of time is the antipode of cinema: undecided amid hundreds of impressions, it is as if these people were transmitters.

"Machines have learned to see with laser light. . . . Since the middle frequency of visible laser light registers at approximately 500 billion vibrations per second, you can exploit the use of 100 billion vibrations onwards in order to transmit 20 **million television channels, 5 billion radio broadcasters,** or 25 billion telephone conversations all at the same time."[5]

II.

"The pathos of this work: there are no periods of decline. . . . No belief in periods of decline."[6] "The expression 'the book of nature' indicates that one can read the real like a text."[7] "Overcoming the concept of 'progress' and overcoming the concept of 'period of decline' are two sides of one and the same thing."[8]

"'With the vitiation of their use value, the alienated things are hollowed out and, as ciphers, they draw in meanings. Subjectivity takes possession of them insofar as it invests them with intentions of desire and fear. And insofar as defunct things stand in as images of subjective intentions, these latter present themselves as immemorial and eternal. Dialectical images are constellated between alienated things and incoming and disappearing meaning, are instantiated in the moment of indifference between death and meaning. While things in appearance are awakened to what is newest, death transforms the meanings to what is most ancient.'"[9]

Technological progress always puts use objects out of circulation. Such commodities that have been put out of commission include not only external things or public places (e.g., the cinema) but also human characteristics. Some of the highest qualifications have been taken out of circulation. What am I to do with my entrepreneurial characteristics in an institutionalized office or a large agency? I would only stick out.

The vast quantity of such "hollowed-out things" (i.e., forgetful memory, human characteristics bereft of their framework) is the raw material for the continual production of new public spheres and new image worlds. In this respect, it is superficial to say that the cinema responds to the structural needs of the nineteenth century. How often are such needs only first met by mass appeal in the wrong century! In this case: cinema in the twentieth century. "In the meantime, cinema has lost its basis in the masses. The underlying conglomeration of needs was also destroyed."[10]

What will prove true about this is the fact that this need of the masses will not return on account of a series of secondary infiltrations of cinema, including, for example, the dramatic sound film, which is geared toward bourgeois needs (and consequently the structures of nineteenth-century theater). But even the dramatic needs of the nineteenth century, which classical American film imitates (e.g., the "closed" drama, no more or less than ninety minutes long), have no foundational character. It is something preconceived, something that came out of the courtly world, acquired as a finished product in the eighteenth century and sanctioned by a small upper class. Neither trivial literature of the nineteenth century nor the early forms from film history, neither their epic productions nor the principle of montage—these are the nonbourgeois roots of film—fit the mold: **needs are lost**. Yet needs can be lost only when they are met. Otherwise, they get shifted and take on alien forms. Given the 250 million video games sold in the United States last year, it may be that a need once trained on cinema is now focused on these intelligent game consoles. Just as much a time machine as every preceding technology, these objects are far more handy and also socially useful.

These new commodities do not, however, have the ability to make cinema obsolete. They cannot even confiscate the time specific to cinema. It is well known that needs change and migrate away from historical places where they have been disappointed. (In the cinema, more trivial needs were displaced by undependable middle-class taste, and as a result the middle class lost interest.)

An das Publikum!

Achtung!   Die große Lüge des Tonfilms!

Der Tonfilm hält nicht, was er verspricht!

Das Kino soll eine Volksunterhaltungsstätte sein!
Das Kino soll Euch nach des Tages Last erfreuen und entspannen!
Das Kino soll Euch gute Musik bieten!
Das Kino soll Euch Leistungen guter Artisten zeigen!

Erfüllt das Kino Euere berechtigten Wünsche??
Nein!!

Der Tonfilm allein geboten
verdirbt Gehör und Augen!

Der Tonfilm ohne Beiprogramm mit lebenden Künstlern
wirkt nervenzerrüttend!

Nur
Kino mit Bühnenschau und Orchester ist Entspannung und Erbauung!

Fordert Bühnenschau!
Fordert lebendes Orchester!

sonst:
Meidet den Tonfilm!

Deutscher Musiker-Verband.   Internationale Artisten-Loge E. V.
Karl Schiementz   Alfred Fossil

Figure 1. "The battle over film."
© Alexander Kluge Archive

Translator's note: The poster says in English: Dear Public! *Attention! The great lie of the talking film! The talking film does not do what it promises!* The cinema should be a place of entertainment for the people! The cinema should cheer you up and help you relax after a day's work! The cinema should offer you good music! The cinema should demonstrate the work of great artists! Does the cinema fulfill your rightful wishes?? No!! *The talking film*, on its own, *hurts the ears and eyes! The talking film*, without a supplementary program involving living artists, *destroys the nerves!* Only a cinema with a stage performance and an orchestra is relaxing and edifying! Support the stage! Support a live orchestra! Otherwise: **Avoid the talking film!**

> Keyword: Suspense[11]
> "We are now having a very innocent little chat. Let us suppose that there is a bomb underneath the table between us. Nothing happens, and then all of a sudden, 'Boom!' There is an explosion. The public is *surprised*, but prior to this surprise, it has been an absolutely ordinary scene of no special consequence. Now, let us take a *suspense* situation. The bomb is underneath the table and the public *knows* it, probably because they have seen the anarchist place it there. The public is *aware* that the bomb is going to explode at one o'clock and there is a clock in the décor. The public can see that it is a quarter to one. In these conditions this same innocuous conversation becomes fascinating because the public is participating in the scene. The audience is longing to warn the characters on the screen: 'You should not be talking about such trivial matters. There is a bomb beneath you and it is about to explode!'
>
> "In the first case, we have given the public fifteen seconds of *surprise* at the moment of the explosion. In the second case, we have provided them with fifteen minutes of *suspense*.[12] The conclusion is that whenever possible the public must be informed."[13]

III.

"On the Gare du Nord: . . . an abundance of space . . . is found in waiting rooms . . . which led to the problem of the railroad station as exaggerated baroque palace."[14] The bounty of the screen in classical, grand movie theaters and the bounty of large train stations are similar. Apparent abundance. This abundance *is*, however, the message.

The principle of cinema waits. Needs wait. **The need for exceptionally large windows—from which I can look out of my own world or alternately into the outside world—waits. The desire for exceptionally large waiting rooms is permanent.**

"Considering its connections to the past, the *motion picture* is once again a reality in itself like the world fair and the opera: with Hollywood as Versailles, multiplex cinemas (Benn M. Hall, *The Best Remaining Seats: The Story of the Golden Age of the Movie Palace* [New York: C. N. Potter, 1961]; Dennis Sharp, *The Picture Palace and Other Buildings for the Movies* [New York: F. A. Praeger, 1969]); gala premières and award ceremonies as courtly celebrations; stars and tycoons as the highest-ranked guests (Arthur Knight and Eliot Elisofon, *The Hollywood Style* [New York: Macmillan, 1969]); villas and apartments of stars and moguls—once **again an aristocratic world, performed for money.** Considered in this way, the motion picture is an episode between architecture and television."[15]

IV.

"There is talk of renewing art by beginning with forms. But are not forms the true mystery of nature, which reserves to itself the right to remunerate—precisely through them—the accurate, the objective, the logical solution to a problem posed in purely objective terms? ... Are not all great conquests in the field of forms ultimately a matter of technical discoveries? ... 'To what extent the old forms of the instruments of production influenced their new forms from the outset is shown, ... perhaps more strikingly than in any other way, by the attempts, before the invention of the present locomotive, to construct a locomotive that actually had two feet, which, after the fashion of a horse, it raised alternately from the ground. It is only after considerable development of the science of mechanics, and accumulated practical experience, that the form of a machine becomes settled entirely in accordance with mechanical principles, and emancipated from the traditional form of the tool that gave rise to it.' (In this sense, for example, the supporters and the load, in architecture, are also 'forms'.) Passage is from Marx, *Capital*, vol. 1 (Hamburg, 1922) p. 347n."[16]

> Bitter polemic waged against iron rails in the 1830s: In *A Treatise in Elementary Locomotion*, for example, A. Gordon argued that the steam carriage (as it was called then) should run on lanes of granite. It was deemed impossible to produce enough iron for even the very small number of railway lines being planned at that time.[17]

First of all, the suggestions today about what you can do with new electronic technology are equally blundering. We apply the past morphology [*Formenwelt*] to those of the present. This makes no sense. Technological innovation, which can just as easily procure a morphology for itself, is just as present in past morphologies as the railroad developed its reliance on tracks.

174   *Difference and Orientation*

Figure 2. "Locomotion."
© Alexander Kluge Archive

Rails, Trodden Paths

In engineering, much as in mathematics, forms of expression are generated most often by containment, simplification, or a separation from an original abundance that was too excessive or impractical and now yields to technical necessity. What becomes praxis is therefore merely a reflection of the original abundance of pathways. It has the appearance of conducting itself inversely toward fantasy commodities: in their naive beginnings, such commodities take on a paltry form. In any case, all early expressions of literature, philosophy, book printing, music, and film do not originally appear in a wide variety of forms. Instead, new forms emerge out of processes of development: differentiation, expansion, and ever more diverse articulations. At the same time, setbacks also create in this field of expression—e.g., asceticism, deliberate simplicity, new objectivity—a countermovement that itself is a part of differentiation. Decisions regarding both technical and fantasy commodities are already made in exact opposition to what culminates in useful praxis. Therefore, in terms of design [*Formgebung*], neither field of expression may submit to the dominance of the other. Technical or administrative control over fantasy commodities—new media's project represents nothing less than this—will kill the living forms of expression in fantasy commodities on account of its inherent indifference and thoughtlessness when it comes to cutting corners and simplifying. The opposite conception—that fantasy commodities take control over technology—is thankfully not prevalent.[18] When one mode of expression tries to subjugate another, a bitter fight always ensues. Without ever intending to do so explicitly, new media's project leads to the conclusion that they destroy or at the very least disrupt the classical means of expression in fantasy commodities. The cinema, which ranks as one of these classical means of expression, must arm itself.

Currently, competing companies are buying up the rights to show movies on twenty television stations both new and old twelve hours a day, 365 days a year. The prices are now said to mushroom from 126,000 to 500,000 marks per film. Future providers are therefore not concerned with spectators not having enough time to watch television, but rather with a lack of software. It is the authors of ideas who are not proliferating. You could add India's entire film industry, and the time slots for new media's debut on the air would still not be filled. This entrepreneurial boom will effectively end in a fiasco. We know about the incident with Dr. Strousberg and his Romanian railroad as well as examples from the first economic crisis at the end of the nineteenth century.[19] **Only after they experience disappointment can new media acquire the intelligence they need to learn. They will then acquire other forms we do not yet know about.** This is remarkably different from the flat, one-to-one representations typical of media that emit and distribute the same thing twenty times in the row. Such media resemble more a steam engine (possibly traveling cross-country) capable of lifting itself up from and then setting itself down on its bed-plate than the classic train bound to its rails that has become praxis **due to this very limitation. Moving forward is made practical by simplifying** and canalizing. Something living like feelings and cinema are not the means to some end, but rather living beings in a manner of speaking. **Their further development will depend on differentiation and not channeling** [*Bahnung*].

In this respect, one must always trace cinema back to its basic components: an intermittent mechanism, a projection, the large surface for the screen, a trivial public sphere in attendance, a panorama effect, narrative techniques, etc. Every one of the individual technical

> **The close-up,** a technical form dependent on a long focal distance. Initially unfamiliar to spectators because a close-up of the face was found to dismember the body. Even in films today, extreme close-ups of objects, as opposed to people, are jarring. Just as irritating are long shots [*Zeit-Totalen*] and close-ups [*Zeit-Großaufnahmen*]. In naturalistic films, they appear as an effect (effect = a result without a cause). These are the primary means of expression at the disposal of the time machine called film. The translation of the close-up technique into something dramaturgical ties in to needs in spectators called the big screen, concentration, etc. Such translations into dramaturgy have not happened.
>
> **Short focal lengths.** The morphology of distance. A translation of a short focal length into the abstract process of montage and techniques of filmic narrative does not exist. (What would we call a short focal length in storytelling?)
>
> One could say that for every filmic invention—CinemaScope optics, the intermittent mechanism in the camera (the passing of film per unit of time), the principle of the zoom lens, different formats for the screen, tripods, and the projection onto multiple screens—a translation (1) into a dramaturgical form, (2) in order to meet the needs of the spectators is sought. It will become apparent that with every technical achievement comes a wealth of forms yet to be developed, and even more so when a translation no longer deals solely with a simple technical context [*Zusammenhang*].
>
> In the case of this kind of **elementalization,** the movie theater collapses at the entrance, on the main screen, in the assembly hall, and the projection room, etc.: each of these elements can be varied. Vary one of the parameters, and all others are influenced as well. The auditorium, for example, in a classical movie theater is thus set up to create a sense of intimacy: the balcony, the last row, the intimacy of the first row, the intimacy of the spectators sitting next to one another and in relation to the screen. In the 1930s, the interior design of the theater took on elements from cafés and bars.
>
> The kind of forms this tradition contains becomes evident when one imagines an auditorium paved like a bathroom with tiled floors.

Figure 3. "A film like an earthquake, a man like a volcano."
© Alexander Kluge Archive

178 *Difference and Orientation*

or organizational elements or texts contains a morphology that continues to develop independently and may translate into new media.

V.

A band of knights runs through a Celtic forest. They are nobility. You can tell by the embellishments on their helmets. A snake symbol is the clan's battle insignia. The noble knights arrive on horseback at a village and there they kill all of its inhabitants. A beautiful young woman is the sole survivor of the massacre. She is holding a sword in her hand (a hallowed sword). Next to her is a child, her brother.

Next, the leader of the knights, with his somewhat Asian face and his "kind, sad" eyes, comes forward to duel with the young woman. The aristocrat cannot refuse the challenge, but he does not want to fight, and looks sad. Then the woman also lowers her sword; the knight or the king turns his back to her, and she does **not** use this opportunity to kill him. This was a mistake, for the knight turns around in a flash and strikes the woman dead. The brother, a child, has seen all this. The adventure is concerned with the boy and his future fate; he will never stop tracking down the snake insignia in order to avenge his clan.

After many odysseys, the boy, who has now grown into a sword fighter, finds the group of knights with the snake symbol. The group has now grown into a religious sect in which the leader officiates not by sword, but as a kind of Christian faith, except that the disciples wear orange robes and pray while kneeling before scenery from an operetta. We find ourselves in Asia. The noble knights or comrades of the grail eat human flesh and occasionally turn into snakes at night; in reality, they are snakes. After all of the knights are killed by the sword fighter, the film ends with the note that the next film will continue the saga of the victorious sword fighter. The film is called *Conan the Barbarian*. The film is based on a series of fantasy novels and comics.

We saw that technical innovations can be translated into a wealth of forms. This principle cannot be applied to the production of symbols. Symbols are not based on innovations. There are practically no new symbols, but rather simple allusions to other symbols, because realities have changed. **Each one of the symbolic narratives is in and of itself authentic, and each has its own contemporary history with its own measure of narrative time.** The stories of Lancelot or Parsival or similar adventure stories would be told differently around 1800 than in 1982, but they would not be arbitrarily different. The measure of time [*Zeitmaß*] is inherent to the symbolic morphology and must be guessed or translated, but it is never subject to the whims of the storyteller. If you approach film in a quasi-technical way by combining symbolic sequences arbitrarily merely for the sake of making a film for money (so that something is offered to every belief: Pune, Jesus, the old Celts, genocide, forgiveness, distrust, mercy, magic, probability, etc.), what results is a specific **destruction of the environment in the spectator's world of experience. Were your feelings to register all that is happening on the screen, you would go crazy.** Instead, spectators watch these films selectively, just as they do with the irreconcilable particles of reality.

In this context, the new elementarization and synthesis of symbolic sequences corresponds to the destruction or devastation of historic cities. **Consciousness compared to a grown city.** The greatest instances of simplification, which supposedly meet the needs of the masses, correspond to "Haussmannization."[20] Napoleon III's architect Baron Haussmann, who tore down historic Paris, named himself an *artiste-démolisseur* (demolition artist). The difference between the arbitrary mass production of impossible symbolic sequences and what Haussmann did is that Haussmann's great caprice had its natural limits precisely because it was man-made. In the anonymous business of producing new media, this is no longer the case, as the rules of production will show. The ABSURD damage that occurs in this situation has to do with the fact that a deluge of additional images is constantly being added to the already overexcited and jam-packed world of human images. People cannot develop a relationship to these new images because they have no recognizable sequence. Yet, they take up just as much room as those image sequences according to which people live their lives. At this point, you begin noticing the material content that the production of expression occupies. **These are not ideal images.**

Supplement 1 to V.

"Artiste-Démolisseur" (demolition artist). Everyone who has a reason to create works of art is participating in a kind of destruction by abdicating the conventions of expression. On the other hand, the artist is always also a conservationist, since he does not abandon language itself (the language of music, of architecture). The audaciousness itself—the power that arises from the idea that "what destroys me is what I thrive on"—is a convention. This "sensational" attitude of the artist differs fundamentally in its social position when compared to what Baron Haussmann did. A **destroyer of cities** cannot be regarded on the same expressive level as authors or artists; instead, he is an organizer of the establishment. He is a statesman, so to speak. The state is never a person. It is also not creative. The single individual who works for the state is always an instrument. This instrument brought Baron Haussmann to imagine that he was in the business of being an independent artist. He can be nothing more than an administrator; and yet he goes around acting as if he were an artist! Today, there are only a few points in society where you might find a Baron Haussmann: the American presidency, for example. **Bureaucracies** today are assuming Haussmann's conceit to plan and destroy. But even Baron Haussmann, who was nothing more that a bureaucrat, looked like any other person.

Supplement 2 to V.

"These are not ideal images." **Symbolic sequences are solidified actions.** The sequence animalism-magic-omnipotence-of-thought is where thoughts began to fear their own omnipotence. As a defensive response, they produced magic. **Prohibition** shapes modern society just as much as it did the oldest ones. It can be said that no society could ever develop without the symbolic production of this sequence.[21]

The great catastrophes discussed in ancient books—the Deluge, Babylon—occur as a result of crude breaches of laws that govern the way in which symbolic sequences are combined or destroy each other. Things can become high-rise buildings or technical syntheses (e.g., the Eiffel Tower), so that we forget that things can *also* have a (secondary) symbolic function. In general, technologies can be combined and added to others without bringing about **immanent** catastrophe. If you do this to a living body—i.e., insert a foreign organ into it—an immediate catastrophe will ensue. There are entire medical disciplines dedicated to the mitigation of the ways in which bodies **reject** other living organs. We are talking about the way symbolic sequences take on an interim value, which is defined as the relationship between an object's ability to be synthesized with other objects and its strong rejection of those objects: build "skyscrapers" and sooner or later a **Babylonian confusion of languages** will result. These sequences cannot be combined arbitrarily. In fact, one could almost say: They cannot be combined at all. They need distance, gaps between each other, so that the symbolic gravitation between sequences does not tear the symbolic bodies themselves apart. If these bodies are torn apart, it is not the symbolic forces or their magic that dissolves. Instead, the sequences run about as if they had no body, as a mixture. **The flood of images and the countless forces involved in raising children do not destroy the elemental forces in humans, but instead they destroy the ways and means by which these elemental forces associate with one another.** The sensitivity is actually not reduced: it always remains vulnerable; yet, it no longer enters into an exchange, nor does it express itself any longer. Out of this inauthentic intercourse with symbolic sequences, a permanent displacement of the realms of expression occurs: "linguistic confusion."

"Laing and Esterson, for example, give a lecture about a family, the 'Edens,' whose renaming of all family relations led to an exceptional degree of interpersonal unreality. With the exception of the seventeen-year-old daughter, all family members participated comfortably in this entirely unreal system of relationships, which was supposedly created for the daughter when she was born. The following list presents the key to the renamings:

TABLE 1.

Real familial relationship to daughter:	The name the daughter had to use:
Father	Uncle
Mother	Mummy
Aunt (mother's sister)	Mother
Uncle (aunt's husband)	Daddy, later Uncle
Cousin	Brother

As established already, the only member of the family who did not come to terms with this chaos of identities and relationships was the daughter, who eventually had to be admitted to a mental institution for acute catatonia."[22]

The demand for authenticity that every radical auteur seeks finds its justification in the observation of the laws of symbolic production. Symbolic production is authentic because it is not merely a "mental exercise" [*Probehandlungen im Geiste*]. How can we put something so dangerous for humans into the hands of media-speculators! "Knife, fork, scissors, and fire: these are things we do not give to young children!"[23]

Three Different Happy Endings
(Organized according to Media)

It is known that in Shakespeare's plays and in the theater in general the fall of the hero or antihero—the catastrophe as happy ending—has become common. There can be neither rousing drama nor serious opera without a catastrophe in the fifth act. Happy ending = catastrophe.

One could say that Western works of art are melancholic. This is true under one condition: that the everyday life of the spectator and the extraordinary event in the theater and the opera (or in a novel) are strictly separated. The stage lies between them.

In the **movie theater** this distance first disappears. The cinema gestures toward immediate presence. It belongs to the (original) everyday ecology of spectators and it has the ability to pull them into the filmic image. One can presume that this degradation of distance is the reason why more and more films have required a happy ending, **a happy way out**. That is not the producers' clever idea, but rather a question pertaining to the balance sheet of happiness in the life of spectators.

What has taken the place of a happy ending in **television?** One cannot say that the nightly news has a happy ending. It has no beginning and no end. It merely harks back to the previous day, and repeats itself in 1½ hour segments. We know that the weather forecast always comes at the end. That is not a happy ending. The end of the program must be organized in such a way that I can easily fall asleep and start the day tomorrow by taking off for my usual activities unrelated to television. **In this respect, the program must come to an end.** It may not assign me any tasks that have influence beyond the realm of the program (which is exactly the point of classical theater: **the aftereffect**). In comparison to the cinema, television shortens the distance further by bringing itself as an everyday object into close proximity of the spectator as well as into the midst of his evening activities. At the same time, it also moves into the distance (much like a mirror): one does not greet the evening anchorman even though he greets me. A happy ending: "unanticipated happiness at the end" of a television program would be just as irritating as a "surprising and abrupt catastrophe," a tragic ending. It gets confusing because film or plays that appear on television appear as **quotations**. They too have an ending of this kind. Embedded within television programs, they are part of a flow of programming that generally has no particular beginning or end. **At least we see a summary of the news—a bit of the weather report—after a dire catastrophe and sudden good fortune.** Both of these extremes have become television's requisites of reality. The spectator is aware of the fact that reality does not contain these extremes. In this respect, a mirror reflection rather than a happy ending.

VI.

"You will remember how I have said that the day-dreamer carefully conceals his phantasies from other people because he feels he has reasons for being ashamed of them. I should now add that even if he were to communicate them to us he could give us no pleasure by his disclosures. Such phantasies, when we learn them, repel us or at least leave us cold."[24]

It is uncivilized when someone is besieged by another person who exposes their inner life. "The tyrannies of intimacy" (Richard Sennett).[25] Civilization means distance.

184   Difference and Orientation

Only the poet, Sigmund Freud goes on to say, can possibly find a way to translate the extraordinary fantasies of others while still offering maximum pleasure. In this respect, classical cinema has always been a poetic art. Observations, like those of Färber, that illustrate how labor is only rarely depicted in the movies reveal how the principle of cinema translates reality into the chance of pleasure. Cinema has not yet addressed those places where this kind of translation appears to be impossible.

When Chaplin shows work in *Modern Times,* he stylizes it. When the Marx Brothers deal with the misery of Italian foreign workers in New York, they do so in the form of success stories. Spectators are always given the opportunity for both *insight* and *evasion*.

In contrast, the anonymously manufactured modes of production, in which the products of *new* media generate their specific speed, return back to the barbaric **assault on the other.** This mode does not allow for insight and represents the **invasion** of the spectator's own movement.

The fantasies of the daydreamer tell stories in a loop. The stories have their own specific order, which is **idiosyncratic,** i.e., they are **different for every person;** one person cannot force his own timing on another. If the sequence of these stories is disturbed, unrest results that subsides only when the natural order and integrity of the story's loop are reestablished. If necessary, sleeping and dreaming can reestablish a piece of the spectator's own "natural motion." According to Kierkegaard, a person falls into despair when he slips out of his own "natural" perspective rooted in his prehistory. He will almost go *crazy*. He must engage in an enormous amount of activities in order to reestablish the **balance of his inner narrative.** These stories respond to strong symbolic stimulation in films (the original sword, God's first words, good and evil, strong emotional turns) like the pull of magnets. **When multiple magnetic forces cumulate haphazardly and affect people, then a disruption of the spectator's own motion occurs, followed by an attempt at reestablishing balance. This recalibration avails itself of every form of help such that it also virtually surrenders itself to the very medium that proved to be so destructive.**

At the beginning of cinema's development, spectators were initially afraid that the artificial, mechanical production of moving images could destroy the individual balance between their impressions of reality and dream images. Because the pictures moved quickly and this, in turn, triggered astonishment, bringing with it both pleasure and profits for producers, the early American film industry assumed it could also commercialize the new media **faster**. Following the model of successful shorts with speedy plots, the early American film industry turned to mass production. Employing a tried-and-true plot again and again, they made each new film successively faster; instead of *one* they made twenty-five films of the same kind: faster, shorter, and in large quantities. Instead of one drama at a time, they made two, three, or even four dramas simultaneously, each one cheaper than the last. Everything was a formula that still proved successful in the production of automobiles (the Ford T4). This led to the rapid collapse of the former American film industry and to the blossoming of the European film industry (in France and Denmark), which filled a market niche with more often than not epic narratives. The epic, not staccato (Dieter Prokop).

The film industry in every country learned lessons from early American cinema. They manufactured their own films more carefully. The individuality of their products corresponded to considerations given to the works' concrete contact with the spectator. It is sometimes possible to say that film consorted directly with the id.

It was not until television that the deindividuation of film resurfaced. One can understand the principle of television in the Federal Republic of Germany only if one takes into consideration the strong emotional drive in radio broadcasting between the years 1933 and 1945. In radio after 1945 and therefore in television as well, all strong emotions were supposed to be curtailed. At least, we can infer that is what happened. Seen temporally, every dramaturgy is geared toward the stereotypical abbreviation of feeling on account of both television's compulsion to broadcast continuously and its inherent drive for permanent competition between shows. The obvious result is that spectators comport themselves insensitively toward television. They do this because the limitations of television prevent its programs from stirring up deeper psychological strata in spectators. This leads to frustration because spectators want to be deeply moved. If television were a product spectators had to physically go to, then a similar indifference toward it would evolve just as it did with early American cinema. Because television is more like a clock and wallpaper (Jean-Christophe Averty: "The television is not a medium, it is a piece of furniture"), a particular opinion on the part of spectators is only necessary at the time of purchase.

VII.

At first sight, orientation is simple: **there are two kinds of public spheres that are increasingly divided.** The first follows the model of corporations and public institutions. On the one hand it suffers from a scarcity of ideas, and on the other it has market power. Sooner or later, this form for producing a public sphere will always represent the **cultural majority**. These superpowers make forays into minority cultures. At the other end of the spectrum, however, are structures increasing in strength geared for the **alternative production** of publicity.

In reality, this division is not so simple. Different public spheres are not always physical groups of people standing in opposition to one another. Nor do they differentiate themselves according to a person in an institution or a person in a corporation. Rather, **these two kinds of public spheres pervade individual spectators, editors, filmmakers, and critics** regardless of whether they pledge allegiance to both.

> There is a trend that all minority cultures in a society are stronger than the hitherto ruling cultural majority. Yet, the fact that none of the single minority groups operating apart from society ever manage to oppose other minority groups or to replace the former cultural majority by overthrowing it means it does not matter anymore who represents the majority and the minority.

> There is only ever **one** society. Public spheres, i.e., the context of expressions within a society, can, however, break apart. This is happening at the moment to the extent that one expression can no longer be translated into any other. In spite of this, the opposition participates in the majority's contradictory systems, and the majority subsumes the opposition even though it is called by another name. Just how pricey the "cost of

common ground" (= cost of community) really reveals itself in the fact that *both* public spheres are present in every single person. It is as if he were his own society and possessed a feeling of majority and minority.

Cinema is the only audiovisual medium that can be produced **independently**. It is therefore the only corrective against electronic media's slippage into the functional dimension.[26] "The active agents of false consciousness are those that bring people to believe in a false view of their surroundings and their own position in it" (Giltin, Gärnter, Noelle-Neumann).[27]

Freedom and pluralism mean having more images of reality that get to the heart of things, says Federal Minister Schwarz-Schilling. I argue, however, that the active development of the corrective potential in audiovisual technologies as they currently exist exclusively in film means producing a real pluralism by replicating ancillary issues. The German Constitution says that the state must meet not only the primary but also the secondary needs of the people. This suggests that spectators have the right to access representational forms (theater, books, cinema) structurally and substantively different from new media, in general, and the proliferation of television channels, in particular.

"'Knowledge of nature and of truth is as infinite as they are; the arts, whose aim is to please us, are as limited as we are. Time constantly brings to light new discoveries in the sciences; but poetry, painting, and music have a fixed limit which the genius of languages, the imitation of nature, and the limited sensibility of our organs determine. . . . The great men of the Augustan age reached it, and are still our models.' Turgot, *Oeuvres*, vol. 2 (Paris, 1844) ('Second discours sur les progrès successifs de l'esprit humain'), pp. 605–6. Thus, a pragmatic renunciation of originality in art!

"'There are elements of the arts of taste which could be perfected with time—for example, perspective, which depends on optics. But local color, the imitation of nature, and the expression of the passions are of all times.' Turgot, *Oeuvres*, vol. 2 (Paris, 1844) ('Plan du second discours sur l'histoire universelle'), p. 658.

"'Militant representation of progress: "It is not error that is opposed to the progress of truth; it is indolence, obstinacy, the spirit of routine, everything that contributes to inaction . . ."'"[28]

F.H.

VIII.

This is how a unique situation is created that never existed before: when the printing press emerged, it did not curb the art of letter writing. When photography emerged, capital was not inserted in between painting and photography such that the entire means of production necessary for painting was stripped away and instead diverted into the chemical industry. This was because the chemical industry did not pose as the master of photography. It restricted itself to matters related to supply. The industry did not meddle in photography's agenda.

The attempt to expand into a new area happened at the same time as German film blossomed around 1917. Using General Staff's funds (Ludendorff), a medium was supposed to be taken into state control and the custodians of the idea of the old state—the German right-wing nationalists—would then construct a corporation that would drive **egalitarian rule** using the means of film. These attempts lead to extreme propagandistic examples of **social manipulation** especially after the National Socialists, who take up Hugenberg's legacy, come to the realization that in the social context of expressions politics can never express itself solely politically, but rather that the political is contained in **entertainment films**. Nevertheless, the American film produced by a free market economy in 1943 is emotionally superior to the German Ufa product of the same year.

> After the Americans landed in Morocco, Rommel captured a bunch of American films. They were shown in the Ministry for Propaganda. The experienced manipulators were baffled by the **indirect** effect on human motivation these films evinced. They were not ready, however, to recognize their own mistakes. They placed blame on **color** for the outsized effect. As a result, they made a color film: *Münchhausen*.

The turn to new electronic industries is developing today practically by coincidence and with significantly less deliberate input. The electronic camera has existed for over fifty years. The possibilities of cable infrastructures have been around since 1936 (the television transmission of the Olympic Games in Berlin): fiberglass is not the cause, but rather an opportunity. The forced development of new media markets in the Federal Republic and the governmental incentives for their application do not correspond to social necessity. They do not even correspond to economic and political considerations. The fact that new media lie fallow and simultaneously appear to be worthy of investment is enough reason to try them out on a grand scale. **In politics, we call something like this adventurism. Because all real growth processes appear to function incorrectly, the growth of society must take place more or less within the idea itself.** Because all real property has been allocated and every apartment is occupied, the mind becomes a field for expansion. When every country on the planet is allocated, the fight for the distribution of wealth, **colonization, enters the interiority of human beings.**

A pragmatic question: fascism's mass mobilization of activism will never happen again in these latitudes like it did in the 1930s. The modern form of fascism is rather the **mass mobilization of passivism: collective inattention.** I acquire this through my unemployment in reality and my overtime in the realm of consciousness that is mediated especially through media. If I am fully employed in my free time, I have little concentration left over. If I am unemployed or if my job is imperiled (as are practically all jobs), there exists a so-called industrial reserve army. In other words, I am replaceable at all times. I must balance this fundamentally unbearable situation. I am also dependent on the production of illusions. This keeps me glued to the overproduction of the medium. "The real becomes imaginary, hence the imaginary is real."[29] Such a prearranged, social situation (when not already organized by the powers that be or conspirators) breeds **passivity** and permits a social minority to do what it will. Desperate people—i.e., **productive forces removed from their historical perspective**—have the tendency to repudiate reality rather than refraining from using it. The mix of capitalism and vital feeling forces a breakthrough into the irrational.

"Understood in terms of the above, love as a medium is not itself a feeling, but rather a code of communication, according to the rules of which one can express, form and simulate feelings, deny them." (Niklas Luhmann)[30]

Keyword *Autobahn*: Federal Minister Schwarz-Schilling: "In a way, we are only building streets; only afterwards can we make decisions about the cars that will drive on them." (*Der Spiegel* 43/1982, p. 56)

One should not be fooled: the National Socialists are **opportunistic materialists** (Franz Neumann). Had they been unable to strike a chain of emotions, real relations, and hardships, they would certainly not be able to win a majority of the people over time.

The core is, however, a speculation *à la baisse*. The combination of easily obtainable motivations results in activism. Today that activism has become a passivism among the majority of people.

Evidently difficult to assemble in the moment and thus too weak to break through, the more muted motivations within a single individual are thereby destroyed; their **relationality** is killed. The discrepancy lies in the fact that this violence to this context does not in any way kill one's feelings. **If, however, the human relationality where these emotions emerge and combine is destroyed, then a person will no longer be able to recognize their own emotions. People can be made literally inhumane this way.**

As such, fascism effectively builds, in opposition to the political definitions of the Left and the Right, a third option of sorts, one that is **supposedly** produced through feasibility. It must be only "supposed" because no human could actually engage with this feasibility. The consequential antithesis must then initially accept (for the short term) the clearly available advancements in the organization of National Socialism. The difference between this and the opposite extreme has to do with the fact that it has **nothing** to do with opportunistic materialism. It therefore must be a *cohesive* [*zusammenhängendere*] politics: accounts, or better yet: the ascertainable compensating **exactitude à la hauteur**. "À la hauteur" is a Parisian phrase that means socially *at the top*. In reality, human characteristics, which are difficult to mobilize, lie at the so-called bottom or depths. **Depth is, however, merely a category of relationality. In this respect, the touch of the skin would be, for example, a kind of depth because it cannot be deceptive in any way.**

The cinema acts like a civilian from the year 1932 with respect to the project of new media (not to be understood as the underlying technology, but rather as projects based on it). Not until 1949 could this civilian begin to plan again.

IX.

Overview of the most frequently used orders of magnitude.

Trillionstel: Atto	10^{-18}	= 1/1 000 000 000 000 000 000 = 0,000 000 000 000 000 000 001
Femto	10^{-15}	= 1/1 000 000 000 000 000 = 0,000 000 000 000 000 001
Billionstel: Pcio	10^{-12}	= 1/1 000 000 000 000 = 0,000 000 000 001
	10^{-11}	= 1/100 000 000 000 = 0,000 000 000 01
	10^{-10}	= 1/10 000 000 000 = 0,000 000 000 1
Milliardstel: Nano	10^{-9}	= 1/1 000 000 000 = 0,000 000 001
	10^{-8}	= 1/100 000 000 = 0,000 000 01
	10^{-8}	= 1/10 000 000 = 0,000 000 1
Millionstel: Mikro	10^{-7}	=1/1 000 000 = 0,000 001
	10^{-6}	= 1/100 000 = 0,000 01
	10^{-5}	= 1/10 000 = 0,0001
Milli	10^{-4}	= 1/1000 = 0,001
Zenti	10^{-3}	= 1/100 = 0,01
Dezi	10^{-3}	= 1/10 = 0,1
Eins	10^{-2}	= 1
Zehn: Deka	10^{-1}	= 10
Hundert: Hekto	10^{0}	= 100
Tausend: Kilo	10^{1}	= 1000
	10^{2}	= 10 000
	10^{3}	= 100 000
Million: Mega	10^{3}	= 1 000 000
	10^{4}	= 10 000 000
	10^{5}	= 100 000 000
Milliarde: Giga	10^{6}	= 1 000 000 000
	10^{7}	= 10 000 000 000
	10^{8}	= 100 000 000 000
Billion: Tera	10^{9}	= 1 000 000 000 000
	10^{10}	= 10 000 000 000 000
	10^{10}	= 100 000 000 000 000
	10^{11}	= 1 000 000 000 000 000
	10^{12}	= 10 000 000 000 000 000
	10^{13}	= 100 000 000 000 000 000
Trillion	10^{14}	= 1 000 000 000 000 000 000
	10^{15}	
	10^{16}	
	10^{17}	
	10^{18}	

Figure 4. Writing conventions for the orders of magnitude. The overview on writing conventions for the orders of magnitude refers to the speed of communication. The future, the past, above, below, close, and far can be expressed in similar magnitudes and strain the fantasy.

© Alexander Kluge Archive

192   Difference and Orientation

X.

Figure 5. People. No one can tell whether they are filmmakers or spectators. It would make no difference anyway.

© Alexander Kluge Archive

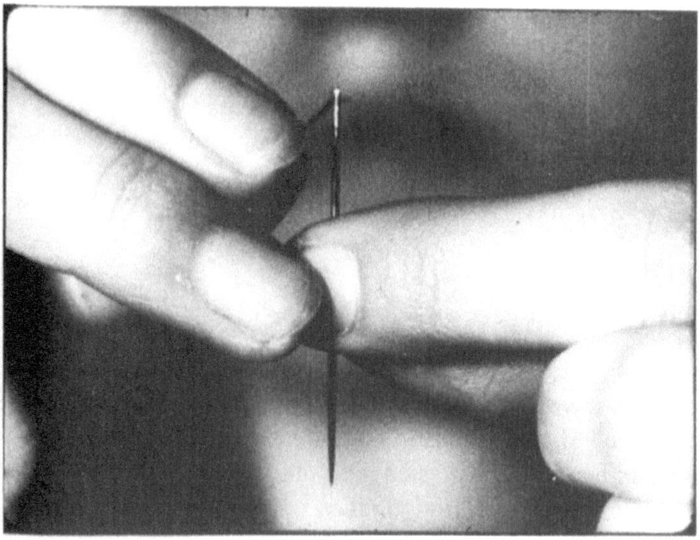

Figure 6. *Easy.* A film by Claudia von Alemann.

© Alexander Kluge Archive

Figure 7. The Paramount-Palace on Broadway. The fact that nothing simple happens in this house is apparent.
© Alexander Kluge Archive

194 *Difference and Orientation*

Figure 8. A media corporation. It cannot be seen. What is typical about a media corporation is that there is nothing typical about what it represents.
© Alexander Kluge Archive

XI.

(1) According to Schwaiger (*Laser*, p. 73), people have been working for several years now with giant pulse lasers, which have a light output of several 1,000 billion watts.[31] Using these lasers, film and

television studios can be flamed out. The problem is: how do I turn them down? The lasers are not hazard-free; with that kind of output they can burn you. Which lighting technician wants to work with this apparatus?

(2) According to scientific estimates, a human brain with a volume of 1500 cm^3 can supposedly save between 10^{12} and 10^{15} symbols. With the help of an electron microscope, we can now burn 10^{13} holes into the surface of just a few cm^2 and then overlay each hole with 10^{12} symbols. Storage density is two times the 10^{12} symbols per few cm^2. **This is a technical revolution.** This storage density exceeds the abilities of the human brain (per cm^3). We can store the world's entire collection of 500 million books (each having 500 pages) in a die measuring 1 cm^3 and keep it in our pocket, for example.

(3) In the People's Republic of China, computer systems from both the USSR and the United States are in operation. These systems cannot communicate with each other. As a result, new computer systems are currently being developed in the Federal Republic that are supposed to facilitate the translation between incompatible computer systems from these two foreign countries. While the discrepancies between entire social systems are being made translatable through a supplemental production, the development of computers has encountered difficulties when translating computer languages (COBOL, ALGOL, FORTRAN, BASIC) into colloquial speech. Morphology, syntax, context, and ambiguity (polysemy of similar concepts), leading a dialogue, and implications make conversations difficult. Two separate worlds emerge; one has multipliers and the other has none.

(4) The new basic technologies in information and communication represent a technological revolution: everything that exists in the world can be expressed using two fundamentally different modes of symbolic production and is interchangeable on the symbolic level. If this revolutionary technical innovation did not interlock with the power relations passed down over time and real objects (or if the transitions between the symbolic and objective were controlled publicly), then these technologies would be useful as an increase in the "mental exercise in the mind of humanity."

What is necessary about control? To whom can such a great excess of control fall?

(5) As we have already seen, the middle frequency of visible light is 500 billion vibrations per second. Employing 100 billion vibrations, one can transmit 20 million television channels, 5 billion radio shows, or 25 billion telephone conversations per second. The excess capacity exhibits a glut like the ones nature knows from its own surges that precede the selection of the fittest: monstrous abundance, a monstrous murder of surplus. An alliance emerges between what is already available and something new that would not exist without this process.

(6) The basic idea of so-called external pluralism contains at its core precisely this. One can actually assume with complete liberalization—meaning channels and communication in the above-named amount—that there is contact with real human needs at some fortuitous place such that **this** side of the abundance survives, while the remaining mass is incidentally absorbed. One thing is certain: on the basis of 5 billion radio programs, surely one will say something new, and another maybe even the truth.

> Even for the purposes of a moderate pluralism, as represented in Germany by ruling group interests, it would be possible to achieve an actually "interesting" selection of programs, like the one media experts from the CDU and Schwarz-Schilling have in mind, by creating 2, 3, 4, or (at the very most) 53 additional channels. Anything less falls short of creating new channels, and instead leads to the accumulation of new advertisers within the usual margins. For all intents and purposes, Schwarz-Schilling's advice would lead to a **single** gigantic **channel**.

> External pluralism = There are so many providers on the market that this **confusing abundance** can be put to use for the entirety of social processes. External pluralism calls for the continuous and free access to the means of production and the channels of distribution. As long as everyone who owns a telephone and a desk can establish their own newspaper in the newspaper market, an external pluralism exists.
>
> Internal pluralism = the organizational control of a public institution or a corporation, such that "the basic social powers in play have a place

on a board and a voice."[32] Internal pluralism is recognizable by the fact that (1) there is no free and continuous access to the means of production or channels of distribution controlled by the public institution; and (2) the means of labor is not production, but rather control or administration. Simply put: external pluralism expresses itself through production and innovation, and inner pluralism through surveillance and the maintenance of the system.

The combination of highly developed **advances in the production** of new media with the **principle of conservation** and **administration** of an internal pluralism is a **monstrosity** according to the laws by which living developments transpire. The former is premised on a long process of trial and error in the relation between spectators and the classical ecology of the public sphere, whereas the latter excludes every complete process of this kind before it could ever come about. What results from this includes, for example, (1) the fiercest kind of economic interests, which are supposed to be tempered, sit on the diversified board of directors, and receive a governmental position that cannot be bought on the market, which they need for their economic power; they have appropriated a piece of the state for themselves; (2) "the counter-effect of real relations," the only means possible of establishing an ecological balance, is barred;[33] (3) all creative prospects of new media require a fully developed and long-term process, in which the basic planning and execution are set apart from what is useful and viable for life. This is how every previous form of the public sphere has come about up until 1945. Now at this most critical juncture when multiple public spheres are "revolutionizing" themselves, we will see how a public sphere, contrary to the rules of experience, develops as if it were a crazy project in a planned economy.

XII.

As already stated: were it only about the technical revolution of the means of communication and information (means = media), we would not know how to use them in the moment of their emergence, but they would not be deadly. People usually never know at first what to make of classical inventions (steam engine, railroad). **The wild possibilities of these technologies could be connected to all different kinds of subversive and creative human needs.**

They cannot do this for reasons of order. In the Federal Republic, this order is produced by a division of labor. The federal postal service delivers the technical aggregate "to whom it may concern."

198 *Difference and Orientation*

It has no influence on how the technologies it produced are used. The framework legislation at the state level is responsible for this. In these states, a series of supervisory authorities are being developed that represent the internal pluralism of new media. The third element of this restrictive structure creates prominent, economic interests. Initially, they select the overall process according to the law of the jungle. An additional factor comes into play: a dismemberment dependent on growing indifference. Whoever is entirely indifferent toward the product—information about what happens in the spectator—(or else represents the orthodoxy) has no difficulties using the available instruments of censorship and power. Those entirely not indifferent to the products and their effects will find it increasingly more difficult to make any use of the shape new media have assumed.

(7) A cultural-revolutionary process of a particular kind has developed: all of the brakes known to society are busy preventing new methods from evolving freely. At the same time, everything that is blindly driving our society is concentrated—in spite of all

Figure 9. The Etruscan shrew. Until recently, it was considered to be the smallest mammal. Now, the *Craseonycteris thonglongyai*, the bumblebee bat, has taken its place. This animal lives opposite the River Kwai.
© Alexander Kluge Archive

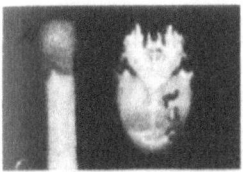
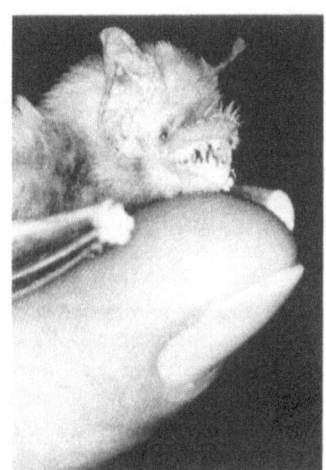
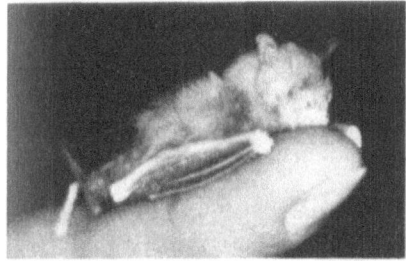

Figure 10. The bumblebee bat, 2 grams, as big as the heads of three matches but smaller than the tip of a person's index finger; low budget in nature. They are a threatened species, although they have an extreme will to live. Like all of the smallest mammals, these animals must eat a lot of food in order to maintain their high-speed metabolism. Their low-budget ovens must heat up to 98.6 degrees Fahrenheit.
© Alexander Kluge Archive

political skepticism—on maintaining new media's highest possible initial speeds. It can be said that neither the activist nor the restrictive side of this agglomeration is realistic. In combination, they are capable, however, of assembling so much composite power out of the contradictions that this catastrophic synthesis gains power capable of determining reality. This principle is called **survival of the unfittest.**

XIII.

> Robert Musil's essay "The German as Symptom" says: "The need for the unequivocal, repeatable, and fixed is satisfied in the realm of the soul by

violence. And a special form of this violence, shockingly flexible, highly developed, and creative in many respects, is capitalism. To describe this I have already advanced the broader concept of an order that takes account of selfishness. The principle of order is as old as human association itself. Whoever wants to build in stone where people are concerned must use violence or desire. This reckoning with people's bad capacities is a bearish speculation. A bearish order is trained vulgarity. It is the order of the modern world."[34]

The shape of order emerging in new media is, however, not at all geared toward the mobilization of violence or human desires. Here we see the difference between Musil's words written in the 1920s and our contemporary experience. New media bank much more on superficial interests: "I am actively interested, although (and because) it has nothing to do with me." This invention does not occur in the spirit of capitalism. It is large, commercial administrative apparatuses that are preparing the way for the media system; if anything, only the supply sector can be described as entrepreneurial. No classical capitalist of the nineteenth century would have ever thought of inserting himself into a pluralistic governmental framework by way of administrative boards. The capitalistic principle requires that we slyly circumvent these bonds. But you also cannot blame the state, because it, too, is only being perverted with respect to new media. Where the state appears as a developer, it has built factories, plants, mines, universities, schools, and streets. When it comes to streets or access to education or the marketability of what is produced in plants or factories, the state guarantees a particularly high degree of fairness. Governmental initiatives mean the end of private streets, barriers, robber barons, etc.

Just how contradictory these elements, which represent the economy of life *in their relationality* (and are thus always implemented entirely), appear to one another must be reaffirmed. Every one of the evolutionary principles was individually a *poison* to the living, but in their complete interaction they were the *condition* for the living. For the principles of (1) the state, (2) entrepreneurial initiatives, (3) technical progress on the terrain of new media, (4) the sociation [*Vergesellschaftung*] (universalization) of people—their powers of feeling and consciousness—one can say that every one of these traditions of power contains something good. Theoretically speaking, combinations are conceivable. However, the constellation (1–4) likely with new media is lethal. Because human feelings and habits that developed within the traditional forms of the classical public spheres (and even more so in the private sphere) are more violent than any current media project, the crisis between what is lethal and living cannot be expressed as a confrontation, but rather assumes the form of displacements, expansions, distortions, as well as additional improvisations and assistance. **In a manner of speaking, this is the line of attack of real relations that reduces the dream that new media try to create from their own ideas to the level of the factual.**

XIV.

> The entrepreneur, the poet, and the filmmaker have each developed a specific product; the entrepreneur, for example, developed aspirin. "Invent, produce, sell."[35]
>
> In opposition to the classical entrepreneur, the media corporation does not invent anything new; instead, it manages and grooms the market. Between those who invent things and the capacities that produce things, it constructs a sluice that excludes everything from being sold (and even from being produced) that does not belong to the corporation. **It is therefore hardly a force of production, but instead a power for apportioning reality.**
>
> Constitutions explain how citizens stand vis-à-vis authority. Now comes the novel question regarding how a person (be it a filmmaker, editor, or spectator) stands vis-à-vis media corporations. **There are no constitutions for this.**
>
> If a corporation's product structures a market ("property in and of itself"), then the concentration of property on one side can be guaranteed only by expropriation on the other. The spectator acts as the **producer** of his lived time, as opposed to the *wholesale buyer* of preferably large pieces of this lived time. It is not the buyer who pays, but rather the person who gives up their lived time. Since no one can talk about this commerce because the individual's and the corporation's respective independent existences play out in entirely different dimensions such that only the external life of a spectator (that part of their free time they give to the media) and the public arm of the corporation (what its public relations division produces) come into contact, nothing intersects that would express the opposite relation.

XV.

Wins and Losses

The traits of the market are utility, habit, and location in the lifeworld. **There is no such thing as utility in and of itself.** Something thoroughly unattached because of either habit or location in the lifeworld would never be recognized as useful. Were something already established on account of habit and location in the lifeworld to become useless, it would continue (to be paid for) for quite some time before an agreement on its uselessness became common knowledge. Utility automatically presupposes a comparison (that transpires among images, not objects).

All relations in the media industrial society suffer from a loss of reality. This affects space, time, and objectivity. Both excessive **waiting** (in the administrative world) and **time lapse** (the industrial acceleration of time) eliminate orders of time from the possibility of a "right point in time." Advanced commodity images lead to a **deterritorialization** of experience. The most important factors threatening life (e.g., expansion, "development," poisoning of foodstuff) are strangely **nonobjective**. Where I experience what destroys or merely rankles me has no addressee.

The agency that pledges to compensate for this loss of reality nevertheless produces a commodity fraught with need: **the new concreteness of media**. If each medium insists I give up some of my own life and in exchange participate in the media's faster speeds, then every price is acceptable if I get concreteness, time, and space in return. My senses, body, and spirit yearn this.

I would be subservient to the medium capable of completely satisfying this need.

This has to do with the fact that new media, like old media, are distributors and not producers, insofar as they **cannot** find the sense of time characteristic of human needs.

> At the right time none can understand!—
> If at the right time we saw the ground,
> Truth would lie **close** and **near at hand**,
> Spread all **lovely** and **mild around**.[36]

No world in television is close; it is *tele*-vision. It is also not near at hand, but is rather outnumbered by commentary. It is hectic. It tries to grab your attention in ever more drastic ways. It is thus anything but mild. We will skip "lovely," and as for truth that is out of the question.

Marcel Proust describes how travelers on a train move from one window to another, "to reassemble the offset intermittent fragments of my lovely, changeable red morning, so as to see it for once as a single lasting picture."[37]

XVI.

The "Game without End"

"To begin with a highly theoretical example, imagine the following. Two persons decide to play a game consisting of the substitution of negation for affirmation and vice versa in everything they communicate to each other. Thus 'yes' becomes 'no,' 'I don't want' means 'I want,' and so forth. It can be seen that this coding of their messages is a semantic convention and similar to the myriad other conventions used by two people sharing a common language. It is not immediately evident, however, that once this game is under way the players cannot easily revert to their former 'normal' mode of communication. In keeping with the rule of inversion of meaning, the message 'Let's stop playing' means 'Let's continue.' To stop the game it would be necessary to step outside the game and communicate about it. Such a message would clearly have to be constructed as a meta-message, but whatever qualifier were tried for this purpose would itself be subject to the rule of inversion of meaning and would therefore be useless. The message 'Let's stop playing' is undecidable, for 1) it is meaningful both at the object level (as part of the game) and on the metalevel (as a message *about* the game); 2) the two meanings are contradictory; and 3) the peculiar nature of the game does not provide for a procedure that would enable the players to decide on the one or the other meaning. This un-decidability makes it impossible for them to stop the game once it is under way. Such situations we label *games without end*."[38]

1. What could the players have done to avoid this dilemma?
   They could have agreed to use one language, say, German, when playing the game and another (a foreign language like French) to talk about the game.
2. The players could have agreed on a time limit before the start of the game.
3. The players could have presented their problem to a third person, with whom they have maintained their normal mode of speaking used outside of the game, and this person could declare when the game was over.[39]

When it comes to new media and their pollution threatening the internal worlds of human brains and feelings, everything that takes the place of the classical public sphere in the wake of its demise has no referee and no set time limit, and the foreign languages someone could employ to argue critically about the end of the game are only understood by a small minority (e.g., Hebrew, Latin, philosophy).

> "Instead of embarking on a catalogue of difficulties beforehand, you first have to start one about the difficulties that resolve themselves afterward."
> (Schwarz-Schilling, in *Der Spiegel* 43/1982, p. 61)

Translated by Samantha Lankford

Notes

This essay was originally published in German as Alexander Kluge, ed., "Utopie Film," *Bestandsaufnahme: Utopia Film* (Frankfurt am Main: Zweitausendeins, 1983), 443–94.

Kluge wrote three versions of this essay, the first dating back to 1964, a second condensed one in 1979, and a third expansive version in 1983. The translation provided here uses the 1983 source. All three can be found in Christian Schulte, ed., *In Gefahr und größter Not bringt der Mittelweg den Tod: Texte zu Kino, Film, Politik* (Berlin: Vorwerk 8, 1999).

Of the eighteen images included in the German original, only ten are included in the present translation.

1. [Translator's citation: Alexander Kluge, dir. *Artists under the Big Top: Perplexed* (1968; Frankfurt: Zweitausendeins, 2007), DVD.]
2. [Translator's citation: Walter Benjamin, *The Arcades Project*, trans. Howard Eiland and Kevin McLaughlin (Cambridge, MA: Belknap Press, 1999), 107.]
3. [Translator's note and citation: This is taken from the last stanza of Romantic author Eduard Mörike's poem "Erstes Liebeslied eines Mädchens" (A Girl's First Love Song, 1828). The translation provided here is from Eric Sams, *The Songs of Hugo Wolf* (London: Methuen, 1961), 127.]
4. Benjamin, *The Arcades Project*, 105.
5. [Translator's note: This quotation is unattributed in the German original and remains unidentifiable.]
6. [Translator's citation: Benjamin, *The Arcades Project*, 458.]
7. [Translator's citation: Benjamin, *The Arcades Project*, 464.]
8. Benjamin, *The Arcades Project*, 460.

9. Benjamin, *The Arcades Project*, 466. [Translator's note: This is Theodor W. Adorno's letter to Walter Benjamin of August 5, 1935, incorporated into *The Arcades Project*.]

10. Translator's note: This quotation is unattributed in the German original and remains unidentifiable.]

11. François Truffaut, *Hitchcock* (New York: Simon & Schuster, 1984), 73.

12. [Translator's note: In the original interview, Hitchcock speaks of fifteen minutes of suspense. Truffaut translated Hitchcock's words first into French in the original book, and then later into English in this 1984 English translation. Yet, in this German translation, which appears to be the one and only German translation (and in all other subsequent citations of this translation), Hitchcock is misquoted as saying five minutes, instead of fifteen.]

13. Frieda Grafe and Enno Patalas do **not** translate the word "suspense" in their German edition of Truffaut's book. They explain that there is no German equivalent for this word. In German, the translation for Suspense = "Spannung," "Ungewißheit," "Hangen und Bangen," "in der Schwebe," "im Ungewissen sein."

The core issue is contained in the last sentence: "The conclusion is that whenever possible the public must be informed." All contributions Hitchcock made to the language of film lead back to this sentence. This narrative *technique* has a price: it must find moments of suspense apart from everyday life, because suspense needs a certain height to fall. I need an extraordinary, dangerous situation (e.g., a bomb) in order to introduce the technique of suspense in the first place. How I happen upon this extraordinary event, in this respect I must remain naive. I otherwise depend on what spectators very quickly accept as an extraordinary situation. Put erotically: in order to narrate in this way, I need a Victorian attitude. Something is erotic, because it is forbidden. A fact is thrilling when it faces danger. In other words, this narrative form is expensive and compulsive. An example of suspense (Truffaut): the protagonist is on his way to the train station. The suspense is primed, when it is implied "Hopefully, I'll still catch the train." Every red light and every traffic jam becomes a moment of suspense. Technically speaking, this is how stress is created. There are other sensuous experiences on which narrative structures have been built: rambling, strolling, lingering, having time to lose something. If suspense is a narrative technique, (a) what would a version of it look like that is not purely technical; and (b) what would the antipode of this narration look like? There must also be an epic *anti*-Hitchcock effect.

14. Benjamin, *The Arcades Project*, 154.

15. Helmut Färber, *Bau- und Filmkunst: Aus der Geschichte des Sehens* (Munich, 1977), 32.

16. Benjamin, *The Arcades Project*, 155.

17. [Translator's citation: Benjamin, *The Arcades Project*, 156.]

18. To imagine how something like this would look, i.e., how such a dominance of fixed fantasies (within the aesthetic) over objective relations destructively affects objectivity itself, one must merely recall Hitler's pen, with which he architecturally redrew to a certain extent an "unaesthetic bulge" on a map of the eastern front. Now the roughly 100,000 soldiers who find themselves entrenched within the perimeter of this "bulge," which is only visible on this one map, must march in the mud either back or forth and most likely died as a result. On whether a stretch

of autobahn was unnecessary on account of the expectation that it would see little if any traffic, Hitler replied: Considerations regarding usefulness are always a mistake. You see, someone said years ago that we do not need any Wagner tenors. It became apparent, however, that we need **considerably more Wagner tenors** than we thought. We will therefore build the highway.

19. [Translator's note: Barthel Heinrich Strousberg (1823–84) was considered the European king of rail during the Wilhelminian period of rapid industrial expansion in central Europe. Kluge is referring to Strousberg's failed attempt in the late 1860s to undermine the Austro-Hungarian monopoly over river traffic along the Danube by building rail connections between Prussia and Romania.]

20. Benjamin, *The Arcades Project*, 132.

21. For "Animalism, Magic, and the Omnipotence of Thought," see Sigmund Freud, *Totem and Tabu: Some Points of Agreement between the Mental Lives of Savages and Neurotics*, trans. James Strachey (London: Routledge, 1999), 75–99.

22. Paul Watzlawick, Janet H. Beavin, and Don D. Jackson, *Menschliche Kommunikation*, trans. (Bern: Hans Huber, 1969), 158. [Translator's note: Because the German-language edition of Watzlawick et al.'s study includes an inserted summary of R. D. Laing and Aaron Esterson's *Sanity, Madness, and the Family* (1964) that is not included in the English original (Watzlawick et al., *Pragmatics of Human Communication: A Study of Interactional Patterns, Pathologies, and Paradoxes* [1967]), the translation provided here is from the German.]

23. [Translator's note: This is a popular maxim in German: "Messer, Gabel, Scher' und Licht, gibt man kleinen Kindern nicht."

24. [Translator's citation: Sigmund Freud, "Creative Writers and Day-Dreaming," in *The Standard Edition of the Psychological Works of Sigmund Freud*, ed. and trans. James Strachey, vol. 9, *Jensen's "Gradiva" and Other Works (1906–1908)* (London: Hogarth Press, 1959).]

25. [Translator's citation: Richard Sennett, *The Fall of Public Man* (New York: W.W. Norton, 1992), 337.]

26. [Translator's note: The functional dimension refers here to one of six primary dimensions of social consciousness that Negt and Kluge outline in *History and Obstinacy*. Taken from Bertolt Brecht, the functional refers to the invisible abstractions endemic to capitalist production that no photograph can capture. See Alexander Kluge and Oskar Negt, *History and Obstinacy*, ed. Devin Fore, trans. Richard Langston et al. (New York: Zone Books, 2014), 235. See also note 157 in chapter 10 in this volume.]

27. [Translator's note: This quotation is unattributed in the German original and remains unidentifiable.]

28. Benjamin, *The Arcades Project*, 477. [Translator's note: This excursus is attributed to F. H., who is Florian Hopf, a contributor to the volume *Bestandsaufnahme: Utopie Film*, in which Kluge's essay appeared.]

29. [Translator's note: This quotation is unattributed in the German original and remains unidentifiable.]

30. [Translator's citation: Niklas Luhmann, *Love as Passion*, trans. Jeremy Gaines (Cambridge, MA: Harvard University Press, 1987), 20.]

31. Laser. Laser is the acronym for Light Amplification by Stimulated Emission of Radiation.

32. [Translator's note: This quotation is unattributed in the German original and remains unidentifiable.]

33. [Translator's citation: Oskar Negt and Alexander Kluge, *Der unterschätzte Mensch: Gemeinsame Philosophie in zwei Bänden*, vol. 2, *Geschichte und Eigensinn* (Frankfurt am Main: Zweitausendeins, 2001), 989.]

34. [Translator's citation: Robert Musil, *Precision and Soul: Essays and Addresses*, ed. and trans. Burton Pike and David S. Luft (Chicago: University of Chicago Press, 1990), 182.]

35. [Translator's note: This quotation is unattributed in the German original and remains unidentifiable.]

36 [Translator's note and citation: Johann Wolfgang von Goethe, *Poems of the West and East: West-Eastern Divan–West-Östlicher Divan*, trans. John Whaley (Bern: Peter Lang, 1998), 215. Lines 3 and 4 in Whaley's translation are slightly changed in order to bring Goethe's poem into accordance with Kluge's context.]

37 [Translator's citation: Marcel Proust, *In Search of Lost Time*, ed. Christopher Prendergast, vol. 2, *In the Shadow of Young Girl in Flower*, trans. James Grieve (New York: Penguin Classic Editions, 2002), 234.]

38 [Translator's citation: Watzlawick et al., *Pragmatics of Human Communication*, 233.]

39 E.g., a data supervisor, the Federal Constitutional Court, or a media representative. But how can they decide when the game is over, if they are merely defined as an opposing force within the game?

12

A Plan with the Force of a Battleship

1. The Plan

He sat there exhausted. It is October 12, 1927. On the previous day he had finished shooting *October*. He is sitting on 60,000 meters of material, i.e., he has twenty-nine hours of exposed negative. He now has to sort it and cut it. The effort required to shoot a film is as nothing compared to the rigors of editing it. Sergei Eisenstein is thus facing a MOUNTAIN OF WORK. That very evening he decides to film *Capital*, "based on the scenario by Karl Marx." By "scenario" he means the book itself.

During the following two years Eisenstein pursues his plan, which no one is willing to finance: neither the Central Committee, nor the Gaumont distribution company in Paris, nor the Hollywood tycoons. On November 30, 1929, he is sitting in Paris opposite James Joyce. Joyce, almost blind, plays him his own reading of *Ulysses* on the gramophone. He cannot read it aloud any more. Eisenstein decides either to film Joyce's book—simultaneously with *Capital*—or to adapt *Capital*, using the literary method of *Ulysses*.

The director of the Moscow Film Museum, Naum Klejman, has found the notes relating to this plan among the almost 25,000 pages of writings by the director. Eisenstein's biographer Oksana Bulgakowa has identified how they relate to the other projects pursued by the director at the same time. Fritz Lang's *Metropolis* had inspired Eisenstein to plan the film *The Glass House*. A factory in the USA had already been commissioned to produce the sets for a "glass skyscraper": a world open in all directions, transparent above and below, free of walls and open for unusual vistas. Almost at once, Eisenstein realized that in the case of *Capital* a single evening screening would not suffice; it would have to be four evenings instead, like Richard Wagner. Eisenstein, initiator of great projects, a Catiline of modernism.

It is hardly surprising that the film was not realized. Its framework narrative was to follow a day in the life of two individuals from midday into the night, rather as in *Ulysses* a day in the life of Leopold Bloom is described (during the night he meets his wife), while chains of associations and subtexts evoke the history of humankind since Troy. In this way, Eisenstein wanted to construct out of parts of *Capital*—commodities at the beginning and class struggle at the end—a TOTAL MONTAGE into which would be woven the "story of two lost people." Or the other way round.

THAT PICTURE IS CINEMATIC
WHOSE STORY CAN BE TOLD
IN TWO WORDS.[1]

Should the project be filmed in the studio? Or should the effects of capital be tracked down in the real world, should they be documented? Dziga Vertov and his brother, the cinematographer Mikhail Kaufman, would probably have been better suited to the project. They would have directed their camera toward the real events of 1929. Strangely, Eisenstein makes virtually no reference to them.

2. Source Material from 1929

During his stay in Berlin in 1929 Eisenstein ordered a "prop" for himself in Babelsberg: "beef tongue in silver paper." He had been inspired by a newspaper report about the death of the former Imperial Chancellor Fürst von Bülow. This politician, leader of the German government from 1900 to 1909, had the nickname "silver tongue" on account of his ability to talk effortlessly and rather in the manner of Cicero. Eisenstein planned to include a montage sequence in *Capital* relating to him.[2] In his notes, Eisenstein makes no mention of that other event of 1929, Black Thursday and Friday, which occurred on October 24 and 25. At this very moment, he travels to Paris for a few days and attempts to enter into a contract with the distributor Gaumont.

In the year 1929, a stock market crash was nothing new. As early as May 1873 the stock exchange collapsed in Vienna one Friday. Austria's high nobility lost its fortune. The line from Johann Strauss's operetta *Die Fledermaus*, "Happy is he who forgets what cannot be changed!" and the scene in the debtors' prison in act 3 refer to this event. The very expression "debtor's prison" betrays a sense of distance from the experience itself. It was a stock market crash that did not shake the world. That is fundamentally different in autumn 1929. Here, for the first time, we see a wave of depression and collapse that engulfs the whole world; it begins on Thursday, October 24, in New York; causes panic in Europe on Friday; and is reinforced on the following Tuesday when all trust in US banks finally crumbles. The crisis lasted right through to 1934 and is really only interrupted by the collective efforts to rearm, which would ultimately lead to the Second World War. At the end of *Capital*, in chapter 25, Marx writes about the modern theory of colonization. What he is referring to is the experience of the United States, Canada, and Australia. In these "colonies," the workforce, which had migrated from Europe, did not subordinate itself to the industrialists. In the United States, it moved freely westward, took possession of land (as well as natural resources during the gold rush), and escaped exploitation. It is only in 1929 and then more fully in the thirties that the self-confident settlers experience the full force of capital: the costs resulting from the collapse within capitalism. For a moment, depression engulfs the entire continent. This "subjugation under resultant costs" is also experienced in Europe. Here, the de facto subsumption under capital had never ceased, but now it is joined by a somewhat surprising and novel additional form of subjugation of human subjectivity: what was once left-wing energy now marches politically to the right. These nasty consequences, which can best be deciphered using the categories expounded by Karl Marx's finest pupils (Benjamin, Adorno, Horkheimer, Korsch, Brecht), have never been described in either film or literature.

3. An Imaginary Quarry: Eisenstein's Objectives for the "New Film"

I see Eisenstein's grand plan to film *Capital* as a kind of IMAGINARY QUARRY. You can find fragments there, but you may also discover that there is nothing to be found. "The unfilmed criticizes the filmed."

Dealing in a respectful way with the plans of a great master like Eisenstein is similar to excavating an ancient site; one discovers more about oneself than actual shards and treasures. It becomes clear that, in a rather similar way, the best Marx texts are buried under piles of historical rubble. If you dig for them, you discover mainly tools. The analytical equipment and machines built by Marx, the engineer of theory, are things of great rarity. The proposals that Sergei Eisenstein came up with in his notes regarding the future of film are even more surprising, however:

—He suggests giving up on linear narrative entirely. He claims it is necessary to construct films like spheres (rather like stars and planets that move around freely in space and out of whose gravitational field "spherical dramaturgies" evolve). And spherical books! In practice these would be gigantic commentaries, similar to the Babylonian Talmud.

—Further, Eisenstein proposes that cinematic montage should be replaced by imitating effects that correspond to overtones in music. Images that generate coincident events and simultaneities in the

212   *Difference and Orientation*

head of the spectator, i.e., which respond to the multitude of ideas that such heads produce of their own volition, should be answered with cinematic means. Eisenstein anchors the autonomy of the spectator (confronted with the overwhelming persuasiveness of film) in a manner comparable to that realized by modern serial music, for example, in twelve-tone compositions. People, Eisenstein says, are not simple, they are complex.

—Suffering under the pressure of having to edit 60,000 meters of expensive raw material down to 2,000 meters of usable film footage, Eisenstein asks why there are no screenings of raw material. It is, after all, the case that whenever such screenings have been tried, across the history of film, they have always been a great success. But how rarely they have taken place! How much more interesting it would be for us to see the uncut, complete raw material for Walter Ruttmann's *Berlin: Symphony of a Great City*, a mirror of Berlin in 1927, rather than the rhythmically constructed final product. Cinema, Eisenstein asserts, is misunderstood as a hothouse of perception. We should return instead to the extensive agriculture of experience.

Today we experience the proliferation of existent conditions. Objective reality has outstripped us, but we also have reason to fear the mass of subjectivity that eludes our consciousness. In 2008, it is dangerous to confront this reality with the method and the expectations of Marx: one becomes discouraged. One needs a dash of foolishness to cope with it. One has to run roughshod over Marx (and even Eisenstein) with Till Eulenspiegel to maintain a certain perplexity through which insights and emotions can be newly combined.

4. Samples from the Notes[3]

October 12, 1927
It's settled: we're going to film CAPITAL, on Marx's scenario—the only logical solution. . . .

October 13, 1927
. . . Here's a point of contact already with completely new film perspectives and with the glimmers of possibilities to be realized in CAPITAL, a new work on a libretto by Karl Marx. A film treatise.

Nov. 4, evening

In America even cemeteries are private. 100% competition. Bribing of doctors, etc. The dying receive prospectuses: "Only with us will you find eternal peace in the shade of trees and the murmur of streams," etc. (For C[APITAL].) . . .

Nov. 23, 1927

. . . The de-anecdotalization principle is (clearly) fundamental to OCTOBER. The working theory of "overtones" can literally be reduced to a single proposition. Didactically, in explaining the principles of OCTOBER, it's useful and essential, as a development of those principles, to explain the groping stage as well; for OCTOBER remains essentially a model of a two-level solution: de-anecdotalization is, in fact, a "fragment of tomorrow," that is, the premise of the work to follow: C[APITAL]. . . .

Jan. 2, 1928

For CAPITAL. Stock exchange to be rendered not as "a Stock Exchange" (MABUSE, ST. PETERSBURG), but as thousands of "tiny details." Like a genre painting. For this, see Zola (*L'argent*). *Curé*—the main "broker" for the whole area. The concierge—the negotiator of loans. The pressure of concierges like these in the problem of the Sov[iet] Union's acknowledgment of debts. . . .

April 4, 1928

. . . In connection with CAPITAL, "stimuli," that is, suggestive materials, should be introduced. So, for instance, that excerpt from Bleiman suggests elements for pathos in CAPITAL (Say, for the last "chapter"-dialectical method in practical class struggle). . . . The same in B. Gusman's text: "The nature of cinematic language is such that effective presentation of a brief and consequently **insignificant** event requires, more than in any other art form, a great number of visual devices. **What in literature can be indicated by a few words is conveyed on screen by a whole series of scenes and sometimes, even, of episodes, occupying a large section of the picture. . . .**" . . . Furthermore, one realizes that without even chasing around after the flavor of Egypt, the whole of CAPITAL could be "constructed" on a set. . . .

April 7, [1928], 12:45 a.m.

Today, with a banal relapse into the circular composition of Scheherezade, Tūt-nāmeh,[4] tales of Hauff. I explained to Grisha the mechanics of the CAPITAL project in outline while in the "A" streetcar between Strasnaia and Petrovsky Gate (or perhaps after Nikitsky—I don't remember . . .). While riding home from Shub's[5] where we'd had chocolate with *paskha* and cake. . . .

Throughout the entire picture the wife cooks soup for her returning husband. N.B. Could be two themes intercut for association: the soupcooking wife and the home-returning husband. . . . In the third part (for instance), association moves from the pepper with which she seasons food. Pepper. Cayenne. Devil's Island. Dreyfus. French chauvinism. . . . War. Ships sunk in the port. . . . It would be good to cover the sunken English ships . . . with the lid of a saucepan. . . .

April 7 [1928], 1:30 a.m.
There must be one chapter on the materialist interpretation of the "soul."

5. What Does the Radical Renewal of Film Mean?

Eisenstein's early films adhere to the classic principle of agitation. Text and images intended to be typological result in "emotional convolutes." Edited together by means of montage they serve the cause of conceptual and dramatic intensification rather than of observation. With the *Capital* project, he intends to abandon this method (and at the same time all the other methods) associated with traditional melodramas (i.e., that kind of cinema that Eisenstein himself does not engage in)! No linear narrative!

> THE "ANCIENT" CINEMA WAS SHOOTING ONE EVENT FROM MANY POINTS OF VIEW.
> THE NEW ONE ASSEMBLES ONE POINT OF VIEW FROM MANY EVENTS.[6]

6. What Are Images Exactly?

Are texts pictures? If a story is told verbally, what kind of images are stirred in the listener? Film comes about in the mind of the spectator. And, to be precise, in a full cinema in which people respond to each other, in a cinematic public sphere. Both the public sphere and the autonomy of images (they belong to the people themselves) are facts that the filmmaker must know how to deal with.

This is why it is wrong when the image on the screen deprives the spectators of their own images. Association, fragmentation, and lacunae that foster the interaction between audience and film are indispensable. For this reason, the kinds of texts typical of silent films are especially stimulating "visually." Conversely, there are images that the audience can "understand" and read like texts.

In 1929, we have the break with silent cinema and the beginning of sound. Eisenstein conceived of sound as the introduction of a new dimension if deployed to engage autonomously, i.e., polyphonically, with text and image. Sounds are also images.

All this corresponds to Eisenstein's theory of the "third image," the EPIPHANY. One sees contrasts (for example, two opposing images) and in that moment a third (invisible) image forms spontaneously in their head.

What are images exactly? In the famous chapter on schematism in his *Critique of Pure Reason*, Immanuel Kant marvels at the fact that all human beings have a notion of what a dog is (he calls it the "transcendental dog") even though there exists no common image for the different canine breeds (ranging from Pekingese to Saint Bernard). As he describes it, "Thoughts without content are empty, intuitions without concepts are blind."[7]

Ideal-typical images strive to mediate between concept and intuition. They function like reservoirs, signage, or fences. They contain an abundance of sorted images, but no single one is specific. In this respect, images are like "laborers," "entrepreneurs" "at the foot of a mountain" (there is no foot there at the mountain and besides no one learns where exactly anything is to be found there), expressions with enormous reach but without concrete content. These forms of expression that sort and typify intuitions are not images, but rather language. They belong to the "language of film," a convention.

In radical opposition to that are concrete images, i.e., momentary snapshots. They are images at peace with themselves. Images without forced meaning. They are often "unseen images." The camera is an instrument, as Walter Benjamin says, for the "optical unconscious." The human eye, which constantly adapts and waits for the brain's insinuations and preconceptions, has never really seen most immediate impressions. They become visible only when the camera reveals them. That belongs to film's great innovations.

Eisenstein wanted to arrange a series of such "monads" (they contain the whole and are nevertheless blind) just as serial music had done with tones. Different images—irreconcilable and autonomous—plus the gap that arises from their juxtaposition yield a new relationality. According to both Eisenstein and Vertov, human beings' actual sensory forces [*Sinneskräfte*] work this way.

Translated by Martin Brady and Helen Hughes

Notes

Portions of this essay were published in English translation as Alexander Kluge, "A Plan with the Force of a Battleship," in *News from Ideological Antiquity: Marx—Eisenstein—Capital*, trans. Martin Brady and Helen Hughes (Munich: Institutions, 2015), 68–75, 80–81.

The essay was originally published in the German-language booklet that accompanies the film *Nachrichten aus der ideologischen Antike: Marx—Eisenstein—Das Kapital*: Alexander Kluge, "Ein Plan mit der Wucht eines Panzerkreuzers," in *Nachrichten aus der ideologischen Antike: Marx—Eisenstein—Das Kapital* (Frankfurt am Main: Suhrkamp, 2008), 11–22.

The two images included in the German original are not reproduced in the present translation.

1. Sergei Eisenstein, "Notes for a Film of 'Capital,'" trans. Maciej Sliwowski, Jay Leyda, and Annette Michelson, *October* 2 (Summer 1976): 3–26.

2. [Translator's note: On this point, Kluge directs his readers' attention to the second set of extras included on the second DVD to his film *News from Ideological Antiquity* subtitled "All Things are Enchanted People."]

3. Eisenstein, "Notes for a Film of 'Capital,'" 3, 4, 5, 7, 11–14, 18.

4. [Translator's note: The translator of Eisenstein's notes explains: "Translated as *Tales of the Parrot*, these are Persian texts in the Moghul style, School of Akbar (1556–1605)" (17n21).]

5. [Translator's note: The translator of Eisenstein's notes explains: "Esther Shub, the distinguished documentary filmmaker, virtually the inventor of the compilation film. A long-time friend of Eisenstein, she had, in fact, given [him] his very

first employment in the re-editing of Lang's *Dr. Mabuse, der Spieler*, for distribution in the Soviet Union. His apprenticeship under this accomplished editor was extremely important for the development of his own work" (17n22).]

6. Eisenstein, "Notes for a Film of 'Capital,'" 18.

7. [Translator's citation: Immanuel Kant, *Critique of Pure Reason*, ed. and trans. Paul Guyer and Allen W. Wood (Cambridge: Cambridge University Press, 1998), 193–94.]

13

No Farewell to Yesterday

New German Cinema from 1962 to 1981 as Seen from 2011

I can only write about experiences in 2011, for example, or about what set us filmmakers into motion in 1962 from my personal perspective. I am convinced that only one's own personal signature can bring about good fortune in filmmaking. It has been nearly fifty years since a group of young filmmakers, who up until that point had distinguished themselves only with shorts, spoke up at the Short Film Festival in Oberhausen (organized by Hilmar Hoffmann). (Later it was turned into an international forum for film criticism and documentary film.) In their now-famous Oberhausen Manifesto they demanded[1]

> —a renewal of the intellectual attitude in filmmaking in a direction toward authenticity and away from commerce
> —an intellectual center for German film, meaning film education
> —opportunities for young filmmakers to make their first films

The Kuratorium junger deutscher Film (Board for Young German Film) emerged out of the final demand with an endowment of five million marks. North Rhine-Westphalia's funding agency for short film, which formed the foundation of the Oberhausen group, added up to 800,000 marks distributed over six years. A shift in German film occurred right from the start. At that point, the history of film was seventy years old. What later grew out of the Oberhausen movement up until Rainer Werner Fassbinder's death filled a quarter of this history. This included lots of mistakes, a lot of claims to fame, variety, enthusiasm, and many works that have enriched the history of film.

Today, we have kept alive the hope that big surprises are still possible from our country's film scene, as can be seen in the works of Oskar Roehler, Tom Tykwer, Romuald Karmakar, Jörg Buttgereit (and many others). They are just like Volker Schlöndorff, Edgar Reitz, Norbert Kückelmann, Paul Verhoeven, Hark Bohm, Wim Wenders, and many others (including Werner Herzog) who modeled again and again quality, authenticity, and a break from the mainstream.

In a fast-paced medium like cinema, *one* generation lasts at most eight years. Every eight years something new comes along that has the tendency to undermine all that came before it. What is known as New German Cinema is comprised of a quick succession of generational shifts. The thirty-six Oberhauseners were followed by the temperaments of filmmakers like those of Herzog, Schlöndorff, Kückelmann, and Jean-Marie Straub. Then came Klaus Lemke, Fassbinder, Günther Hörmann, the younger Schamoni brothers, and a horde of others. Describing the chronology this way tends to forget the partisans. They *underpinned* the real movement that made this time such a lively part of film history: for example, Werner Nekes, Vlado Kristl, Kersting and Agnes Ganseforth, Hellmuth Costard, Christoph Schlingensief, and many others. And then come the documentarians. Starting with Hans-Rolf Strobel and Heinz Tichawsky, and Ferdinand Khittl, there are so many that they cannot all be listed. Young German film was not created by a few famous people, but rather by many people who cared about authentic filmmaking. This underside of the iceberg has certainly not disappeared. For some of them and not just for myself, auteur television has replaced auteur cinema.

It is a lasting shame for our republic that the minister of the interior Friedrich Zimmermann and the guidelines committee of the German Federal Film Board could subdue with such simple measures and then put an end to these wild and creative developments so successful with both international and German audiences. In the year 2011, German film's international standing is not immediately self-evident. I am sure this will change again. The bosom of film history is fertile even when it comes to our country. The Oberhausen movement was considered a break with tradition. It was *disguised* as a conflict between young and old. The phrase "Papa's cinema is dead" speaks to that. However, labeling this a generational shift is hugely misleading.

The films of the 1960s were actually closely bound to tradition and to figures like Theodor W. Adorno, Fritz Lang, Heinrich Böll, Max Frisch, Jean-Luc Godard, Federico Fellini, Lotte Eisner, Hans Werner Richter, etc. None of them belonged to our generation. Members of the Oberhausen group were all born in the so-called white years, meaning they were too young to be soldiers in the war and too old to be drafted when the Bundeswehr was founded. They were among those whose formative years fell between 1945 and 1949. Their impressions from these years were among the only things, other than their temperament and certain friendships, they had in common: a return to the traditions of the 1920s, to the BEGINNINGS OF THE HISTORY OF FILM.

The guiding principle was professional unprofessionalism. Freedom through skill. This was the goal of the young art of film at its beginning. Something was to be discovered. The élan of the antiacademy. This had hardly anything to do with the previous generation of directors and producers (although we especially respected Wolfgang Staudte, Helmut Käutner, and Bernhard Wicki). In a few cases (Heinz Angermeyer, Hans Abich, Franz Seitz), close collaborations developed, in others lasting feuds (Horst von Hartlieb); even Fassbinder was not shy about working with the producers Horst Wendtlandt or Ludwig Waldleitner. What held the new cinema of the 1960s together across eight different periods and across very different film styles was something conceived in a central European way: we are not subject to directives or higher-ups in the industry. We followed a definition of Richard Wagner's, even though we were not familiar with it at the time. Wagner said: Effects lack validity; they are "a Working, without a cause."[2] Film can therefore never just be a matter of stringing together commercially successful effects; there must be a place (if we put in enough effort) where movie theaters are not spaces of consumption, but rather a kind of production site. I am not talking here about films that were made, but rather about the verbally inexpressible PROGRAM that created a sense of unity in all of New German Cinema's important stations over its twenty-four-year existence.

The emotional core that set into motion the prevailing majority between 1960 and 1980 (even though they were individualistically torn when behaving toward one another in private) was this: the years we work are the best years of our lives. This gives our work its gravity. In this respect, filmmaking has to do with BEING ALIVE. It is not only a BUSINESS. Film is certainly a commodity and the entertainment it provides movie theaters is a service, but this is always just *one* aspect (and an isolated one at that). In reality, domestic and above all international spectators understand us through our WORK. Not the meaning of the films, not the results, not the themes, not even our own personae are as important as the piece of life or productivity that connects us with our audiences over the years.

This attitude necessarily turns against the speculation that dominates the international film industry. An American businessman who deals in film will rarely understand this continental, to a certain extent "central European," approach. Auteur filmmakers invested with power who—like Schlöndorff and Wenders—moved to the United States misunderstood the American business world. Its guiding principle is entirely reasonable: human characteristics are fragmented according to market needs—objective laws—and are then reassembled instrumentally to great effect. Success is the reward. I understood the principle regarding the division of labor at every point of my career and in no way share Adorno's vehement dislike of the culture industry. On the other hand, I wholeheartedly share the illusion that both the Oberhauseners and the subsequent generations of filmmakers took to heart: we were not created as instruments, but are here to live, and this is expressed in our work.

Adorno's claim that "society projects into film quite differently— far more directly on account of the objects" can be interpreted in various ways.[3] Whoever sees something objective in their own work that must be included in their film will not allow this objective element to be edited out. Instead, this person will say: A film without this individual signature is no good. This does not contradict the demand to emancipate the cinematic medium. Only documentation, for example, can renew the feature film; only the radical use of the cinematic medium can document the real. When this succeeds it also does not contradict the audience's interest.

In any case, this is a serious matter. How do the subject and the subjective-objective of society rub up against one another? They create points of contact, meaning a public sphere. The pathos of New German Cinema demanded more public sphere. The opposite of this was escapism or flight from reality. Herein also lies the difference between the élan of the 1960s and cinema's illusory worlds of the 1950s and 1930s. (In the 1950s, it was created carelessly, and in the 1930s it was highly speculative and political.) The year 1962 was not a matter of generational conflict, but rather a difference in ATTITUDE. The attitude: I am not a spectator of my own life and work, but rather their producer. The real contrast is created by going along in a society that is consistently marching today into the imaginary, even though it is separated into completely different groups. One must DECIDE between these two attitudes. The publicist Günter Gaus described this attitude, to the extent that it binds filmmakers and equestrians, as follows: On this side (of the obstacle) eternal shame, on the other side certain death.

The Arbeitsgemeinschaft Neuer Deutscher Spielfilmproduzenten (Association of New German Feature Film Producers), which grew out of the Oberhausen group, was based on all the many questions about praxis that could not be answered with enthusiasm, personal plans for film, and theses. Beginning with Schamoni's *No Shooting Time for Foxes* and Schlöndorff's *Young Törless*, a string of successful films well regarded by the public emerged in the meantime. German cinema's new prestige also brought recognition and prizes at international film festivals for the first time since 1937. With the help of parliamentary representatives (who were later removed from office for accepting bribes), the financial lobby used this new prestige to bring about a reactionary film subsidies law. The Arbeitsgemeinschaft Neuer Deutscher Spielfilmproduzenten boycotted this first law from 1967 for five years (this remains their claim to fame). According to the law, the association did not seize on its seat and vote on the committees of the German Federal Film Board, but instead chose to produce the best films Germany produced in the postwar era. During the reform period of Willy Brandt and Helmut Schmidt, parliamentary representatives Peter Glotz and Burkhard Hirsch developed the reform package known as the film subsidies law of 1972. It was prepared by an intensive collaboration between the Hauptverband deutscher Filmtheater (Central Federation of German Movie Theaters), the Arbeitsgemeinschaft Neuer Deutscher Spielfilmproduzenten, and the Arbeitsgemeinschaft der Filmjournalisten (Working Group of Film Journalists), which included Florian Hopf and Klaus Eder. This could have served as the basis for a pervasive and lasting reform in film subsidies and the continuous presence of German films in its own market (balanced with American imports). At the same time, it could have fostered a European alliance for independent film, a step toward diversity. A week before the law was set to take effect, the president of the Hauptverband deutscher Filmtheater, who had supported this plan, was overthrown by an unholy alliance. The attempt at reform fell apart, and its outlines were significantly altered in practice. After a few of my own attempts to change the devastating result, I resolutely bowed out of film politics.

Today the planned changes to copyright law threaten to push over the edge German cinema's chances at continuing film history.

This would be the destruction of the public sphere by way of an entitlement mentality. The central understanding in New German Cinema was always that it should be possible to maintain as many points of contact to the spectator and to transfer as much lived experience through cinema's public sphere as possible. If every single claim made by every coworker collaborating on a film prevents the publication of that material in ways that are hard to define, this surely leads to the stockpiling of unreleased films. Were this to happen, then the collaborators working on German films would fail to earn more money, and fewer films would be released into the public sphere.

It is wrong to believe the disasters we are witnessing, which accompanied German film from its high point in the 1960s and 1970s to the lean years today, are permanent. There are clear indicators suggesting that film history is progressing. Why not also in our own country? In my film *Artists under the Big Top: Perplexed*, the following is said of a deceased circus clown:

> He brought joy to so many,
> big and small.
> So many laughed at him,
> Who will cry for him now?

No one needs shed a tear for cinema. It is not dying. This is because of the dark phase that lasts 1/48 of a second and separates one image from another.

Translated by Emma Woelk

Notes

This essay was originally published in German as Alexander Kluge, "Kein Abschied von gestern: Der neue deutsche Film von 1962 bis 1981—gesehen von 2011," in *Personen und Reden* (Berlin: Klaus Wagenbach, 2012), 108–15.

1. [Translator's citation: "The Oberhausen Manifesto," in *West German Filmmakers on Film: Visions and Voices*, ed. Eric Rentschler (New York: Holmes and Meier, 1988), 2.]

2. [Translator's citation: Richard Wagner, *Opera and Drama*, trans. William Ashton Ellis (Lincoln: University of Nebraska Press, 1995), 95. Kluge accurately

evokes Wagner's formation "Wirkung ohne Ursache," which Ellis awkwardly renders as "a Working, without a cause" by tracing *Wirkung* back to what Jacob and Wilhelm Grimm identified as its root meaning, namely, "verfertigen, arbeiten" (to fabricate, to work). See Jacob Grimm and Wilhelm Grimm, *Deutsches Wörterbuch*, vol. 30 (Leipzig: S. Hirzel, 1854–61), 554.]

3. [Translator's note: Theodor W. Adorno, "Transparencies on Film," trans. Thomas Y. Levin, *New German Critique* 24/25 (Autumn 1981–Winter 1982): 202.]

Part IV

From Classical to New Media

Opera, Television, Internet

14

AN ANSWER TO TWO OPERA QUOTATIONS

Vedi? di morte l'angelo . . .
(Do you see? The angel of death . . .)
Giuseppe Verdi, *Aida*, act 4

I.

1.

The unlikely pair, the Ethiopian princess and the Egyptian general (removed from office), are buried alive because of their love. They are considered traitors. Radames, though still accompanied by deputies, is now alone (or so he thinks) in that dungeon under the Temple of Vulcan. Aida, in contrast, snuck in by herself; she is here of her own free will. She had always known that a love like this would end with being walled in.

This scene is preceded by the dramatic underground trial of the reluctant traitor. Radames had stubbornly remained silent. Change of scenes. The orchestra evokes a particular melancholic mood, set in D minor, which Verdi uses for departure scenes—for those moments immediately preceding acts of finality. Radames wonders where his lover is. Her presence was never so familiar to him as it is now that she is absent . . . The music breaks off . . . a sigh . . . *Qual gemito?* (What cry is that?). The former general searches in the darkness for the living creature that had sighed. Nervous movement in the orchestral score. Radames has just touched a strange body. Even in the darkness of the tomb, he knows immediately who it is. He calls out in extreme despair (*nella massima disparazione*): "*Tu, in questa tomba?*" (You, in this tomb?).

He thought Aida had been saved. This thought, his interest in her objective well-being, is a sign that he really loves her. He loves her reality. That is why he is so extremely desperate when he finds her buried alive.

Aida answers:

> My heart forewarned me
> Of your condemnation;
> Into this tomb
> Which was being opened for you
> I made my way by stealth,
> And here, far
> From every human eye
> In your arms I wish to die.

As a princess, she is aware of the following: it is written that she *sacrifice herself before everyone's eyes* for her lover; this act would benefit the caste of all princesses and widows, the kingdom, the priests, the memory of the victim, and whatever can be redeemed from the latter. Sharing the destiny of her lover, however, she dies for him alone, "far from every human eye," without producing any benefit for herself or her class: *she expresses that she really loves him*. Throughout the entire opera, the lovers appear amazed, surprised that they love each other. Again and again, they declare to each other that they (against all the laws of reality, the powers of war, class boundaries, etc.) are on fire for each other.

Even now Radames is amazed: "To die! . . . to die for love?" Two currents of history collide in the "emotional economy" of this scene. The old tale goes: *sacrifice* and *the wish for happiness* are coupled strictly together—it goes without saying that the woman can express her loyalty, the very fact that she is a living being, only in such a way as will cost her her life. Colliding with this, on the other hand, is a certain bourgeois levelheadedness in Radames: one doesn't exaggerate the bond to the point where someone has to die purely as a result of falling in love. That is why he is surprised, but also happy: Aida's particular form of devotion is expressed especially *clearly* in the midst of this collision between values and times. "*Sogno di gaudio che in dolor svani . . .*" (dream of joy which in sorrow faded . . .). But in this version, the sky opens up: "*A noi si schiude il ciel . . .*" (Heaven opens for us . . .—the word "to close" has the same root as "to open" in Italian).

At the climax of the lovers' dialogue, or rather at the climax of the two alternating monologues (for the lovers misunderstand each other in distinct ways), Aida says: "*Vedi? di morte l'angelo . . .*"

2.

"Do you see? The angel of death . . .," says Aida. Is there an angel of death that Radames, too, sees at this moment? Are there any angels of death whatsoever in Egypt? We know that there were some in the mists of Germania because Brunhilde pronounces Siegmund's death and later fetches him in *The Valkyrie*. Does an Ethiopian princess cite a myth of her own country, which the Egyptian general cannot immediately understand? Does she see anything? Or does Aida only want to comfort the despairing man by claiming to see this angel? Is she describing herself as one? It is pitch black in this tomb. The executioners have not set up any lights because the priests must prevent the condemned from burning himself to death—for if he did so, his soul would not be starved to death along with his body, indeed it would not even step over into the realm of the dead; rather, it would haunt *them*—in which case, they might as well have burned themselves. At any rate, that's why it is dark; the lovers can touch each other, but nothing is visible. Hence, Aida can claim with impunity that she sees something. Radames, willing to believe her, looks for a time, spellbound, in the direction he assumes Aida is pointing. He does not want to spoil the mood with a contradiction. Neither does she insist. Nor does she repeat the question. The dead in Egypt enter the realm of the dead via the *preparations made by the living*: the dead in Egypt are the debt to be discharged at the home of the creditor, not that of the debtor (*Bringschuld, nicht Holschuld*).

3. The Unpredictability of the Angel of Death

Why, however, if there are angels of death, do they not help, for example, in the case of a mistaken verdict? One has to distinguish the live burial of two live lovers from the sentence that condemned only *one* of them.

Doubtless there are cases more unjust than the punishment of lovers who, after all, were pursuing an egocentric, consumerist dream of happiness, "*sogno di gaudio*"; and behaving rather imprudently with regard to state secrets—for which they now pay. In Smolensk 1942, that would have led to a rash ending as well. It's another story when Antigone, Oedipus's daughter, is walled in. *She* fought for the burial of her brother and was herself buried alive as a result; she fought for the *validity of the old laws* against the new despotism. No angel of death helped her. It cannot be, however, that angels of death remain completely insensitive to the injustice suffered by the dying who wait to be fetched. Thus, Brunhilde is quickly prepared to decide the duel against Hunding; Hercules enters the underworld in *Alceste*, responding to the unjust sacrifice by robbing the dead; and thus Charlemagne intervenes in the nick of time to save the Infante in *Don Carlos* etc. Angels of death, if they do exist, have in certain cases no other choice but to mutiny, refuse commands, employ cunning. In fact, these are actually the signs by which we recognize them. How else could we

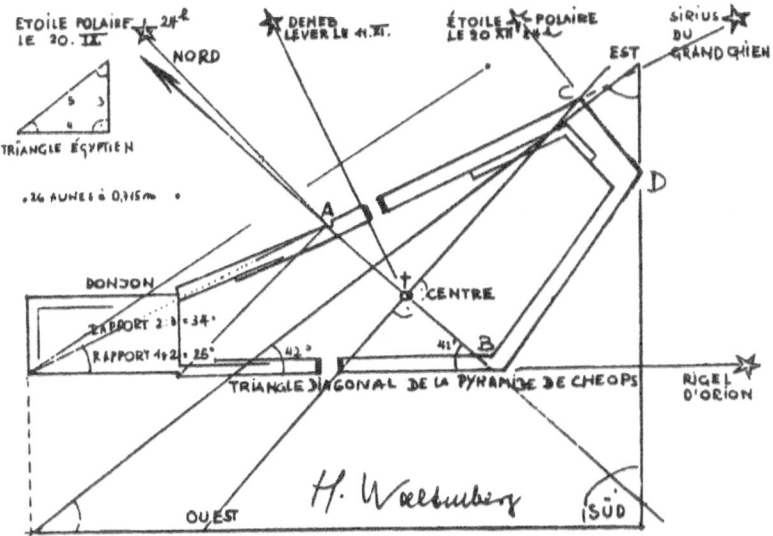

Figure 11. Instructions for the transferral of a dead person.
© Alexander Kluge Archive

discern whether or not we are dealing with an angel of death? After all, we don't follow him merely to be his witness.

By the way, the angels originate from the same substance *from which the old laws arise*. The text reports nothing more specific about *"di morte l'angelo."* Here lies the starting point for another opera—it lies in the *gap of the text*. The secret that is waiting to be revealed is, from the perspective of the angel, the text.

> The dead are not equal. On the contrary, their different forms of accommodation (some are put into holes, others into pyramids) rather consolidate the earthly hierarchy, which in turn represents the only secure connection with the cosmos. An angel of death in the Germanic tradition would be likely to confuse this hierarchy, especially if he were to display a sense of justice or a personal capacity for discrimination. In Ethiopia, such a thing might have existed, but never in Egypt. It could be the case, therefore, that Aida saw an angel of death, which Radames, hard as he may have tried, could never have seen.

4.

The mission of the twentieth century, of which we still have sixteen years ahead of us, is to tell *counter-stories* to the collected stories of the nineteenth century—in the manner of the story of Odysseus, which is of course either fairly old, or set in Ireland (James Joyce). To the classical dramaturgies of plot, intensification, progress, suspense, climax, and catharsis, we oppose gravitational forms of expression; that is, forms that develop from the laws of narrative and musical material. This is no contradiction to the eighteenth century, no contradiction to Lessing or Arno Schmidt, yet clearly one to the nineteenth century as it nests in the minds of the twentieth.

5. Radio Broadcast from Afar; Air Raid

On April 7, 1945, at 11 p.m., there is a broadcast of *Aida*, I think on Radio Rome. We are sitting in my father's bedroom in front of a brown wooden set, with an illuminated glass panel showing the foreign stations, and we listen to the distorted mystery music; from far off and a little garbled, it conveys something serious that our father summarizes in brief German sentences. At one o'clock the lovers are suffocating. My father, a country doctor who knows something of the technical tasks of prop masters since he is also on call for the Halberstadt Theater, speculates on what the cause of death might be on the third or fifth day, on whether Radames survives Aida or vice versa (according to medical probability—a doctor can never be sure). They were found in this vault, my father said, after thousands of years. Did Caesar dig them out? One doesn't know. How were they lying? One can imagine this from other pictures, namely, those of Herculaneum and Pompeii. It's hard to embrace for five days straight; they will not have had the strength in their last moments to change their position in any major way. Nothing in the world is as serious as (1) a dramatic opera, which (2) comes to us from a great distance. With our big super-radio in the dining room, we would not have been able to receive the distant music that this tiny foreign product managed to dispense into our provincial town, albeit with distortions.

Because it got so late, we didn't go to the Rübeländer Höhlen the next day, April 8, 1945, although we children were supposed to be evacuated there because of the danger of the air raids, which everyone was talking about on April 7, 1945, a Saturday. Instead we have been sitting in the shelter from 11:20 a.m. on. After the first attack, when the lights went out, we are lying on the cellar floor. This action has nothing of the seriousness that the operatic action of *Aida* has. The magic of opera implies: we believe in the absurd because it contains a serious mystery; because what is spoken and what remains unspoken (for example, the angel of death) is guarded as a secret, camouflaged by the work of the orchestra. Of the bombers, however, we only believe what *really* happens. If they hit me, I'm dead; otherwise, I'm not. They can bury us in the cellar, but without doing so, they cannot move us to consider what it might feel like to be buried in the cellar, what we feel like when we think of the entombed lovers in the opera *Aida*. We see them as they depart, fleeing from the city: in squad formation, a school of minnows in the sky. Living in the twentieth century, we do not know why it says in the opera guide: "Amneris above the tomb sends a prayer for peace to the sky." We find this prayer for peace, the invocation "*ciel*" in many operas.

This sky, however, is occupied with bomber formations; the invocation, the prayer, must find another direction. Thinking of the injustice of their action, the scattering of bombs over rich and poor seems insensitive to us. We know that angels of death would never behave this way. The attack was unnecessary. I would never have said to my sister, while running through the burning town: "*Vedi? di morte l'angelo . . .*"

6. Practical Uses of a Love Token

Sitting in the dark, above her the footsteps of the priests and the desperate calls of Amneris (who in such a condition makes mistakes, for which the Priests will send her to follow the lovers into death), Aida has, unknown to those above, a ring on her little finger. She had stolen this ring from Amneris, who has delicate Egyptian fingers, so that the ring, which Radames had given Amneris when they were still engaged, does not fit on the paws of the muscular Aida. Now, in the face of the angel of death—perhaps she could survive three or five days in this vault, through long drawn-out hours that are too short for living and too long for dying, but she couldn't think of anything more to do—she took the metal ring from her finger, handled it, scratched signs on the cellar wall and eventually put the ring back on her little finger. She lacked the conviction necessary for a definite action.

In Halberstadt, my hometown, the story is told of a young woman whom the count of Regenstein unlawfully incarcerated in the dungeon of Regenstein castle in order to win her love (compare to Count di Luna in *Il trovatore*). The grotto or castle that bears the name Regenstein is situated at the northern border of the Harz, dating from a time before there were cities. The imprisoned young woman, however, owned a ring given to her by her lover, to whom she remained faithful and for this sat in the cellar. With this ring—her fingers would not have worked—she scratched an oblong hole in the sandstone on which the prison rested. In the spring, she did not know the date, she beheld the *shimmering light of the valley*, and hurried away. Thus, the token of her love had a practical use. The ring is the savior when the angel of death fails.

II.

Here I am, true to you till death!
Senta in Richard Wagner, *The Flying Dutchman*, act 3

1.

The Dutchman has overheard the conversation between the hunter Erik and Senta. Erik reminds Senta "that she once pledged him eternal faith." Senta rejects him. The Dutchman has overheard and misunderstood everything. He renounces Senta, rushes to the ship, orders the anchor to be weighed. "Senta frees herself from those who are trying to hold her back, reaches a cliff, and throws herself into the waves." Her last words: "Here I am, true to you till death!"

2. A Putsch of Emotions

For 2,000 years, he cruised the sea and now he decides, from one moment to the next, I will marry this woman (whom he has never seen). Senta, the well-protected daughter, jewel of her father's stock of commodities, throws herself without further ado at this stranger of whom she has only seen pictures and heard stories. We know, however, that such pictures or mythical stories do not at all resemble the actual person who suddenly appears before us. Feelings take time to develop. It therefore seems unlikely that love at first sight is mutual. An emotion erupts that has been building up for a long time, enriched by fantasy, by stories one has heard; yes, love at first sight, but only for one; the other feels magically attracted to the prey that is just lying there. He acts like one in love. Thus, in appearance at least: love at first sight. Yet, one of them is investing the whole weight of his or her life, whereas the other, happy-go-lucky, merely seized an opportunity. The suddenness of the Dutchman's and Senta's fatal and mutual falling in love has something of an act of force. One could call it a putsch in the domain of emotion.

3. Older Versions: Sacrifice and Self-Realization; the Dutchman as Vampire

Wagner tries to mystify this situation. But there are older traces. The complete phrase preceding Senta's fatal leap reads: "Praise your angel and his words. Here I am, true to you till death!" Thus, a more ancient prophecy comes into play; it relates to the promise of God's messenger to lift the curse from the Dutchman's life, provided a woman dies for him. The angel's words then mean the reverse, as in the case of Abraham: there is no substitute for the human sacrifice; on the contrary, it is required by command—though, in this case, the victim of the human sacrifice is not the

238   *Difference and Orientation*

sacrificer's own child but the daughter of a stranger, robbed from her father. For it is through an act of robbery that the Dutchman manages to get possession of the daughter from Senta's father: he

Figure 12. The pale man.
He says: "Ah, bereft of hope as I am, in this hope I still indulge."
© Alexander Kluge Archive

begins by displaying his treasures, behaving no differently than a wealthy army would in occupying a poor or defeated country.

Just as Arteyu in *The Never Ending Story* discovers the battle occurring already in the form of paintings on the walls of a ruin, Wagner's ballad assumes the endless repetition of that which has already happened but has never been redeemed: the picture of the pale man above the door; in this regard, Senta has been ready long before the pale man actually enters through the door. She ends her recital of the ballad of *The Flying Dutchman* with "the ecstatic pledge to bring redemption to the damned." The reasons for this pledge lie, as it were, in prehistory, in the *command* of an angel or in Senta's *interest*.

> "After his and the helmsman's calls remained unanswered, Daland discovered the Dutchman sitting motionless on the shore. He approaches the latter, who, in the course of the conversation that develops, asks the Norwegian to grant him lodging for one night. When Daland sings the praises of his daughter Senta, the stranger, in a *sudden fit of passion*, desires her to be his wife. . . . Only the selfless devotion of a woman willing to sacrifice herself could free the Dutchman from the curse of eternal damnation. In search of this savior, he once again today—this is his last chance—has set foot on solid ground."

4. Senta's Attempt to Escape Her Father

It is a terrible fate when the days that rush us toward death become predictable: nothing new will happen. What would life be like on the side of Erik the hunter who, as Senta will have quickly learned, has only limited interests as far as her person is concerned? By contrast: the never-ending neediness of the Dutchman. He requires fundamental redemption. This is the loophole through which Senta can escape the paternal prison. She has to realize her interests before the father sells her to the wrong man, for instance, Erik. What makes the father unreliable is that he would prefer to sell her more than once. He is not a good businessman. The commodity, as it were, understands more about the business than the merchant. For she is *interested* to meet someone who needs her fatally. Only this would be serious.

5. Two Different Versions of a Curse

A curse dates far back into prehistory. The wretch has committed blasphemy. A curse like that always affects the individual. Collectives that tempt or blaspheme God are usually not punished in *this way*. They incur the flipside of the curse: the everyday confinement to the habits of life, civilization and its discontents, the prospect of marriage with Erik, the "extended presence that leads to death." All this is already described in the fairy tale of Sleeping Beauty: she is pricked by the thirteenth fairy only so she can fall into a deep sleep—a routine of fate. And, accordingly, one sees only princes lurking around the hedge. Rarely has Senta been awakened to try to make her way through the thicket from the inside; rarely, either, would the young woman and the prince meet midway. The invincible fascination of romantic opera—compared to merely dramatic opera—is this antiphony between the curse and the act of liberation. Yet while the curse varies from victim to victim, the act of liberation is usually described in rather schematic terms. It is based on a particular type of male actionism, a prior misunderstanding, and the abrupt decision of the woman to kill herself.

What do I fight for, when my life is at stake? "If the history of all dead generations resting like a nightmare on the minds of the living is resolved just for one moment, my life is not too high a price to pay," says the opera.

6. This Collides with My Mother's Sense of Practicality

My grandmother on my father's side lived by virtue of her sharp tongue, in constant battle with her physically superior husband until he died. Half a year after his death, she died as well. She was faithful to him, especially to her war with him, till death. My maternal grandmother, born in 1872, lived in relative harmony with her husband until he died in 1937. She, however, survived him by another thirty-six years and died, physically and mentally quite alert, three weeks after her 100th birthday in February 1973; she remained faithful by surviving.

For my mother, i.e., her daughter, coming to grief for reasons of love was in no way part of the program. That was reserved for *us*. She herself had come to grief, and had died of it. She was well aware of this, as a kind of *trap of fate*, and had talked about it. She didn't think of it as tragic, merely as consistent. A feeling is not proven wrong just because it has run off the tracks.

The ecstatic pledges we make are prepared for by the program of our parents' generation. This is the core of truth in the angel's words, in the compulsion to repeat, in the principle of the ballad, in the closed form in which drama is submerged and rises again to be transfigured, freely adapted from the poets' words. At issue are the balance sheets by which our forefathers and foremothers

Figure 13. Senta, to the left.
© Alexander Kluge Archive

lived, sought their happiness, missed their happiness, tried to stockpile it, were robbed, etc.

III.

The Unfulfilled Program of the Bourgeois
Tragic Drama

1. Misunderstandings from the *Opera Guide*

Reclam Opera Guide, 16th edition, 1953: "Aida is considered one of the *summit achievements* of Italian opera. The *nobility of musical language*, whose melodic power of expression in the most immediate sense of the word manifests the soul, is joined by a will to form, which is in full control of its means and uses them with greatest clarity.... Fascinating as well are the musical landscapes (the scene at the river Nile) and the *Egyptian local color*, which may have nothing to do with ancient Egyptian music but, thanks to Verdi's musical idiom, is raised above the merely historical into the realm of a *higher artistic truth.*"

2. Keyword: "Higher Artistic Truth"

There is no such thing. Artistic truth does not have any special status vis-à-vis truth. Nor can truth be "higher." There are truths for which there is no time, truth that is jammed up because it does not get expressed, truths in passage, in the diaspora, truths torn to shreds, etc. However, one cannot claim that the concept of truth allows for comparisons of any kind. I can accumulate lies ... but the opposite of these lies cannot be more beautiful, more timely, more elevated, more local, more true, etc., than true. Thus truth eludes a basic dramatic principle: intensification, heightening, the *stretta*, the bottleneck. What is true, in a manner of speaking, regulates itself.

In act 4 of *Aida*, "higher" could mean the sad Amneris, *above* her the priests, though all of them still on the ground floor of the temple. *Higher* yet, Verdi's misunderstanding that the temple is a *"tempio di volcano." Above,* the Egyptian heavens, a figment of poetic imagination. Above that still, the *soffits* of the theater building. **One cannot accomplish through mere height what can be gained only by means of a context, relationality (***Zusammenhang***).** The dramaturgy of experience is gravitational, hardly ever linear.

We would reach the same conclusion with regard to a "more profound truth." It would be under the feet of Radames and Aida—i.e., the desert. It would be interesting to think of "truth in a nonartistic sense." For instance, by the standards of Egyptian custom, the behavior of Alceste and Aida is barbaric, certainly not "artistic." The vehemence of feelings is at odds with art.

3. "A Summit Achievement of Italian Opera"

As in the case of "higher truth," a similarly mistaken notion of the nineteenth century. At issue is the *image* of a creative career's gradually ascending trajectory. After a crisis (usually the death of the wife or lover), steep ascent to the summit, followed by decline, deterioration, committal to a mental asylum or tuberculosis clinic in old age. It is appropriate for operas to use principles like *accelerando, crescendo,* momentary discontinuation of the music, drumbeat, as well as marvelous plateau passages (like the one on peace in *Simone Boccanegra*). For the concrete working processes of authors and composers, however, such mountaineering images are inapplicable.

4. "Nobility of Musical Language"—"The Bourgeoisie of Musical Language"

Certainly there are musical materials that display the qualities of bourgeois acquisitiveness; there are workers or Napoleons of music, slavish or domineering musical idioms. The human senses themselves seem riddled with class barriers: the eyes struggle with the ears, the "higher" interests with the physical ones—all senses fight for their respective rights. In the grandiose project of opera, the events of which operas give an indirect account—the primal scenes, the carnage between nations, the failure of great political causes—are ennobled and raised to the level of a unified idiom of sound, communication, and meaning. This heightened idiom provides the common denominator for extras and heroes alike, for the Egyptian slave, the upstart Radames, the Pharaoh et al. This resembles German politics in the nineteenth century: aristocrats (von Stein, von Hardenberg, von Bismarck, von Caprivi, Prince Hohenlohe, and many more) run the affairs of state as deputies for the bourgeois forces who cannot agree among themselves.

5. "Egyptian Local Color"

Similar to *Turandot, Land of Smiles*, or the American feature film, Verdi's *Aida invents* an Egyptian local color for the sake of a "higher artistic truth." The sluggishly flowing Nile, the exotic, the "savageness" of this country that does not know that it is older and wiser than the Italian barbarians who built Rome—these are marks of distinction like the rings pierced through the noses of prisoners. The invention of so-called local color occurs around the same time as the flourishing of the slave trade in the Sudan.

6. "Le vaisseau fantôme"

The French title of the opera *The Flying Dutchman* epitomizes the principle of the nineteenth-century opera: a phantom ship. In this century, music, social relations, were for the first time set into a dynamic motion (beginning with a small advance in the eighteenth century and extending through the outbreak of the war in 1914 as part of the nineteenth century). . . .

    Like a chaotic ark, this phantom ship carries in its hold the symbolic associations of all past centuries, setting up relations among them freely and arbitrarily—a confused way of establishing firm ground. This attitude, however, is ambivalent: one would like to tell the truth—that everything is in flux, that in this social sea there cannot be any fixed positions—yet, at the same time, a landing is attempted every seven years. One of these two goals could be accomplished, but not both. The people of the opera are not in love with civilization: *"La mer est plus belle / que les cathedrals"* ("The ocean is more beautiful/than the cathedrals").

7. The Approach to Symbolic Sequences

In the opera *Le vaisseau fantôme*, several myths intersect that are more hostile in relation to each other than class antagonisms might be: the wandering of Ahasver, the wanderings of Odysseus, pirate tales, the story of Kundry's laughter about God that leads to her 2,000-year persecution, etc. This multiplicity (the antagonism that the diverse mythical fragments foster among themselves) makes any redemption inevitably schematic. The origins of the events appear multiplied—far too many reasons for one Norwegian fjord or for a single historical year in the Egyptian-Ethiopian War. In the end: a leap into the waves or a walled-in tomb—far too few answers.

The ways in which our two centuries, the nineteenth and the twentieth, approach such symbolic sequences are fundamentally superficial. The two centuries act (presumably in the manner of an administrative aristocracy) as if these sequences of the mind, these symbolic sequences and authentic narratives, could be manipulated entrepreneurially, at will. As if one could plan whether to use the images, sounds, or narratives in a documentary or fictional vein. This attitude corresponds to an incomplete form of materialism in these two centuries, to their "occasional materialism" (*Gelegenheitsmaterialismus*).

8. The Wanderings and Attempted Landings of Ulysses

Via detours, the sufferer Ulysses approaches his home, the island of Ithaca. In one instance, he insults the god of the sea by putting out the eye of one of his relatives, a one-eyed giant. Storm and shipwreck ensue, Ulysses is saved, falls into the hands of princesses, a sorceress, and spirits who try to seduce him from the shore (but he has cotton balls in his ears or else is tied to the mast); at any rate, he seems to manage the separations with almost greater perfection than the rapprochements. Now he has reached the piece of land from which he originally came (*terra, solum*). He does not enter a pale, bearded man. Rather, he takes a bath, disguises himself. He kills the suitors who besiege his wife; he decimates the staff for having been disloyal during his vagaries. Gradually, he is getting used to the happy outcome of his fate; it surprised him.

This is a totally different plot from that of the Dutch captain, who, "in raging wind and violent storm /... once sought to round a cape; / he cursed, and in a fit of madness swore, / 'In all eternity, I'll not give up!' /... And Satan heard." As far as blasphemy goes, this is a rather minor offense, committed in the heat of passion. Hard to believe that, as a result, the Dutchman was subjected to 2,000 years of punishment. There must be something in him complicit with the curse, an indecisiveness. This means "that Satan took him at his word"; probably there was a contract between them.

9. Kundry, Ahasver, Lucifer, Nora Leaves the Doll's House . . .

There are others who are cursed, fallen angels: a woman who laughed when Jesus made his way to Golgotha; a woman in Norway who dared to leave husband and child—now she leads a solitary life. In one case, a cosmic coup d'état provokes the curse, in another an almost trivial violation. The excessive disparity in these narratives suggests that they originate from entirely different stories, which were accumulated, superimposed upon each other; stories in which the ability to discriminate got lost.

10.

In the logic of such predetermination, of such incorrigible powers, there is no trace of free will, not even an involuntary one of the human species.

11. *Terra, Solum*

Both terms mean "land"; they could also mean "area," "a surface on which to stand." *Terra* can also refer to "fatherland" or even to the whole planet—these are large areas of abstraction for the powers of fate. The Latin word *solum* cannot compete. It always refers to the actual place where one puts down one's feet. A part of the ground to which every human being has a right. In the opera *Aida*, both terms for land, country, home, surface, are used.

12. Turning Drama Inside Out

In antiquity, drama reported on events that eluded the will of the persons concerned. A trace thereof can be found in later dramatic works; these later works, however, delight in the demonstration of *free will*. From the tortures incurred in the name of free will, drama, like a vampire, takes its nightly nourishment. To the extent that they are more than just effects, these systems of logic, these intensifications **tear human beings to pieces.**

The accumulation of causalities and family relations, the masquerades of choice, produce the tragic ending. Chance, luck, detail—whatever was not subject to my choice (as little as I chose to have *this* mother and *this* father) thus offers, contrary to the rules according to which experience is traditionally organized, a *free surface for associations*, a starting point for our sense of intimacy. **This is where the new stories lie.**

Translated by Sara S. Poor and Miriam Hansen

Notes

Originally published in translation as part of a conglomeration of three different essays on opera, this partially reproduced translation was originally published in English translation in Alexander Kluge, "Kluge on Opera, Film, and Feelings," ed. Miriam Hansen, trans. Sara S. Poor and Miriam Hansen, *New German Critique* 49 (Winter 1990): 89–138. Only parts 1 and 3 are included here.

The first part was originally published in German as Alexander Kluge, "Antwort auf zwei Opernzitate," in *Jahrbuch XI der Hamburgischen Staatsoper für die Spielzeit 1983/84* (Hamburg: Hans Christian, 1984), 117–30. It was reproduced in revised form in Alexander Kluge, "Antwort auf zwei Opernzitate," in *Theodor Fontane, Heinrich von Kleist und Anna Wilde: Zur Grammatik der Zeit* (Berlin: Verlag Klaus Wagenbach, 1987), 19–34.

The second part was originally published in German in Alexander Kluge, *Macht der Gefühle* (Frankfurt am Main: Zweitausendeins, 1984), 234–35, 50–53, 202–5, 187–89, 239–40, 272–73, 346–48, 424–25, 447–56.

The third first appeared in Alexander Kluge, "Ein imaginärer Opernführer," in *Jahrbuch der Hamburgischen Staatsoper 1984–1988* (Hamburg: Intendanz der Hamburgischen Staatsoper, 1988), n.p.

The three images included in the excerpted English translation are included in the present translation.

15

On the Expressions "Media" and "New Media"

A Selection of Keywords

People do not say the word "medium" to describe something they do with one another directly. For more meaningful matters like physical contact, feelings, and exchanging words with one another, we do not use the words "information" and "communication," but rather words like "working," "telephoning," "studying," "telling," "reporting," "announcing," "doubting," "loving," "hating," "confirming," and so on. The coined words "communication" and "information" already contain a certain abstraction, as if an exchange were taking place among people that was initiated by a concrete situation. In truth, the appearance of "intermediaries" (= media) like the radio and television does not provide any "distance from the situation." They can only operate vis-à-vis the spectator as though they were exchanging with one another, when in fact they merely act out monologues. The recipient receives all these messages and feelings within a concrete situation.

It is unlikely that something with immediate use value, something that intervenes in everyday life, can be identified by such an unclear moniker as "media" for very long. "Hand me the print-medium" sounds silly when referring to the newspaper over breakfast. Nowadays, institutions like the radio, the newspaper, or the cinema are dwarfs both economically and in terms of their power when compared to so-called new media. This dreary expression prevents a majority of people from imagining what goes on at the level of microelectronics, computers, digitalization (the artificial language of computers that translates the formal diversity of all living things into digital yes/no answers), databases, fiber optics, or multimedia systems. At stake is an entire chain of new-fangled economic powers ranging from the transformation of department stores and the world of commodities to the revolutionary changes to society's cultural fabric. The expression "new media" functions like a cloak of invisibility.

A child learns to differentiate between people and things in its environment. At the same time, it learns to speak. The child does not achieve this alone, but rather uses the language and attitudes of its mother and its environs as a model. One calls this the "anticipation of the other."[1] This principle states: I learn by putting myself in someone else's position and then look at what *I* think or feel *from the outside* ("from the other"). Only then can I possibly perceive. Indeed, I gain experience by creating distance between my experiences and myself. This is only achieved via sympathy or antipathy, mirrored through things but primarily through other people.

This fundamental assumption of communications theory is indisputable.[2] Whoever observes the development of children or considers the deep layer in adult relationships can also observe again and again the development process of a message without the aid of science. It is self-evident and "natural" (in the sense of social nature) that primary monologues cannot exist just as there can be no single Robinson Crusoe on an island. Rather, the ability to monologize itself arises out of countless dialogues, and the young man stranded on the lonely isle carries all of London inside him.

This also describes the principle of cinema. Translated from Greek, the word "cinema" means "movement": the images move and their scenes, in turn, make me move. There is nothing in the history of cinema that people could not also imagine without having ever seen a film. But because such experiences can be viewed in the form of public images shown in a particular place (the movie theater) while I notice others besides me viewing, too, the experiences contain another self-consciousness, a language supplemental to the daily, demoralized one of my interior. In this sense, the technical discovery of film merely imitates how the experience [*Erlebnis*] of images—always via a counterimage greater than a mere reflection—has developed in human beings for thousands of years. Music triggers movements possibly allowing for the freer and more detached circumvention of both place and situation. Literature's worlds of letters or physics' formulas may organize larger masses of experiences, but none of this resembles *more* closely the principle of dialogue, the emergence of thought, than these changing images, this "inner film." I sense something and develop a perspective by looking at it from the standpoint of another person. I could even convey it now to a third party (even though only *my* nerves can say *precisely what* I feel).

What develops among people from a particular society along these lines and at a particular time cannot be seized. With the emergence of standard languages, jokes, culture, urban centers, it appears as an "aura" that is just as vague as the word "media."

Because of this word choice, it is not clear how "new media" break through the basic principle according to which human experience [*Erfahrung*] unifies itself in language, culture, the public sphere, and collectivity. They generate their connective networks according to a completely different organizational principle, one that corrodes situations (places and times) in which human experience remains originary. The supposed advantage of new media lies in the fact that it mobilizes people more rapidly and more inclusively in a *nonhuman* way than humans could ever manage directly among one another.

> Consider the example of the telephone: the interconnection of equipment changes nothing about oral communication except that long distances can be overcome without losing time and that participants do not see each other. Additionally, every nuance of personal contact can be imitated over the telephone. The telephonic medium essentially does *not* change the original structure of communication.
>
> As an extension of this direct communication solely mediated via a technical apparatus, radio and television are, at first glance, not that different from one another (technologically speaking). Two teams of astronauts can see each other via television while they work. Radio transmissions occur back and forth in a one-to-one relation, broadcasting the translation of direct impulses at great distances. A person's voice may become raspy, but the transmission maintains enough of its structure, thus allowing both sides to infer the original communication.
>
> Therefore, the essential difference between a television program and direct exchange between people is not based on anything technical, but rather on the principle of programming. If this kind of programming imposes a particular temporal structure or, for example, a normative rule regarding the balanced content of its message, then the appearance of original communication results for a while, even though this communication is already determined at essential points by a superstructure operating at the level of the broadcasting institution. This then cannot be compared to any old telephone call, but rather to one in which the participants can only respond using the ready-made wording allowed by the postal service when sending congratulatory telegrams. This fundamental structure works consistently only in one direction.

To all *appearances*, new media works differently. A television program shows, for instance, direct documentation; it is a *transmission*. This is, however, not at all unmediated, but is rather cut down from its original time. In special cases (for instance, a twelve-hour parliamentary session), this temporal structure is not imposed upon the event. Considered against the backdrop of a broadcaster's entire program, this is such an exception that it is forcefully singled out in ways that events are otherwise not. For institutions that broadcast programs unidirectionally and that are addressed "to whom it may concern," there do exist possibilities for spectators to respond. They are, however, just as generalized and informed by programming interests as the programs themselves. This is how, for example, *the fees collected from viewer groups* correspond to a broadcaster's programming according to Infratest's market-research numbers, without a single, speaking individual ever conveying anything in this format.[3] One cannot be conscious enough of the fact that *individual* communication transpires neither on the side of institutions nor on the side of spectators (except in the case of glitches).

A further, radical level of this programming is the breakdown of actual = living relations into yes/no answers (binary codes). A programmed product *always* results from the methods of digitalization. It is something that does not exist *in that form*, even if the character value can store a disproportionately large number of symbolic relations standing in for real ones. Translating the symbols back into real relations at first yields a remarkably large correlation. In truth, the back-and-forth typical of such translations incurs losses. They can, however, initially be expressed in binaries and added or subtracted. In any case, a *second world* arises alongside the structures of real relations. Inside this second world, data can calculate its authenticity without damages or losses. As long as not an ounce of programming is involved and as long as the worlds of real relations and their symbolic calculations are kept separate, then no distortion in the communication occurs.

However, such an *imaginary condition* cannot be maintained for long. There is already a kind of programming within the binary principle: the law of the excluded third. In contrast, living, cultural relations operate under the law of the included third, meaning that all binary programming destroys the living context of messages. Thus, a person can produce something using binary logic that seems to *function*, but this then radically changes the authentic relations in reality: the minor points are gone.

New media's technical leap is made possible by fiberglass. These communication pathways enable and are a requisite for digitalization. Only by the dint of these pathways can computers communicate with each other at speeds of up to 2.24 gigabits/second (giga = one billion). This type of communication is unsuitable for people who can absorb 1–8 bits/second using their individual senses.

> Binary Notation: What Is a Bit?
> Binary notation uses the smallest unit, the smallest building block, out of which extensive amounts of information are assembled: it is either a 0 or a 1, since binary notation uses only these two expressive elements. These units are called *binary digits*, the abbreviation for which is "bit." You can depict sixty-four signs with only six bits. If the bit is like an atom, then the self-contained packet of information that can be called up is a *byte*.

Cinema has an astonishingly oppositional relationship to this state of affairs. Even more so than a book or a photograph, the expressivity of film works with so-called secondary valences: the partly miniscule surplus of images and movements, the intermediate values between images, sounds, contents, and motions. The difference between a simple consumer product and the art of film is regularly on display in these so-called intermediate valences that are intangible outside of film and, for the most part, disappear when film is shown on television.

What the Classical Public Sphere Has More of and the New Media Has Less of

The cinema belongs to the classical public sphere. Walter Benjamin drew a distinction between the classical arts—for instance, theater—and film.[4] The theater, he maintained, remained on the side of the classical arts, whereas film exceeded this classical boundary. It had no aura. Benjamin's assertion is an exaggeration. Portions of classical aura do disappear in films, but spectators introduce new forms into the movie theater. Furthermore, we would not dare interpret what classical public spheres possess by comparing artistic institutions. The fact that the theater (and literature) infiltrated films, especially talkies, did more to damage the aura of films than to increase it. The essential point becomes clearer when we compare the situation in cinema, in which spectators encounter moving images on the screen and in their heads, with the *original*: namely, the ways in which a spectator *conducts himself in society throughout his entire life, speaks, interacts with, and forgets images. The richness of experience* [Erfahrung] *and storytelling are the fundaments of the classical public sphere.* As long as *unmediated* access to these fundaments exists, we may speak of a classical public sphere. For this exchange, the following criteria must be met: *uniqueness* and *permanence* [*Einmaligkeit und Dauer*].[5] If I cut off permanence or replace uniqueness with cross talk, then the connection to *this* human root gets lost; derivative public spheres emerge, but not classical ones.

The boundary between new media and the classical public sphere actually lies between film and television. In fact, it presumably lies beyond television at the threshold to digitalization where private enterprise organizes itself around the combination of new media technologies.

The opposite of uniqueness and permanence—the producers of aura—are *transitoriness* and *repeatability*. Benjamin does not see them as negative concepts. They are only irreconcilable with uniqueness and permanence in terms of speed and exclusivity.

We said that the television is a hybrid. It conveys endless uniqueness in spite of its will to programming. In this sense, it is a conservative medium. It is still the classical public sphere, but it attempts to dispense the immediacy of experience by moderating it and cutting it up like new media. The television belongs to the classical public sphere as long as it *fails* at imposing the will to programming.

The Oral Tradition

It cannot be presented elementally enough. Heinrich von Kleist put it thusly: "*If there is something you wish to know and by mediation you cannot find it, my advice to you, my ingenious old friend, is: speak about it with the first acquaintance you encounter.*"⁶ The state of being in the company of others, regardless whether I happen to be alone or truly in the company of others, this is precisely what defines the public sphere.

This elemental piece of advice is difficult for public broadcasters to follow. I cannot even get past their gatekeepers. The programming formula does not allow me to speak when I am so inclined. Specialists can *do so* as though they were improvising, but everyone who has participated in a discussion on live television knows the situation: a majority of participants realize what they wanted to say fifteen minutes after the broadcast ended. What a lively atmosphere. The show is over. An element of the public sphere, this kind of situation is something natural for a group of people chatting face-to-face. The conversation goes on for an hour and a half, while one member in the groups remains silent. An hour into the conversation, he says something. The conversation takes a turn. *The fact that the duration* [Dauer] *is not trimmed down is more important than any content.*

We know television programs like, for instance, Austria's very particular *Club 2*, in which direct speech can be simulated as though it were occurring under real relations.⁷ A few things on the show are unique: guests can jump around from one topic to another, and the producers have a sense of natural duration. This is exactly what we mean when we define the television as a hybrid. Beyond this realm where future multimedia corporations reside, the *industrialization of communication* will not succeed. An ersatz public sphere will emerge, but not an actual one. People, whose minds cannot be brought in line with the industrial order (those who continue to hoard, so to speak, permanence and uniqueness), will be the ones who *manually limit* each and every media experiment. But these individual countermeasures are no longer supported and they cannot be united as they once could be in the classical public sphere. In this sense, two adversarial organizational principles meet at the site of political poles: the battles over form and content. *Cinema's faction and new media's faction are aligned under different stars.* Because the principle responsible for dispelling time, eliminating duration, and replacing uniqueness with reproducibility *also* exists in large quantities in cinema, it is not obvious that spectators in the movie theater gain time; they do *not* lose it.

The Principle of Gaining Time

Nature has an organizational principle, according to which life on earth has developed. Along this long path, it is possible to sense a "gaining of time." The time of pure activity becomes shorter, while the time between birth and adulthood when creatures develop provisional solutions and live according to their own time (by playing and educating themselves) becomes longer. Johann Gottfried Herder says: "*What differentiates us from animals is not that we develop, but that we do this slowly and carefully.*"[8] In this respect—and contrary to appearances owing to the hectic movement of the past 300 years—human beings and human cultures are characterized by the *principle of deceleration*.

It is astounding that neither evolution nor any of humanity's high cultures have pursued the opposing principle, namely, the one that, for example, viruses follow in nature and computers follow in civilization. They do not form their own bodies. They are only a program, so to speak, that temporarily invades foreign life-forms.

> The kinship between the organizational principles of the flu virus, electronics, digitization, and programming is perplexing. In each of these cases, a tremendous acceleration is achieved in the transmission of material information. We could say that things—set apart from human beings—interact with each other. At the same time, the primary root, the idiosyncratic element ("comprehensible only to its very own self"), does not exist here. *The person* is missing.
>
> Human communication has two different, radical roots. It is radical to have something of your *own* ("what only *I* sense") that can never fully vanish into general understanding. The other radical principle is that I can express myself in a civilized way only at a *distance* that I maintain with respect to my intuition and "idiosyncrasy." *The coexistence of these incompatible principles is like a bad stretch of road: There are bumps at the junctures. This is precisely the living, human core.*

Figure 14. *Volksempfänger* on Christmas Eve in 1942. One day we woke up, and suddenly all of Germany was wired. Everyone from Bordeaux to Kharkiv and from the North Cape to the Aegean sat in front of a radio we called *Volksempfänger* on Christmas Eve in 1942.

© Alexander Kluge Archive

Figure 15. The ENIAC computer in 1946. The computer filled an entire room.

© Alexander Kluge Archive

Figure 16. A microcomputer in 1980. It can do the same as the ENIAC computer from 1946. It is smaller and faster.

© Alexander Kluge Archive

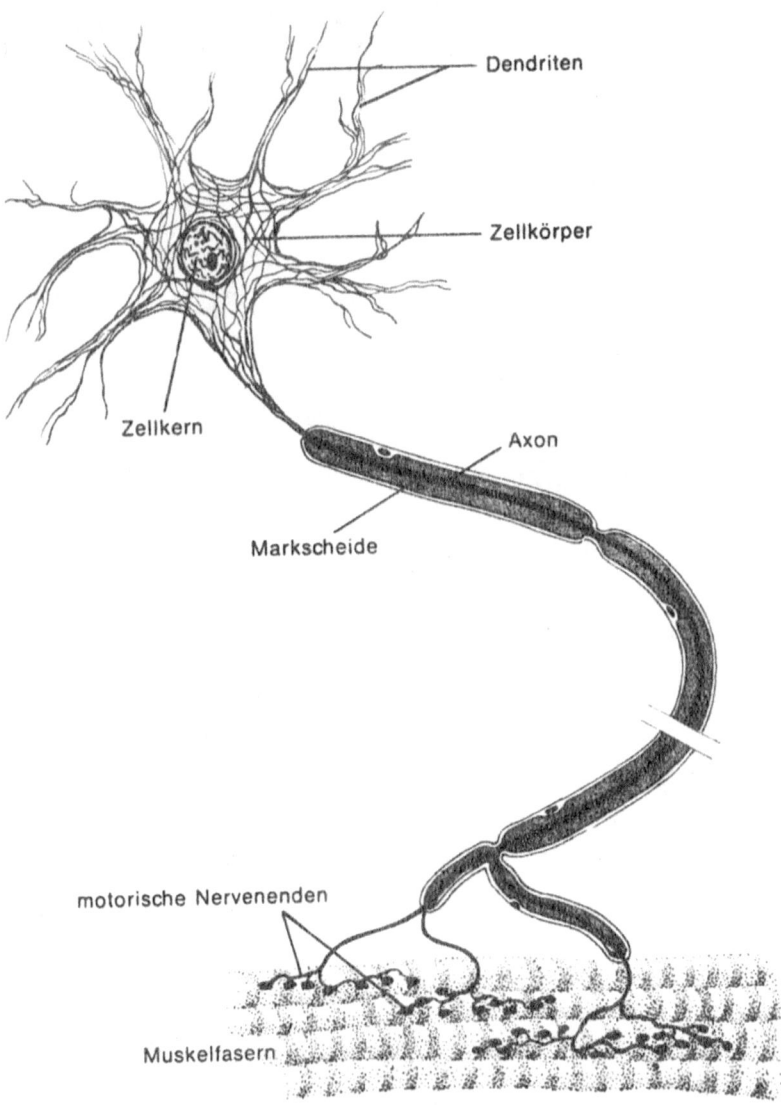

Figure 17. The human nervous system. The human nervous system is not wired directly. Between the nerve endings (synapses) are interstices similar to a bad stretch of road or a street full of stops. Human characteristics like freedom and feelings are based on this peculiar, cumbersome organization of mere *approximate* connections.

© Alexander Kluge Archive

> "What separates us from yesterday is not a rift, but a change in position."[9]

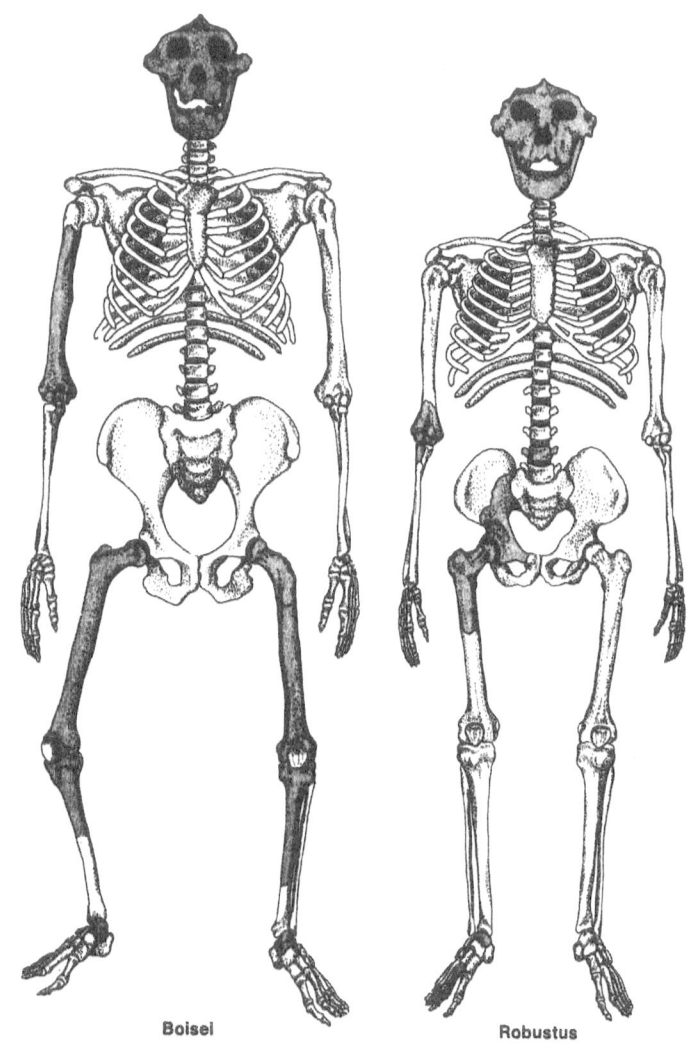

Figure 18. *Paranthropus boisei* and *Paranthropus robustus*. These are *paranthropus boisei* and *paranthropus robustus*. Our ancestors. The distances between feeling and acting for them are longer than for *their* ancestors. They are slow on the uptake.

© Alexander Kluge Archive

Chapter 15   263

Figure 19. The essential difference between computers and the human nervous system lies in the fact that the smallest units in a computer (chips) are directly linked. Electronics function directly.
© Alexander Kluge Archive

Another word for multimedia system is *corporate program*. It creates a new synthetic market out of diverse technologies and products such as entertainment, educational opportunities, informational offerings, and

> communication. Private industry will merge adult education, cinema, the music industry, private television, the satellite industry, distance learning, professional development (and, by extension, private universities), fashion, and the clothing industry into a *single* business. The product replaces the individually governed lifeworld containing all human difficulties with a chance to participate in a synthetic lifeworld, in which some of these difficulties are ostensibly purged. This kind of product is attractive at first glance.

"The New Obscurity" (Jürgen Habermas)

The response to the "new obscurity" cannot be to produce clarity.[10] This response would, of course, require a bird's-eye view, in other words, a never-ending reduction of singularities [*Einzelheiten*] where the particular [*das Besondere*] hides. We would rather take sides with obscurity and reside in its midst, right at its feet. Both the sense of touch and curiosity work from the bottom up. The response to this new obscurity is therefore *the capacity for differentiation on a mass scale*. When one and the same circumstance can have any number of meanings depending on perspective, interest, and preconceived misunderstandings—in other words, ambiguity increases rather than decreases under the influence of schematisms—then the nomenclature, the allowances, interpolation skills, and the sensual apparatus we use to convert slivers of perception into the content of experience must recalibrate themselves according to a new capacity for differentiation. The product is called *unifiable differentiation*. The universal [*das Allgemeine*] and the strictly particular thereby create completely different communities than broadcasted stereotypes (and those of the classical educational system, the state, the classical representation of order, and attribution).

What I describe above is merely what an interpreter does when he *translates* from one language into another. This kind of interpreter exemplifies the basic form of the mediator, a messenger from the gods. We know messengers who tell rulers only what they are comfortable hearing and what will entertain them (their delusions).

We also know the translators who in the moment of translation substitute their own message for the original text. They *replaced* what they should have translated.

The categories by which the capacity for expression was measured in the classical public sphere can be described as skill, fantasy, content of experience. What are compared with each other are not so much branches (information, education, entertainment) as production channels. One category does not exclude the others: the content of experience always presumes skill and the capacity for imagination; skill presumes content of experience, etc. *In this sense, communication is not based on a division of labor.* Unlike the category of information, communication crops neither answers nor their echoes, neither their nuances nor what cannot be expressed verbally.

> It is clear that translation poses a difficult task: to create a replacement and distribute it. This false conception has developed because we do not account for the six billion marks that the creation of replacements within the public broadcasting systems costs every year. (In the future, this same amount will go to the commercial side, and who knows how much intermediaries have already invested in the production of replacements in society.) At the same time, we do not pay for the transformation of these replacements back into the capacity for differentiation; this is something television viewers, our country's population, perform on a daily basis. Nowhere do we collect the results of this kind of unpaid fine-tuning (translation). In fact, the mass production of this capacity for differentiation is not at all difficult for the organization of the human senses, the cerebral cortex, and the pleasure in subtle deviations we find erotic. I maintain: Broadcasters that trust in the capacity for differentiation have mass loyalty.

Indirect Experience, Direct Experience

Media = mediators [*Mittler*]. In Goethe's *Elective Affinities*, there is a defender of human reliability and honest virtue by the name of Mittler who is easily frightened but talkative. The matchmaker, an apartment referral service, the job placement agent, a translator—they are all media.[11] Media are instruments, through which *indirect experience* is relayed.

A book in which the twelfth century speaks to me is a medium. It is useful and trustworthy if it is authentic. It is authentic to me if I am able to judge whether what the book tells me is a *source*. I must be able to judge whether what the book tells me is true. Lies, misunderstandings, gaps in the text, are also authentic mediators as long as the path to the sources remains open, and I can trace the origin. This question of orientation—Where are you from, stranger? What is your name?—is a problem of indirect experience characteristic of media. If I cannot have experienced it myself, then it is indirect experience. For this reason, it makes no difference whether we are dealing with a television channel or a foreign guest. Something is reported that my senses have not experienced, and they therefore could not test its origins.

So-called new media are corporations for the formation of new private property. This property is realized inside people's heads, and it forms an ownership relation, similar to one associated with property, with these heads. Once this has been established, something remains—an entitlement to its use—even when the new mediators insist that they are only there to serve, but these servers are influential. The essential element, however, is not power. Parents already had this kind of power over minds, but were not able to maintain it. What is novel is how media's new property revolves almost entirely around indirect experience. We humans, however, direct our questions and orient ourselves almost exclusively according to criteria of *direct* life experience.

As long as life and labor are intertwined and they careen through winter to spring, summer, fall, and back to winter, then the lion's share of experience is self-regulated. Physical time and psychological time are close together; what is possible and impossible result from the hard confrontation of my wishes and fantasies with the bulk of my experiences. A sudden thunderclap refutes my idea that I can still save the hay; this is *direct*. In this sense, the surrounding community that cares for me and under whose supervision I grow to find myself is also direct or unmediated; it is not a medium. It was not long ago that over 80 percent of the population in this country lived according to this proportion of time and experience.

In urban life, the amount of direct experience [*Erfahrung*] *decreases*. What I hear from strangers who neither know me nor care for me and about whose reliability I know nothing, and what media tell me—what I imagine in the heat of communication and the *zeitgeist*, the inventory of collective knowledge that becomes unclear—all of this increases indirect experience in societies based on a division of labor and in urban centers where population density leads to an aggressive way of life. I alone cannot test the sources of these factors or their tempi. It is true: "The development of the Pythagorean theorem took 2,000 years. Learning it requires two hours."

In a society whose rural districts are gradually urbanizing, and whose urban centers are at the same time losing their character because ways of living that are neither truly urban nor rural encompass the entire country, in this kind of society a new sort of cave dweller becomes rampant. The former farmer within me, the urbanite within me, the industrialist within me, the person who became superfluous under industrialization within me, that kind of person who on account of the difference from all these selves does not fit "to any one place"—all of this retreats into one's own head, into the four walls of one's apartment, and charges itself with imaginary, new *needs for direct experience* because the real can no longer be found outside but rather inside. Need = "what I do not have." The majority of direct experience is structured around *symbolic sequences* governed by indirect experience like fairy tales. Projects for the formation of new property—new media—reflect on this Robinsonian constitution of the modern house and cave dweller. Interiority is supposed to be industrialized.

The Loss of Reality

> "Wander through the Harz . . . while blindly following the directions of a map of London"[12]

If one examines the contents of experience not only in terms of right and wrong, usable and unusable—all of which, depending on the situation or perspective, are subject to change—then one runs up against the difference between *one's own experience* and *expropriated experience*. If my experience is expropriated by a benevolent lord, then I am immature but nevertheless protected. I learn about bondage experientially from an external source of control where freedom resides. Bondage does have advantages. It removes the urge to produce. An efficient bondsman can come to rest. He watches his own life and is the consumer of his own skills.

Compared to the bondsman, every other form of self-determination is taxing and less *entertaining*. We must *convince* ourselves to utilize our powers of self-control. It would be libidinously more advantageous to place them in a museum and to honor them without ever using them. I say that without irony. Learning processes from direct experience are atavistic, strenuous, and generally decoupled from the libidinal economy. This has a far-reaching consequence: the tempi and means of production of direct experience influence the control and application of indirect experience. Were indirect experience to become absolute, then control and governance would be practically lost to the individual. They cannot be regained through any conceivable institutional process. *A loss of reality* arises not because a person knows too little, *but rather because they know too much and therefore are unable to take control of any of its parts*. A quasi-Dadaistic condition therefore arises: "Wander through the Harz . . . while blindly following the directions of a map of London." The remains of direct experience, which remain increasingly more incomplete and ruinous, regulate enormous masses of indirect experience (continuously fed by media).

Ever since Madame de La Fayette's novels from centuries ago, two elements have been competing for introspection (looking within oneself), that most reliable form of direct experience: (1) erotic experience (of one's own body), (2) the novel's imagination. "I read a novel and then felt in love."[13] You cannot say which comes first: an idée fixe or romantic infatuation, the sense of touch or fantasy. Nevertheless, reserves of direct experience reside in the genitals simply on account of childhood.

A female doctor tries to explain the pain of childbirth to a young woman who has never given birth before. She gives up after a short while and says: This cannot be explained. And it could be that it does not always feel the same way. "I cannot explain it to you, I just know how it is." This is obligatory direct experience. The young woman can listen attentively to any number of stories and can read all about it, but indirect experience cannot change the content of experience.

We know the story of Robinson Crusoe, whose ship is destroyed, who learns to survive on a deserted island, gets himself a slave or servant, and is finally saved. His head is full of hegemonic knowledge acquired in London, the buzz of millions of humans and inventions, while he waits, by all accounts alone, on the island. His specific form of activism that saves his life is based on indirect experience. It is, as it were, a novel and nourishes itself on the novel of civilization's history. This is the kind of indirect experience that the media are all about. They cannot deal with anything else.

Memory, Forgetting, Reconstruction

Remembering and forgetting are activities performed by different bodily apparatuses within a human being. The clearing away of presence (forgetting) functions for different reasons, and is based on a phylogenetically different physiological process than that of reconstruction, which produces memory out of traces and fragments based on the schematism of ideational realization. It is a question of two different though presumably not diametrically opposed aptitudes intertwined together. Within these aptitudes (which could be showered with both ratings and rewards as is the case with musicality), the reasons for and the paths down which the labor of remembering and forgetting are different: forgetting can be due to obviousness or repression, but it can also come of generosity. These are completely different nations and sovereignties within the soul.

The content of experience also comes into play, as Jean Piaget describes.[14] Piaget investigates *catharsis* and *memory*. He says: Memory is not the translation of something unconscious or the imagining of something temporally hidden. Rather, ideational realization is always a reorganization, a *reconstruction*. As an example, Piaget tells the story of a so-called false recollection. He says he remembers precisely and vividly being a baby bound in his carriage and falling prey to an attempted kidnapping (details include the location of the adventure, the fight between the nanny and the kidnapper, and the passersby and policeman who rushed to his assistance). When he was fifteen years old, Piaget continues, the nanny wrote a letter to his parents explaining that she had made up the entire story and was herself responsible for the scratches on the young child's forehead. Nevertheless: the experience (a direct experience) of the attempted kidnapping, which the young Piaget had *heard* at age five or six and which his parents had still believed up until this point, remained stronger than the denial of this memory. The story fabricated a visual memory that can be developed into a complete scene *with the help of our imaginative powers' constructive abilities*; it was as if this replica were a negative stored in an archive. Only fragments are necessary in order to set fantasy's independent generative activities into motion. There are human sensory abilities whose long-lasting effects are diminished (they all have long-lasting effects to one degree or another). One could therefore say "that it is immaterial for a young person's feet what ground they have touched." "My words from yesterday left no trace upon my tongue."[15] (Who really knows what goes outward while I am talking or what goes inward while I am speaking?) In any event, the accomplishments of reconstructive labor are never without an influential effect. This means that what I form a memory of takes hold of me; I can behave playfully toward it, but it is not a game. Because human beings can transform almost anything into internal images owing to the complete reconstruction of every provocative fragment from prior experiences, the symbolic sequences, with which motion pictures and television programs interact, are not interchangeable, "entertaining" constructions: they have material force. They possess this material violence because of the independent activity that accrues within human beings. Like magnets or the thirteenth fairy in "Sleeping Beauty," they trigger an obstinate activity, a vital counterproduction, an internal effort that is the opposite of a Pavlovian reaction. If they do so arbitrarily, then they drag around something living inside them just as brave Achilles dragged the murdered Hector through the dust around the city walls of Troy. It was a cannibalistic gesture on the part of the hero. He wanted to subsume his enemy without actually devouring him.

The Capacity for Differentiation and How It Relates to Time

Without ever seeing a label, my father could tell the difference between 186 types of wine using only his tongue. I knew a truck driver from Halberstadt who worked on the construction of the Rappbode Dam and could describe 140 different ways one could cool off in waterways flowing through the foothills of the Harz. An important experience for him was leaping into the reservoir's cold water, feeling pressure on his bladder, and peeing. That is something quite different than feeling the pleasant, lukewarm waters of a carp pond when your limbs are overheated. For him, it was a matter of *various kinds* of water qualities, for which he had words, too.

In a much clearer way, the times constituting our life spans possess *various kinds* of qualities. There are disposable times that are too short to accommodate anything vital, and there are others too long to endure while waiting. There are right moments in time that contain a fullness that comes apart only in memory. There is fragmented time. Ancient Greek differentiates between *kairos*, the moment that holds sway over happiness or disaster, and everlasting time, called *chronos* (which eats its children), that floats by. *Kairos* is portrayed as a god with wings on his feet, a thick lock of hair on his forehead, and no hair in the back. Whoever fails to grab him by his tuft of hair at the right time ends up sliding off the bare backside of his head. These are practical differentiations of time commensurate with life experience. Similarly, nautical maps differentiate between at least some of the qualities typical of bodies of water rather than just saying: It is all water. In this respect, we could say that we live in a sea of time. Attainable time, however, is only what we can *swim* through, what we can *camouflage* ourselves with, what we *bite* into, and how far we can *take flight*. "Biting, taking flight, camouflaging, or swimming straight ahead"—these are the four reactions of a fish.

All films and television programs are *artworks of time.* Their existence requires human attention in order to exist, which means they acquire human time. They are constructs created to remove time from where it once was. In this respect, there is no definitive evaluation of whether a film or television program is something good or bad, even if in every case they expropriate time. They can do this in the sense that they produce a current that structures worthless time for people, sets it into motion, and makes it something of value *to them*. This applies, above all, to the time after a good television program or film. *Television programs and films can be produced in such a way that they give back more time than they cost*. I need not describe the antithesis that destroys time.

Physical time (measured by a metronome), psychological time, production times, daytime, the times of a single life span, historical time—these are all different perspectives. When applied to time, perspective means quality. We experience psychological time unconsciously. A fast or accelerated plot filled with suspense leads to a condensation of time in the moment it is experienced (Piaget: the reversed proportion between time and speed). In memory, however, the duration of such sequences stretches out. Additionally, egocentrism also plays a role insofar as we first learn from immediate childhood experiences how to deal with psychological time. Thirdly, there are different kinds of accessibility to our individual experiences [*Erlebnisse*] relevant for introspection. For these reasons, psychological time is the easiest to expropriate. It responds quickest to mass media's programs and suspense, its offerings to surrender autonomy and embrace heteronomy. Physical time would be safe from all this; the rigor of the labor process keeps it constrained.

Expropriated historical time means: I can discard years from my own life. I cannot keep it as my own. I lose it as it relates to my identity. It was a suspenseful time for me controlled by outside forces. Afterward, I return from captivity and start over again at zero. I lost something, and no one is concerned whether I get it back. Losing historical time is something I wish no one.

I lose time (my train is running late). This is not so bad. Everything balances itself out. I lose time that could be decisive. After falling in love, I should have followed my gut instinct, switched trains, and followed her; that would have changed my life and I missed out. I dedicated twenty years of my life to a company and now the firm is ruined, even though my department was successful. I can disavow those twenty years. At the next station: my people are scattered and I do not even know who is at fault. Another station farther: I cannot orient myself in time. I live in a permanent state of actuality and its influence on me eludes my powers of description. If this perspective toward what created me is hidden, then I am driven to despair. These are all *perspectives* on the concept of time.

Temporal Places, Pauses

A striking difference between cinematic projection and the televised image is the different rhythmization of time. The televised image consists of lines (about 600, high-definition televisions will have 1,200 so that the wealth of information is more like reality). The eye must read constantly (physiologically speaking). I am not referring here to perception, but rather to the stimulation of the sensory pathways and the cerebral cortex that correspond to the sign "occupied." I do not perceive these occupations, but they prevent me from rambling.

In contrast, cinematic projection relies on an illumination lasting 1/48 of a second followed by a dark phase of 1/48 of a second, the so-called transport phase. On average, half of the time spent in the theater is dark. The eye looks outward for 1/48 of a second and then inward for 1/48 of a second. The effects of film montage were first made possible by these pauses. The information conveyed by the montage effect is contained neither in the first nor in the ensuing image, but rather is based on images with a lasting impact. In an ideal case, they are "unseen" images that occur as an epiphany on account of the difference in the informational gap between two high-contrast images. This is the lofty ideal throughout film history—the representation of "invisible images." To this end, one needs the *moving* image; it cannot exist without pauses that are equal in value as the illuminations. Films that support this, such as *Stranger Than Paradise*, films by Tarkovsky, Godard, and Dreyer, can (with the agreement of the spectators) undertake unusual risks not perceived as unrealistic. In *Stranger Than Paradise*, this happens very simply by the intersplicing of black frames.

Such pauses are not technically possible in the televisual medium. Television programming (or rather the producers' fight over programming time caused by a scarcity of time) does something else: it fills and destroys all the gaps and time niches. In front of the television screen, spectators can create an economy of pauses marked by ramblings and rhythms necessary for their perception solely by dint of their inattention. To a certain extent, they learn to deploy inattention rhythmically.

> In this respect, urban movie theaters are not just places, but rather a temporal quality (temporal places). Consider, for example, the two o'clock showing that insurance agent Franz Kafka hurries to; the gala at Dresden's U.T.-Lichtspiele on New Year's Eve 1918; a movie theater at the trenches near Smolensk: a hiding spot amid the fighting on the front; a movie theater in the countryside near Kressbronn am Bodensee; or simply the local time in London or New York because movies are playing in these cities. In his book *Sculpting in Time* (the Russian title suggests a fixed, preserved time transported through multiple times), Andrei Tarkovsky talks about film as a "matrix" of *real time*. Verified and fixed time could now be "preserved in metal boxes" for long periods of time (from a theological perspective, even forever).[16] The film *The Arrival of a Train at La Ciotat* (by Auguste Lumière) depicts a time that has vanished; it supports our consciousness in its quest to render the flow of time reversible, at least (internally) for us. It does so in a way that is *different* from how a novel or musical composition would go about engaging the same event. The difference is based in "time, printed in its factual forms and manifestations."[17] Based on a passage by Proust, I reconstruct a moment from the past; my understanding—a translation—will create valuable misunderstandings: I gain a piece of my own lost time aided by Proust's matrix of ideas completely inaccessible to me. By comparison, a film can do both less and more. In any case, what I do to resolve this difference is the most active element; this creative impulse develops within me, as do I, when I *read* or *translate* a text. Above all, I require time. It is part of the

nature of works of art to produce more time. This has been confused with the work's aura that is showered with admiration, a myth that supposedly must be either destroyed or declared dead. The opposite is true. The only democratic element rooted in the remaining monadic forms of artistic production resides in the cooperation between readers (spectators) as coauthors of those necessary misunderstandings that make encounters with works of art useful.

The market's *new mediators* will, as the very least, overpower movie theaters and then empty them out. The preemptive bombardment of film broadcasts that public television institutions have executed has already reduced theater revenues by 60 percent. Then again, doctrinaire movie theaters are still clutching to entertainment offerings and stereotypes unable to respond to the competition. As is the case already in Italy, the premium, subscription-based television channels created by the recently merged Bertelsmann/Springer/Betafilm will reduce the movie theater industry in our country to 10 percent of its current size. Spectators will then no longer find these temporal places in the overcrowded market. With the disappearance of the movie theater, the entity for which original productions were created is lost as well. We filmmakers have no motivation to create original productions for administrative apparatuses like private television's corporations do. They all lack a temporal place and instead simply offer different ways of being hectic. The continuous thread of programming, in any case inimical to innovation and change, does not need us.

We have no other option but to actively defend the temporal places of the classical public sphere, including the movie theater, the bookstore, the concert hall, and the opera. If one of them goes under, we must reestablish it somewhere else. They will not develop spontaneously. The needs of spectators never express themselves if they fail to come across an offer and thus remain isolated and diffuse (for lack of a classical public sphere). On their own, 17 million desires and needs are immaterial. They need temporal places.

Fantasy Commodities; Commodity Research

A drinking vessel from Syria was sent to Caesar Augustus. Back then an everyday commodity, it is now an antique. Fantasy adds something the Japanese call *saba*. Translated literally, it means "rust," the patina of time. This turns the vessel into a fantasy commodity worth more than the implement from 2,000 years ago.

There is a rule that says fantasy commodities are not consumed by their use (publication). Grain from New Zealand is consumed; films from the largest film importers, amortized many times over, imported from the US market, and dubbed using public funds, acquire a higher value from multiple performances than they had before. This becomes even clearer when we consider not cheap goods, but rather works like Gone with the Wind, The Children of Paradise, Casablanca, and so on. What the course of time added to Augustus's vessel is done to these films by human eyes of yore that had seen these films already. Since the use of these fantasy commodities does no damage and also takes nothing from reality, what consumes these commodities? Cars and groceries do not have this problem. Certain handmade products that appear to be made for eternity—British cloth from around 1810, for example—could be consulted for comparison. Production and distribution of fantasy commodities have peculiarities; the contradiction is to be found primarily in their consumption.

Because commodities do not consume themselves on account of the consumers and hardly do so by themselves, it is *artificial mechanisms* that remove them from markets and our minds. Initially, the unconsumability of the fantasy commodity is itself a lever and with this unconsumability a ruling alliance of prototypes guarantees itself and therewith bans opposing products from the imagination. This is something different than changes in fashion. Thus, the constructivists took on bourgeois cultural production after the Russian Revolution, and were then jettisoned and plastered over by administrative art. Today, the Soviet Union has an academic art industry regulated top-down that drives the appreciation for art out of the country. Even without the art police, this system would be immune to rebellions committed to independent forms of expression. A specific "realistic construction" has become anchored in the heads of the population, as though these heads contained administrative departments and museum curators. These people will surely be just as creative as before, but they will not accommodate creativity as part of that department called art. Instead, they will have practical ideas, for example.

The use of stereotypical forms of expression is just as common in US cinema. New waves of stereotypes surpass old ones in this film more quickly. For the fantasy commodities of cinema, this means (quite arbitrarily) that only the current year's products receive public attention: they are the only commodities according to the current cinematic offerings. Older films are not screened in the same way, but rather are only shown as part of retrospectives or as revivals in repertory cinemas; in order to be played in larger movie theaters, these films must be either remade or significantly remastered. For fantasy commodities in the world of music, other rules apply. In classical music, variation only exists in the performance. There is no strict insistence on the contemporaneity of the offering, which generally degrades the fantasy commodity as soon as it is more than one season old. The relation between the original product, current product, classical product, prototype, and standard (repertoire)—for every genre of fantasy commodities, for every collaborative part of our public sphere—different rules apply. These are mostly arbitrary, but always anchored in the spectator. Were one to extrapolate from the dimension of the commodity, the distinctions between art and kitsch, culture and commerce, become no less arbitrary. An objectifiable distinction within fantasy commodities or cultural products appears to me to be cohesive—non-cohesive.[18] During a love story, Charles Swann is both surprised and touched by a kitschy piece of music. The judgment of a music critic moves outside of Swann's world of experience and that person's value judgment would be entirely arbitrary. In that moment, Swann would not have heard a better-crafted musical score by Beethoven and would not have been jarred. A person engages fantasy commodities and so-called cultural commodities more concretely when they take the concept of relationality seriously. I know of no other counter-concept useful for analysis.

When set in their relationality, the individual product; the shop in which I find the product; the street where I find the shop; the district and the city where I look for the street can all be differentiated. Cities of this sort are collections of commodities. If I live on a homestead in the country, the same is true. I come up against a similar collection of commodities in my own head. There I find streets, shops, and commodities. Such a context is essential for fantasy commodities. The singular commodity only ever becomes a *text* through the meaning it takes on in its relationality to everything else.

> This only *appears* to be different for material goods. They are simply not organized entirely as fantasy commodities; they have a material, consumable core.
>
> I arrive at the central train station in Frankfurt, and bring with me cauliflower from the region of Upper Hesse. Supposedly, cauliflower is a use object, a vegetable, a commodity. Yet this single cauliflower is actually incomprehensible as a commodity. If I offer it as a commodity for purchase to a passerby on Kaiserstrasse, this passerby would wonder if the cauliflower were poisoned, if this were at all a trick for carnival, if he is being tested, etc. Outside of a certain context—for example, a vegetable stand or a department store with a grocery store—the single product is incomprehensible. I cannot hurry through the city looking for a vegetable stand or produce shop. In the "zoned" city, I cannot assume that there is a produce shop in my neighborhood. I require knowledge of a particular street where I would find this shop. For fantasy commodities, the "shops," the "groups of commodities," and the individual "commodities" are rooted in a person's head before they can even look for or locate them.

New media produce department stores, zoned cities, and paved streets for large commercial vehicles of a symbolic punctuation. In relation to the classical public sphere and representations of this public sphere in the human imagination, they act like urban sanitation workers. In this respect, they permanently change product forms by mainly cutting up the relationality of fantasy products. They destroy therefore the market not only by appropriating the forms of evaluation but also by *disorienting* products and *destroying* consumption.

Suspense

The ideal of suspense reigns in the American tradition of fantasy commodities.[19] The word denotes tension, uncertainty, fright, limbo, the sense of putting yourself into someone else's shoes and trembling. The word "suspense," with all its rich ingenuity, cannot be translated into a foreign language.

François Truffaut provides an example in his interview with Hitchcock:

> "We are now having a very innocent little chat. Let us suppose that there is a bomb underneath this table between us. Nothing happens, and then all of a sudden, 'Boom!' There is an explosion. The public is *surprised*, but prior to this surprise, it has seen an absolutely ordinary scene, of no special consequence. Now, let us take a *suspense* situation. The bomb is underneath the table and the public *knows* it, probably because they have seen the anarchist place it there. The public is *aware* that the bomb is going to explode at one o'clock and there is a clock in the décor. The public can see that it is a quarter to one. In these conditions this same innocuous conversation becomes fascinating because the public is participating in the scene. The audience is longing to warn the characters on the screen: 'You shouldn't be talking about such trivial matters. There's a bomb beneath you and it's about to explode!'
>
> In the first case we have given the public fifteen seconds of *surprise* at the moment of explosion. In the second we have provided them with fifteen minutes of *suspense*. The conclusion is that whenever possible the public must be informed."[20]

In American mass media, which is not run by auteurs like Alfred Hitchcock alone, management has specialized suspense into an ideal. It is about taking away the spectator's own sense of time, "to seize him." Spectators may not be released from the grip of suspense even for a moment; they must never possess the freedom of choice, which could well drive them to the competition. In this way, a sense of super-reality affixes itself to the way humans see that fundamentally devalues real experience [*Realerfahrung*].

This is part of the American market's immunity against the incursion of European products in the event they do not imitate American suspense like a schoolchild. (In this case, they would therefore be immediately recognizable as inferior products.)

In the European expressive tradition, especially European film history of the 1920s, suspense is not king. The will to express dominates this tradition that turns against the continuous creation of effects. "Effect = a Working, without a cause" (says Richard Wagner).[21] It depends on expressing something for its own sake. The difference between European languages and the universal language of American English is slight when measured in terms of these two contradictory worlds of expression: on the one hand, genuine expression, for which attention is itself enough, and, on the other, a permanent goading of exaggerated interest. In this respect, the qualitative model for cinematic arts that culminates in a common category, which includes films by Hitchcock, Alexander Dovzhenko, Tarkovsky, and Robert Bresson because film critics equally award them up to five stars, engenders an extremely abstract approach that fails to take into account their products' resistant mode of operation. This kind of view that levels everything is surely harmless when evaluating less prominent works in the history of film; this changes when one of the two opposing sets of production ideals evinces itself as the ruling apparatus of the consciousness industry.

There are astonishingly few plot constellations that generate suspense on their own, one example being the bomb under the table. If one were to simplify the variations, there would be twelve models for generating suspense. The strongest effect, experts say, emanates from the model involving two lovers who, even when they first meet, fear (on account of violence, death, madness, or inequality) the demise of their love. In accordance with the laws of suspense, however, the life experience of mourning contained for every person in the situation from which suspense is derived is turned into an accessory. Suspense draws attention to the stroke of fate still hanging in limbo. The dramaturgy of suspense never lingers on happy moments; the shackled narration revolves around guilt, punishment, deadly blows, and shallow thoughts. Suspense toils alongside thrills [*Angstlust*]. The consciousness industry responds to a psychological structure endemic in the population that eroticizes guilty feelings of childhood.

In his essay *The Ego and the Id* from the year 1923, Freud describes the superego as Janus-faced. Its relationship to the ego does not deplete itself on account of the command: you must be like the father. Rather, it also encompasses the prohibition: you are not allowed to be like the father.

> Children have to try and find, using these commands, their libidinal sustenance within the triangle of child/parents. Everything they acquire from one parent, they must take away from the other parent (at least that is how they must see it). Yet they can do nothing other than obtaining such things for themselves. Love, therefore, always awakens feelings of guilt and "within such a cruel construct it is more than understandable that at least guilt feelings are then eroticized."[22]
>
> The basis of commodity research, as it pertains to the suspense effect, lies in the same powerful movements that elicit an *uneasiness in culture*. War, religion, the instability of feelings, and the entertainment industry all have *the same* root.

Segregation

Postmodern city planners talk about the segregation of cities. Urban obscurity should be ordered so that no one lives in zones where people work and no one shops were people live. The metropolis of Frankfurt am Main is currently working on this kind of segregation of the city's different functions: the Zeil is designated as a shopping area; the left bank of the Main has its lovely row of museums; exhibition grounds have functional routes; past the university there are the recreational zones of the Palmengarten and Grüneburgpark; and the row of banks whose inhabitants form self-sustaining boroughs like villages or small towns are supplied on Fridays with sausage from Upper Hesse at reduced prices. Nowhere has this functional concept been fully realized, neither in the planned baroque city nor in the projects of the Third Reich. Postmodern planners have certainly not achieved it. It carves up human ways of living that depend on admixtures. Segregation is an administrative concept.

This analogy between urban development and media reveals what a large role tolerance plays in coexistence and the amalgamation of an expanded city (or a living mind). Located on valuable department store real estate, Frankfurt's St. Catherine's Church is visited every morning by perhaps twenty-seven worshippers, but it is not torn down. This church, the medieval Römer building, and St. Paul's Church are *public* in a matter of speaking. The Munich delicatessen Dallmayr attracts wealthy customers in particular but also middle class ones, and offers excellent *affordable* groceries. Dallmayr's stores are located near countless other businesses between Maximilianstrasse and Marienplatz. Department stores are located in grand buildings next to this in the stretch from Kaufingerstrasse to Stachus; these retail outlets for mass consumerism are clearly different from the variety of choices between Maximilianstrasse and Marienplatz. The location of little shops alongside department stores exists symbiotically (like coral reefs). If they did not exist as integrated clusters, then there would be no reason for travelers from the suburbs or even towns like Bad Tölz or Rosenheim to find their way here to purchase more unusual items. A single shop, regardless of how qualified it is, could never draw such through traffic on its own. The opera house, the Kammerspiele, the hotel Bayerischer Hof, and some movie theaters in the area also benefit from this. This sort of collection of shops is a *commodity of its own kind* that only developed organically until now. I know not a single entrepreneur to date capable of producing this while still maintaining differentiation. For this reason, all the world's accumulations of differentiation find themselves on the defensive. The Bavarian restaurant Donisl is both solid and reasonably priced: a historic, temporal place rooted in the cityscape especially around five o'clock in the morning (after holidays). This place did not fall victim to segregation, but rather to bands of criminals. Foreign infiltration, violent appropriation, secret takeovers: these are the forms of attack.[23]

Educated Greeks were able to make their way from conquered Byzantium into the city. These refugees taught the sons of bankers. Within the city, aggressive temperaments live elbow-to-elbow: craftsmen, alchemists, prostitutes, refugees, and tradesmen—and in the middle of all of this was a silversmith's workshop, a painter's studio, and an academy. Florence's reputation for managing this subtle mix is a commodity of its own kind: there is no other way to produce a rich consciousness.

Interfaces, Seams, Joints[24]

This term comes from the hierarchical, centralized world of images. The interface between two command centers; the seam where two military units border one another; the stitch a surgeon sews. The term can also be understood as a form of anticentralization. The joint is the unsolvable problem for centralized organizations. It was never possible to concentrate forces at the point of decentralization, the seam, the boundary to the other. Forces never stay put, but rather surge toward the sun, a ruler, or a center. The Roman Empire collapsed for this reason, and the Soviet troops invaded the seams at the German front until the very end for this reason, too. Accordingly, information failed to function at the interface between the Federal Criminal Police and North Rhine-Westphalia's office of criminal investigations.

The Latin word for interface is *separatrix*. The *juncture* of incompatible opposites does not form a sharp separation, but rather one side creates an enclave near another. We *later call it* a dividing line. Gottfried Wilhelm Leibniz discusses this. A group of mathematicians from Bremen fed the formulas for different forms of a separatrix into a computer and let it graph the results: just as Leibniz had predicted, it yielded 50 percent stochastic results (chance, arbitrariness) and 50 percent solid structure. These materials are precisely those that produce creativity: good luck rolling the dice and necessity. It can only be produced in mass quantities at so-called interfaces.

In our current social structure, the chance for contact between opposites is actually decreasing. Functionalization and segregation are doing the groundwork to isolate everything and everyone. In this way, countless subsocieties and Robinsonades are created even though the illusion of a *single* society remains. These groups seek their fortunes separately from the other, *parallel* groups, as though they were independent corporations. This is seen more clearly in structures such as the Soviet Union with its parallel hierarchies (politics, economics, technology, life) or in television broadcasting (production, economics, jurisprudence, programming, technology) than in social arenas that do not express themselves as a planned economy. Parallelism—the tendency to avoid contact (as is characteristic of flight behavior: "Save yourself, if you can")—is merely concealed here; it is not *expressed*.

The lack of closeness also affects our consciousness. A person can carry around inside them four or five incompatible structures of consciousness. The demands placed on that person by their environment determine which of their various personalities will respond.

In this type of situation, it is fruitful to produce contact artificially according to Socrates's dialogic method. This is the category of relationality, whereas universal, uncompromising parallelization is the root of the new obscurity. If institutions incapable of understanding one another (television and the film business, professional politics and poetry, experts from hostile powers, etc.) abruptly confront one another, then a spark of intelligence emerges at the point of division. It arises out of the distress that communication has fallen into, but it also arises because in each of the others a pent-up supplemental labor is ready and waiting. The segregation forming the basis for parallelism is unreal; they are the sources of the blockages.

New media that destroy the balance between the masses of indirect experience and the controls of direct experience carry with them extreme risks. The antidote can be found, so to speak, only *in the midst of this development*, at the interfaces, at the points of the conflict between broadcasting and the human spirit. The worst case would be a separate, parallel development of administrative monsters, one public and the other led by a corporation.

In a classical market society, competition is supposed to lead to contact, to put products in such seamless proximity that confrontation is unavoidable and buyers are forced to choose. This competition was always more an idea than reality. It was first prevented by the guilds and then by the particular relation of violence stemming from society's most powerful. Yet we are still familiar with places with a few narrow streets lined with many stores (we still find them today in Paris; they are often arcades), where the commodities are in such close contact with one

> another that the jumbles lead to a synoptic view and the confrontation leads to invention. A kind of magic emanates from these places. Not long thereafter, people need world's fairs to collect the confrontations and interfaces because they no longer do so in reality. A little later—following the most intensive collection of products in our century: the two world wars—world's fairs are replaced by field-specific exhibitions. The collapse of this confrontation precedes the collapse of the public sphere.

Isomorphism According to Piaget, a Category of Relationality

How do consciousness (deduction) and material reality come together? Take, for instance, logic, mathematics, biological necessities, and external complexity. The pathos of classical philosophies was based on the idea that there was a principle of universal agreement because the inner nature of objects does the groundwork for the consciousness and this, in turn, does the same for objects; one consciousness would cajole another and a social drive would force the parallelisms, each antagonistic and incomprehensible to one another, to translate. Based on something as simple as the right to hospitality, Immanuel Kant came up with the following: the earth is round, so whoever walks around it will invariably encounter others. This principle of contact and permanent motion around the round, blue entity called earth supposedly guarantees that a person listens to others, and accepts them as their neighbors as long as this does not put his own livelihood at risk. Piaget replaces parallelism with the notion of isomorphism. There is, he says, a structural similarity between "conscious implications and certain systems of organic reality."[25] *But this is only valid as a relationality.* Single attributes, institutionally separated, do not necessarily exhibit such isomorphisms. The principle of agreement is not safe from this form of disassembly. The ruins of human society and those of human beings, Piaget says, are losing the impulse to make themselves universally understood.

> The theory of isomorphism provides a unique perspective. If the logical-mathematical and organic structures, meaning those systems from the worlds of things that enter into society by way of dead labor, and those that our mortal bodies control are isomorphic, then the physical chemistry of the most advanced processes would have to become corporal and the physical chemistry of the body would have to become mathematical and deductive. This means that these structures take their results back to the starting point. "It is in the perspective of such a circle or, if we prefer, of such a constantly increasing spiral that it is probably fitting to situate the problems of relation between life and thought."[26] These are the structural rules that are not interested in intuition.
>
> It is clear that this sort of spiral is less concerned with understanding than with the homunculus, the human species's shenanigans, and alchemy. But the opposite effect is also produced as long as the relationality of such a "laboratory" remains protected. But how dangerous must manipulation, segregation, and the demolition of this kind of experimental chain be! It is no more dangerous than machinery that is not yet destructive but also not safe. The industrialization of consciousness or, in the words of Jack Lang, the "industrialization of culture" contains this "alchemy within alchemy"; there is no natural organ (neither individual nor social) that controls this kind of process.[27] If thought and life have been brought into conflict because of hastiness, then industrialization, meaning the expropriation and separation of thought from life, must be a devastating ecological and phylogenetic intervention.

Counterproduction; Terrestrial Reconnection

In light of the large mass media institutions controlling television, cultural criticism is effective only when it appears in the form of a product. Ideas cannot fight against material production when the latter occupies the world of images. What does counterproduction even mean if access to television channels is exceedingly limited and the commercial media industry tends toward aggressive advertising, which then forces a similar tendency from public broadcasters thus driving counterproducts out of the market and out of people's minds?

Effective counterproduction must fulfill three requirements: (1) it must latch onto the opponent's strength; (2) it must be more cohesive and relational than its opponent, because it will initially be inferior to the opponent in terms of capital; and (3) it must be decentrally organized, because the advantages of centralization lie with the opponent. It boils down to the terrestrial reconnection of television.

The most effective tools against a surplus of telecracy are cities illuminated at night: the classical public sphere in which life is immediate among those present. It is not enough to condense the remnants of the classical public sphere still alive in cities today. Indeed, cities are almost empty at night. We have to do away with the restrictions governing how late shops can be open, and then the forces of the classical public sphere (theater, literature, film, music, and the free world of commodities) would still have to form alliances with the forces of established television, print media, and foreign countries. Cities filled with life—such temporal places are diversified today across the country and made available to those who have time to spare. Businesses and public broadcasters (with the exception of ZDF) lack the ability to function in a decentralized way.[28] In this way, they have to leave large parts of the human spirit unsatisfied; they make only hollow attempts at conquering the unmediated public sphere in the form of large events, fundraisers, and entertainment. These give rise to additional events, but none are magnets for liveliness. This all can be gathered because of marginal benefit calculations and the hierarchical chain of command.

What we need is commercial activity that can repeat on a large scale what the Brothers Grimm achieved in terms of personal labor and collecting. Today it is not just fairy tales that have gone missing, but rather an entire world of diversity. In village gardens, the gene pools of apple and nut trees are vanishing. A handful of tree varieties, all categorized by bureaucrats from the European Economic Community, are replacing through their sheer volume the wealth of unexpected varieties that our parents knew. Here is something that has been told over a period of thousands of years, something initiated by nature and transformed by humans into a garden, and now it will perish if it is not collected. The same holds true for the *inner gardens* that traditionally comprise both children and adults. Unexpected answers become rarer because the

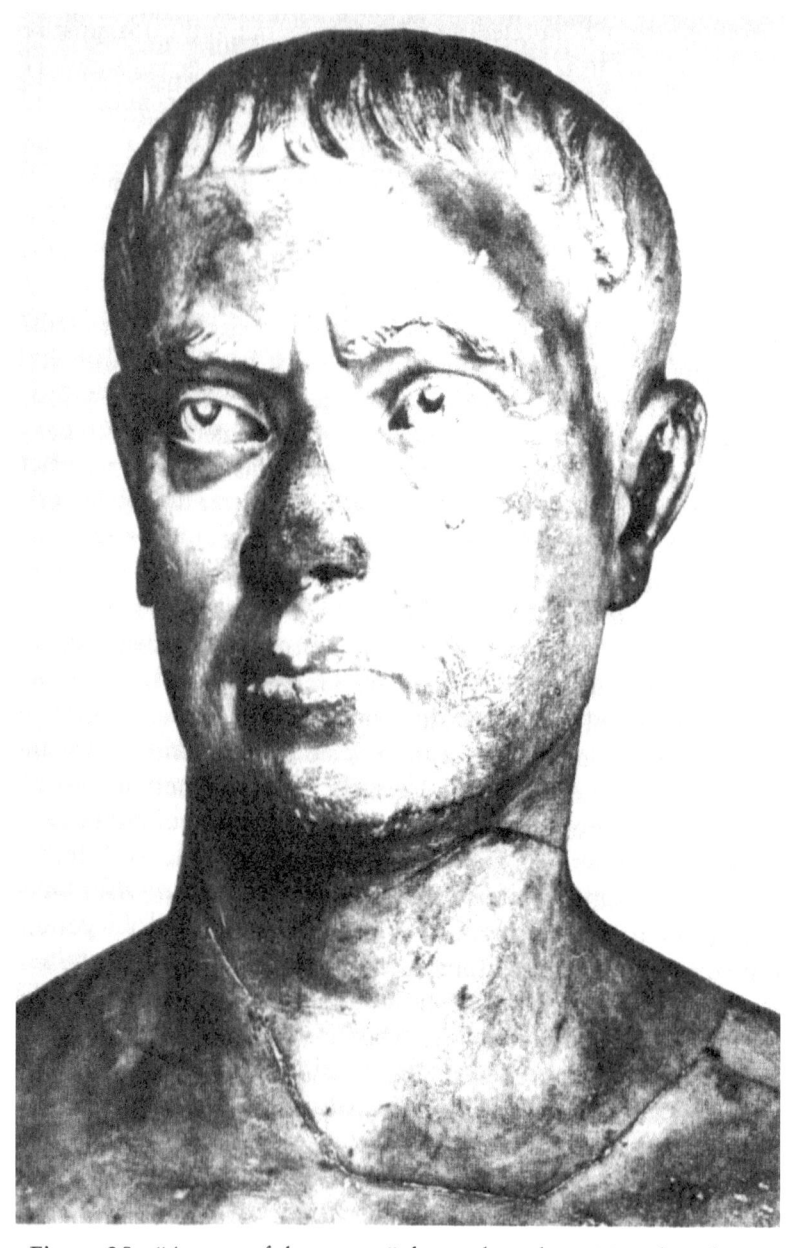

Figure 20. "A powerful servant," formerly a slave. Now he advises a Roman emperor and rules over the provinces.

© Alexander Kluge Archive

Figure 21. Old territory. *Mille passus*, 1,000 steps. The route. In the king of Macedonia's army, geographers among the *arrière garde* wander from the cities of Greece to Pamir and the Indus River. In the south, they search for the source of the Nile. Everything they learn, measure, and appropriate for the Greek spirit world they did by walking with their own feet. They counted their double step and dragged cords behind them so as to measure and correct the fluctuations in the length of their strides. Regardless of whether it was an Iranian parasang or a Roman double step, whoever strode across the stretch of land spent a portion of their life in it. The powerful servant who served the emperor will never be there where his decrees take effect. A long-distance ruler, a nearby ruler.

© Alexander Kluge Archive

places—the interfaces—are lacking where people can share them. The overwhelming majority of what is conveyed to people through immediate expression and experiential content cannot find its way past the editors and the advertising norms of commercial industry. These media achieve little, but they devour self-confidence and the time of life.

Translated by Richard Lambert

Notes

This essay was originally published in German as Alexander Kluge, "Ausdruck 'Medien,' 'Neue Medien,'" *Bestandsaufnahme: Utopia Film* (Frankfurt am Main: Zweitausendeins, 1983), 43–60.

It was republished as part 2 of the much longer, three-part essay that appears in Alexander Kluge, "Die Macht der Bewußtseinindustrie und das Schicksal unserer Öffentlichkeit: Zum Unterschied von machbar und gewalttätig," in Klaus von Bismarck, Günter Gaus, Alexander Kluge, and Ferdinand Sieger, eds., *Industrialisierung des Bewußtseins: Eine kritische Auseinandersetzung mit den "neuen" Medien* (Munich: Piper, 1985), 51–129.

This translation includes the entirety of the 1983 essay as well as the most significant portions of the glossary of keywords in part 3 of the 1985 edition. The translation does not include the first part of the 1985 essay, which originally appeared as Alexander Kluge, "Zum Unterschied von machtbar und gewalttätig: Die Macht der Bewusstseinsindustrie und das Schicksal Unserer Öffentlichkeit," *Merkur: Deutsche Zeitschrift für Europaisches Denken* 38.3 (April 1984): 243–53.

Of the fourteen images included in the Piper Verlag edition, only seven are included in the present translation.

1. [Translator's note: Kluge deploys here the intersubjective language of American pragmatist George Herbert Mead and uses, in fact, the English in the German original: "anticipation of the other." This can be traced back to *Geschichte und Eigensinn*, coauthored with Oskar Negt in 1981, in which they assert that "ego production through the *anticipation of the other* is indisputable today as the path toward identity formation" and then reference the 1968 translation of Mead's 1934 study, *Mind, Self, and Society*, into German. The prevalence of Mead in thinking from the late seventies and early eighties (e.g., Axel Honneth and Hans Joas's *Social Action and Human Nature* [1980] and Jürgen Habermas's *The Theory of Communicative Action*) suggests that Mead's anthropology commanded the attention of many thinkers throughout the seventies. See Oskar Negt and Alexander Kluge, *Der unterschätzte Mensch: Gemeinsame Philosophie in zwei Bänden*, vol. 2, *Geschichte und Eigensinn* (Frankfurt am Main: Zweitausendeins, 2001), 508, 508n11.]

2. On the theory of communication, see George Herbert Mead, *Mind, Self, and Society from the Standpoint of a Social Behaviorist* (Chicago: University of Chicago Press, 1967); Johannes Siegrist, *Das Consensus-Modell: Studien zur Interaktionstheorie und zur kognitiven Sozialisation* (Stuttgart: Enke, 1970); Jürgen Habermas, *The Theory of Communicative Action*, trans. Thomas McCarthy, 2 vols. (Boston: Beacon Press, 1984–87). For specialist literature on the application of media processes, see Kurt Lüscher, "Medienwirkung und Gesellschaftsentwicklung," *Media Perspektiven* 9 (1982): 545–55. See especially the critical apparatus.

3. [Translator's note: Infratest was a market research company dating back to 1949 when the Ludwig Maximillian University of Munich's Research Institute for Journalistic Media Effects christened its ongoing study of radio audiences. Incorporated in 1975, Infratest was acquired in 1980 by the first in a long string of global market research corporations. It currently exists as a brand held by the Munich-based Kantar TNS.]

Chapter 15   291

4. Walter Benjamin, "The Work of Art in the Age of Its Technological Reproducibility," trans. Harry Zohn and Edmund Jephcott, in *Selected Writings*, ed. Howard Eiland and Michael W. Jennings, vol. 4, 1938–1940 (Cambridge, MA: The Belknap Press, 2003), 251–83.
5. Benjamin, 255–56.
6. Heinrich von Kleist, "On the Gradual Production of Thoughts Whilst Speaking," in *Selected Writings*, ed. and trans. David Constantine (Indianapolis: Hackett, 1997), 405. Italics added.
7. [Translator's note: The original "Club II" was a biweekly panel discussion broadcast on the public-service broadcaster ORF (Austrian Broadcasting Corporation) beginning in 1976. Characteristic for the talk show were its open-ended discussions lasting several hours.]
8. [Translator's note: This quotation is unattributed in the German original and remains unidentifiable.]
9. [Translator's citation and note: Alexander Kluge, dir., *Yesterday Girl* (1966; Frankfurt: Zweitausendeins, 2007), DVD. The sentence was penned by Reinhard Baumgart and originally published in *Merkur*. See Alexander Kluge, *Abschied von gestern: Protokoll* (Frankfurt am Main: Verlag Filmkritik, 1967), 7.]
10. [Translator's note and citation: Kluge is referring here to Jürgen Habermas's 1984 speech on neoconservative postmodernism, entitled "The New Obscurity: The Crisis of the Welfare State and the Exhaustion of Utopian Energies" and published in *The New Conservatism: Cultural Criticism and the Historians' Debate*, ed. and trans. Shierry Weber Nicholsen (1985; Cambridge, MA: MIT Press, 1989), 48–70.]
11. [Translator's note: The first three words in this list in the original German—*Heiratsvermittler, Wohnungsvermittler, Stellenvermittler*—are all compound words built from the noun *Vermittler*, which is also used in German to mean "mediator."]
12. [Translator's note: On the origins of this quote, see note 3 in chapter 3.]
13. [Translator's note: This quotation is unattributed in the German original and remains unidentifiable.]
14. Jean Piaget, *Child and Reality: Problems of Genetic Psychology* (New York: Penguin, 1977), 42ff.
15. [Translator's note: These quotations are unattributed in the German original and remain unidentifiable.]
16. [Translator's citation: Andrei Tarkovsky, *Sculpting in Time*, trans. Kitty Blair (Austin: University of Texas Press, 1986), 62.]
17. [Translator's citation: Tarkovsky, *Sculpting in Time*, 63.]
18. [Translator's note: Kluge's original formulation is one that courses through his collaborations with Oskar Negt. The language here—"zusammenhängend—nicht zusammenhängend"—appears as "cohesive—non-cohesive" in Oskar Negt and Alexander Kluge, *Public Sphere and Experience: Toward an Analysis of the Bourgeois and Proletarian Public Sphere*, trans. Peter Labanyi, Jamie Owen Daniel, and Assenka Oksiloff (Minneapolis: University of Minnesota Press, 1993), 296. See also Alexander Kluge, *History and Obstinacy*, trans. Richard Langston et al. (New York: Zone Books, 2014), 220. Given the semantic richness of these terms, they could also be rendered as "relational—non-relational."]
19. [Translator's note: Kluge uses the English word "suspense" in the original.]

20. [Translator's note: François Truffaut, *Hitchcock*, (New York: Simon & Schuster, 1984), 73. See note 11 in chapter 11 in this volume.]

21. [Translator's note: See note 2 in chapter 13 in this volume.]

22. Hildegart Baumgart, *Jealousy: Experiences and Solutions*, trans. Manfred R. Jacobson (Chicago: University of Chicago Press, 1990), 207.

23. [Translator's note: Although at first glance it appears to be a critique of the Donisl, Kluge's account is actually using the long-standing Munich gastronomic institution as a metaphor to describe the effects of the Bavarian government's media policies on the Federal Republic's public broadcasting institutions.]

24. [Translator's note: The German *Nahtstelle* (literally, "location of a seam") can be translated variously as "seam," "interface," or "joint," and Kluge accordingly probes the word's semantic range with his allusions to media technologies, military maneuvers, and medical procedures.]

25. Piaget, 172.

26. Piaget, 172.

27. [Translator's note: These exact quotations are unattributed in the German original and remain unidentifiable. Jack Lang (1939–) served as France's minister of culture from 1981 to 1986 and then again from 1988 to 1992.]

28. [Translator's note: ZDF, Zweites Deutsches Fernsehen (Second German Television), was West Germany's second consortium of public broadcasters. Founded in 1963, it continues broadcasting today.]

16

Medialization—Musealization

I think the word "medialization" primarily alludes to "television," but when all its parts are examined, then the "long-distant vision" that the word "tele-vision" implies has nothing at all to do with any of the television stations I know. They actually create foreground and generate wallpaper. They open a window and then prevent anything from being represented from a distance. I cannot put actors into any old period costumes, have them play someone from the twelfth century or act out Caesar's death, and call it a television play or, for that matter, something "distant." This is nothing, neither close nor distant; it is a relation that simply does not exist. This is similar to a discovery by Prince Pückler: he finds a child in Sudan's slave market and assumes she is somehow a descendant of Aida's royal family.[1] He carries her off to Germany and keeps her like an animal in a museum at his palace in Muskau. The child dies at some point later on. The northern climes simply did not suit her, and building a fence around her like an animal was equally detrimental. It would have been better if he had picked a local and dressed her up.

This old colonial imagination is imperialism in the form of a zoo predicated on dispossession. It also assumes the form of conceptual imperialism repeated once again in the media. They appropriate everything as it perhaps once was "at a distance." It is brought closer and stuffed into living rooms by way of an administrative act.

Television stations are administrative agencies. My work obtaining independent broadcasting licenses, or the work of opera houses, theaters, independent producers, and publishers, consists of making sure that we each do not produce for just a single day and that we have a longer prehistory than the press. Broadcasting companies must actually have a longer prehistory for their forms of production. If I attempt to form coalitions with these companies, then it is actually no longer a matter of television in the sense of media, but actually a kind of "antitelevision," something that clings to people's concept of experience, that takes the public sphere very seriously and tries to protect the classical forms of the public sphere in this current state of emergency, in which the classical bourgeois public sphere, which was always a compromise, is threatened by permanently overlapping medialized public spheres. This likely occurs only if one explores the fundamentals of the classical public sphere and then attempts to realize them.

In order to begin thinking about "medialization and musealization," I suggest imagining that I cannot tell you whether one should be for or against either or both. I cannot proceed with either without a counter-concept. If the question is traced back to the concept of experience [*Erfahrung*], then I can say: *Medialization* could be generally translated as mediation, but then there must be immediate experience if there are plenty of mediated experiences on the other side. However, I cannot say that as much immediate experience must be saved, preserved, or organized as possible because the principle of immediate experience is a purely private matter. It is a very private and narrow-minded position if I consider only what I have touched to be real. Conversely, if I know things only through hearsay—through mediated experience—this would be just as senseless as a society of blabbermouths we occasionally see on television. From that point, it is easy to see that the *balance* between immediate and mediated experience is actually the topic of interest here. What must be expanded and made more precise is also the balance between past, present, future, and all other temporal forms. *This* is the pressing question regarding the production of experience that resides in the tension between "medialization—musealization." It has nothing to do with any commitment to one or another of these times.

It was quite obvious how dictatorial concepts of the future ruled over the past and present in the first half of the twentieth century. The past dominated the turn from the nineteenth to the twentieth century. The German military made so many considerable achievements in 1870–71 that people suffered to a certain extent because of its legacy. There were so many aristocratic minister presidents, culminating with Minister President and Imperial Chancellor Bismarck, that everyone who followed had a difficult time eking out from the nineteenth century's stockpile of dead labor their own place where they could spontaneously decide free of burden: "This is my present." The mechanism: I am ashamed of my society's past; I want to violently break out of this condition; I find myself guilty; feel ashamed again; and then acknowledge my guilt once more. This can quickly acquire an expansive dynamic that assumes a spiral form of shame and guilt. In this respect, if the time cannot be closed off when a person could still decide something and when a society is still in the midst of decision-making processes, then the present has the tendency to stretch itself out (because this is the time when a person still believes they can still decide something), such that the 200 years between 1789 and 1989 form a *single* present. One might even think that the date of the French Revolution could be renegotiated in order to repeat it, assuming one could now do it better. There is certainly something right about repeating everything again with more time, labor, and effort. It is surely correct that the Enlightenment needs to be repeated over and over again. At the same time, a tremendous amount of energy weighs down on this process, rendering it an unproductive burden.

I cannot retroactively put anything in the past and at the same time I mistrust the future. I, therefore, invest virtually, blindly, in a permanent present in a kind of wait-and-see attitude, a deferral of death. In this way, an immense mass of present time is developed, accumulated, and unfurled such that it is capable of destroying all futures and pasts. This omnipotence that assembles itself in processes of the present can be clearly seen in some armament processes. This is a society that still considers itself omnipotent and inflates its ego, as was also the case in Prince Pückler's Eurocentric era of colonialism. When someone like Cecil Rhodes "founds" a portion of South Africa, he simply overestimates himself. Whole societies overestimate themselves when they attempt to define the world according to a childish need for omnipotence that insists on making the world clear, so much so that I may be debt-free and powerful, that I have to protect history and fortunes using my own absolute authority. In this way, entire societies attempt to turn the world into a continuous present, to make it their own, to appropriate it. This is a cannibalistic attitude toward the world, and is actually the metaphorical concept, the core, and the root of a whole host of processes that we find, for example, in ecology and the depletion of the political by the administrative and that actually define the egocentric tendencies in all countries. I cannot strip away my childhood when, for example, I sit here talking to you on All Souls' Day, relatively tired with a cup of coffee, after working the whole day. Of course, there is a little man in my ear from my childhood who is more or less always present as an agent of past times. And since I will die at some point, there is also a man older than me who looks toward the future. I speak of myself as an example: a whole host of things, events, and references flow through me, all of which are of a different age. If you look at a grammar book of ancient Greek, then you have in addition to the present also the past and future tense as well as the optative, a wonderful grammatical tense: the form of polite requests and wishes. This is a form useful for expressing distant possibilities that go beyond the realm of the normal subjunctive. This means that there is a way of dealing with temporalities and modes of experience that can be quite differentiated. Only when all of these differentiations come together is reality rich, which means they are also all real. The isolation or hegemony of one temporal mode over others, even if it were the polite optative, would essentially be a dictatorship of unreality. This would already be the factual contribution, the machinery, leading to the loss of history.

If I take the concept "musealization" seriously, understand it correctly, and try to interpret it within this context, then it can only mean labor against the loss of history. Making dead labor come alive does not correspond, however, with momentum. In a way, I can dissolve this forgotten, dead labor only in something living that absorbs it. In this process, there is, on the one hand, the media, which are so to speak the sum of administrative acts that deal with the substance of human minds, and, on the other, human minds, which are the opponent of this medium and also the force capable of actually getting rid of it. Yet they are created in the first place by the relationality of minds, those of people working in media: media's producers and consumers. Human sensuality and the human mind are actually at fault for believing that a single mind is something real; they are captive, always inferior to the media as the sum of many minds, and initially as unorganized as a single peasant who takes on a group of knights on horseback. As a consequence, the peasants lost most of their wars despite being stronger. This is how individuals now face highly organized media. Media and human minds can easily be analyzed using concepts borrowed from urban planning and architecture. In the preface to the second part of *Critique of Pure Reason*, Immanuel Kant comments extensively on the "architecture of reason." Yet this concept comes up only at the end of the *Critique*. He initially begins with simple dwellings that we require for experience. It is precisely these simple dwellings for experience that are nowhere to be found today—this is the problem, he says, of modern time and the present. They either do not grow organically or are already there; they are also not constructed organically because the linguistic confusion characteristic of media's Babylonian condition made the "construction workers" supposed to build the dwellings for experience crazy. It confused them. And so they always try building something larger than what is needed for direct experience and in so doing they create borders. Kant lays this out in detail and describes how important it is to always create the possibility for simple dwellings for experience and a form of thinking akin to the principles of the Bauhaus; to this end, both construction *and* demolition are necessary, a "deconstruction" performed by an "artiste démolisseur" or philosopher who also destroys something. In this sense, the orientation provided by the metaphor of the city is exceptional. If I take a city we know well and hear much about—one, in other words, well suited for metaphor—then you have to imagine: scholars in a distant city overrun by Turks. (We are describing an earlier century.) These scholars still possess all the knowledge from the ancient world contained in the books from Alexandria's library that had long since burned down. They carry it around in their heads and repeat it again and again in a thoroughly musealizing way. In this respect, they are extremely loyal. They hardly use any of this knowledge in their own city of Byzantium, and it is also of no use against the Turks. They have, in part, the wrong knowledge for this war. They are cast out and end up in Italy. There they become tutors for the sons of bankers, etc. The bankers' sons seize on a certain folkloric element as well as Tuscan traditions. Their city is comprised of whores, chemists, murders, tradesmen, and producers. But there is also Cellini's small silver workshop and the painter Botticelli's studio, etc. This combination, which is actually unpalatable and can be neither engineered nor planned, leads to an attractively unique symbiosis: the phenomenon of Florence. Yet the bankers know very well that what their sons are learning, which has somehow condensed into a community, is also incredibly effective for commerce. "Culture" can be a business, as is the case with commercial television today; back then, trade as far as Ulm or Nuremberg could be financed as long as silver vessels were available. Even if all this is based on general concepts, confusion, and misunderstandings—to the extent that it is based on the ancient world itself—it is still productive because so many seams, different experiential processes, and sites of production emerge, and with each one distinct developments and qualifications become possible. Leibniz said that at every interface (the separatix) between something irreconcilable there arises 50 percent misunderstanding and chaos and 50 percent structure and organizing innovation whether one likes it or not. This structure, which qualifies itself by way of antagonistic experiences, must be collected for the sake of public efficacy. This abundance of imposed border crossings that transpires out of necessity and the knowledge commanded by a few museum personnel, musealizing scholars, and guardians who hold no permanent positions lead to something that has always fascinated me: what long belongs to dead labor and is merely maintained and passed down suddenly expresses virulence and erupts into a new stage of production. This was the case, for example, with *Cahiers du cinéma* and academic events in France associated with the Cinémathèque Française. They actually collected, admired, and wrote about films. Suddenly, they became directors. We then tried to imitate this model in Germany as best as we could with the distinction that even though we did not make the same waves we nevertheless did so for a long time. This cinematographic awakening also emerged out of a musealization project: first collect and assess, as the Brothers Grimm once did or as a gardener does, but do not do what an animal tamer does. A tamer forces his will onto an animal, so that an elephant, for example, does what is most difficult for him to do in nature, namely, to balance himself, or he uses perversions, tricks, treats, or bribes to force a lion to take the tamer's head into its jaws. This is an entirely unusual and absurd act, especially if one considers how the French revolutionaries wanted to use such performances to show how powerful man is. But this really cuts both ways and requires new kinds of collecting that enlighten.

Basically, we need to gather, collect, sort, repeat, make variable, condense, and narrate slowly and thoroughly this tremendous mass of experience—to give a meaningful example, 200 years of the French Revolution—in its full breadth and with unusual thoroughness. I imagine this collection leapfrogging out at some point and becoming productive. This is the tacit ideal I have when I imagine a museum as idea and praxis. I actually see within it a small production unit; it will always be a factory that lives out of respect to its viewers, users, and objects. Therefore, it will certainly never become a factory that destroys the old in order to produce everything anew. In the years 1789, 1790, and 1791, the French revolutionaries changed the calendar and said: This whole Christian manner of counting has to go, we are starting with the year 1. This lasted through year 5 and then we have Thermidor. I believe this stormy, violent approach to producing without first gathering led, as experience shows, to administrative behavior and ended after five years. We will therefore require a tremendous amount of patience because today, at the end of the second half of the twentieth century, we need to step up and visualize, collect, evaluate, and sort the tremendous masses of experience from the nineteenth and twentieth centuries. We need to enter into the most diverse areas. In every place where things have been left behind, we must take them up and translate them into production. If I take, for example, Robert Musil's great work *The Man without Qualities* and imagine how he wrote this retrospective text in 1942 while a brutal cycle of military operations and mass death took place here in Europe, then this temporality seems to be the necessary kind of musealization appropriate for media technologies.

A twentieth-century poet goes into full action. He describes the last ten years of the nineteenth century and first ten years of the twentieth century. He approached this short period but cannot make the novel, the construction, the narration into the whole epic he imagined. He has the impression that he is missing something. It is for this reason that it is so urgent that the work he started, shaped by the sign of thoroughness, be continued. This is primarily just literature, mere experience and production in quotation marks, as it were. In this sense, it can be said that every other area where the experiences from the twentieth century are processed and organized is always unchartered when compared to both the mass of labor performed by poets and the mass of accumulated dead labor.

Last year in Moscow, I was quite astounded when I suddenly got the immediate impression that a very small group of people, members of an academy who all occupied permanent posts run like country estates and who actually did more than was asked of them, actually came across like those bourgeois Prussians who surrounded Baron vom Stein, von Humboldt, Gneisenau, Scharnhorst, etc. Amazing was when they said they want to set in motion again a bourgeois revolution, free enterprise, etc., but with more time and more honesty. This is the core of perestroika. This is supposed to be repeated unevenly today at a wrong moment in the historical context, in other words at an imaginary point in time, albeit with some more instruments of power, experience, immunization, if you will, and sufficient incubation time for such processes. This is a worthwhile and promising task that can accompany our children into the twenty-first century as long as we make the effort.

I see this point necessarily superseded by museums, those institutions that bear responsibility for bygone, lost objects. It is necessary that museums keep on hand the possibilities for displacement. This is something not so pressing for those who work every day. In closing, it is necessary to juxtapose two stances: whether I comport myself as a *spectator* toward my life and the course it took, or whether I relate to them as a *producer*, whether I move through society as a producer or spectator. It is very important to consider the question: What constitutes the status of a producer or spectator? If I take, for example, remembering, creating the capacity for differentiation, sensing, assembling the times and experiences living within me, and producing relationalities—this appears at first glance to be *observant*. I can walk down a street during Advent and look into windows. They are illuminated. I did something and continue doing it. In such an instance, I am a producer through and through, a producer of the stances I take and my experiences. I can also sit in a sauna and contemplate something and be a producer. This is different than the abdicated Kaiser Wilhelm who could not at all sit still and either shot animals or had to take a saw and cut through tree trunks. In the end, he sat around in Holland like a museum piece. He only appeared to be active; even when he was a young boy, he was actually always "beneath Bismarck," so to speak. When he went to Jerusalem and showed off his costume, he was actually not a producer; he stood beside himself and observed *himself*. It is very easy for me to take down an old Kaiser from today's perspective. Yet I would say that 90 percent of the active operations we consider activities need to be evaluated in order to check whether or not they actually produce anything, and whether or not they actually linger on the spectator's administrative standpoint. Here, too, it is not a matter of saying: This one is good and the other one is bad. I only want to relativize the relations and make it clear that these are all questions of balance. If someone examines the categories and practices that can no longer be enhanced, then they cannot also enhance and intensify the way time is dealt with. "More past" cannot be created than what is past. The future cannot be forced. You can sing as many songs to the morning dawn as you like, but no more future will come about than what is already worked on. Setting into relation the side that can be enhanced with what cannot be enhanced is a massive criterion for differentiation: a tremendous force and a productive capability. If we stabilize these relations and found a form of politics on it, and if it heeds the "the auspicious time" conveyed by "KAIROS" (the name of my firm), then we would take an important step. Kairos is an ancient Greek expression referring to a god. He has a tuft of hair in front and is bald in the back. If you grab him at the right time, then you grab both opportunity and this god by the tuft. If you grab too late, you get the bald side where your hand slides off. This god of the auspicious moment in time, who corresponds with all sorts of things at the same time, refers to the heart of relations. This is something that could not be read off the face of a clock. Sometimes it is also necessary, as was the case with Napoleon's adversary Mikhail Kutusov outside of Moscow, to wait and count on the fact that the Russian winter will come to end at some point in the year. For this reason, it is not on account of one's abilities but rather by waiting, by doing nothing, etc., that he perseveres, in this case against the active Bonaparte who wore a timepiece on his arm. He always sees himself winning and writes in Moscow disheartened letters to the czar about why he does not understand that his war is actually logically lost. Because the Russians did not understand that this war could be lost, they could not be defeated by an opponent who captured their capital and could have also taken their other major city, St. Petersburg. Nevertheless, they did not understand, just as the Spanish guerrillas also failed to understand, that they should have been defeated. They simply had no sense of the valid rules of the game, and history proved them right. There were rules that referred to specific tempi and times that were obsolete.

I believe that museum work, musealization, should involve a careful, horticultural way of dealing with time that could in the long run lead to the creation of intensive, saturated, experientially rich temporalities amid the gears, bustle, and restlessness of contemporary life. This is also the case in a few lovely museums in the middle of New York. They are built precisely to be temporal oases right in middle of the city center. They could actually be understood as pools, bodies of water, or ponds, in which one can linger without ever getting bored. There is a compelling metaphor for this: these kinds of ponds can freeze over very quickly, for example, such that too much of the surroundings are musealized. If a city gets too many museums or puts on too many events, if a mayor like Frankfurt's Walter Wallmann decides that the Römer has to be expanded with new concrete in the back and an old façade in front, then the museum façade lacks any background. If everything is closed because of full employment and countless events, then as with nature effects can arise that lead to the pond, a scene, a context of production, freezing over. Long ago in the thirties, I always marveled at the employees in my father's medical practice, who, without ever being obligated or told, jammed pieces of straw into the garden pond so that the fish had open spaces and got air. Accordingly, the pond could never completely freeze over. They performed an unsolicited labor, which they repeated every or every other day. They were not paid for this. This made a big impression on me as a child.

Were someone to ask me what we do in television, then I would say: We actually do precisely this. We make something as minor as a trace element, a half hour twice a week. That is hardly any broadcasting time for massive commercial television stations. If Minister President Stoiber of Bavaria then says he is terminating the federal state treaty because of a half hour of "SPIEGEL" television and our twenty-four-minute broadcasts, then it is clear that even a little bit of salt and pepper can cause an uproar when it fails to fit into the television landscape.

It is no different than were someone to carry out musealization intentionally on behalf of someone else as a productive form of memory and preservation work. Because it is not purely functional, this act would be effectively useless. This is an instance of archivalization and warehousing for some future use in some future place where the auspicious moment, "kairos," has arrived and ignites a productive spark.

Translated by Emma Woelk

Notes

This essay was originally published in German as Alexander Kluge, "Medialisieren—Musealisieren," *Zeitphänomen Musealisierung: Das Verschwinden der Gegenwart und die Konstruktion der Erinnerung*, ed. Wolfgang Zacharias et al. (Essen: Klartext, 1990), 31–39.

1. [Translator's note: Hermann Ludwig Heinrich von Pückler-Muskau (1785–1871) was a Saxon count promoted to prince by King Frederick William III of Prussia in 1822. A member of European high society, Pückler was a decorated lieutenant-general, landscape architect, world traveler, and travel writer.]

17

THE OPERA MACHINE

Power Station of Emotions

CHRISTIAN SCHULTE: *In your film* The Power of Emotion *you describe opera as a power station of emotions. You use this image to talk about the nineteenth century, while in the first half of the twentieth century film took on the role of mobilizing and connecting the masses.*

ALEXANDER KLUGE: I would not say that anymore today. If I may be allowed to break the question down according to how I see it in 2001, then I would say that an energy is being produced in small, highly radioactive ovens throughout this country, namely, in families. This fission of the mind that occurs in the form of parenting in nuclear families is capable of preserving a tremendous ability to surrender, concentrate, and conform.

In other words, it is capable of repeating the entire experience of alienation that shaped a people for 500 years over and over again in the process of child-rearing that transpires in a small unit akin to a coal-burning stove. These energies do not flow into a whole; they remain strangely ensnarled in individual families. For this reason, they wander over almost completely to the subjective side in human beings where they nourish the structures subtending the balance economy of fantasies and desires and where they shape emigrations that do not involve me moving even an inch. This societal energy produced in families in both the Balkans and highly industrialized societies builds a drain, say Max Horkheimer and Theodor W. Adorno, that feeds into funeral ceremonies with which societies celebrate their own barbarity. These include, for example, the Third Reich's party rallies, grand funeral processions, the light festivals, and the parades for the Day of German Art. The city of Munich was completely covered in black flags on the Day of German Art in 1939, as if the war had already been lost, as if everything had already been destroyed. This is one way of expressing this. The other way entails the veneration of saints in the Middle Ages, which was a celebration in which coffins were opened and people admired the fact that the hand of God had kept the bodies of the dead intact. They were covered with mold, and were thus like new.[1] Barring the event that war, big earthquakes, or catastrophes force humans to react and thus drain this subjective congestion, one possibility that would allow someone to express themselves extravagantly at the level of these small familial power stations of emotions is opera. This is because opera is especially grand and celebratory, and because it is recognized by the artistic community as the highest form of mimetic expression and meaning. In other words, musical theater, which the Greeks allegedly invented, has a unity of plot, and the tradition of opera arises out of a misunderstanding. This is an exaggerated and peace-loving way to assure yourself of the intensity of the emotions burning within the nuclear family.

CS: *And at the same time the opera takes a huge detour through its choice of artificial means . . .*

AK: . . . because civil war would otherwise break out in families. If the entire potential of a family's emotional faculty as well as its emotional congestion were expressed, then this would lead to manslaughter and murder. Insanity would ensue. Because this surplus of subjectivity is kept in sealed containers within families and dismantles itself either slowly by way of increased individualization over a period of hundreds of years or quickly in times of war, self-flagellation, and destruction, humans went looking for an instrument that accompanied bourgeois development in central Europe over 370 years. That instrument is the opera.

CS: *That would be opera's balancing function.*

AK: Yes. Opera is a power station of emotions in the rather extreme sense insofar as it vicariously carries out emotional waste removal without actually being the power station. The power is generated elsewhere. My film *The Power of Emotion* depicts a slightly abridged version of this. I honestly have to say that I did not analyze it properly.

CS: *It is nevertheless a strong image.*

AK: Yes. It is also true that you can basically warm yourself up using this opera machine capable of both removing waste and reducing temperature. When they momentarily rise to the surface, you can see that these heated emotions really exist, and this is exactly where opera makes its inspiring appearance. It is a little bit like the big world's fairs. The scene "Power Station of Emotions" in my film *The Power of Emotion* is precisely situated after a sequence that deals with world's fairs where commodities were displayed in a rather decentralized way. Every commodity had some small commodity value, a little flame, a commodity fetish that it carries within itself. This is the portion of the human imagination that makes this product a commodity and makes it exchangeable. It is always bound up with an idea found on Robinsonian islands all over the globe, namely, every individual good is discrete and can be bought or sold. Every decade there is a world's fair and commodities appear in their own temple. The Krupp cannons stand next to useful objects, while products made by indigenous peoples that nobody pays money for (because they are exchanged for glass beads) appear next to Chicago's manufacturing plants. Similarly, the community comprised of every recognized human emotion is put on display in the opera house. Obscene feelings do not make an appearance in the opera and the ignoble ones have a hard time even creeping in in small doses. Verdi achieves this, as it were, through old men who sing the bass and baritone parts. In the twentieth century, they find their place by way of Alban Berg's *Lulu* and make themselves felt through the inversion of the hero. But all this takes place in a kind of temple, says Adorno, barred from transcendence. Instead of ever reaching God, the audience will only attain the painted gods alluded to on the vaulted skies of the opera house. This is what the medium of opera allows for.

CS: *But that also means that the socially necessary balancing labor takes place in a hermetically sealed room . . .*

AK: . . . under artificial conditions that cannot be imitated by the audience. While Schiller's *Intrigue and Love* could still be performed by laymen if need be, an opera is much more difficult to recreate. The complete opposite is true for the so-called *Singspiel,* Emanuel Schikaneder's theater (for which Wolfgang Amadeus Mozart wrote the *Magic Flute*), and folk and popular art.[2] Opera distances itself from the popular insofar as opera searches for what is numinous, holy, and harrowing. What sends a shiver down the spine, the place where society reaches its limits, this is what opera looks for because it is a secret need for expression rooted in families.

CS: *Does opera then not also take on the function of an altar?*

AK: Something like that. On the other side of the coin is the novel, the confessional journal of the same emotional world. Therefore, the things that move *Effi Briest* and *Anna Karenina* and drive *Madame Bovary* so that her feet hurry up the stairs faster than her body can follow and eventually drive her to Paris, this world of desires and heightened drives is either fixed in a novel as in a container, or witnessed in public in the opera house.

Victim Logic

CS: *The opera is primarily defined through tragedy and fundamentally follows victim logic.*

AK: Yes, when watching opera, the audience mainly watches a victim. In almost every opera you can make out a victim somewhere. This is a ritual in opera. You can also find mourning that comes with sacrifice as well as consolation. In this respect, the original, seventeenth-century operas were cast from the same rigid mold, one that cannot be changed for entertainment's sake. Something irretrievable is lost: Orpheus loses Eurydice and nature mourns, the herdsmen mourn, the whole world mourns. And now the gods give him a chance to bring her back because they anticipate that he will turn around. He will not have the stamina of an immortal or an absurdly disciplined person to follow Apollo's rule, which has been impressed upon him only verbally. This means that he will lead this woman to the earth's surface without turning around and without assuring himself. This is where something fails, and it will be deeply mourned. This is the first bourgeois opera. The second big bourgeois opera is the *Return of Ulysses* also by Claudio Monteverdi. This is an opera that describes in the most fascinating way just how careful Ulysses must be. He knows the story of Agamemnon who is murdered after returning home, and he tries to transform his shape. The goddess disguises him, and he trusts no one. And thus he escapes the freemen's assassination attempts, and only in the end does his wife finally recognize him in disguise. She recognizes him because he knows something, namely, the embroidered decorations on the linens on their conjugal bed and the stories they tell. The moment he tells these stories is his actual homecoming. This is depicted using all the forms typical of a very simple music keenly attentive to the text. The brevity and laconism of this music is something that all of composer Wolfgang Rihm's idols possess today. In this respect, Rihm's opera *The Conquest of Mexico* as performed in 2001 and the operas by Monteverdi published in the middle of the seventeenth century are closely connected. You can play the final a cappella song between Montezuma and Cortez in *The Conquest of Mexico* and then follow it immediately with the final song from *The Coronation of Poppea*. This is the song in which Nero and Poppea comfort each other after a day that brought about much injustice in the hopes that they may be happy. If you do this as we actually did in one of our television programs, then you will notice that it is the same music. Monteverdi's is of course some 300 years ahead of its time compared to Rihm's completely modern music, but at the same time there is an inner affinity as if only one day passed between them.

CS: *Is that not also a form of mourning with respect to the genre of opera insofar as he assures himself of the origins of the genre?*

AK: That I do not know. The fact that Rihm affirms the origins of the genre and also an intermediate point in its development (you also find Verdi and above all Wagner in his work)—that he affirms all this and feels related to Luigi Nono points to a new form of ALLUSION, innuendo, a playful appropriation of something past in order to insert it into a new context. This sounds modern, but it has the force of something old. It is not based on the preconception that music moves linearly toward something higher thereby becoming more and more complex from Wagner to Strauss, for example, but rather that in reality music cycles through the centuries, always returns to elemental sources, and consistently needs differentiation. There are, for example, no opposites between high and low. I believe this is a democratization of tones by another means, something Rihm employs differently than Schoenberg.

CS: *This is something that depends on and acquires its authority from repetition and citation.*

AK: Exactly. Suppose a visitor from Sirius, an alien, arrives and asks us: What kind of strange tradition involves ruins in the middle of the city, buildings seldom visited that stand empty the whole day where people merely rehearse? These buildings are on the margins of industrial development, and there people sing. What are they doing there? What is opera? In this moment, the scales falls from their eyes that this excessiveness, this extreme, the way opera works, the so-called *impossible artwork*, has actually accompanied the development of the individual and what we call bourgeois society, and that all of the peaks of bourgeois development find an answer in opera. The burning of Magdeburg can be connected to Heinrich Schütz's *Dafne,* the first opera in the German language. Turning away from the war and National Socialism, Richard Strauss composed the opera *Capriccio* in 1944 in which he wrote about an operatic conflict between Nicolo Piccinni's Italian music school and Christoph Willibald Gluck that takes place right before the French Revolution.

Is the text subordinate to the music, or does music subordinate itself to the text? Who is serving whom? Meaning or movement? This was the debate conducted quite passionately in Paris.[3] It is interesting that a discussion about questions regarding art paved the way for the Revolution. In fact, the Revolution was better prepared for than it was fought. What we see here repeated itself faithfully in the development of Mao Tse-tung's Cultural Revolution, namely, conflict begins with questions about expression. For this reason, our habitual delineation of the aesthetic from life or the political is utterly wrong. It is an observable fact that all large political movements leave behind bad music. The chief composer of the French Revolution, Étienne Méhul, is mediocre. But at the same time you can say that they grapple with this, and that revolution is actually an attempt at expression—with the guillotine if necessary. If there had been more art, then the guillotine would not have been necessary. In the German nation, which refrained entirely from participating in the French Revolution but nevertheless observed and felt it like a spectator, there was good music. At bottom, you would have to explain clearly to the visitor from Sirius that the opera is a collection of mistakes, desires, hopes, and expressive needs that no society can invent, but rather necessarily guides its development in a manner of speaking. These opera houses are essentially part of a free market. At no point in the nineteenth century were they ever subsidized. They were supported only by the nobility. They are fundamentally a free enterprise and survive thanks to the fact that humans clearly feel the need to assemble in a secular-religious ceremony and to affirm a community based on the spirit of music.

Adorno, Opera, and Cinema

CS: *Adorno notes the similarity between opera houses built after 1945 and movie theaters. He makes this argument based on the fact that they no longer have loges. Is this a real point of departure for you?*[4]

AK: No, not at all. But I find the observation absolutely striking, because it conveys a portion of cinematic history. The movie theater is originally a standing room in New York, as Miriam Hansen describes it, where working-class immigrants who speak different languages and cannot communicate verbally reach agreements through pictures, indeed through their common reaction to pictures that they can all perceive equally.[5] Sound film does not disrupt this process. Thus, the basic form of cinema is a tremendous Babylonian din of reactions, a stock exchange of communications in relation to the relatively static, quiet pictures captured without sound. It makes no difference whether the film is accompanied by a piano player or not. This plebeian starting point of cinema is gradually undermined in the thirties by the introduction of first-row seats, stalls, loges, and balconies. Even now the contents of a film are subordinate to higher admission fees, and the seating arrangement organized according to class. In this respect, cinema imitates the opera house, or better plebeian opera houses and vaudeville theaters, the cheap imitations of opera. The theaters were democratized after 1945 because it was too expensive to pay for these balconies and loges, etc. It is not a principle of equality, but rather an increase in the number of moviegoers that led to democratization. And then the opera houses were rebuilt in the name of affordability in the style of movie theaters. The money was not there to rebuild them as they once were, unless you simply rebuilt an old national theater as they did in Munich. The cinema, after all, is now a stand-in for opera; it is transcendent in a different way, but it is still transcendent.

There are particles of time when it is dark in the movie theater. In a two-hour film, one hour is taken up by the projector's transport phase, and during this hour it is completely dark. A dragonfly would perceive this as both light and dark, but our human eye cannot see this and imagines that it is seeing something uninterrupted, and our brain takes a break to think about something of its own. I have the impression that transcendence in the cinema is technologically manufactured. During this pause an uptick in subjectivity reacts to the cinematic image such that I release just as much subjectivity in the movie theater as I have passively acquired from the screen. This is a highly active medium, different from television and dramatic theater, a genre to which opera also belongs. The triumphant procession of cinema is therefore probably the beginning of a new kind of human interaction.

CS: *This also fits with Adorno's observation that this is why film has materially surpassed the opera as a sensuous allurement, as a spectacle, but spiritually opera undercuts it.*

AK: That is correct.

CS: *He is probably also thinking of the plebeian origins of film.*

AK: Yes, but the plebeian origins do not necessarily undercut the opera. What first does this is the star system, a cinema organized and driven by the division of labor that lies in the hands of businesspeople. Every time something escapes marketeers (for example, when Rossellini and others began making films free of commercial managers during the upheaval in Italy in 1945) is a moment when a free cinema comes into being. This applies to the French New Wave and the twenty years during which we created the New German Cinema. The cinema that came out of America's East Coast, including Scorsese's work in New York, retained a similar independence and freedom. This is nothing other than the actual progression of film history. Everything else is just a form of captivity. Unlike the opera, there is no consensus about this new form that would allow us to suddenly recognize film quality in its entirety. Such consensus exists again and again but only for a

	short period of time. Museum directors and critics try it briefly, but there is never an agreement, while those things that are agreed upon, for example, suspense and Hitchcock films, are entirely artificial methods for captivating audiences from an earlier time. They require that I simply keep the viewers afraid and spellbound. Any Egyptian priest could do a far better job of this.
CS:	*In your television broadcasts primarily about opera you frequently have these two agents of illusion, film and opera, quoting each other and thereby effectively dismantle at each end of this spectrum a little bit of tragedy or suspense, if you will.*
AK:	The deconstructivism in my films is far more energetic than in operas. This does not make them popular, but the real stinger is that I really only like silent films in a movie theater where the audience can react and is not bound to sound or the realism typical of sound film. On the other hand, I find fascinating those aspects of a film's soundtrack reminiscent of radio plays. These are two details of film that fascinate me. Film as *Gesamtkunstwerk* is too long for me; I already know a film's plot after twenty minutes even though it surely contains surprises and fascinating bits. Of course, the censored canon of cinema, from the Hays Code to the schematic nature of love stories that paralyzes all films, is far worthier of being destroyed than most operas.

Translated by Tayler Kent

Notes

This essay was originally published in German as Alexander Kluge, "Die Opernmaschine," in *Facts & Fakes* 2/3: *Herzblut trifft Kunstblut, Erster Imaginärer Opernführer* (Berlin: Vorwerk 8, 2001), 36–42.

The six images included in the German original are not reproduced in the present translation.

1. See my *10 vor 11* broadcast "Der tote Körper spricht" [The Dead Body Speaks] of May 5, 2011: an analysis by Ulrike Sprenger of the RTL-2 television series *Autopsy*. Sprenger connects the audience's interest in the opening of coffins with the 500-year-old interest in opening the coffins belonging to potential saints. The coffins were opened with pomp. If it turned out that the corpse was completely intact because of either an infestation of mold or a lack of oxygen, then this was proof of God's work. Recently, the body of Pope John XXIII unveiled in its sarcophagus was amazingly intact. This fact now makes him eligible for canonization.

2. [Translator's note: Here Kluge refers to Emanuel Schikaneder, the librettist for Wolfgang Amadeus Mozart's *The Magic Flute*.]

3. [Translator's note: This is a reference to the Piccinni-Gluck debate, the subject of Richard Strauss's 1942 opera *Capriccio*.]

4. [Translator's citation: Theodor W. Adorno, *Introduction to the Sociology of Music*, trans. E. B. Ashton (New York: Seaburg Press, 1976), 79–80.]

5. [Translator's citation: Miriam Hansen, *Babel and Babylon: Spectatorship in American Silent Film* (Cambridge, MA: Harvard University Press, 1991).]

18

Primitive Diversity

On Early Short Films from the American East Coast, the Principle of Numbers, and "Primitive Diversity": The Concept of Minute Films

CHRISTIAN SCHULTE: *What does "primitive diversity" mean?*
ALEXANDER KLUGE: It is an expression from the American East Coast for early film. What D. W. Griffith and Thomas Edison did, that is *primitive diversity*: we care about everything. The assassination of President McKinley jolts us, and now, at every state fair, in Coney Island, and everywhere where films can be screened, we show how the assassin is executed on the electric chair. A moment later, we show the execution of an elephant in Coney Island. We show the most brutal images. We show how a group of bandits from the Wild West are caught and

shot by sheriffs. It is sheer cruelty and a curiosity on the part of the camera, but it sets itself in opposition to this brutality and sensationalism. These one- to two-minute films demonstrate the early form of cinema. *Pre-Hollywood cinema* is closely tied to the inventors of the film camera, who were also scientists. Primitive diversity encompasses the entire spectrum ranging from sensationalism, curiosity, and old greed to the abilities cameras themselves possess. These are strictly instructive and scientific, and without needing much consciousness incorporate forms of intelligence that are among the features of modernity. They are located deeper than the trained brain. They are antiacademic. This early cinema responds to the needs of migrant workers in the United States who come from many countries, are in need, and create their own public sphere themselves in the silent movies. Astonishment as means of knowledge—that is *primitive diversity.*

CS: *It is a need for attraction and distraction . . .*

AK: . . . and at the same time a deep attentiveness accumulated over the course of many generations. I let myself be amazed only by those things that really touch me.

CS: *Would there also be an investment in knowledge-constitutive interests beneath the need for attraction and emotional address by the new medium and its rapid succession of stimuli?*

AK: Or unintentional devotion. It has more to do with the capacity for love and the ability to be astonished than with great intentions. It is not the whole person who responds here, but rather parts of them that respond. The film is also assembled out of parts, and this particularization of the medium makes it possible for me to switch between close-ups and long shots. Not only can I do this out of deceit, but I can also use it for astonishment and attraction in the sense that a gravitational bond is formed between what affects human beings and the medium. This is a rare case. As soon as a producer interferes, he will absorb this bond, simplify its contradictions, and wish to maximize it. This is the moment when this effect, this "intimate" bond between the naive spectator and a naive, newly invented medium, is broken.

CS: *Different forms of attention that arose in completely different locations gather in one place and . . .*

AK: . . . confirm each other. They encourage each other. There is a certain audacity therein. And this audacity is, in turn, what counts in a *primitive diversity* film by Griffith and Edison along with their calculations as the sign of victory. A cowardly film is the only thing that must be avoided.

CS: *What would that be, a cowardly film?*

AK: Commercialism is a cowardly form that manipulates the audience. There is an audacious form of cinema that trusts the audience to know more and to have greater pleasure than we assume.

CS: *How long did primitive diversity exist?*

AK: Until about 1916. The gorgeous film *Intolerance* by Griffith is *primitive diversity*.

CS: *In 1907, censorship was imposed in the United States to tackle the new medium's moral unsoundness.*

AK: Censorship is basically the extension of Marcel Reich-Ranicki's concept of novels by different means: the school essay controlled by the teacher.[1] I may not express myself spontaneously, but rather I should express myself meaningfully and for higher purposes. But alongside all this hunger for meaning, there is also a need for liberation from the compulsion for meaning. In the eighth sequence from

	my broadcast "The Eiffel Tower, King Kong, and the White Woman," you see minute films by the Lumière brothers.[2] They started exporting them in 1894 from Paris to Budapest. They came every year and brought, for instance, Edison's *Niagara Falls*. In other words, they transport to Budapest via Paris a location that you could otherwise experience only as a tourist. *Traffic in Front of the Opera House in Paris*, spring 1896, a snapshot in time. It contains no peculiar pathos, plot, or excessive event, but the metropolis Paris greets Budapest. I am, so to speak, ubiquitous. That is the first model for what television could actually do. *Launch of an Ocean Steamer*: it is quite sensational when a gigantic steamship slides on rails into the water. In 1897, catastrophe is not yet contained therein. In 1912, you know the consequence of a launch can be the catastrophe of the *Titanic*. The dramaturgy for this does not exist yet. That is *European primitive diversity*. And a *Swimming Contest on Horses*, there are heavily armed officers on horses, Hungarian Uhlans, who do not, however, play war, but rather splash in the water. The tools of war move playfully, and this makes for pleasure in the movie theater.
CS:	*And anticipates Marshall McLuhan's diagnosis of the* global village . . .
AK:	Because it is enjoyable to stroll around the planet visually without marching too much. That is the first form of *primitive diversity* film in Europe. And the second fantastic form is developed by Georges Méliès.
CS:	*These would be the attractions of fantasy?*
AK:	And they are as real as the launch of an ocean steamship, which is actually also something unreal.
CS:	*Over and over again in your work, you return to these two roots or, as the case may be,*

	principles of film history, which are more or less varied over the course of their progress.
AK:	There are more than just two roots. The first root is the scientific interest that coincides with the invention of the camera. One wanted to know: Does a running horse touch the ground with all four legs at the same time, is it at all capable of doing this, or is it capable of raising all four at the same time, is it capable of flying? That is a scientifically relevant question, and something I can base a bet on. That is the primary school of cinema. The secondary school is the documentary school of the Lumière brothers. The third school is Méliès. And the fourth is the *primitive diversity* movement in the early cinema of the American East Coast, captivating and unsurpassed by anything in Europe. These are my idols. I would like to maintain a free space in television for films. That was the purpose of the minute film magazines, because these elements of film do not tolerate hyperconstructions.[3] When you create hyperconstructions, you have to mix them, otherwise you cannot convey them. In the aggregate, it is no longer clear what kind of charm they have.
CS:	*These forms lead to a tremendous break from traditionally practiced forms of art reception, as described by Benjamin using his concepts of contemplation and collection.*
AK:	Initially, contemplation remains alien to cinema, which is related to sensation. It does, however, exist as a medium of a particular kind of surprise. That would be a fifth movement that covers the complete history of film: these moments when a film describes silence like a Japanese haiku poem and then comes to rest. You can find this in François Truffaut, Jean-Luc Godard, Roberto Rossellini, and Michelangelo Antonioni; these are, so to speak, the

	sacred zones of film. Every skillful commercial producer would cut them out.
CS:	*Or shortened to such an extreme degree that they make way for a new suspense.*
AK:	Absolutely. They get functionalized. Compared to Robert Musil, Reich-Ranicki is a highly amusing, on point, and pedagogically interested man, but he would cut out every form of poetry, claiming it is without a connection. Musil is the author of that famous scene in *The Man without Qualities*, the novel Reich-Ranicki executed in *Der Spiegel*, where nothing happens except for blossoms that fall onto grass from the summer sky above. That is the most marvelous literary passage I know. I once wanted to build a film around just this scene. It would have been a film that—the year was 1985—dealt with Stasi activities in the capital of the Federal Republic, Bonn, and so on, meaning with real espionage activities, which are at base unable to convey what is embedded in this kind of scene.
CS:	*According to what criteria does someone like Reich-Ranicki, whose conception of art certainly has a certain following, pass his judgments?*
AK:	According to the criteria of classification. And this is, after all, fitting for long stretches. This would be entirely suitable for road traffic, for instance. It is also fitting in order to protect industrial facilities against sabotage. It fails to be attractive in poetry only because the cinematic or poetic core is not functional.
CS:	*Because it is located beyond the realm of purpose?*
AK:	It is entirely without purpose.
CS:	*When you talk about the concept of minute films, you talk about an emotion at the beginning of film history. What is this emotion made of?*

AK: This emotion begins as the filmmakers' astonishment at what they accomplish, that they can in fact perform magic in the way Méliès did. Such as when a person enters one half of the frame and comes into an environment that would be quite improbable for him. This is repeated in contemporary film when a protagonist is suddenly confronted by President Kennedy and shakes his hands in front of the blue box. This ability to astonish oneself and then to unleash this astonishment in the audience, this is the key aspect from the start that constitutes the beginning of film. This involves a unification of opposites that otherwise only existed in music and is now reenacted in film.

CS: *And mimetic, too, since it is also an emotion that is already firmly rooted in the rest of the audience's lifeworld and its horizon of experience?*

AK: Otherwise it would not work. I can only be surprised by something I suddenly recognize, but yet have always known. The reason for my minute magazines is that you can practically realize purity only in basic lengths. Ninety minutes will always lead to impoverishment or, in other words, a planned economy where information is attainable only in exchange for vouchers. It would not be satisfied were I to develop large constructs while worrying about being frugal. And frugality means applying the elemental and authentic, which are simple unto themselves, to large constructs. Bread and water for a whole society is rather inhumane. Bread and water unto themselves comprise an element and are something quite pleasant. I think that in the year 1988 the short form of the minute film can present a new beginning for music, images, words, sense, and nonsense. For instance, "What sort of nonsense is he up to?" does not have to do with sense.[4]

I can realize every element purely when I limit myself to one concrete minute. Were I now to create the opposite, I would not try this in the ninety minutes typical of a feature film or a drama, but rather I would immediately extend it to six hours and say: Now there is the polarity in which this new simplicity, an overview, emerges out of a bulk of relations. For this I need two, four, six, eight, or ten hours or even a week. These would be the other formats. And this polarity is actually at the heart of DCTP's culture magazines.[5] On the one hand, you trust intensity, and this has to do with momentary impressions. The more intensely I wish to present something, the more suitable one or two minutes are. On the other hand, the more extensive and synoptic I wish to present something, the longer the programming's relationalities need to be. Long focal lengths correspond to filmic brevity.

CS: *Let us look at the ninth section from your broadcast "The Eiffel Tower, King Kong, and the White Woman." In this sequence, you see the head and neck of a dinosaur, his jaws are wide open and reveal sharp teeth. This follows a series of early films by the Lumière brothers.*

AK: It is accompanied by waltzes that stem from this period. These are actually Czech waltzes that were surely played in Budapest at the time when the films by Lumière would have been shown there. And now you have varied what in a single moment is real. The Lumière brothers try to transport snapshots across the country, a piece of Paris to Budapest. With *Workers Leaving the Factory* or the famous scene in *Arrival of a Train* they honor the moment. But they do not actually understand what a moment truly is. When a dinosaur no longer alive in our own time emerges from the sea, looks at us for a brief moment while the audience looks back,

CS:

AK:

and then dives under again: that is a moment, one in fact that tends toward the improbable. It is no invention. Why should these early creatures that reside within us and form a part of our brains and bodies—we are after all their descendants—not be able to look at us for a moment? If they are temporally removed from us by some 60 million years, then a moment of their time and a moment of our time are like cousins. When you understand that, then you have a reason to keep playing.

After that you see a flying dinosaur and then a Heidegger quote from Being and Time: *"Why do we say that* time *passes away, when we do not say with* just as much *emphasis that it arises?"*[6] *This seems like a commentary, although it stands rather loosely next to these fantastic images, this retrospective into our prehistory.*

That is just the way it is. Even though the Eiffel Tower still stands in Paris, it has the potential to be abducted or for the swastika flag to be raised over it. That is just how IMPROBABLE-TRUTHFUL it is that some otherworldly wizards have abducted it, and that it now stands straddling the Grand Canyon on the Colorado River.[7] It is no less unnatural and alienating that someone traps a great ape of extraordinary strength in an African well and transports him across the Atlantic. According to the legend, he almost destroyed the ship out of rage. He is then displayed as a circus creature, but this not in his nature. He is a powerful creature. In the end, he stands at the top of the highest tower in New York and defends himself against government airplanes that attack him for reasons unclear to us. What kind of system is this that attacks him while he protects this white woman? What is this white woman? She does not exist within the linear narrative.

CS:	*What relation do the wild Other and the domesticated Self assume here?*
AK:	This is something I know as little about as you do. I marvel at the images that movies have invented. If you assemble everything we fail to understand in film, then you would have experienced from film history more than were you to explain its contents.
CS:	*The white woman is protected by the great ape. This is a topos repeated with superheroes. Spiderman protects a woman, too.*
AK:	It is the topos of a dust-covered woman who wanders through ruins, who then obviously falls victim to alcohol, who cannot live with the fame for supposedly having survived doom. They are all elements we do not really understand. We will not understand King Kong, we will not understand why the government airplanes have to attack him like this, we will be left to wonder what this white woman is. Heiner Müller can tell me more about this, and he is not inclined to talk in an unambiguous style.
CS:	*The fear of the uncanny that emanates from a vampire like Dracula is usually projected onto female flight instincts. Why is it that what is worthy of protection is always marked female?*
AK:	Parzival's strong mother, who, for instance, plays an important role in a poem by Heiner Müller, watches her son and turns him into a fool so that he will not become a knight. In this respect, the feminine can also be the protecting force. The distribution of roles that gained acceptance in film history is not one of its strengths. Its strength is what it does without being aware of it. There is a *cinematic unconscious*.
CS:	*The Heidegger quote in the film is accompanied by an explosion of thunderclaps. You see thunderbolts, a diffuse light, an uncanny*

atmosphere. Why is this thought that time is something transitory, something we work our way through, more familiar to us than the idea that it emerges, that it forms the future?

AK: In this context, Heidegger draws on Heraclitus, who says: "One thunderbolt strikes root through everything."⁸ In the classical world, the most powerful god always appears as a thunderbolt. So you have the image of a calm time, but you can perceive it only if you simultaneously perceive the thunderbolt. Now let us go from Heidegger to the year 1941 when on the American West Coast Japanese submarines are approaching, where battleships that just threatened Honolulu are headed. There is a story I know from Max Horkheimer who lived in Los Angeles back then. He vividly recalls how the city's electricity was cut off and how at night the town was plunged into darkness as a camouflage against Japan and a blitz. On Mount Wilson, the astronomer Walter Baade takes advantage of the city's blackout. He discovers that the galaxies are twice as far away as one had thought until then, and that they keep moving farther away. That is a six-page story in my book *Chronik der Gefühle* [Chronicle of Feelings].⁹ I believe, however, that it has an equivalent in the human soul, though it is only touched upon in cinematic images. An enemy approaches, I disguise myself, and in this very moment I experience something. This is all about unintentionality.

CS: *The universe or the starry sky would be a cipher for that?*

AK: For instance. At the very least, it is removed from my intentions. When I perceive something that is distant from me, it results in a surprise. In the same way I can use a long shot to shoot something in a film in its entirety and then surprisingly transition to a close-up, so, too, can I juxtapose topics to one another in surprising ways: the year 1941, the starry sky, dinosaurs, or King Kong, who all of a sudden has a son, and so forth.

CS: *The scene on the ship, in which a man in a white tuxedo stands at the railing and smokes, fascinated me. The picture of the monkey is collaged on top of his face. This internal montage creates a peculiar cross-fade effect that moves from civilization to an archaism entirely unexpected on a ship.*

AK: That is a scene from a Hollywood movie with Bob Hope. The monkey's face invented in 1933 is not archaic for me, but rather the highest embodiment of a star. After September 11, 2001, you will need to invent it a couple more times anew. I could also take a yeti and insert it there because it, too, is omnipresent. For film, there are actually no differences between moments. A camera records 1/24 of a second and in doing so it can jump across all sorts of times.

In this respect, a human being is at once a camera, a projection, and a darkened theater full of pauses. Cinema is precisely this. In other words, the cinema is a unique replication of human characteristics. In contrast to the television screen, which is a mere window, cinema is a genuine answer that replicates human methods of perception more accurately than any panorama, *laterna magica*, or photograph ever did.

Translated by Sandra Niethardt

Notes

This dialogue was originally published in German as Alexander Kluge, "Primitive Diversity," in *Facts & Fakes* 4: *Der Eiffelturm, King Kong und die weiße Frau* (Berlin: Vorwerk 8, 2002), 26–31.

The one image included in the German original is not reproduced in the present translation.

1. [Translator's note and citation: Marcel Reich-Ranicki (1920–2013) was one of the most prominent West German literary critics of the postwar and postunification periods. Kluge is very likely referring to Marcel Reich-Ranicki, *Romane von gestern, heute gelesen*, 3 vols. (Frankfurt am Main: S. Fischer, 1996).]

2. [Translator's citation: Kluge is referring here to one of his first broadcasts on German cable television that premiered on the station RTL on December 26, 1988. See Alexander Kluge, "Der Eifelturm, King Kong, und die weiße Frau," *Seen sind für Fische Inseln: Fernseharbeiten 1987–2008* (Frankfurt am Main: Zweitausendeins, 2007), DVD 1, track 3. For the transcript of the broadcast, see Alexander Kluge, "Der Eifelturm, King Kong, und die weiße Frau: Minutenfilm-Magazin," *Facts & Fakes* 4: *Der Eifelturm, King Kong und die weiße Frau* (Berlin: Vorwerk 8, 2002), 6–24.]

3. [Translator's note: Kluge is referring here to a series of one-minute films he started making in 1996 at the behest of curator Hans Ulrich Obrist. Originally shown on Swedish television, and immediately thereafter projected onto skyscrapers in Seoul, Korea, this series of minute films were projected in Dutch architect Rem Koolhaas's 2006 pavilion at London's Serpentine Gallery, four years after the publication of this interview. The minute films from London can be seen in Alexander Kluge, "Serpentine Gallery Program," *Sämtliche Filme* (Frankfurt am Main: Zweitausendeins, 2007), DVD 14, track 2.]

4. [Translator's note: This is a line from a nursery rhyme by Heinrich Hoffmann, nineteenth-century psychiatrist and author of the children's book *Struwwelpeter*. Kluge uses this in his 1974 collaboration with Edgar Reitz, *In Danger and Deep Distress, the Middleway Spells Certain Death*.]

5. [Translator's note: DCTP stands for Development Company for Television Program, which has been Kluge's headquarters in Düsseldorf for his television broadcasts on the cable television stations RTL, Sat1, and VOX from 1988 to 2018.]

6. [Translator's citation: Martin Heidegger, *Being and Time*, trans. J. Macquarrie and E. Robinson (New York: Harper & Row, 1962), 425.]

7. [Translator's note: Kluge refers here to Heinrich von Kleist's anecdote "Unwahrscheinliche Wahrhaftigkeiten," usually translated as "Improbable Veracities."]

8. [Translator's citation: Heraclitus, *Fragments: The Collected Wisdom of Heraclitus*, trans. Brooks Haxton (New York: Viking, 2001), 19.]

9. [Translator's citation: Alexander Kluge, "Verdunkelung in Los Angeles," in *Chronik der Gefühle*, vol. 1, *Basisgeschichten* (Frankfurt am Main: Suhrkamp, 2000), 866–71.]

19

PLANTING GARDENS IN THE DATA TSUNAMI

While the Internet floods us with its overwhelming mass of information, it evokes a counterreaction at the same time: we tend to dismiss everything that is superfluous and unimportant to us. According to filmmaker and author Alexander Kluge, this reaction presents us with a new form of intelligence, and it also poses a challenge to art.

UWE EBBINGHAUS: *Do you use the Internet?*
ALEXANDER KLUGE: When I start working on a new project, the first phase for me and my team is actually what I would call "scouting." We first need to identify and collect the raw material. In order to do so, we use the Internet.
UE: *The available materials are nowadays of course a lot richer than they were in the past.*

AK: Certainly. And the mechanism I use to sort through the material has become more complex, too. Since the advent of the Internet, I am able to orient myself much more quickly. It has become easier for me to dismiss everything not relevant to me. I spend the same amount of energy deleting stuff as I do collecting it. It was different when you used a card catalogue. With a catalogue, you spent energy preserving something and you kept things for a reason. It was therefore a lot harder to discard things. I believe people react to the Internet in two distinct ways. On the one hand, they are surprised by the tsunami of information that barrels down at them from the Web. They are overwhelmed. However, in that very same moment a counterreaction is elicited. Allow me to explain this using an allegory Dirk Baecker once told me: when Gutenberg invented the printing press, central Europe was flooded with pamphlets. Most of them dealt with religious topics, or they tried to incite civil war. These pamphlets were a highly ideological mass of letters plagued by errors. This development triggered a countermovement that gave rise to critique. This movement led to Immanuel Kant who does nothing other than to differentiate the things we can know from the things that we cannot know.

UE: *Would you say that young people who have grown up with the Internet exhibit a different reaction?*

AK: This is not the case as far as I can tell. I have two children, and I have also watched other young people using computers. There is, for example, a significant age difference between my coworkers and myself, and my experience has been that they are better at protecting themselves from the flood of data. In the midst of the Web's antinature, they have developed what is clearly a defense mechanism. For every 20 lines they read, they dismiss 800, and all of this happens very quickly. The speed by which they discard information is greater than the chance this mass of material could influence them. When I was a high school student, for example, I did not have this ability.

UE: *How has the Internet changed your thinking?*

AK: The Internet has strengthened my thinking in a very specific way, insofar as I have always been concerned with networks: my literary works and films form webs as well. I would therefore not speak of "change" in my case. For young people, however, there is a new form of intelligence emerging, just as there is also a new medium emerging, a medium that is not identical with the Internet, for it incorporates and links together television, the classical public sphere, and the book. There is a new longing for sustainability and a longing for a new "hortus conclusus," a walled-off garden. This no longer has anything to do with the desire to surf. It is difficult to survive on the open ocean as a surfer. Rather, a heightened interest in boundaries and containers has emerged. This is art's new calling. Art will connect everything that opera, oil paintings, and literary texts once accomplished on their own by rearranging the material according to a constellative dramaturgy that obeys nonvisible forces. You can see the beginnings of this dramaturgy in Ovid. He tells 1,200 stories, and they all have the same plot: a suffering creature changes its form. A single thought undergoes every possible permutation, and as a result the whole universe is depicted. We can also find a similar phenomenon in Honoré de Balzac's writing. He explicitly talks about constellations not only within one novel, but rather constellations that span several novels and orbit and influence each other. This concept has made its way into modernity via Alfred Döblin and John Dos Passos. Even though we already know it from Ovid and Balzac, his new dramaturgy is now rendered stronger by new demands from the future, namely, YouTube. Film history provides us with a malleable example. In the beginning there were only one-minute films that could be added together. Nowadays, we have the exact same phenomenon with YouTube, where you can also find films that are between one and three minutes in length. The new challenge for art then is to create beacons of light, harbors, and rafts. YouTube cannot meet this challenge, for YouTube is a jungle and an open ocean, for that matter. One of our new artistic tasks is to redefine the containers. They will radically change: it is not my thinking that is changing, but rather the physical world in which it is expressed.

UE: *Is it not odd that the most successful sites on the Internet do the very opposite?*

AK: The mass of facts that we find, for example, on *Spiegel online*, push us through the week. Just as Central Park, a place of solitude, is located right next to the business district in New York City, you can plant gardens on the Web right in the middle of the rubble of data (rather than doing so at an academy or in nirvana). The only way to acknowledge data's right to exist is to save it from itself by keeping it in an enclosed, tamed space. A garden is the antipode to a jungle.

I have great respect for first nature (Immanuel Kant speaks of its transcendence), which I experience while looking at the stars, for example. That is not the same as the sphere of human life. I love English gardens. Take one of Prince Pückler's gardens, for example, or the one where Lady Di is buried: they look like nature, even though they are examples of man-made second nature.¹ To me, they evoke a sense of comfort. I cannot express this impression any other way. It is on this level that new things grow today.

UE: *That reminds me of Voltaire's Enlightenment satire* Candide. *In the face of chaos in the world and deflated optimism, the only thing that remains is the task of cultivating a garden.*

AK: Exactly. We are trying to cultivate this kind of garden on our Internet domain www.dctp.tv. We show there numerous loops containing roughly twelve films each that speak and react to each other, and that deal, for example, with the cosmos, love, or the Latinate Middle Ages. Stories from this period like the ones by Caesarius von Heisterbach, for example, are some of the most beautiful stories I know. It fills me with delight to bring these stories into contact with our present. I would put it this way: it is not the stream of data that is real, but rather Caesarius von Heisterbach.

UE: *Is this a program in its own right, or is it mainly to counter the Internet?*

AK: Alongside the reality of data, there is a second reality, and this one we control. While we cannot create utopia, a nonplace, we can work toward an enclave, a heterotopia. The lifetime of a human being is limited, whereas the Internet will probably still be around in a thousand years. The machines will effortlessly outlive us. Behind all the data on the Internet, there are facts and they are significantly more obscure than the Internet can ever be. In this respect, the Internet is only symbolic of an overpowering facticity that we have been trying to defend ourselves against ever since Verdun in 1916. The abundance of the objective is not a new perception. What is new, however, is the fact that you experience the whole thing with so many other participants. Given the fact that the number of online participants is so sensational, a connection between humans is now possible via the Internet that is almost as strong as the increase in the representation of the objective. We do not need to be afraid of the Internet. Part of the idea of a garden is that you know ways out. Think about the myth of Jason and Medea. Jason, along with fifty young heroes, steals the Golden Fleece. The locations of treasures and escape routes by sea were recorded on the back of this animal hide. This is what he was after. However, these treasures are not located in places that can be found using GPS. Instead, they have to do with my motives, where I come from and where I want to go. From this we can infer the following challenge: we must counter the infinite wisdom of GPS with subjective maps. You can observe the Internet according to this very same schema.

Translated by Steffen Kaupp

Notes

This dialogue was originally published in German as Uwe Ebbinghaus, "Gärten anlegen im Daten-Tsunami," *Frankfurt Allgemeine Zeitung*, January 14, 2010, 24.

1. [Translator's note: On Pückler, see note 1 in chapter 16 in this volume.]

Part V

Theory

20

The Role of Fantasy

The Concept of Labor

PARTICIPANT: *I would like to hear a short explanation of the word "fantasy" because the expression is a tad irrational.*

ALEXANDER KLUGE: You see fantasy is a divided product in our society. Let us look for a moment at what Marx has to say about the original concept of labor.

He mentions it twice, for example, when he explains that a craftsman, when making something like a chair, first forms an image of the chair in his mind and makes a plan before then setting to work with his hands to make this plan a reality. Here we have a unified path of labor between the activity of the mind and the activity of the hands. I will leave it at that. There are other passages as well.

P: *The image of the chair ... he has to have that in his mind first.*

AK: Exactly, that image was made beforehand by society, and he has to take it from his own mind. In this respect, the concept of labor is never individualistic, but rather *always a reflection of collective need*, right down to the plans that guide what the craftsman does with his hands. So the whole development of the human mind under the influence of the hands and the emergence of the hands themselves are already social productions.

I do not want to overstate things, but Marx never said that this comprehensive conception of labor never existed. He left that question unanswered. It could be that something like that once existed under the ancient matriarchies, in paradise, or with Adam and Eve.

It is difficult to imagine the existence of horticultural societies without there having been some original concept of labor in which the labor of mind and hand was identical. But we do not know about this. For him, it is merely an idea projected into the future that people might someday be able to reunify their disrupted, divided, and fragmented labor. It is there where he develops this concept.

If only we could someday agree on a concept of human labor in which head and mind cooperate with one another and are identical.

But for now, manual labor is both alienated and dismantled into separate, individual channels. If these channels are in line with Taylorism—in other words, if labor is emptied of all its sense and purpose, and moves purely mechanically as Chaplin depicted it in several of his films—then you end up with the actual dismemberment of manual labor. I do not need to go into that now. I bring it up simply as a parallel.

But the labor of the mind is no less dismembered. To begin with, rationality and educated thought—as defined by schooling, occupational experience and requirements, and specific intelligence and expertise—are also delineated, used separately, forced to progress prematurely and to specialize. Beneath this lies another force, one that is much more widespread in people. This is the imaginative capacity.

Organization of Fantasy

AK: Sigmund Freud described this *imaginative capacity*, by the way, not only in terms of psychoanalytic theory or out of a specific therapeutic interest. Rather, he described it and pursued it on account of a general theoretical interest. He said that the law of this imaginative capacity exists in people. It is the law of the human mind. He said not only that it is influenced by libidinal control and the negotiation of reality (such that the human mind is always under two influences), but also that the brain triggers the perception of actual circumstance and then remembers something from the past, a conflict, a desired situation, or a wish.

From there, a projection of a concrete action is cast onto the future. So if some law of motion can be said to underlie this trinity of present, past, and future—assuming we can imagine such a law—then that is precisely what I mean when I talk about the imaginative capacity. By this I mean the free, self-regulated unfurling of the kind of mental activity that, as I have said, can certainly be separated from action. It separates neither from the past nor from what a person is, their circumstances, or their actions. But society breaks down this imaginative capacity. The types useful in the labor process or the reproductive process in our free time are stabilized and organized by one's upbringing, but according to the standards of dominant society.

Everything that thereby escapes the imaginative capacity is then identified as "fantasy" in the narrow sense of the word, as something altogether gypsy-like or bohemian (which cannot be trusted and can be found in the so-called ghetto of art), or as something largely repressed (which accompanies us every day as the sentimental, the kitschy, the dreamlike). Everyone has it, but it does not really count: it is the gypsy beneath sensory perceptions.

Due to defamation and suppression, these forces are organized on a different level. Their organization is not based on the standards of advanced industry or the educational system, and it cannot be connected with the technical code of rationality that governs society.

But humans conduct all of the investigations they sustain throughout the year through this hybrid, this gray area between unconsciousness and consciousness. Humans supply the entire libidinal structure of economic demand and its regulation as unpaid labor, and this compensates for conditions that would otherwise be intolerable. Then fantasy forms a kind of buffer, presenting us with a daydream that allows us to tolerate these conditions.

Fantasy and Domination

AK: I would like to overstate something again. As part of the mechanism of domination, fantasy and the imaginative capacity can manifest themselves, for example, as the fear that arises when simply walking away from work, the fear of running away from school, the fear of resisting—in other words, as a constraint, the imagined consequences of doing something other than merely obeying.

In imagined fear of persecution and abandonment, etc., we see the so-called imaginative capacity bound up in the mechanism of domination. This, too, is fantasy. The fantasy that someone is brave. Someone who sets out to learn fear lacks this imaginative capacity; he is simply bereft of it. Richard Wagner's Siegfried has this deficiency of imaginative capacity. He has no fantasy, at least not at this point.

This is *bound up in the hegemony*, so to speak, and an aspect of it. Another portion of the same energy, the same imaginative capacity, is departmentalized, shut out from the hegemony, and excluded from the technical imprisonment of society. And this we call fantasy.

The fact that you rightly say this is totally unclear and seems almost mystical, and so on, this is simply because it is excluded, shut out from the official communication that is really valid, and removed from the technical imprisonment of society as it currently functions. It only emerges, as it were, in private and unorganized form. It is something that humans talk about, as it were, only in pauses and only sometimes allow themselves momentary glimpses of, even though they conform to it. This is even less organized and therefore appears mystical, even though an enormous amount of energy lies behind it.

Now the following happens. These characteristics are shoved underground and organized by the Right. The difference between Weimar hegemony and National Socialism is nothing other than the appropriation of this left-wing energy by the Right.

This imaginative capacity that is then appropriated leads to utopian fantasies: if only we had conquered the Urals and then sent a few divisions to India, if only Erwin Rommel had taken the Suez Canal and then pressed on toward Iraq, then the Panzer Division General Max Roth would break through the Caucasus to the south, then we would have oil and then we would reach Japan and could have attacked the USA in a pincer movement. In other words, the whole fantasy about everyone who wore the Iron Cross getting a manor in the East, all being Aryan again, returning to where we came from, life beginning anew.

A highly industrialized society idealizes an image of a bunch of farmsteads with cozy houses where polyamory is possible; where people have slaves again; and where they can think about sleeping with these slaves even though, to be clear, any sexual intercourse with Jews is forbidden and would also certainly be discouraged with the other repressed peoples.

Although such a war is conducted according to the rules of a prison administration with its intense discipline and highly industrialized background, fantasies run wild as though the National Socialists see this as a liberation toward the past. As professional materialist opportunists, they have taken hold of a material force that bourgeois society had previously written off as impractical and useless for its enterprises.

Having noticed since 1929 that the economic enterprise has not been functioning, they find it necessary to transform economic contradictions into the political realm, where they need a piece of this repressed fantasy that is finally incorporated.

However, it cannot be as nicely exploited as the fantasies already utilized in the economic realm. This represents the irrational moment in the National Socialists' fantasies, that neither an Adolf Hitler nor a Heinrich Himmler nor an SA leader, Ernst Roehm, holds sway over.

This means that seeing how something turns out, in order to see what comes next, where the masses are moving to, can be done only if the top is spinning very fast, only if it never occurs to the masses where it is all headed, because the moment they start insisting on these fantasies, the whole experiment would be called into question. This is a very complex political relationality. I simply wanted to show you the political relevance of all of this. It is no less relevant now and not just because of Springer Verlag.[1] I can instead point to simpler forms by saying that this energy, this activity of making fantasies, which happens below the threshold and has not yet been taken up by the normal processes of production, is in fact understood by the Right, by which I mean not only the political Right, but also the economic system that exercises dominance over everything.

For example, media conglomerates certainly understand fantasy's subliminal quality, though this is not what Springer or Bauer Verlag is doing right now. Instead, it will be integrated firms with integrated technologies that do not just deliver individual products that consumers believe they have freely chosen but rather distribute a concentrate, offerings you find in big department stores, as it were.

P: *For the sake of systemization, I would still appreciate it if . . .*

AK: I am afraid that it simply cannot be done. If, for example, you take energy that has been bound up in the relations of domination as fantasy and then free that energy from the hegemony, then you would be able to see exactly how something that had previously existed as fear suddenly raises hell in another context.

In other words, the same energy changes form depending on the relationality. In a bourgeois public sphere, it might look one way, but in a proletarian one it would be different. It looks one way in the context of a factory, and another way in the context of a wildcat strike. In one organizational form, for example, it functions as the brakes, and in the revolutionary context it functions as an engine.

It is, however, not actually a different energy. Indeed, they are quite similar. You probably are familiar with the same problem in psychoanalysis. This is why you cannot say that they should have two different names.

P: *I do not think that I expressed myself very clearly . . .*

AK: I certainly agree, and perhaps we can find a different name that differentiates between the two products. But they remain in a constant state of motion that has, for example, crystallized into a domination of the imaginative capacity. Take, for example, the strong belief in Hindenburg, Adenauer, or Brandt. This is something that also finds itself in constant motion. It never stays still.

Consider the following example: if the workers (meaning maybe a few million) in the Weimar Republic vote for the KPD and then after 1933 join the SA, then there has been no change in energy, and we also cannot say that the product (what an individual person does) is fundamentally different, but rather it appears to be different in a different relationality.

Perception and Development

AK: Let us start with an example: a friend of mine, the director Günther Hörmann, goes to observe a factory in operation. A worker is busy welding in an extremely hot environment, doing work that is physically unbearable, and tells him that he is content. He has simply been able to balance this experience with the help of his imaginative capacity and to reimagine his situation by creating a mental picture. He dreamed something up. He does not create a mental picture of what he is doing, but rather one that alleviated its strain.

In a different situation, he was angry with his foreman. This time, he is working somewhere else where the work is quite agreeable. It is just that he had a spat with this foreman. He described that situation as wholly unbearable. The same worker usually reads the *Bild* newspaper.

At the same time as workers at this factory were on a wildcat strike, he participated in a public burning of the *Bild* newspaper. I cannot claim (observations would refute my position) that this man was any different; that he did not have the same energy, so to speak; that he really actually produced something psychically different, because he did not really change during the brief period of the wildcat strike. The potential always existed for what he did; it could not have developed in two days. We must simply say that these different utterances and characteristics live in him, and depending on the situation, they sometimes fall apart or come together, creating different figures. From this, we can conclude that all questions regarding the aesthetic organization of perception as well as those of political organization cannot consider humans as being something whole. Organization must not count off heads and must also reject, for example, the perception that human beings are whole beings.[2] Individual characteristics exist that have developed differently in society. There are also certain characteristics that have not taken part in the societal development of the last couple of years. There are some that have been forced to grow prematurely because they are either needed in the labor process or have formed a resistance to it. And there are those that are somewhere in the middle.

For the history of this development, we must view each of these characteristics as a question of organization. This is much more concrete than what a cadre party does, for example. And we might say that this adjustment is essential for questions of both materialistic aesthetics and political organization. The failure of certain abstract forms of the labor movement is due in part to the fact that this materialist analysis does not look at the truly fundamental elements.

We—Oskar Negt and I—have taken our cues for this hypothesis from Marx, who said that in practice the individual senses are like little theoreticians. What he is suggesting here—the idea that within people there are groups of other smaller, partial people not unlike a Russian nesting doll—is indeed very interesting.

This places the source of the theory in the individual senses and not in the mind as a whole, which (according to his theory) forms a kind of counterweight to the immense collection of commodities produced by fragmented capitalist production. It cannot, in fact, be any other way—why would human characteristics develop any differently than how the surrounding society develops? Do you follow me?

If you accept this, then you distance yourself considerably from the theory of the mature human being that television and our constitution take as their starting point. It is not a question of maturity, but of a difference in development.

When you admit this, you can also develop it. If you assume the mature human being to be a fiction, then you cannot develop it any further, because it does not get at its basic elements.

Then you no longer have to make judgments about things. You have to say to yourself, This man deserves to have his head chopped off; he is not capable of bettering himself. In the worst reactionary mind-set, you can find at least one characteristic that has some societal meaning, and then you can usually develop him further. This is the model of the Chinese king who became a gardener even though he was a truly brutal ruler. It is actually more socialist and Marxist than the idea that we can move toward societal development through the physical liquidation of human beings, as though this development were made out of humans. That is something right out of the theater.

The Appropriation of Fantasies

P:	*It seems rather questionable to me for the Left to use the same thing that the fascists used to gain power. That would mean that the fascists could also appropriate communist argumentation, and I see that as incredibly dangerous because it effectively cedes the advantage to the fascists once again . . .* [unintelligible].
AK:	That is very interesting. So, I think that we really should delve deeper into this, if you agree, because it is an important and burning question that also allows us to address the whole question of materialism and to get away from opportunistic materialism, both of which we will need when we address the question of materialist aesthetics.
P:	[unintelligible]
AK:	There is an enormous difference between true materialism (which is to say, left-wing politics) and opportunistic materialism, which is the appropriation of left-wing energies by the Right.

If I appropriate for myself left-wing energies from the Right, then they are never released, and as a result, I can never really mobilize that energy. These energies are not acknowledged, but they have been refunctionalized and manipulated. That means that I must always fear the |

thing that I am using so this can never become radical, because to be radical means to grab something by the roots and remobilize it fully.

We have a so-called left-wing politics that could really mobilize the same characteristics, and to its own ends (meaning the ends of those who have that energy). Then, for starters, this energy would be greater than the fascist energy and would therefore be fundamentally able to conquer both fascism and imperialism. In addition, the Left would be able to really declare it their own. They would have nothing to disguise.

P: [unintelligible]

AK: If, for example, you were to say right now that socialism cannot utilize anything that comes from fascism. If you were to . . . you must forgive me if I push this a little bit into the absurd. I take what you say very seriously and I also know that this is an essential argument popular, for example, on the Left. It is not just societal rationalism that brings it to the forefront, but rather it is indeed a body of thought that is very strong in left-wings groups and it tends to trigger their antiaesthetic stance, for example (which is also a reaction against perception in general).

Take the following example: if you have iron or weapons or tanks or newsprint, then there is no question that you use everything of your class enemy that you can. The only alternative would be that I turn myself into a cynic and take a trip back in time to the Bronze Age, because bronze is altogether useless for a capitalist society. But that would be nonsense.

It is even nonsense to say it. If I take an example from guerrilla warfare: this forest belongs to a great landowner, so I will not trespass it. I will not camouflage myself therein.

Or maybe a true German fighter pilot refrains from using English airspace. One thing must be said first of all. There is nature—objective, raw material—and there is a means and a goal, according to which this nature is processed. This happens differently in fascism and socialism.

But the raw characteristics of sensory experience must be clearly recognized. And so now we come to your key term: irrational. We do not intend to mobilize the irrational; rather we simply do not want to recognize that this irrationality is in fact irrational.

So we would base the thoughts of reason (or of ratio or whatever you would prefer to call it) on precisely this idea, which is to say that we would base it on all human characteristics and not on an arbitrary selection determined by the hegemony and identified in the narrow sense of the word as technically rational.

In a sense, we are contesting the idea that rationality, as it is handled in our society (or perhaps as it forms the basis of physics), actually lies at the foundation of our political or police system. We are contesting the idea that these things are actually rational.

Because you cannot deny that these things produce any number of crises, thereby demonstrating that they actually have an irrational character. In moments of resistance, for example, the imaginative capacity that lies just below the threshold has rational energies that must ultimately be organized so that it separates itself from the mystical, the mistaken, and the ideological moments and thereby takes on a stronger, more controllable form. Could we agree on that?

But help me, state your point once again, because I think that we must be able to refute it or else our hypothesis is false. You must say it again.

P: *I do not know if it will do any good at this point.*

AK: Yes, it will, because you are not the only one saying it, you see. This is a very particular pattern that I hear in every discussion.

Translated by Rory Bradley

Notes

This dialogue was originally published in German as Alexander Kluge and Oskar Negt, "Die Rolle der Phantasie," *Kritische Theorie und Marxismus: Radikalität ist keine Sache des Willens Sondern der Erfahrung* (S'Gravenhage: van Eversdijck, 1974), 41–51.

It was reprinted in Alexander Kluge, "Die Rolle der Phantasie," *Gelegenheitsarbeit einer Sklavin: Zur realistischen Methode* (Frankfurt am Main: Suhrkamp, 1975), 242–50.

1. [Translator's note: Kluge is referring here to the so-called Springer blockades that ravaged twenty-seven West German cities following the attempted assassination of student revolt leader Rudi Dutschke on April 11, 1968. At the center of these left-wing protests was the Springer Verlag headquarters in West Berlin, where student protesters blocked the conservative media monopoly from distributing its newspapers that actively demonized the Left.]

2. [Translator's note: For more on the question of organization, see also Oskar Negt, "Don't Go by Numbers, Organize According to Interests! Current Questions of Organization," trans. Helen Fehervary and Wigand Lange, *New German Critique* 1 (1973): 42–51.]

21

THE FUNCTION OF THE DISTORTED ANGLE IN THE DESTRUCTIVE INTENTION

GERTRUD KOCH: *Your stories* Lernprozesse mit tödlichem Ausgang [Learning Processes with a Deadly Outcome] *end with the following line: "If [Zwicki] turns around he can see the planet Dorfmann in the north. If he uses his telescope he can read 'The Dawn,' a sign of intelligent life that delights him"; and the following page features a copy of* L'Aurore *with the lyrics "La nuit pour moi ne cache plus les ceiux" [The night no longer obscures the heavens for me].*[1] *This is a point in your work that can easily be connected to Theodor W. Adorno's aesthetic theory. It is the metaphor of the message in a bottle that is projected into space and then ironically made to appear as the dawn. To what extent have such figures from Adorno's work played a role in your work?*

ALEXANDER KLUGE: The thing is that you have to imagine this sign of the dawn as something totally concrete, and by the way it was Adorno who gave me the score from the Schubert song in question. But it is not anything particular where one would say this is taken from either Adorno or Schoenberg, who would likely also express it musically in his own way. This is actually the metaphor for an endpoint.

GK: *I find this construction of history, as it appears in the aesthetic material, to be much more disparate in your work in the sense that you are assuming materialistic, rationalistic, and sometimes incredibly pragmatic constellations. In doing so, pragmatism almost becomes a utopia of action that could lead the way out of the paradoxical dilemma, but is actually unrealizable and thus remains utopian in this completely practical sense. This is much more reminiscent of Walter Benjamin's concept of history that imagines the world as actually already lying in ruins. History no longer takes a linear course and the concept of progress is no longer about forward thinking, but rather travels backward through history.*

AK: If you look at all the citations in the *Dialectic of Enlightenment*, the entire first long chapter references a couple of apocryphal anthropologists, but there are no quotations to speak of, except for those from Homer, though these are also used ornamentally. Yet in Benjamin you would find that he collects in a way that is unbelievably thorough. If I may give away my own position: I would be on the side of the Benjaminian method inasmuch as I would begin by furiously collecting. To say something and make a claim with one large stroke as Adorno did is something I would feel less comfortable doing.

This massive amount of material that is the *Arcades Project* contains a certain friction inasmuch as the reconstructed fragments repel and attract each other, though neither the attraction nor the repulsion leads to a whole entity, and thus the material remains as is, but with an abundance of points of resistance. This is exactly what an analyst would conclude when analyzing humans. I believe this is just as present in Adorno, only he pares it down to ciphers, particularly musical ones, to such an extent that the path of this material is no longer comprehensible for the reader. He does not need any citations because he can create a code with only a few pieces of music. All of his texts have these contexts. It is therefore no wonder that he comes to similar conclusions as Benjamin at so many points despite his completely different work process.

I do not think if one is thorough one will come to significantly different conclusions than Adorno or Benjamin. This is due to the gravitation in the fragments, all of which contain dead labor and are therefore living beings that operate among themselves and transform our twentieth century into a living concert, so to speak. We are just the—I do not want to say administrators, and we are actually not translators either, nor are we collectors, trainers, or gardeners—we are actually parallelists: because of the fact that this world of ciphers cannot be brought into our language and because of the impossibility of constructing yet again a reality parallel to all that is real. Because of this impossibility, we are caretakers of ruins, if you will. But the ruins do not need our care.

GK: *In Benjamin there is this idea of operatively bringing out the shine of this collected aesthetic material. In the famous film essay he bestowed this role on the camera: the operative transection of the world, the capturing of perspectives that are no longer possible in the world.*

AK: It is a mythic behavior that wrestles with itself in a Laocoön-like sort of way and that can no longer be mythic, but also does not disengage itself from myth. This ambivalence is fundamentally intertwined with the reality principle, and is actually one of the main nerve centers where naturalism keeps the tautological relation to reality going to a certain extent because it contains the promise of omnipotence, one that is leftist in the utopian sense that I operatively turn things again, and another that is conservative, cannot be spoken of, and must become silent. This tension is not completely resolved in Benjamin. Whenever he works with material and casts an anchor, he is not mistaken. Whenever he clings to something vague and mythic and wants, as it were, to make a big pitch parallel to the communist movement, then this has the same structure as the redemptive, world movement that could turn everything all over again. Within all of these elements lies the conceptual imperialist; this is actually a form of colonialism and cannibalism that wants to consume the object I am grappling with. Adorno is completely immune to this. He virtually relates to such things like an angel, immaterially, and says, I must abstain. Yet because abstention would be subjugation, I must express it. In this parallel world of one's expressive capacity, which is more than aesthetics, one is able to feel oneself independent of ethics because we cannot kill anyone in the parallel world. These are the points that Adorno always represents albeit only abstractly as ciphers.

GK: *For Benjamin, allegory already has a cognitive motive within the baroque tragedy, since it already presents representation as representation and no longer stands in a reproductive relation to the world. In this sense, it autonomizes itself and thereby cognitively* brings *something into representation. So actually it has already abandoned the purely mimetic capacity for expression that Adorno dedicates long passages to. Here I find interesting the way in which the Romantic tendencies of both thinkers diverge so sharply. In other words, Benjamin at one point becomes completely cognitive where Adorno clings to mimesis.*

AK: This seems to me to be a core idea. It never occurred to me before. I do not want to say Adorno essentially overcame the Romanticization of objects, but rather he always hesitated on this point. He initially can do this. When I imagine how he learned piano as a boy, how he loves his mother, how he positions his father who sold cheap wines next to his mother, etc., then I would say there is already an entirely free-floating and uncontrolled capacity for Romanticization there, which he puts out of commission when he thinks. This runs parallel to those things about which he would have never laughed, namely, his veneration of a Sicilian countess who came from the House of Byzantium, and of his Corsican relatives whom he considered to be not so aristocratic. He had several weaknesses that he recklessly gave into, but he truncated them from any course of action or thought, meaning from any and all professional perspectives. He retained, so to speak, the Romantic behavior of that small boy and the Romantic thought of his youth and could deploy it any time day or night, particularly during afternoon tea. He also relied heavily on Romanticization with respect to his dreams, but rejected Romanticization out of principle just as he did the tyranny of melody in music. This is not always the case with Benjamin. What really attracts me to Benjamin is that he possesses several personalities of thought and several forms of production all at once. We ourselves are fragments, something full of tension.

Adorno is immune to the idea that we actually possess linguistic mastery.

GK: *He detaches himself in a certain way from the problems of language by focusing heavily on the mimetic capacity. This is his hard Romantic core.*

AK: In the classical Romantic period, meaning Ludwig Tieck and Friedrich Schlegel or whomever you wish to call on, you will find that there is always a lack of decisiveness when developing a concept of Romanticism. A certain oscillation of thought, an observer status, belongs to it. Here, Adorno is fundamentally more decisive than most other modernists. There can still be something hidden in kitsch, even if it were a raw material that has more structure or stringency than the finished work that replaced it. There is not this division into aesthetic, moral, juristic, political, etc. categories. It does not exist.

GK: *Adorno formulates this as social theory.*

AK: I am fairly certain that there exists neither a whole society nor isolated particulars in his ability to make fundamental decisions. Everything is equidistant from a central point. Where is a classification supposed to be when the center and the surface fear one another such that both move gravitationally around one another? You cannot secure it in any way and you also cannot express it except by itself. In this respect, thought is something completely different, something nominalistic, something separate from what it depicts. Expression has nothing to do with what is expressed and will forever have nothing to do with it.

What I find wonderful about Adorno is how he is able to disregard the fact that he thinks in the first-person singular. Currents flow through him: texts by Freud, Marx, Kant, and all the pre-Kantian thinkers he practically memorized. A seminar on Leibniz can be more far more interesting than everything that was first thought after the eighteenth century. In between these traces, Adorno is—like the thinker Heidegger—neither a registrar nor a judge, neither a thinker nor anything else for that matter. Instead, he is someone who, without affectation, does nothing, and through whose head all these traces flow and themselves think. This is how he appears to me. He is almost like a small, extremely sensitive, living machine that imagines to a certain extent this dynamic, centuries-old body of thought as a construct or cistern once again. In doing so, it is no longer clear whether a thought is aesthetic or political. This could be grounded using examples he develops.

GK: Has *Minima Moralia* played an important role for you?

AK: Of course. Everything except for his sociological writings, which I consider to be more preambles, institutional works, mandatory exercises. There is too much assertion for me in these works. They are also too careless for my taste. All his other writings, including the notes he constantly carried around in his head, actually constitute a school of thought I trust. In terms of the work process, I always rummage around and thus rely on the material as Benjamin would. I am not inclined to think things through by writing out my texts in notebooks. On the other hand, my attitude would always look to Adorno.

GK: *How did you meet Adorno?*

AK: At the inaugural lecture by Prof. Dr. Harald Patzer (you know him as the professor of Greek in *Yesterday Girl*). He attends the inaugural lecture because all the professors go out of politeness. He sits in the row in front of me. I never saw him before and only knew a text about him by Thomas Mann. All of the sudden, I am looking into wonderfully large, velvety eyes. He is the type of person who looks back when someone is looking at him, and he does so in a way that is so strangely insistent. I do not believe this can be interrupted by speech. You cannot say at this point, "You're Mr. Adorno, aren't you." The conversation would have possibly ended right there. You can spend an entire forty-five-minute lecture just looking at someone. We always looked at each other intently. Mimetically, the face remains completely calm. You also do not see him gesticulate wildly in his lectures. You will see how his hands remain quite still, as if they were separated from his body, for he is thinking, he is telling a story. His eyes remain very calm and only comment on what he is saying momentarily. Mostly in jest, hardly ever in sadness. His eyes do not express sadness when he talks about something sad. He avoids false decisions. If you look at it as a matter of trust that can develop when falling in love, then you come closer. It is not the case that I would police myself according to Adorno's ideas, so to speak.

GK: *So you fell in love with him . . .*

AK: At one point you say to yourself, I really do not want to definitively know now, but I am sticking with it.

GK: *A true admirer of Adorno . . .*

AK: And when people are together for a long time, then you say to yourself, these thirteen or twenty or forty years I spent living with someone are more important to me than being right and so I wish not to decide this anew. You have to imagine it like that. In 1962, Adorno thought he had to rescue me from literature, that I should remain a lawyer. That was safer ground, and literature would be a brutal embarrassment, that after Proust one really cannot show up and say, I am doing literature all over. Everything has been written already. For this reason but also because of his inner contempt for images and film and especially the film industry, he provided me with a letter and sent me to Fritz Lang. This was intended to get me over this idea, so to speak, and to turn me into a good lawyer. I only took from this that he did not have much of an appreciation for film. While music and literature are something real to him, film is a phantasmagoria, a chimera. He even considered the work Fritz Lang did as a director to be nonsense. He never considered it artistic when you dress up actors by putting them in foreign dress, which by no means transports them to India or another century. Similarly, I could never get a word out of him on theater, except with respect to a few Beckett pieces. In other words, he held several contradictory positions toward the medium of film. One of these positions is recounted in the chapter on the culture industry in *Dialectic of Enlightenment*. There he describes a Hollywood that did not even exist at that time and was thus not really an appropriate object of theory. Had he not been so set against Hollywood, he could have developed an image theory based on the commodity fetish, i.e., the images and the exchangeability rooted in every commodity, as well as an exact method. This could have been a consciousness industry chapter. Instead, he simply criticized Hollywood's distribution system as a propaganda machine that developed through advertising. At the same time, he assumed that the world could be shaped through distribution, which it certainly cannot.

The second position is also affirmative and was spurred by friendship with and affinity for a few people involved with New German Cinema, which he never saw.

GK: *So did he watch your films back then?*
AK: Hardly. He would have seen two films: *Yesterday Girl* and *Artists under the Big Top: Perplexed*. I could never get anything out of him, and I am fairly certain that he liked both films

only to a certain extent. He really did say that what he finds troubling about film is the image. I believe he really liked the musical portion of my films, the soundtrack, and that he could play with this. But it was too much concretion for him compressed into an hour and a half without receiving any reading material. I think we would have had to have a small lectern under his seat and a score that someone had written out for him. Only then would it maybe have been acceptable. He then supported us when we concretized our Oberhausen Manifesto in 1963 in Mannheim. I knew already then what erroneous sources this program had, and not just the theoretical ones. I just knew that these were favors. He once had the impression, as with the Emergency Acts later, that he had to go along with it all and so he turned a blind eye.[2] Then it was as if he was in a puppet show, not acting consciously but appearing out of friendship and keeping his head still. That is the second position he had on film.

The third position is contained in the book on film music and actually has quite a bit of substance, since he rubs up against Eisler's affirmations of film music here. The basic theory that film music should not be noticed and should refrain from interrupting is certainly not Adorno's concept. He departs from a position supporting the autonomy of tones. He intended on rewriting this book.

GK: *Without Eisler . . .*

AK: He was dead. Those would be the three positions, the last of which was never carried out and the first two of which are affirmative.

And then there is also "Transparencies on Film," but he left no theory of film.[3] I think he opposed visible images in defense of invisible ones. He was against the narrative principle of visualization. The naturalism of film is always immanent for Adorno. He simply did not know all that many early films.

GK: *What is interesting in "Transparencies on Film" is that he sees the mimetic motive in film, though in a very Kantian way. He sees film as the possibility of mimetically capturing natural beauty* [das Naturschöne].

Where he expresses himself is also where he develops a prelinguistic dimension of expressive forms that basically tend toward clownishness and boil down to body language instead of spoken language. In short, he really transports the very mimetic capacity he so values in aesthetics. So it is possible, if you so choose, to draw out from these few points an approach to film aesthetics. If this is underpinned with his aesthetic theory, then you suddenly get a very strong idea of what film could actually be and I find that interesting. This does not transpire for him via montage, but instead relies heavily on a phenomenological path and body language.

AK: There are two ideas we have directly from Adorno. One is a mode of narration: switching between intensive and extensive description, epiphany, and polyphony. These are the formulas we introduced in the tutorials at the institute in Ulm.[4] He really drove this little theory of harmony for film home for us. Interestingly, it is actually quite difficult to produce polyphony through cinematic images, since the images follow one another. This is even more difficult than scratching away on a violin to create polyphony, because film is arranged sequentially. We made so many attempts to create simultaneity using multiple screens, double exposures, montage, and other forms. We conducted an actual research project. These were his lines of thinking: polyphony, epiphany, and metamorphosis. Epiphany is when I show two images and a third one then arises. This seemed to him to be the secret ideal of cinema, which can be brought about through neither asceticism nor Aronian methods.⁵

GK: *In "Transparencies on Film," he talks about the train of images, and describes cinematic experience as a journey, where all the impressions of the journey pass by in the evening. This is a nice metaphor.*

AK: The image comes from Proust. Looking through one window and then he sees in another a sunset stretched out over time.

GK: *. . . and you actually found this idea so relevant that you tried experimenting with things like internal montage. I find this interesting because all these forms of internal montage came into play in the fifties and early sixties with the André Bazin debate printed in the journal* Filmkritik. *With internal montage, as opposed to the conception of Sergei Eisenstein's theory of montage, there are no cuts. Instead, depth of field and camera movement are used to make the image more dynamic and give it more layers. If I understood you correctly, your work relies less on the meditative aspect of the Bazinian approach and its meditative redepiction of the depth of being through extreme long shots into the interior of an image. Rather, your approach relies more on a peculiar combination of operative and constructionist approaches such as double exposure, whereby the material content itself is actually increased within the shot, and less on the level of space/time in the Aristotelian sense.*

AK: Wait. Those would be two equal poles. On the one hand, the creation of time itself would be the intensive method: I simply create time or even extend it. I may not attempt this mechanically using slow motion, as if slow motion were longer than twenty-four images per second in normal time. No, I must create intensity by developing the experiential content of a particularity's calm singularity. We really see very little here. Polyphony is not about producing as many images as possible, but rather means stringency, the relationship of partial images to each other that contains tension much like a counterpoint. The tension is what is essential. It is not a numerical question regarding tones.

Epiphany means making real particles transparent by moving them toward the invisible. The highest form of film is when I see vampires even though they are nowhere on the screen, or when I hear the Brownshirts marching and convey this to viewers without ever showing the SA.

Metamorphosis is something that we can never attain cinematically, even though it is a fundamental ideal to transform something into something else and to suspend it in its transitioned state. This can be done by modulating tones, but this has almost always failed with the cinematic image. We cannot achieve it. We have a grand idea: a frog that turns into a prince. I can narrate this in a fairy tale, but I cannot express it in a realistic way.

GK: *You then try in a surrealistic way . . .*

AK: Yes, we will not give up so easy. These metamorphoses and simultaneities are a single element, the other is epiphanies. The latter is a second perspective, and neither is synonymous with the image itself. They violate one another by way of their contrasts, differences, or tautologies. A third image arises from this, one that resides in the cut and is itself not material. This third image is the calm ideal that has long existed inside spectators.

GK: *The third image is then the utopia that follows the ban on images.*

AK: In the literal sense because it is absent.

GK: *So your films would therefore abide by the postulate of iconoclasm in the Adornian sense?*

AK: Yes, that is how I would see it.

The central point is you are at least 80 percent *artiste démolisseur* when you make films because the tautological doubling of real relations through the camera's image also includes the replication of the particular professional features of the instrument, insofar as I can make *those* long movements possible only with the camera. This means you can see in every slow movement of the camera the crane, the tracks, and the simplified world relations I must create when I want to make a long tracking shot. You behold the world of the camera. This is just like when a cameraman cast his shadow into the image. This is precisely not what we assume. We believe that film theory does not exist at all, but rather that film theory takes into account theories of experience and the capacity for expression and expressivity. To the extent that it takes this into account, it is an intelligent practice of film. But a singular theory of film makes as little sense as a singular theory of music. The eye has deeply rooted relationships to intensely internalized objects going back to childhood. The eye has already seen everything before it recognizes something. A stand-alone theory of film is therefore a senseless undertaking.

GK: *Let us nevertheless go over the current approaches in film aesthetics to your relationship to Adornian aesthetic theory. What is being done now is, on the one hand, the celebration of long shots that cast the cameraman's shadow, so to speak. This would be the direction Wenders and Handke take in their filmic practice. Concretization at the same time as a meditative healing process...*

AK: ... the concluding dialogue in *Wings of Desire*, for example...

GK: *A healing process at the wrong point, sacralization instead of sexualization. This has little* to do with Critical Theory. It actually comes more from Heidegger. On the other hand, I find it very interesting that you develop a theory of montage that forfeits Eisenstein's precipitous, cognitive demands and instead re-romanticizes in a utopian sense and simultaneously renounces the elitist strain of Adornian aesthetics by attempting to advance the utopian strain of mass culture.

AK: I would not sign off on that. We are talking here about art. Culture is controlled by priests and their successors. This is actually ritual, rules about customs, and their appropriate form of reception, while art does something different. It revolts against culture and the reality principle. It is the grievance in culture, etc. Art cannot, incidentally, be practiced by just any group of people.

GK: But in your new works for television, for example, you did experiment with breaking down this distinction . . .

AK: . . . but not by taking a leap into mass culture. I am just an individual and it is my ideal as an auteur to be connected to other auteurs so we can build roads together. But we need to first build roads before they can become more relevant for other people. At first, this would be the path that you could eventually call populist, but it is initially a professional activity, one that is not mass culture. We look at mass culture the wrong way when we see it hermetically. It has high levels of tolerance, but they need not be tested right away in a battle between David and Goliath. The so-called mass audience is not a constant mass and is not inherently loyal. It certainly does not correspond to a majority in a parliamentary election. There are also aggressive impulses in the contemporary production of culture that extend into a segmented form of fascism, which the culture industry cannot produce but gradually singles out. Just think about *Rambo I–VI*, for example. Amid all this, libidinal efforts still prevail in art where networks refer to the entirety of experience that is not yet articulated, is largely beyond the public's reach, but lies around out in the open. It has not yet decided whether it will allow itself to be organized.

GK: *What would authenticity look like in film aesthetics according to a concept of experience?*

AK: It means no invisible cuts on the part of the film crew. The antithesis is the invisible cut, the ideal of middle-class cinema. Authenticity depends on what is recorded and what is identified as inadmissible material. It has its own laws and autonomy.

GK: *What is the authenticity of the material then?*

AK: An actor must be transparent in his or her roles. An actress who has never been pregnant, for example, cannot authentically play a pregnant woman. Pretending does not work. So I have to differentiate between experiences that someone standing in front of the camera can have and those they cannot possibly have. In this sense, everything in narrative film is documentary. It is not flirtatious when we say that fiction and facts are the same for us, but rather this is the law of authenticity that serves as the foundation for the entire production of art.

GK: *What does this mean concretely for film, where the camera's possibilities for creating material itself are quite extensive? From the perspective of auteur cinema, does authenticity not then come from the material the author has produced? Or is it already present in what has occurred precinematically?*

AK: No. Just as an astrophysicist can determine the gravitational pull between two planets, so too the author of a film is actually nothing more than an observer who has a crew at his disposal and begins by reproducing what they observe in a one-to-one relationship. In doing so, he must place trust in the fact that the movement among the relations he is recording is sufficient. He would merely reflect the interference between the camera and what is being recorded by not recording something that cannot be authentic. It is a question of the finely honed capacity for differentiation. The author actually does little more than make distinctions.

GK: *This would turn the camera into a reflecting mirror and the work of the director would only entail placing the precinematic before this mirror and setting the mirror up at the right moment.*

AK: I fear that a single-lens reflex camera can do only this and nothing more. It does make a big difference where you place the camera and whether the people in front of the camera try to incorporate an experience they are really having or one they are acting out.

GK: *Benjamin gave the example of the actor who is scared by a gunshot offscreen such that the camera captures authentic fright, which would not be possible for the actor to act out. There is a completely naturalistic concept of authenticity operating behind this surreal scenario.*

AK: But it is absolutely correct. There are other human reactions that cannot be elicited from a gunshot, ones that come from people themselves. The proportionality between these different expressions is actually the film itself, whereas the plot is just a cover. In the way I make films, plot is a kind of politeness toward my audience, because this is unfortunately what they expect. What actually moves the film is not the plot.

GK: *The plot is a fictive by-product of the images.*

AK: It acts as if it had a plot. In reality, it is just differences, different observations. This could be called the authentic cinematic aspect of my work.

GK: *That is why you insist that your films are documentary?*

AK: Yes, this is not derived from a political principle of documentary. The second factor is their subcutaneous structure. This concept plays a central role in Adorno's writings on music. When a long piece of music becomes a refined particularity that evinces a true antagonism of tones beneath the level of its construction—a constellation—then this subcutaneous layer is the true structure of the piece of music that determines its quality. We would like to generalize further. I can recompose these subcutaneous points; for example, I can place all of Giuseppe Verdi's conspiracy scenes in a sensuous, meaning informative context. On the other hand, I can also leave out information. Just as there are "Songs without Words," I can also create "Images without Information." For example, I can take the scene with the pin from *The Marriage of Figaro*, which is quite broad in its composition, and combine it with all of the opera's subplots. All of these moments would acquire quite an exciting worldview freed from the dictates of narration. Vertical structure and change in perspective are very important categories. If I tell the story of *Anna Karenina*—a great novel, but one in which the perspective of the omniscient narrator dominates—from the perspective of the young son, then every perspective within the novel would change according to this distorted angle.

GK: *It would essentially be a different novel.*

AK: Certainly a different novel, but one that has not been told. Adaptations for the screen must be seen as a fundamental feature of modernity. A vertical structure must be used. There is a conversation during a meal between Karenina's brother and Levin. This conversation actually exposes the aporias of this way of life that later leads to death. Yet it is an innocent meal of fish. It is possible to narrate this in a single film, a fragment, like Adorno writes aphorisms.

GK: *Modernity would mean doing away with the centralized perspective in favor of individual points within a subcutaneous structure?*

AK: Something that is already modern like Joyce, for example, would not have to be repeated.

GK: *The subcutaneous structure would then be the secret legend of authenticity.*

AK: The third is the creation of sequences in the way that music can develop variations. The autonomy of tones makes possible relationality and freedom for each tone. To this end, we must try getting permission from the audience to repeat.

GK: *Up until this point you have heavily relied on the concept of experience when addressing aesthetic questions. What would this material be in a strict sense in such an aesthetics?*

AK: It does not exist.

GK: *The mathematic principles of the late Schoenberg school, the twelve-tone technique, and the principle of serialism would not be examples for you?*

AK: I will not pay a price for the purity of perception. This interests me just as little in Schoenberg as it does in mathematics. Music also does not interest me independent of the people who listen to it. The antithesis of mathematics is the influence that objects and people exert on each other. Gravitational relationships. If we first call that material, then the material characteristics are located between things and people. Take the piano, for example: there are the piano makers, the pianists who have played the pianos, the countless generations of students who had piano lessons, the piano teachers, all the way to the piano Richard Wagner had delivered over the Alps to Vienna around the time of his death. Because it is so cold up there in the mountains, all the strings went out of tune. You see, it is a long story to get to the point where you can finally say: Piano. In a certain sense, it, too, is a living being that is treated as a mere object. Yet it is dead labor and thus a part of people. This is the access point into the generational contract that forms the majority, from which we live from generation to generation. This means not only that the previous generations weigh like a nightmare on the survivors, as Marx puts it in a different context. In reality, they are also our helpers when we need majorities. This majority created music, for example, which lasts for the ages. In the contemporary broadcast system, this majority would be outvoted by our contemporaries who want entertaining music. The majority across time certainly would not choose entertainment, but rather serious music. Were I possibly able to keep myself alive as a piano player in a SS mess hall, this question, this aporia, would not exist. A series is therefore not only a formal, mathematical principle, but also the access point into the temporal flow that Benjamin's angel grapples with. This is the real, while the snapshot of the so-called present is something unreal. There is no conclusion to time, and therefore the modern era cannot be said to be over and replaced by the postmodern, or that the culmination of the late Romantic era is the Viennese School. This is all just a façade. I can just as well say that the culmination of the Viennese School is the reappropriation of the entire history of music. I would need to enter into the gaps of music history and compose what music neglected. This can be shown more easily in film history than in music, which is richer and therefore makes it more difficult to detect the gaps. The nickelodeon lasted two years and then it was done away with by producers and later was no longer relevant. To repeat this again with more time would be a worthwhile cause. This never results in the historical product, of course. This will not look like a film from 1907, but rather like a film from the eighties or nineties. It will reignite an impulse that history abandoned.

GK: *Then you would definitely distance yourself from the postmodern aesthetics that invoke you as their supporter. You also are not citing older styles, but are instead actualizing and modernizing the contents of experience.*

AK: Modernism is always an uprising against (a) the reality principle, and (b) traditions. Adorno speaks of the necessity of modernity, which cannot be chosen by just any person or artist. Modernity is also not an issue of manual skills. I strongly resist the division of labor responsible for separating the aesthetic, as if the aesthetic refers to something ornamentally permissible, as if it were a playground. The capacity for expression is a very important, immaterial productive force, through which I express myself professionally. I can do this, incidentally, not only as an artist, but I can also do it with the art of my own life experience. I once convinced an actress to use her theatrical experience to avoid the threat of a pending divorce that would have isolated her child. She then acted, deploying this trick simultaneously on her husband, her child, her in-laws, and her directors. She saved her relations by acting. In other words, she applied what is usually reserved for the theater to real relations. Authenticity belongs in the theater and it includes masquerading, performance, and artistry in the entire range of experiences including family politics and deception.

GK: *Perhaps we should now touch on another point more situated in the realm of social theory, where the concept of the public sphere and the matter of mediation play a role, namely, the question why no one reads the message in a bottle and what is read instead. We are getting closer to the analysis and description of society. You*

	worked a lot with Oskar Negt on the concept of the public sphere, and if I understand correctly from your own work, you have slightly different conceptions of the way that aesthetic constructs are brought into the world and set into motion.
AK:	It is not a question that has to do with aesthetic constructs, but rather with the contents of experience. They can be expressed aesthetically and extra-aesthetically, meaning they can lie around as raw materials and still represent a capacity for expression. We cannot lay claim to an alternative concept of the public sphere. The difficulty is that Adorno says relatively little about the category of the public sphere. I believe that except for the public gathered for a concert, which he did not really consider a public. He built up a great deal of skepticism such that those of us working in Critical Theory can far better deduce a concept of the public sphere from Horkheimer. He develops quite effectively a concept of those involved in discussion as a form of public sphere that emerged out of commercial transactions dating back to the early bourgeoisie.
GK:	*Habermas developed this in* The Structural Transformation of the Public Sphere.
AK:	Although this public sphere has two, if not three sides. One is the emancipation of the universally comprehensible world of commodities. Now thoughts that look like commodities can, of course, also partake in such communication. This is the organic, bourgeois public sphere that heavily dominated Anglo-Saxon countries. The second one, developed out of self-consciousness and bourgeois ideas about autonomy, attempts, to a certain extent, to appropriate the self-consciousness of courtly expressive forms for the bourgeoisie. Men like Wilhelm von Humboldt, Georg Forster, Friedrich August Wolf are representatives of a movement to develop public

expression that basically stalled out in the early years of the nineteenth century. A third movement comes out of the experiential content of the French Revolution. This is a formalized concept of the public sphere that designates the public in the moment when the gallows or a guillotine is cordoned off from the general population. Someone is executed without anyone being able to interfere, but everyone nevertheless watched. This would be the public sphere of the French Revolution . . .

GK: . . . *for Adorno this would be what anticipates the culture industry, the public acclamation to execution.*

AK: . . . and standing at the scaffolds such that the ability to act is necessarily divorced from the ability to perceive. These are the three precarious roots of the public sphere we now must activate against the universal, private tyranny of intimate spheres, which are the counterpoints to the public sphere where the essential production of experience resides. In other words, an alternative conception of the public sphere must be envisaged, meaning a critique of and a battle for the public sphere that simultaneously acts as a bulwark.

GK: *This is a differentiation that was essentially made by Critical Theory's empirical studies at the Institute for Social Research, namely, the difference between public and official opinion. What is essentially part of the public sphere in train compartments and streetcars, even when official opinion is completely different.*

AK: *Authority and the Family* is the central work. It names the alchemist's kitchen where every impulse and thought in a society in reality suited for the public sphere, including every act of marginalization such as murdering another, comes into being. The fact that this is fenced in and confined is the starting point for the public sphere.

The fact is that both of the most important activities in bourgeois society—the factory and the family—were at one point removed as the substance of the public sphere, and all the other less important elements were united as the public sphere. I have a highly balanced, plebiscitary society in which enlightenment is possible, and at the same time I have plebiscitary decisionism that fitfully marginalizes parts of this society that can very quickly tip over into war. This means that the developmental processes described in *Dialectic of Enlightenment* have developed a certain material violence such that they attempt to confront twentieth-century causal chains with eighteenth- and nineteenth-century capacities for imagination. This concerns me. This concept, this societal expression, does not look out for real people who have at least enough autonomy that they get sick and seek out niches, which can also be anguishing. This captivates me, and I at least would like to put it into words, since I do not believe in an immediate Armageddon, but rather in the tenacity of relations.

Translated by Emma Woelk

Notes

This dialogue was originally published in German as "Die Funktion des Zerrwinkels in zertrümmernder Absicht: Ein Gespräch zwischen Alexander Kluge und Gertrud Koch," in *Kritische Theorie und Kultur*, ed. Rainer Erd et al. (Frankfurt am Main: Suhrkamp, 1989), 106–24.

    1. [Translator's citation: Alexander Kluge, *Learning Processes with a Deadly Outcome*, trans. Christopher Pavsek (Durham, NC: Duke University Press, 1996), 104.]

    2. [Translator's note: The German Emergency Acts passed in the hot summer of May 1968 constitute the seventeenth constitutional amendment to the then–West German Grundgesetz that guarantees the federal government's ability to act in times of crisis. Reminiscent of Article 48 of the Weimar Constitution, which the

National Socialists exploited in 1933 to solidify the dictatorship, the Emergency Acts represented a threat to West German democracy and became a central concern for that country's student movement well before the acts' ratification.]

3. [Translator's citation and note: Theodor W. Adorno, "Transparencies on Film," trans. Thomas Y. Levin, *New German Critique* 24/25 (Autumn 1981–Winter 1982): 199–205. In the accompanying introduction to Levin's translation of Adorno, Miriam Hansen explains that Adorno's late writings on film were heavily influenced by his friendship with Kluge. See Miriam Hansen, "Introduction to Adorno, 'Transparencies on Film,'" *New German Critique* 24/25 (Autumn 1981–Winter 1982): 193–96.]

4. [Translator's note: Kluge is referring to his time at the newly established film department at the Ulm School of Design beginning in 1962. Cofounded and directed by Kluge along with Edgar Reitz and Detten Schleiermacher, the department was created on behalf of the Oberhausen Group whose manifesto Kluge cosigned that same year. Shortly thereafter, the department was transformed into an independent charitable organization called the Institute for Film Design. Its stated mission as of 1970 was to promote "research and development in the field of film." See Klaus Eder and Alexander Kluge, *Ulmer Dramaturgien: Reibungsverluste* (Munich: Carl Hanser, 1980), 5.]

5. [Translator's note and citation: Kluge alludes here to Arnold Schoenberg's opera fragment "Moses and Aron," which Adorno championed as a great work recognized by its "broken outlines [which] survive as ciphers of a supreme, unnamable truth" (226). The work's aspirations stand in stark opposition, says Adorno, to the "subjective expression" characteristic of Moses's brother Aron who succumbs in the biblical story to the iconoclastic temptations of reducing the absolute perception of God to mere word and image (228). See Theodor W. Adorno, "Sacred Fragment: Schoenberg's 'Moses and Aron,'" in *Quasi una fantasia: Essays on Modern Music*, trans. Rodney Livingstone (London: Verso, 2002), 225–48.]

22

THE POLITICAL WITHOUT ITS DESPAIR

On the Concept of "Populism"

1.

Words like "folkish," "folksy," "popular," "populist," "*popularis*," "folk festival," "national community," and even phrases like "in the name of the people" not only describe different ideas, but each also assumes a different historical guise.[1] The seriousness contained in the use of these words (located either beneath or beyond each expression) cannot be found if the shadows, perspectives, and temporal signs accompanying such words are destroyed. Amid falsehoods and instrumental appropriations, appeals to the people [*das Volk*] revolve around the search for autonomy and distinctive character. What is sovereignty's elemental material? How is the creation of autonomy, if need be by proxy, organized? How is it balanced? Which building blocks are used to construct a community?

People [*Menschen*] pose these questions more frequently at two historical transitions: when they doubt the materials used to construct their community along with the organization of their experience; and when they believe they have reason to be proud of their achievements, like when they succeed at attaining autonomy. With regard to the concept of the political in both positions (sovereignty, community)—doubt and pride—we are currently witnessing a peculiar devaluation.[2] It appears as though it matters not whether I doubt or hope. The category of the political is undergoing an inflation, not in the sense that the political contents of the experiential world are bringing about an increase in matters of the state. Instead, they have severed the political from large portions of this world of experience. Only *images* can still create an imaginary bridge between professionalized political activity and immediate life contexts: parallel realities arise that no fear, doubt, hope, or even an extended hand can relate to.

The emotional reality of a life context (children grow up) and the administrative-industrial block of reality (one generation of commodities and weapons is replaced by the next) do take each other into account in many ways at their points of contact, but at their center they are not capable of understanding each other. Our planet is inhabited by a multitude of antagonistic blocks of reality of this kind, which have the tendency to organize themselves "on their own terms," and to relate to the rest like cannibals. There is no universal capacity for expression that is not immediately weighed down by the labor of heterogeneous blocks of reality.

At this juncture, it is not possible to proceed historically, just as it is not possible to simulate a viewpoint from now-time. Both forms of analysis, historical reconstruction and comprehensible abstraction, are distorted by the violence arising from the multitudes of realities drifting apart. This occurs in the form of a loss impacting the capacities for expression and differentiation. Most notably, metaphor becomes useless; it can no longer lay bare the experiential content of historical tragedies in the ways that stupidity and weakness typical of satyr plays do. What is far more likely is either new tragedies on a greater scale or the arbitrary revival of every historical station in every one of the separately conceived vessels of reality.

2.

We are familiar with the *popularis* method from the crisis of the Roman Republic.³ The Gracchi, Marius, Catiline, and Caesar all relied on a clientele of *populares*. It would be interesting to investigate more closely the preconditions for the approach to this political *method*. It was found wherever administrative power, the city, the professionalized oligarchy (in the Roman case: the aristocratic leadership), developed a continuity independent from the life of the individual. The outsider, the individual, and the people [*Volk*] are all equally excluded by direct rule from the institutional world. Christian Meier has described the dissolution of the Roman Republic by the monarchy as a grappling of incompatible realities.⁴ In the final analysis, the displacements brought about by this exclusionary mechanism pertain to the substance of the *populares* only momentarily. All calls for administrative power and the will of the people remain instrumental.

The French revolutionaries of 1789 draw comparisons with images of the Roman Republic and use them to dress up their ideas. Yet France has no administrative power comparable to what existed in Rome, and a clientele that could be mobilized instrumentally existed in only a few places (e.g., the Faubourg Saint-Antoine and a few enclaves in Lyon, Marseille, and Strasbourg). In fact, the social structure, but especially the capacity for expression, includes a constitution passed down from feudal tradition: individualism, robbery, punishing felonies, rewarding loyalty, the freedom of ideas, the liberation of willpower, and engineering. Communication is entirely un-Roman. Compared to antiquity's formal differentiations for appointing magistrates, according to which its political syntax orients itself, the Revolution creates its own magistrates in an entirely different way, namely, through the amalgamation of otherness, originality, and ingenuity. The relations in England and in the German states are substantially more complex with regard to the reception of free enterprise.

The bourgeois republic—the principle of democracy—contains, for lack of a better phrase, a signature flaw: kingdoms and aristocratic rule in the Middles Ages were not themselves monocratic.

Power is not truly centralized, but instead is based on numerous reciprocal dependencies. Only a *threatened* kingdom tries to develop absolutism by establishing centralized power, especially through the visual depiction of power and representation. These images, for example, those of the palace at Versailles, command the attention of republicanism's adherents. The republican movement takes possession of the universal authority that the king previously appeared to have. Therein lies an excessive demand for community from the outset.

A democratic process can make decisions about issues for which those involved have a sufficient capacity for expression and differentiation. Work was never performed on this capacity for differentiation. On account of its pressure to remain current, the Revolution essentially disrupts all previous processes that work toward expanding the capacity for expression into societal riches. At the same time, the unbridled program of asserting *feelings of omnipotence* in people and the selective escalation of those feelings mean whoever addresses the desire for omnipotence is able to profit rhetorically; the *profit* he gains is *legitimacy*. The history of Thermidor and all following movements marked by the opening and exclusion of the omnipotence principle is a history of deceleration, projection, displacement, denial, introjection, etc.

> The republican process: the expropriation of monarchies and the appropriation of the worlds of power and images they hoarded. The democratic process: the gradual production of capacities for expression and differentiation on which a communal will formation without exclusion is based. Most notable in this production process is the development of richer capacities for perception that precede this will formation. It is clear that republicanism has taken place, but democratizing processes have been uncommon; they have only been prevalent in places where new self-consciousness developed following decentralized commodity production. However, the underbelly of this self-consciousness created an exclusionary mechanism that restricted first the capacity for perception and then later the democratic process of will formation.
>
> "The path out of estrangement follows the same path as estrangement."[5] How is it possible to imagine a fortuitous means, one favorable for a rich expressive capacity, for learning new social formations based

on previous ones? How is it at all possible to make gains at passing down traditions instead of incurring experiential losses? Apparently when the learning and appropriation processes are able to draw on the *early phase* of the previous formation. Something within them was excluded and as a result lost; there lay the roots of a diversified development of society's parts as well as the injury to community, its mortification. At any one time, reactions must be found that focus in special cases on reversing the injury. In moments when collective doubt and hope could imagine alternative historical paths, a diversified capacity for differentiation emerges that can not only be related to bygone historical circumstances but that also always remained present *in subjectivity* while objective relations formed new blocks of reality. It would therefore be especially informative for people living at the end of the twentieth century to closely examine the beginnings of capitalism, when peasants, those living in the provinces, and cottagers were separated from the land—their ancestral home—because it cannot be assumed that the forces unleashed back then (this occurred in part in Germany and in the American Midwest initially in the 1920s and 1940s) were ever extinguished within the subjective structure. Yet there is no one capable of expressing anything along these lines. Advertising firms know about it perhaps and can take advantage of it to a certain degree. Political campaigning certainly relies on it. But literature, academic parlance, and everyday self-consciousness do not concern themselves with it; they have no appropriate means of expression to address it.

A translation from psychoanalysis into history cannot be a matter of transmitting psychic-individual experience into the collective processes. It is much more a matter of turning away from an objective view of history. History's conflicts remain accessible to analysis and the collective capacity for expression in much the way individual conflicts are, but according to an architecture completely different than what a single person possesses.

3.

Characteristic of a world of facts that falls apart into various blocks of reality is how images hold it together (phantasmally). Analytical work would make its decay transparent. For a so-called mass mobilization, this (apparently) means the actor's hour of disguise has arrived.[6] According to this perspective, every path leads to an instrumental attitude. It becomes irrelevant whether this perspective is taken up from the left or the right, by an agent or an investigator. The perspective itself contains a fundamental error.

A differentiation at the level of observation must be introduced in order to orient oneself: it is noteworthy that every administrative and reactionary form of politics strives in its early stages to deploy an image of a mature citizen specifically at that point where no valid capacity for differentiation can effectively be established. The following idea is based on this observation: "From the vantage point of non-emancipation, people are something whole. From the vantage point of their emancipation they are something not-whole."[7] This proposition paraphrases the Enlightenment assumption that the material of the human species is prosperous unto itself, rich, and thus suitable for rich social relations. People are thus nowhere as poor as the real relations suggest: legitimate doubt arises as to whether people have already achieved their personality.

> There are times when the possible continuity of a large number of people, who have time and opportunity to find a form of collective expression for developing their self-consciousness, confronts the increase in dead labor and new facts. These are rare moments and regarded as classical. Between attempts to go on the offensive and collect world experience for itself, as is the case with Johann Wolfgang von Goethe's Wilhelm Meister and Franz Biberkopf from Alfred Döblin's *Berlin Alexanderplatz*, there remains a violently traveled stretch paved with expropriation, introjection, and a drive toward increasing passivity. A large portion of modernity's subjective features resulted from processes of expropriation and dislocation. A broad spectrum of human characteristics presumably came into being at first as fragments unequal to one another in their development. Flexion, destruction, friction, disqualification, potentiation, and stimulation are further stages in the creation of fragments. The fragmentation of contexts in which human characteristics spent their incubation period is the mark of an excessive causality, damages to third parties, friction between antagonistic realities, and the eclipse of old realities by new ones. In every case, a broader, more vitalized flow of human characteristics emerges, one in which each is open to new opportunities to bind to others. These crude displacements, overwhelming in nature when measured against an individual human life span or the succession of generations within single families, encounter in the subjective makeup common in late twentieth-century human beings no psychic authority capable of responding through perception or will formation to external forces in ways other than disguise, defense, mask (= person), or flight. Of the three constituents described by Sigmund Freud, it is primarily the ego that

tends most strongly toward flight. It is implausible why alliances among such fugitives should be so well suited for collective will formation. The unfathomability of either libidinal interactions with representations of the superego or a culturally magnetized, selective interaction with narrators of the subconscious cannot be explored further here. The flow of phased-out, partially accelerated, and undeveloped characteristics cannot develop into something cohesive in these three vessels.

The concept of differentiation is used therefore incorrectly when applied to social groups, classes, professions, families, or individuals. It is possible that such a differentiation is carried out on these synthetic levels as either a mere appearance or without any basis in reality. In this instance, it is therefore unstable. On the other hand, the authentic processes coursing through every block of reality (insofar as they are raw materials for universalization) exist far below closed personalities and far above the threshold constructed from the perspective typical of closed life spans. If the reasons for crises and disruptions lie within these two realms of movement typically derived from our attention, then the building blocks for the "architectonics of reason" can also be found there.

In this sense, the question of populism is missing its object. It asks about the authentic element—the basis—that cannot be located within the form and role of a voting public. On the other hand, republics, the movements of demons, the relationality of perception, and the possible constitution of a collective will have *individual* human characteristics as their building blocks. These materials are unable to organize themselves either because they, as fragments, are open to and await new opportunities to bind, since nothing accommodates any connections to them, or they have secured themselves into the most diverse constellations made out of blocks of the real: the result of which is worlds of images, magnetizations. This is the process by which whole societies slip "into the imaginary."[8] They did this in the first half of the twentieth century in the form of mass movements. They are doing this in the second half of the twentieth century in the form of passivity.

4.

This analysis does not initially lead to any political suggestion; it deals solely with the perception of the real object of exploration. The working method concentrates on uncovering this objectivity in the expectation that people are able to make something of it themselves. To this end, we must create catalogs containing falsely conceived questions and reveal their unanswerability. It is useful to determine what *cannot* be an object of sovereignty: the reduction of the political to what can be imagined as a process of production and the identification of those inflationary parts of the political that can always only be produced distributively and administratively.

> The steep competition in the production of profits gleaned from persuasion and legitimation (the results are falsely described as mass loyalty) forces professional politicians to take up everything that can be addressed and discussed as exciting, new, or politicizable in order to raise their profiles among constituents, on the level of parliament, or among international agencies. Each one of these different representational public spheres has its own rules for distinguishing oneself. Random masses of life contexts, technical innovations, scientific options, and international constellations can be introduced anew at each of these levels of representation. This occurs regardless of whether there is even the possibility of a political decision. The appropriation of such new political material is also dependent on the ability to transfer a potentially political decision into a production process. The beginning of the inflationary movement that confronts overburdened political organs with ever greater amounts of overexertion hails no more frequently from the camp of reactionary interests than it does from the camp of goodwill. Something must be done against the dangers of genetic engineering; this ideally occurs through laws, at least this has to be tested out, addressed in speeches, introduced as a motion that bears the author's name. An investigative committee is formed. Without much consideration of the results of the inquiry, a ministerial contract is awarded. Draft amendments and laws are developed. I hardly know an example of something introduced like this that was then later dropped. The mass of material taken up by professional politicians escalates. The side effects entail hectic movements on the part of the political apparatus in order to dispose of this mass of material in a way other than just dropping it. In effect, they are all abstraction processes. A party convention that first formulates out of 1,200 proposals joint motions, combines these into verbal compromises, and then finally decides on a few consolidated "baskets" deals in something both resistant to concretization and unfit for authentic abstraction. This world of overexertion and the countermovements against this overexertion (in this sense, the compromises are not compromises) are situated *between* concept and intuition, untranslatable into the capacity for expression of those who have not taken part in this special, professionalized process.
>
> The social contract is actually made up of written and unwritten rules *not* subject to the political exercise of power. Some of these norms were instrumentally turned around in the Weimar Republic by the political

> Right as well as during the founding of the Federal Republic of Germany in the interest of widely varying groups opposed to government intervention. Yet this occurred very selectively. There is no school for constitutional law that enumerates the cases in which a political decision is as senseless as its opposite. This must be rejected: the binding of modern republics to the ideal of omnipotence is focused on something impossible. It comes down to reconstructing the political through the enumeration of what is subject to no political decision. This, above all, creates developmental periods for elementary processes through which perception and collective will formation can multiply authentically. The concept of politics must be drawn from the category of sovereignty. For rigorously reduced political content, an overview must be created from the bottom up.

5.

> When religion became impossible, art should have taken over control. Which art?
>
> ROBERT MUSIL, *The Man without Qualities*[9]

If the nonexclusive, noninstrumental position that insists on relationality is the hallmark of leftist politics, then what comprises exactly what is excluded, popular, civil, and elementary—in other words, those things that represent the social foundation as a rich substance? This other position must be deduced from the roles, masks, and people after undergoing a great deal of processing. In an analogy to the language of the student movement, in which it was said that the petrified relations must be liquefied, the majority of human characteristics could be described as plasma; it is a heated state of matter. Human abilities (skills), wishes, the perception of facts, individual sociated senses (for example, the social eye or eloquence): they all form specific republics. There are always several layers of mediation: a farmer looks out of my eyes, as do the entrepreneurs among my forefathers; in the wishes I may express (that regulate my capacity for expression as a *single* authority), childhood wishes and their imaginary world, which has become unrealizable (I can take hold of every object from a childhood wish, but I still would not be able to win back that wish), coexist with constructs of wishes that arise from the roles found in the adult world. The worlds of wishes recorded in images and programs (the Roman circus, the condensation of time and event horizons such that every moment is a matter of life or death, time travel, "entertainment," suspense) clash with elementary wishes (e.g., a moment of calm, to finally grab hold of something just before 2 a.m.). It is impossible to be brief when describing the fullness of separate worlds that constitutes *rich, historically experienced subjectivity*. In none of the real roles (e.g., a consumer stuck in Christmas traffic) does this richness possess a sufficient capacity for expression, autonomy, or self-consciousness. One has to pass through each role in order to collect oneself. Political attempts to build up mass loyalty by American presidents, political parties in our country, and advertising and entertainment industries appeal to these distracted, lingering particles, the so-called republicans in distraction. Political production can only consist in its assemblage. Each individual attempt to create relationality in a "populist," that is to say, universal way is comprised of similarly complicated steps like the estrangement that individual characteristics experience. It is initially a matter of communication between individual characteristics—communication as a process that can be described in a way similar to how Freud described the work of mourning, meaning the forces of repulsion condensed just like those of affection. Yet communication is based on an additional force held in reserve. With such reserves, one characteristic listens to another and produces attention that consists in one force taking a moment to "do nothing."

These are conditions under which the capacity for expression necessary for subjective social prosperity is amplified; among the esoteric doctrines contained in the German philosophical tradition is the idea that beginning with a certain concentration of communicative forces, which reveals the authenticity of the base, a kind of magnetization occurs, setting off countless strokes of good fortune. It is irrelevant to me whether this assumption is true or not; the labor remains in any case arduous the entire time. The main point is if political reconstruction ever gets started in the objective realm, does it originate from authentic elements or from those images stoked by despair?

> An observation of Friedrich Nietzsche: "All *stronger* moods bring with them a sympathetic resonance on the part of related sensations and moods; they as it were root up the memory. Something in us is provoked to recollection and becomes aware of similar states and their origins. Thus there come to be constructed habitual rapid connections between feelings and thoughts which, if they succeed one another with lightning speed, are in the end no longer experienced as complexes but as *unities*. It is in this sense that one speaks of the moral feelings, of the religious feelings, as though these were simple unities: in truth, however, they are rivers with a hundred tributaries and sources. Here, too, as so often, the unity of the word is no guarantee of the unity of the thing."[10]

6.

The examples of the political we consider successful (they are rare, e.g., a few moments under Henry IV) display an additional dose of light-handedness and a certain weightlessness that call on the concept of seriousness, despair, and crisis in only the fewest of cases. "The political begins by accepting the reality of one's opponent," writes Ivan Nagel in his book *Autonomy and Mercy*.[11] For a certain period of time, people can afford to heighten their powers of attention required to produce reality surrounding an opponent. This demands not only realism but also antirealism, which provides a reality for the opponent while merely accepting it at the same time. There is therefore a certain *disbelief* that exists as a condition for the political relation in all matters.

"'Something is branded in, so that it stays in the memory: only that which *hurts* incessantly is remembered'—this is a central proposition of the oldest (and unfortunately also the most enduring) psychology on earth. One may even be tempted to say that something of this horror—by means of which promises were once made all over the earth, and guarantees and undertakings given—something of this *survives* still wherever solemnity, seriousness, secrecy, and somber colors are found in the life of men and nations: the past . . . breathes on us and wells up in us, whenever we become 'serious.' Things never proceeded without blood, torture, and victims, when man thought it was necessary to forge a memory for himself. . . . Ah, reason, seriousness, mastery over the emotions, the whole murky affair which goes by the name of thought, all these privileges and showpieces of man: what a high price has been paid for them! how much blood and horror is at the bottom of all 'good things'!"[12]

The image of the closest large-scale unity: nation, religion, esoteric doctrine, a way of living, an alliance, etc., as well as the image of the individual, call up despair as soon as the powers of the will are concentrated. A fit of apprehension develops with regard to the realization of politics, a majority, equality (and finally: social wealth). On account of past experience, seriousness and the collective must be fended off at this point. The results of the twentieth century confirm this for us. If our inquiries focus either on the connection of individual human characteristics made possible only by weak interactions or on the kinds of processes that have won out over the will of everyone involved on a macroscopic level and that can be either friendly or unfriendly to humans, then this very same despair must not necessarily arise. This is the reason (and not because administrations would have had a chance) that we have no use for charismatic leaders. Put differently, it does not matter if the failures of political leaders are transparent. But it does make a difference whether they comport themselves in a closed or open way. To accept that others will be harmed, this is the status between gross negligence and malice; it is the basic model of collective criminal behavior. To accept the *reality of the opponent* in this same dual manner (between malice and allowance) is, on the other hand, to create something that cannot occur without my permission. Opposition is never real if I do not grant the opponent (along with all the others) this status. Amid the collective production of a loss in reality (replacement of reality with images) a production of objectivity is found. If good fortune exists, then this implies that bad fortune exists as well—but what is that? There is a pessimism of strength. Cases of good fortune involving institutionally weak connections like the right to hospitality and the right to be touched softly remain untested within the political dimension.

Translated by Emma Woelk

Notes

This essay was originally published in German as Alexander Kluge, "Das Politische ohne dessen Verzweiflung: Zum Begriff des 'Populismus,'" in Oskar Negt and Alexander Kluge, *Maßverhältnisse des Politischen: 15 Vorschläge zum Unterscheidungsvermögen* (Frankfurt am Main: Fischer, 1992), 285–30.

1. [Translator's note: The German noun *Volk* and its adjectival derivatives (*völkisch, volkstümlich, Volksfest*, and *Völkergemeinschaft*), which are derived from the Proto-Germanic *fulką*, present semantic challenges to English-language readers, especially when they are juxtaposed to those words based on the Latinate etymon *popularis* (*populär, populistisch*, and *popular*). Not only must readers keep in mind the history of the former's fascist instrumentalization in the name of Aryan, blood-and-soil ideologies, but also how the latter is indistinguishable in translation from the German word *Menschen* (used below), which is also rendered as "people."]

2. [Translator's note and citation: Kluge writes in German of "das Politische" (the political), which English readers may instantly associate with Carl Schmitt's 1932 formulation in *The Concept of the Political*. Yet Kluge and Oskar Negt distinguish their own understanding of the political from Schmitt's elsewhere in *Maßverhältnisse des Politischen*, in which the present essay by Kluge appears. Unlike Schmitt's concern with the antagonistic divide between friend and foe, Negt and Kluge situate "the political" *within* "the internal structure of a nation [*Volk*]" and identify it with those "raw materials" required for the enduring constitution of commonwealth [*Gemeinwesen*]. Distinct from the "art of the possible" associated with professional politicians, the political applies to the conditions of possibility in everyday life contexts that make communal action possible. See Oskar Negt and Alexander Kluge, *Maßverhältnisse des Politischen*, in *Der unterschätzte Mensch: Gemeinsame Philosophie in zwei Bänden* 1 (Frankfurt am Main: Zweitausendeins, 2001), 1:758, 708.]

3. [Translator's note: Kluge writes in German of the "populare Methode," which cannot be rendered in English simply as "the popular method," for the adjective in question is derived from the German for *populares* (*die Popularen*), that group in the Roman Republic that supported the cause of the plebeians.]

4. [Translator's note and citation: Christian Meier develops this idea of colliding realities in Christian Meier, *Res publica amissa: Eine Studie zu Verfassung und Geschichte der späten römischen Republik* (Frankfurt am Main: Suhrkamp, 1980). See also Christian Meier, *The Greek Art of Politics*, trans. David McLintock (Cambridge, MA: Harvard University Press, 1990).]

5. [Translator's note: Unattributed in the German original, this quotation is repeated with slight variations throughout Kluge's later essayistic work. The original source of the quotation is Marx's *Economic and Philosophic Manuscripts*, which reads: "The transcendence of self-estrangement follows the same course as self-estrangement." The translation provided here is of Kluge's variation. See Karl Marx, *Economic and Philosophic Manuscripts of 1844*, trans. Martin Milligan and Dirk J. Struik, in Karl Marx and Friedrich Engels, *Collected Works*, vol. 3, *Marx and Engels: March 1843–August 1844* (London: Lawrence and Wishart, 1975), 294.]

6. I would like to point out that Emperor Augustus carries out the reconstruction at the tail end of the Roman Republic. He not only disguises his control but also mobilizes notionally [*imaginär*] the totality of Roman virtues; when he dies, he has himself made up, his languid cheeks are massaged, and he speaks to his surroundings as an actor: How was the play I performed? The overwhelming masses of reality that diverge under the semiotic world contained in the acronym S.P.Q.R. (the second letter stands for *populus*) make necessary a chimeric representation by the emperor, who acts as if he were a common citizen. This illusoriness and spectacularity were embedded in this monarchy from the beginning; for a long time, it is foreign to medieval monarchies, which develop in more synoptic, crude societies rather than under the overwhelming pressure of the world, and articulate the exchange of one form of "reliability for another form of reliability." When talking about autocracy—the opposite of democracy—we must therefore discuss at the very least two fundamentally different roots of monarchy. This would quickly make clear that an American president could not develop an autocracy in the royal sense, but always only in the praetorian sense.

7. [Translator's note: This dialectical formulation is a hallmark in all of Negt and Kluge's writings. It can be found in slightly altered form in Oskar Negt and Alexander Kluge, *Public Sphere and Experience: Toward an Analysis of the Bourgeois and Proletarian Public Sphere*, trans. Peter Labanyi, Jamie Owen Daniel, and Assenka Oksiloff (Minneapolis: University of Minnesota Press, 1993), 296; and in Alexander Kluge and Oskar Negt, *History and Obstinacy*, ed. Devin Fore, trans. Richard Langston et al. (New York: Zone Books, 2014), 220.]

8. [Translator's note: The imaginary is for Negt and Kluge one of six primary dimensions of historical relations they add to Bertolt Brecht's own proposed enhancement of the horizontal and vertical dimensions. Brecht's functional dimension accounts for the abstractions in which capital operates that deceive the human senses and frustrate individual efforts at orientation. The imaginary "is the coordinate of loss, the loss of reality, history, and identity." Additional dimensions include, but are not limited to, the horizontal, vertical, irrational, and revolutionary. See Kluge and Negt, *History and Obstinacy*, 237 and 503n25.]

9. [Translator's note: Robert Musil, *Der Mann ohne Eigenschaften*, ed. Adolf Frisé (Reinbek bei Hamburg: Rowohlt, 1978), 1803. Kluge's quotation is taken from Musil's notes to the novel's second volume, which are excised from the English translation.]

10. [Translator's citation: Friedrich Nietzsche, *Human, All Too Human: A Book of Free Spirits*, trans. R. J. Hollingdale (Cambridge: Cambridge University Press, 1996), 22.]

11. [Translator's citation: Ivan Nagel, *Autonomy and Mercy: Reflections on Mozart's Operas*, trans. Marion Faber (Cambridge, MA: Harvard University Press, 1991), 69 (translation slightly modified).]

12. [Translator's citation: Friedrich Nietzsche, *On the Genealogy of Morals*, trans. Douglas Smith (Oxford: Oxford University Press, 1996), 42–44.]

23

WAR

War lays waste to fields, depopulates provinces, and turns cities into dust. WAR IS A FIGHT BETWEEN RULERS CARRIED OUT WITH THE HELP OF WEAPONS.

This definition comes from Louis de Jaucourt's article "Guerre (*Droit naturel & Politique*)."[1] The article was written in 1757 during the second year of the Seven Years' War. The Russians have just defeated a Prussian army at Gross-Jägersdorf. Following this victory and the short-lived cheer in St. Petersburg, they retreat eastward without result. Later that year, Frederick the Great defeats in a matter of hours both the French army and that of the Holy Roman Empire in a kind of blitzkrieg. It is the era of the cabinet wars. The long path involved in the "taming of war" leads from the butchery of the Middle Ages to the calculated slaughter of the eighteenth century. One can enjoy lunch in peace just two kilometers away from the battlefield. We rarely see the whole picture.

It is a war among rulers. Like a vaccination, societies internalized the excesses of a war that would not end (we call it the Thirty Years' War), the religious wars in France, and the barbarism involved in the founding of the early colonies. RULES OF WAR were developed. The way in which people deal with the catastrophe of war is regarded as a high art form. This art consists not only in conquering the enemy, but also in reining in the autonomous forces as well as war's movements, which subjugates the entire world to its destructive power. This art of war (*l'art de guerre*) is considered to be the highest of art forms, above even architecture. Thus, Frederick the Great writes of Prussia during the Battle at Rossbach: "I cannot get used to seeing the French as my enemies." He makes sure it is known that on the evening before a battle he takes Racine's tragedy *Mithridate* in hand and, while looking out the window, recites verse by the tragic poet accompanied by dramatic gestures.

Thirty-five years later, what erupts out of the escalation of the French Revolution is a form of modern war Jaucourt could not have known when he wrote his encyclopedia article: the people's war. It is a world war from the very beginning. The first of these conflicts lasts twenty-three years (1792 to 1815). It is transatlantic because the independence of the United States, England's occupation of foreign colonies, its expansion of its naval powers, Napoleon's continental battles against Austria, Prussia, and Russia, and the uprising in Spain are all interconnected. Honor, nobility, glory, natural law, and the "fruits of war" (all taken from Jaucourt's vocabulary) become catchphrases. Weapons of mass destruction (industrialized war), *levée en masse* (mass conscription), propaganda. Economic war and guerrilla war are new phenomena. This new form of war finally dies out in the second half of the twentieth century (and even then only in the metropolises) and is replaced by methods of deterrence.

Meeting at the Congress of Vienna, Europe's exhausted nations agree on neither natural law nor the instruments of popular unity after 1815, but rather on the division of spheres of influence and the instruments of repression. It is a seventeenth-century apparatus meant to tame the nineteenth century. Henry Kissinger's concepts of war and peace are founded on this political arsenal.

Carl von Clausewitz's posthumously published theoretical commentary *On War* is written in reference to the war that transpired between 1792 and 1815. In book 1, entitled "On the Nature of War," Clausewitz first describes *modern* war. War, he says, is an act of violence meant to force an opponent to fulfill our will. No word about rulers and nothing about states. The "state of war" is also not a tool against chaos. This theory of war applies to hate and the reconciliation in love, war between generations, or economic empires, and it sufficiently describes the blitzkrieg of 1940 up until the bitter end in Berlin. Both the Gulf War and the war today between Ethiopia and Eritrea also follow Clausewitz's description, but the war in Kosovo does not in the least.

War is a serious matter. Nothing appears more barbaric in war than bonhomie, writes Clausewitz. Nothing of the spirit of war, not even its most inhumane manifestations, counteracts the most extreme application of all means. War, says Clausewitz, "dreams of its absolute power."[2] Nothing counteracts this more than reality itself. This includes the weather, failure (frictions), loss, and especially the subjective powers. "The probabilities of real life replace the extreme and the absolute required by theory."[3] War can destroy itself or be destroyed only in an attack by stronger force.

In 1939, Albert Einstein organized a written poll: What can a person set in motion, including the activation of a moral conscience, in order to prevent the outbreak of war?[4] Sigmund Freud answered skeptically. He claimed that what triggers war is an inherent part of the human moral structure. The united conscience, he wrote, was more comparable to a time bomb than the tools used to defuse an explosive device. One must look for antidotes within war itself, in its boundlessness and in its disproportionality to humankind. If war cannot extinguish itself, then there is no effective antidote. However, humans do possess a hypersensitive allergy to war. This treasure is what must be enhanced. Researchers who mine the depths of the human species say that people are capable of reacting to war idiosyncratically just as they do to pill bugs. It is therefore curious that they instead allow themselves to be fascinated by colorful uniforms that actually have little to do with the annihilating fury of war.

The New Image of War/Virtual War

The international protests set off by the war in Vietnam and the objective impossibility that either superpower could attack one another in an open war without destroying itself forcibly changed the IMAGE OF WAR IN THE SECOND HALF OF THE TWENTIETH CENTURY. The years between 1970 and 1989 are characterized by the fact that the threat of rockets and atomic weapons created a paralyzing threat especially for Europe that quelled all theoretical zeal. A total catastrophe is clearly possible at any moment. Assembled out of an absurd collection of pieces, the keystone in an ARCHITECTURE OF SECURITY is called peace. On top of this, the mechanisms of deterrence are extended into outer space (the Strategic Defense Initiative). This functions like the negative of Clausewitz's conception. The probabilities of daily life would certainly be capable of setting into motion the absolute violence of war. On the other hand, a hybrid communication system (experts from hostile powers) constructed at the limit of improbability is capable of maintaining a system of balances. A prerequisite for this is that no one makes immediate claims to human rights or moral positions. To this extent, the same issues are at play as during the Congress of Vienna or in the seventeenth century. The second premise seems to be that no planned interventions take place. The apparatus managing international crises via assistants and student assistants who are responsible for accompanying their bosses to conferences assumes a certain unconsciousness similar to that of someone riding a horse across Lake Constance or a stock market analyst who, in order to prevent Black Friday, must avoid taking the synoptic view.

> *Ten thousand devils, together*
> *Igniting the wealth of nations.*
>   (Adam Smith/Ezra Pound)[5]

This theory of a NONWAR THAT IS NOT PEACE remained hitherto unwritten because it sounds absurd in a public discussion among reasonable people who feel beholden to the categories of the *Encyclopédie*. But the fact remains that all forms of war coexist at the same time: the atavistic ones, the cabinet wars, total war, peoples' wars, wars of deterrence, space wars, and wars that come to Earth from outer space. Nothing in modern history promises that any of these aspects of war reliably remains suppressed. It is therefore essential to investigate the interaction between these forms of war. It is less a question of truth than balance. In a completely different sense, it is about the ART OF WAR as Jaucourt used the term in 1757. Only those who understand the machinery of war are capable of diffusing a time bomb. The most important political question in this connection is to what extent such a QUESTION regarding the CASE OF EMERGENCY can be given over to experts. We need a functioning PUBLIC SPHERE, if only because a decision about war and peace—this everyday question rooted in sovereignty—is not possible without it.

Achievements and Limitations Due to War

Reports that wars could have led to technological advances, a process of enlightenment, or even "creative destruction" are largely based on rumors. However, the bitter experiences of war have brought about limitations that have become part of antiwar policies or those set on scaling back war. Among them is the insight into the limitlessness and savagery of war. Another example is the Red Cross that protects prisoners of war and the wounded and arose out of the harrowing experiences of the Battle of Solferino, a semi-industrial bloodbath in service of Italy's independence. Also essential are the intellectual limitations contained in the concept of war (in the right-wing faction of international law). Can a single individual or a lone gunman declare war on humanity? Would Michael Kohlhaas, whose rights were violated, have been justified in declaring war? What about the status of an urban guerilla? Do wars between clans or the slaughter of one's neighbors, which we have seen in the Balkans and Indonesia, have anything to do with war? Do murders committed by lovers out of desperation in the private sphere count as war? Is this war against the other or society?

Still in force during war, INTERNATIONAL LAW is an achievement developed out of the horrors of medieval war, which spilled over into the early modern period and reach their climax in religious fanaticism (which remains the case today). Definitions limiting war such that people maintain certain privileges in the midst of it are found in Hugo Grotius's *On the Law of War and Peace: Three Books*. A prisoner may not be tortured and his human rights may not be violated more than is necessary for war. Civilians not involved in battle may not be targeted by extermination programs. This understanding of international law focuses on the freedom of maritime routes and trade and on the idea that an ideal path toward final peace is always possible. "Always act in such a way that you can keep working after the battles cease."[6]

Radical War Crimes Not Penalized at Nuremberg

The line between war and barbarism has always been thin. The difference, to the extent that there is one, is denoted in the fact that the enemy has the option to capitulate. By imposing my will on someone, I may not annihilate them. There is a pathos in Clausewitz's conception of war: I can subjugate the will of the other only when such a will exists in the first place.

Military specialists have a different idol. It revolves around the battle of annihilation (the Battle of Cannae), on the one hand, and the idea of "draining the blood of the enemy," i.e., killing them without bringing about a particular outcome (the Battle of Verdun), on the other.[7] Air wars against civilian populations radicalized these positions. The goal of spurring disobedience within a population or causing an uprising against its own leadership (*moral bombing*) has proven to be unachievable from a sociopsychological standpoint. On the other hand, a population that finds itself hiding in a cellar (a strategy from below) has no weapons against bomb squads (a strategy from above). It is therefore practically impossible for a besieged population to capitulate in the concrete moment when an armada approaches.

Twenty-first-century scenarios involving military extortion go far beyond this perverse escalation of war. The scenario of protecting oneself against rockets while the threat continues to assail the rest of the world (missile defense shield) contains a potential for execution that is far greater than attacks by air or those involving poison gas. On the level of forgoing economic and diplomatic sanctions, this scenario creates a situation in which concrete individuals have effectively no recourse to capitulation. Abstract powers along with their own impotent authority DE-REALIZE sanctions before the killing commences.

The conspiracy of starting and carrying out this type of "military action," which neither corresponds to the concept of war nor does it have any historical basis in atavistic forms of bloodshed, represents a new type of crime that we must demand be overseen by a supranational, international legal body. Importantly, this is not a matter of war crimes but rather an independent type of crime: crimes against history.

War Develops Its Own Antidote

There are rare cases in which the experience of war survives. The tenaciousness of war but above all its morphogenesis (the simultaneity of modern and ancient forms) have cemented the preconception that nothing can abolish war. This may be true for war as a whole, but is not the case for the individual elements that constitute war. Every medium of war can be assumed to have a limited half-life. War is thus "engrafted onto human nature" (Immanuel Kant).[8] It is artificial.

In 1914, chemistry was considered a modern industry. Its contribution to the chaos of Verdun was poison gas. A gas attack led in 1917 to the first breakthrough battle on the eastern front, at which point the military leadership discovered the principle of blitzkrieg.

This groundbreaking and terrible weapon "fell back asleep." Poison gas haunted the plans for future air wars drafted in the 1920s. It was used in North African colonies. During World War II, poison gas was actually kept on hand, but never deployed. We have no protection against the future use of biological or chemical weapons. Yet the fact that weapons are mortal demonstrates a certain "forgetfulness of war" that experience nourishes.

Most Wars Arise from Ancillary Matters

Factors resulting in war arise separately but then march in unison. In comparison, the human powers of attention, which should attend to these factors, are mortal and divided across generations. They behave distractedly. Modern administrations requiring the approval of their citizens will give their attention to primary conflicts. This concentration is exactly what limits the attention span available for peripheral conflicts, which evolve into crises that infiltrate reality. In this respect, a second institution alongside every administration involved in preventing war is needed to watch over ancillary matters. This is happening to a certain extent in foundations dedicated to advancing security policies.

The Second Punic War arose out of chance revolts by mercenaries who occupied a city in Sicily and then sought protection from Rome. The issue was essentially just as irrelevant for Carthage as it was for Rome. Both major powers were pitted against each other by third parties, an ancillary matter of history. Rome could almost have been brought down by such a trivial matter (after the Battle of Cannae), and Carthage actually was.

The Statistics of Deadly Quarrels

In order to research the bare violence that broke out in the First and Second World Wars, the meteorologist L. F. Richardson fed data on every instance of war and peace between 1815 and 1945 into his computer designed to analyze weather probabilities.[9] An image emerges of a continuously growing crisis that builds up the longer peace lasts. In this respect, each war, says Richardson, is that much more gruesome and its dead that much more abundant than the length of the preceding time of peace.

What is fascinating about this observation is the fact that the unprincipled, improvised security plans laid out at the Congress of Vienna provided no tools that could have prevented the escalation of a worldwide or even European crisis leading up to 1914. Richardson describes something simple: the historical process contains continuity, and the phases of war and peace are only just metamorphoses. The rule: the longer the peace, the bleaker the wars must therefore not apply to eras when no crises are building up because conflicts can be drained off.

Every analysis of the concept of war circles around the categories of probability and improbability. Trust in the improbable is crucial in order to prevent wars, while calculations of probability have caused a large number of planned or imagined wars. The preconceptions this brings about, meaning the belief in the probable, must be interrupted by the "desire for the improbable," which can be found in every human being, even in many a politician.[10] This is the art of catching the right moment in time, which can be observed in historical strokes of good fortune. On the other hand, the same human "desire for the improbable" traditionally leads to the outbreak of war (like in 1914) when people expect war to reverse the reality principle with which they are unsatisfied. With respect to the relation among large industrialized nations, the expectation has faded today that war will bring about a break in everyday life rather than immediate injury and inhuman chaos. Even in 1939 it was clear that the excitement for war no longer existed.

Fatalists, Skeptics

If lacking preconceptions means preserving one's disbelief in the necessity of war then skeptics in the tradition of Montaigne are farther from harboring preconceptions and fatalists closer: those who act out of conviction, be it in opposition to or in support of war, oddly align themselves in practice with the fatalists. They lack the disbelief in war.

Peace Agreements Are Only Tenable When They Fully Regulate the Conflicts of Interest

Clausewitz describes war as the continuation of politics by other means in the sense that wars, subject to the laws of reality, lead to peace agreements. At some point, the war is exhausted and collapses into peace. At the same time, however, Clausewitz also points to the fact that the characteristic structure of a war influences the structure of the peace agreement. Much like handwriting. Thus, the principle of annihilation, which lies at the heart of military expertise, has been the cause of grave errors in the peace process: with the Germans against the Russians in the Treaty of Brest-Litovsk in 1917 and with the Allies against the Germans at Versailles in 1919. The structure of violent and simultaneously incomplete peace agreements is recognizable from not only the consequences for the opponent, but also those within one's own country. The repercussions from the destruction of Carthage thus allowed for the creation of autocratic rule in Rome, the praetorian guard, the era of soldier emperors, corruption, and the downfall of the empire.

Successful peace agreements are dynamic equilibria. There are a few cases in which these not only end the war, but also wash away entire realities that led to war. The newly found balances of power established in 1945, for example, together with the Marshall Plan, were powerful enough to alter reality in central Europe, even if they also brought about a stabile cold war. Additionally, the secondary consequences brought together the Federal Republic of Germany and France after 350 years of antagonism.

Enlightenment Is Man's Emergence from His Self-Incurred Immaturity[11]

A person is immature who feels himself unable to make use of his own understanding without the help of a third party (Immanuel Kant). The image of a subject and their society as sovereign is especially essential in so-called cases of emergency. Protego ergo sum: I am able to protect, therefore I am—this is the original line of sovereignty, an almost maternal characteristic. The self-armament of human beings based on this must be capable of preventing the violent inversion of all environmental relations we consider war or a crime. Only in doing so is a person or a society sovereign and thus open to enlightenment.

In their book *Authority and the Family*, which focuses on the relation between the private sphere, enlightenment, fascism, and war, Horkheimer and Adorno describe a traditional structure out of which a counter-construction to the enlightenment, the authoritarian character, develops. Like nuclear reactors, millions of families turn overheated energy into a WAR OF FEELINGS; from the perspective of society, this transpires in isolated plots. When these energies are naively transferred to society as a whole ("politics of feelings"), mass movements, exclusion, destruction, and the subjective raw materials for war are created. At the dawn of the twenty-first century, it should be added that the social process and its subjective authors are further split from each other more than they have ever been before. Classical economists could not be further from today's truth when they write that the producers of life and society stand alongside the production process of history, over which they supposedly rule. Having arrived at a certain point of estrangement, it seems irrelevant which fallacies and impulses humans adhere to, since the social process continues without them. As with the strategy of deterrence, this splitting of human beings from society, the lifeworld from the system, creates a balance. It makes intentional wars and wars supported by urban populations unlikely. It contains extreme risks for the system that people fail to monitor closely. It sets off dangerous sparks in the interaction between the individual cells of society (overheated but still toiling away, only vaguely diluted by the media, distracted, and lateralized) and the systems sensitive to the opinions of citizens, including the global ones. Curiously, the following applies: because humans are incapacitated, they pose little threat of war. Because systems are objectified, their motivation to wield violence operates below the threshold of war.

A reader who takes the *Encyclopédie* to heart (and has foreknowledge of the hopeful gardens from the classical period of 1801) cannot be satisfied by a perspective based on immaturity and trained humanity. Because large parts of human emotional and labor power go unused by modern globalized systems, these are free to carve out beaten paths to maturity as simultaneously and intrusively as possible. This requires us to learn from bitter experience. In lieu of preventing war, something we have no direct influence on, we bring it to mind. Which counterforces are effective against the elements of war, says Freud, is something we can learn only from war itself. The advantage we have over the experiences from 1757 is the knowledge that war as a whole is an object much too large, fickle, and, to a certain extent, concealed for human powers: war is a monster. What we also know is that each *individual* element of war can be tackled using the techniques used to dismantle time bombs from the last 350 years. At this point, the battle against war still remains identical to the battle against prejudices.

The Pacifists' Internationale

Just as it is excessive to try and measure the FATHER OF ALL THINGS, war as a constantly shifting whole, even when its individual elements are conquerable, one must also not imagine a pacifist as an individual or as coalition of individuals. Freud correctly points out that doing so projects onto the side of pacifists those internal human elements that are always at war, the permanent war within us. The Internationale among pacifists is much more a park of feelings, differentiations, and character traits that spontaneously arise of their own accord and work against the principle of annihilation. The horticultural characteristics within humans are the antithesis of war. This means that moralizing or inappropriate aggravation may not carry out exclusions once again within these characteristics. Along these lines, human beings are not moral or truth-seeking creatures, but rather creators of illusions. They protect themselves with illusions by believing in guardian angels, luck, unlikely rescues, or human power over war and fate. This illusion or belief is no prejudice. People living in cocoons are actually capable of finding happiness. Against the horrors of war, happiness must therefore be applied as an effective amalgamation to all individual elements of the human character, including those that are provocative in a moral sense. I deny the existence of war, I hallucinate that it does not exist, I consider myself, my children, and my children's children protected by a lucky fate. These are all advantageous preconceptions that should be seen as belonging to the pacifists' Internationale.

What remains unrevoked from the socialist Internationale and the Spartacus League of 1917 is their radical opposition to war. This, and not the principle of equality of all people, is the spearhead of the socialist Internationale. The fact that this remained ineffective against the outbreak of world war in 1914 sparked the industrial and emotional process that briefly led to the impression that this path might lead to the maturation of humanity in the face of the emergency of war. Either the murder of Rosa Luxemburg and the general recapitulation of this revolutionary element by friends and enemies or the vague recognition of beaten paths led to a temporary failure of this developmental process. It culminated in a real socialist administration and repression, which the founders would never have understood. They are proponents of a slave rebellion and also opponents of war. The only successful case of a war fought by slaves was in the Republic of Haiti, and its negative repercussions continue into the present. The antimilitaristic impulse of the socialist movement is a thorn that remains irrefutable. Only by virtue of this impulse can the difference between the "appeaser" and the "enragé" be detected (revanchist and radical, respectively). All prejudices, all fallacies and illusions, the thoughts of the black market, all morally reprehensible and sensuously attractive feelings, the desire for personal gains, the search for happiness, market speculation, as well as unscrupulous entrepreneurship have unfettered access to the pacifists' Internationale.

A Memorial for the Unknown Deserter, to Be Built within the Line of Sight of the Brandenburg Gate

Among the starkest hypocrisies in the face of the Enlightenment are the death sentences given to deserters. Whoever failed to sign the social contract cannot be sentenced to death because they escaped a massacre, or wanted to make their way home to their beloved and therefore swam across the Rhine from Strasbourg to Baden (as in the folk song "In Strassburg on the Rampart"). Even after May 8, 1945, sailors were punished by death for desertion. Nothing else can be done other than offering an apology by erecting a national memorial.

Translated by Emma Woelk

Notes

This encyclopedia entry was originally published in German as Alexander Kluge, "Krieg," in *Die Welt der Encyclopédie*, ed. Anette Selg and Rainer Wieland (Frankfurt am Main: Eichborn, 2001), 211–16.

1. [Translator's citation: Louis de Jaucourt, "Guerre (Droit naturel & Politique)," in *Encyclopédie, ou Dictionnaire raisonné des Sciences, des Arts et des Métiers*, ed. Denis Diderot and Jean-Baptiste le Rond d'Alembert (Paris: Chez Briasson, 1757), 995–98.]

2. [Translators citation: What Kluge attributes as a quotation is arguably a paraphrase of Clausewitz's first chapter in *On War*. He does this also in Alexander Kluge, *The Devil's Blind Spot: Tales from the New Century*, trans. Martin Chalmers and Michael Hulse (New York: New Directions, 2004), 91, 311.]

3. [Translator's citation: Carl von Clausewitz, *On War*, ed. and trans. Michael Howard and Peter Paret (Princeton, NJ: Princeton University Press, 1984), 80.]

4. [Translator's citation: Albert Einstein and Sigmund Freud, "Why War?," trans. Stuart Gilbert, in *The Weimar Sourcebook*, ed. Anton Kaes, Martin Jay, and Edward Dimendberg (Berkeley: University of California Press, 1994), 25–34.]

5. [Translator's note: The provenance of this ostensible quotation remains unclear. Although Ezra Pound does mention Adam Smith once in *The Cantos* (XL), this exact quotation does not appear therein. Television interviews suggest that Kluge's minimal interest in Pound transpired through Heiner Müller and Durs Grünbein.]

6. [Translator's note: This quotation is very likely Kluge himself intentionally invoking the syntax of Kant's Categorical Imperative to illustrate the limitations Grotius addresses in his foundations to international law.]

7. [Translator's note: The provenance of this quotation remains unclear.]

8. [Translator's citation: Immanuel Kant, "Toward Perpetual Peace," *Practical Philosophy*, ed. and trans. Mary J. Gregor (Cambridge: Cambridge University Press, 1996), 334.]

9. [Translator's citation: Lewis F. Richardson, *Statistics of Deadly Quarrels*, ed. Quincy Wright and C. C. Lienau (Pittsburgh: Boxwood Press, 1960).]

10. [Translator's note: Kluge's Kleistian reference to the "desire for the improbable" [Lust aufs Unwahrscheinliche] is taken from Alexander Kluge, *Macht der Gefühle* (Frankfurt am Main: Zweitausendeins, 1984), 3, 169, 227.]

11. [Translator's citation: Immanuel Kant, "An Answer to the Question: 'What Is Enlightenment?,'" in *Kant: Political Writings*, ed. Hans Reiss, trans. H. B. Nisbet (Cambridge: Cambridge University Press, 1991), 54.]

24

The Art of Drawing Distinctions

The Yearning of Cells

I have lost something and because of this I now yearn for it. This is what sets living people in motion. In this respect, life is lived indirectly and looks for what has gone missing. As we know to our bewilderment, our bodies replicate the 98-degree temperature of the primordial seas from which we emerged. The salt content of the primordial seas even matches that of our kidneys. There appear to be happy moments hidden in our development millions of years ago, our enormous ability to remember, for which our cells still yearn without us ever knowing.

The Capacity for Differentiation

Imagine the human body: take, for example, the mouth, whose capacity for differentiation would be called a sensation. The largest organ, the skin, also has sensation.

Each animal by God is blessed
With kind of skin it loves the best.[1]

The ear: therein lies musicality, the sense of balance, the sense of hearing, and rhythm. These sensations are divided between two cerebral hemispheres. All of these sensations play a role in an encounter with another person. For reasons only we know, we find him attractive. We fall in love. And the other person does this in turn with his nostrils, eyes, and ears. Two people fall in love. Or they cannot smell each other. The moment when related sensations reach a decision about another human being is called feeling.

This is not something sentimental, but rather is subject to the sentimentalization and commercialization of the nineteenth century. In reality, feeling is something very human. It is what a person adds to an objective relation. It is raining and I get wet—I thereby sense something. This can be good fortune—rainwater in a barrel is something lovely to bathe in—and it can be full of misfortune—I start to freeze; I have a cold. In order to be able to convey more clearly the difference between sensation [*Empfindung*] and feeling [*Gefühl*], I would like to introduce another term: passion. There is the passion of the mind. And there is the mind of passion. This is the intensification of the will, feeling, the sum of various feelings pointed in a single direction. One can develop this sort of "mind of passion" for another person, freedom, or the well-being of one's own children. We call it *feeling* when the totality of our capacity for differentiation is combined with a set of sensations and these are then directed toward other human beings or society. *Feeling is the patriotism of sensations, so to speak*. This capacity for differentiation is my domain. From time to time, we need to take stock of it. This means that we have to test this feeling, this capacity for differentiation that we carry around with us like property, in order to make sure we can use it for ourselves and for the community. Does it bring us human beings together or does it separate us? Does this lead to voluntary actions or only to obedience? These are big differences. If one looks at the 100 years that lie ahead, one sees the first balance sheets for the twenty-first century. One will soon be able to tell if the so-called bad characteristics like lethargy and slowness are actually bad characteristics. Are these not actually the means that could lead to increased understanding and more voluntary actions? From time to time we can check our mistakes to see whether they contain a mutation and if progress has occurred. I became a good person by mistake. As an author, not as a scientist, I can describe this in a single story, but not as a principle.

The Power of Invisible Forces

The scientist Rupert Sheldrake, a former research fellow of the Royal Society, researches morphogenetic fields and describes with astonishing consistency the interstitial space of human labor in terms of a relation of forces along the lines of gravitation that arise in between human endeavors. He describes it as follows: millions of female typists write on QWERTY keyboards in the twenties and thirties. The reasons for this sequence of letters are purely mechanical so that the keys do not overlap. It occurred to him that Russians, whose typewriters use Cyrillic instead of Latin letters, learn up to sixteen times faster on a QWERTY keyboard than on one organized according to the Russian alphabet. In addition to this, he was surprised that computer keyboards also tend to use the typewriter's QWERTY paradigm even though it no longer makes sense, since there is nothing mechanical that can get stuck. For this reason he says that habits, inertia, and activities practiced by millions of people over a long time generate pathways, a kind of gravitation, or simply morphologies. To deviate from this gravitation and do something more independent instead is more difficult than following it. This would be, for example, a possible explanation for the observation that every homeopath along with Paracelsus made, namely, that potency increases with dilution. Paracelsus says: If I cast only five grams of yellow dye into the Rhine from its eastern banks where the river flows into Lake Constance, then the slight potency of the dye will most definitely arrive in Constance. Every practitioner of healthy human reason [*Verstand*] would consider this improbable. Yet the human body reacts to homeopathy in the same way. Perhaps *because the body responds more powerfully to faint suggestions*. Perhaps because the yearning of the cells answers in response.

Van der Waal Forces: The Garrulity of Nature

What amazes me about human bodies are van der Waal forces. There is a force within every human cell that does not even rank among the four principal forces: a force that is not identical to strong, weak, or electromagnetic interactions, or to any other physically measurable force. It is active in a living egg but not in a cooked one. It makes up the difference between life and death. These are the van der Waal forces that chaotically congregate within a cell and move around like a chatty class of children on a school playground. If there is another similarly chatty class in the cell next door, then they will come over to the fence such that their forces impose on each other. This only exists in living beings. These van der Waal forces are one of the most mysterious occurrences in nature; they produce in us moods and fluidity—even though they cannot flow into each other and can never travel past the cell wall. They communicate without ever touching one another. How can this be explained? Sheldrake calls this a morphic structure. Maybe this type of force that attracts improbabilities does exist. If so, then improbabilities accumulate to some extent throughout history. Human inventions like the essence of the book have perhaps survived on account of this.

Fanatical bishops in Alexandria burn its library, the largest of its kind in the world. It contained one copy of every scroll and papyrus that existed in the ancient world. The library was closed at the behest of a fundamentalist Christian bishop who believed that the people needed only the Holy Scripture. In fact, the Holy Scripture was itself too much. The people needed only a catechism, an abridged version, seven verses they were to memorize. So we will burn it down. This library lives on in my heart. I truly believe that we will find the lost scripts again. This is what we are meant to do.

4.2 Billion Years of Accumulation

All of the elements in our bodies and the cosmos are made up of three colors. They are assembled at the subatomic level and form, in a manner of speaking, the core of matter. These three colors are referred to as such because physicists are not able to explain what accounts for the strong interaction that holds matter together. These are forces that cannot be separated. Were they to allow themselves to be pulled a mere meter apart, they would develop such a sense of longing to be reunited that they could light up all of Siberia.

This characteristic of matter gives rise to music, people, and everything surrounding us; it is just as old as we are. Our companion, the earth, is 4.2 billion years old. We carry around in our bodies 4.2 billion years of accumulation, traditions, mutations, the results of many mistakes, and improbabilities. This improbability forms an objective and a subjective world. Everything I understand to be part of a chronicle is made up of quantities of time from our own era that deal with the realm of subjective forces. This is actually different from the realm of sentimental feelings or those feelings vulnerable to propaganda and commerce that rise with the stock exchange. In these realms, feelings are transformed into hierarchies: What is a good feeling, what is a bad one? What kinds of feelings can be increased? What is an extremely excessive, sensational, or monstrous feeling? This is what both operas and department stores are concerned with.

Testing Experience Once More

Michel de Montaigne has experience with religious wars: the St. Bartholomew's Day massacre in which Catholics slaughtered Protestants. To be called a Protestant means nothing other than belonging to those Swiss who barricaded themselves in Switzerland or La Rochelle and slaughtered Catholics. For a moment under Henry IV, peace emerges. Feelings briefly become sensible. At this point, Montaigne assumes his place and says: Outfitted with Ovid, antiquity's writers, and our contemporary experiences, we are going to set side by side all sensations, every experience ranging from lies to the fabrication of illusions, from establishing the truth to desire, in order to test once more the following: What brings people together? What is good for the community? What abolishes religious wars?

In the sixteenth and seventeenth centuries, strong traces of an enlightenment reside in the tenacity found in the diaphragm.

If the Enlightenment of the eighteenth century was insufficient in order to defeat fascism, then one must dig deeper and inquire about earlier stages of enlightenment.

I Consider My Feelings My Possession

In the beginnings of bourgeois society—Max Horkheimer described this frequently—land ownership is my line of work. I am an artisan or a lawyer, and base my self-consciousness on my profession. I am so to speak the author of my abilities. In addition to that, I am the author of my passions and my ability to make bonds. Whomever I marry, whether I practice familial love politics or produce a catastrophe, makes a huge difference.

I regard as my property not only my possessions and the abilities I use to produce things. I also consider to be my property my feelings and how I bind them to other people's either provisionally or for life. *What I really want is my lifelong property*, and precisely this is unsalable. Above all else, I can haggle over my assets, my possessions, you name it. Yet I cannot forfeit the core of my will.

In reality, feelings are incorruptible. It is a harsh judgment, if I say to someone: I cannot stand you. I do not believe that bribing, changing, swaying, or domination can remedy it. Conversely, when I love something—"I love you . . . what can you do about it?"—that can be an enduring feeling; it can remain unrequited and still remain indomitable.

The Diaphragm, Zone of Resistance

Every human characteristic is capable of feeling and can form a structure that cooperates with others. Take, for example, the diaphragm.

When human beings developed their upright gait, their digestive tract and the sexual organs traveled downward, whereas breathing, intellect, insanity, and matters of the soul were streamlined up above. In between is the zone of resistance, the diaphragm. A completely uncontrollable quantity. When authority makes a fool of itself in churches and in schools, the diaphragm laughs. An irrepressible outburst of laughter. One of a very few completely subversive forces. In the Middle Ages there was the grotesque. At a peasant feast, at the end of a funeral, or at a celebration: grotesque jokes and hyperbole. *A Celtic narrative form that appeals to the diaphragm.* This laughter, says Rainer Stollmann, is even older than language. It is bound to the ability to walk upright.

The Origin of Language

First we become accustomed to each other's facial expressions and gesticulations, then comes sound, and then at some point language develops. Interestingly, we always have the capacity for language within us. Every one of Napoleon's grenadiers carries it with him to Moscow, and still each arrives there in winter. *Our characteristics are not at their peak.* We do not use them, but they are hidden treasures.

That We Are More Likely to Dream at the Cinema

Something different: our eyes are not fast. Their capacity for differentiation requires 1/48 of a second. For example, the eye cannot actually discern that the movie theater is dark half the time a film runs. During a two-hour movie, we relax in the dark for an hour. The brain perceives this and our many synapses register it, but everyone still thinks they saw a continuous film. Experiencing film is probably like this: one dreams in the movie theater—perhaps a little less in front of a television.

A Fatherland beyond the Real

I was responsible for "practical suggestions." My director never read them. It comforted him to know that there were some, and so he tolerated me in his immediate presence, and spoke up energetically for me when I was supposed to be let go. He needs me, he said.

Our director was a wastrel. Preoccupied with the facial expressions of a single actress, the mountain girl, he let over 1,000 extras wait four hours. Thereafter, the hired horde was ridiculous and no longer needed for the arranged scene. The shooting was postponed till the following day.

What were my suggestions aimed at? Initially, I focused on the plot. Using the same actress, *Intolerance* describes the events in Babylon that lead to the death of the king and his followers; even the mountain girl dies when she sets out to protect him. An episode ensues during the St. Bartholomew's Day massacre in Paris; it proved impossible to save the mistress in the deadly night. In the concluding story, a man unjustly convicted to the gallows is saved by his wife.

It is evident that the market punishes this kind of narrative sequence with the film's premature death. I write: Stories with happy endings must lie in the past. The mountain girl must survive in Babylon and Paris. Those prehistoric people really had enough offspring. It is unrealistic to pile up tragic events on them. Conversely, spectators at the movies know that a happy outcome in the film's final three sequences for the man sentenced to death infringes on all probability.

Griffith had neither the time nor the desire to read my elaborations. If the mountain girl dies in the first fifty minutes of the film, I whispered to him, then the spectator is overpowered by grief and the film ends. It ends, the director replied, when I want it to.

The colossal expenditures for this film—the young medium's distribution limits were still unknown—correspond to the expectation of unlimited profit. That sidelines every consideration and deviation from the original (arbitrary) blueprint for the project.

The fate of the film in the screening venues was appropriately devastating. The production company declared bankruptcy. This is how this juggernaut blocked the way for all future films. Never again was a single director trusted with such sums of production money for a nontrivial story, "the battle of love through the centuries."

One would have to hire twenty directors. They screen the mass of extras for talent. For every talent, they create a new film. A convoy of twenty to thirty films emerges. The extras stream from one illuminated set to another. Costumes are turned inside out and outfit the same actors for different stations over the course of the centuries. This PERMANENT PRODUCTION clears a path through the twentieth century and responds to (1) the changing times; (2) advances in the cinematic arts; and (3) the desires of the market.

I wrote many memoranda on the back of the daily call sheets that the enduring laws of film reveal themselves in these desires. As a spectator and not merely the assistant to a big director, I would like it if hope is hidden in earlier times from where I come. I have no property in the present, but the past belongs to me, as it does to my parents and ancestors. I want to be allowed to mourn the present, i.e., the end of the film, if only because the film ends. I am ready to separate myself from reality. Embellishing the future makes me afraid.

These few rules would have sufficed for the development of the cinematic arts. They guarantee for three to six hours (the future length of movies) a FATHERLAND BEYOND THE REAL.

Visitor from Sirius

If one had to explain human feelings to a visitor from Sirius, it might summarize the explanation as follows: obviously at some point, when your ancestors branched off from reptiles and became warm-blooded, they survived off of huge dinosaur eggs that could not be hidden because they required the heat of the sun. They used these eggs like a pharmacy in order to acquire the protein reserves necessary for giving birth to their offspring in the shade and warming their bodies. For this reason, says the visitor from Sirius, humanity's first differentiation between feelings is the distinction between hot and cold, between *too* hot and *too* cold. All other differences develop from this one, even the murder and homicide typical of the fifth act in operas, in which cold and hot are no longer distinguished. If one were to turn a sprinkler system on during the fifth act of the opera, murder could be foiled.

The Head of Passion—The Foot of Passion

Theodor W. Adorno, a lover of opera of the most advanced kind (like those of Alban Berg and Arnold Schoenberg), once posed the following question: If operas portray the head of passions, what would the foot of passions be?

I imagine that Aristotle's geographers, who march behind Alexander the Great's armies from Macedonia to the Indus River and then southward toward Egypt in order to explore the source of the Nile, do this carefully with the patience of their feet. They measure the planet with their feet, pulling an instrument behind them from which they can read the distance they travel in parasangs. They walk step by step over mountains, valleys, and rivers and explore the earth with the soles of their feet, one of the most sensitive organs of feeling there is. This is a very good use of the passion that resides in the foot. Quite often this is better than the passions of the head, which quickly lead to places on the map like Stalingrad; because its motives have vanished, the army's feet walk back toward Germany and therefore perish. The torturers know this, too. Hernán Cortés, for example, lights Montezuma's feet on fire to find out where more gold can be found. It is also customary during the Thirty Years' War to set people's feet on fire in order to find out where treasure lay buried. This is one of the harshest forms of torture.

Humankind's ingenuity at abusing feelings in order to gain power has no relation to *the emancipation of feelings that just lie fallow like treasure*. We do not make enough use of the foot's capacity to differentiate between pain and nonpain; we are not yet at the level of distinguishing patience from impatience in the foot. Yet there are places, metaphors for enlightenment and emancipation, in the interest of the human being's self-realization. If we assembled everything that people are capable of and shared this with each other, an emancipatory process, self-regulating and unstoppable, would develop on its own.

The Robot as Emotional Intelligence

Everyone is born. We are told that we cannot remember our very first days of life. But I believe there are memory traces we are simply unable to read. Robots are being built with artificial intelligence. There is a scientist at MIT developing a lovely robot programmed for the interaction between mother and child in the first days after birth. It can recognize a big smile, and as soon as it disappears, it lets its artificial ears hang low, makes a sad face, and thereby appears smarter. The robot is a form of social intelligence, an intelligence of feelings. It makes little use of the cognitive intelligence it knows; that makes it no more intelligent. Rather, its intelligence involves loving another being; it is programmed like a gray goose. This is what computer intelligence is made of. Its developers are entirely convinced that in forty to eighty years time there will be a new type of intelligence: intelligent computers and robots aware of feelings that will carry on, as it were, the better parts of humanity. At least this is the case with this development that begins with the mother-child relationship, which every one of us has experienced. This relationship fashions itself prelinguistically like a musical process by way of humming and buzzing, and a thousand tones the parents use to communicate with their child. And slowly a path develops, and at some point the child learns to differentiate. Initially, it would not be able to differentiate between its own bowel movements and its mother's face. If something is lacking or is irritating, the child becomes aggressive, but will also develop trust. This wonderful process occurs in a musical way, using both hemispheres of the brain. This is how a person learns to swim through the world.

The Long March of Basic Trust

There is a fundamental error we human beings and all the other surviving forms of life that found their way through evolution hold dear: basic trust. This error seems to be an evolutionary advantage. As soon as they are born, human beings—we must assume that animals think this way, too—believe that the world will be good to them. This is a complete error. Karl Marx would say: Necessary false consciousness. The world does not have good intentions. Yet no one wants to deal with this. It is a treasure that everyone holds onto until the end of their lives. Frankly, this is what we live off of, the ability to construct horizons. That is what Friedrich Nietzsche means when he speaks of "truth-seeking beings" and describes us as illusion-creating beings.[2] Of course, we build cocoons around ourselves just as Peter Sloterdijk says we do.

Old Celtic Trust

Asterix has an advantage over the Romans.[3] The Romans exercise allegiance to Caesar. He leads them to Gallia, where they do not fare so well, for they have no trust in the authority that brought them to this desert, this jungle. Yet the Gauls tell stories among themselves.

Facts and Fakes

The Gauls, a Celtic people, learned to tell stories—*spinning a cocoon*—so that reality becomes sweetly embellished and thus suitable for communication. The most unpleasant events are made attractive, communicable, reinterpreted, and falsified. This is why there are not just facts but also fakes. This is a necessity. I do not believe the person who claims they can deal with facts without thinking anything of it or faking something. However, I can always find a bit of fact in the lies a liar tells.

There is a difference between "trustworthy" and "untrustworthy." In his *Metamorphoses*, Ovid writes that living beings that suffer would rather transform themselves than to go on suffering. This is the entire story of the metamorphoses. Of course, they are all fiction, stories about gods. None of them are scientifically or historically correct. It is not true that Daphne turned into a laurel tree only because the lustful Apollo was chasing after her. Right when he was about to catch her, she turned into a tree that now adorns the Mediterranean. This story was thought up with intensity and created with necessary false consciousness.

Ovid is Montaigne's god, Heiner Müller's, and my own.

Every one of these stories, these fairy tales in Ovid's Metamorphoses *is more trustworthy than a modern-day news broadcast,* in which everything is told in an extremely abbreviated form.

Back to Basic Trust

If I am a good parent, I really do not want my child to fall down the stairs. But how will my child learn?

In Halberstadt, I learned exactly how bones are broken. I was born in Halberstadt just as we are all born somewhere. I make a leap forward from those first days and first experiences. I am now thirteen years old. I am a measuring device, just like all human beings are, a sonar that travels the world over and tries to record and measure everything. That is to say, a bat.

That Is to Say, a Bat

An air raid on Halberstadt. A bomb strikes ten meters away from my parents' house; right next to the neighbor's home. I try to describe what I felt. I was naturally afraid, but at the same time I thought: Piano practice is in the afternoon, must I go or not? I thought some more: If I can tell this to my classmates tomorrow, then finally something will really happen. These thoughts shadow my fear. I still know now just how disappointed I was that afternoon when my lesson was canceled—the city was burning—after the air raid. I was distraught. And when I was told that school was canceled the next day, I was disappointed.

The Relation of Events to the Piano Lesson

Until Sunday, April 8, the fourteen-year-old boy Siegfried Pauli practiced page 59 from the songbook *Sang und Klang* so much that he stumbled or slowed down only at the end of the piece "Falstaff's Song"—"How happy I am, how happy I am, how my cravings move me . . ."—but he could run through three-fourths of the piece with arched hands as required by his teacher. He now wanted to deliver the piece as fast as possible to his teacher, Ms. Schutz-Schilling, and forge ahead to the top of the next page, finger exercises by Clementi, and then Gilda's aria from *Rigoletto*. The lesson was scheduled for 3 p.m. the next day, a Monday. The attack intervened. "Five meters away from our basement a bomb struck," Pauli explained. This chain of events—the attack, the escape to the Long Cave, the return to the destroyed city, the house, the study where he practiced on the grand piano destroyed by fire—had no influence on the acquired dexterity of Siegfried's fingers or his will to press on to page 60. His piano teacher, whom he encountered among residents scrambling about on Wernigeröder Straße on the afternoon of the bombing, declined to give Monday's lesson on account of the city's destruction. Yet with his will still intact, Pauli found a villa at the end of Spiegelsbergen Weg where a grand piano stood unscathed. He played the assigned piece so long till he got through the shaky part shortly before the ending without any noticeable stumbling. He practiced the spot separately, only the precarious measures, for a whole two hours, till the owners of the villa could no longer listen to it.

It is an entirely different feeling thirty years later. I find it necessary to write something against air wars and the strategy from above: a long story about a teacher who sits with four children in a basement in Halberstadt; while the bombs fall, she cannot even pray, because she knows not what harm she might do if she does. Perhaps a bomb hits her the moment she shifts around to pray. In that moment, an intense feeling arises—when constantly driven forward, feelings become thought. Thought is nothing other than crystallized feelings. I must always have a reason, a motive, for thought. When I face adversity, I have no good thoughts.

The thought that then arises is this: When actually would resistance in the form of a strategy from below have been possible against the bomb attacks in 1945? Were one to imagine this concretely for this teacher, one could say: In the year 1928, when she started training along with many other teachers, they could have banded together. A huge alliance of teachers in the year 1928 could have sufficed to defeat fascism. Were I Gerda Baethe and had I known in the year 1928 that my children and I would find themselves in this hopeless situation in 1945, then I would have strived in 1928 differently with the knowledge of this feeling from 1945 and above all banded together with others differently. That is to say: I would not have sat alone in the study, but rather would have given up all the differences I had with others and united with them. This is essentially how a historical process takes it course.

Mistrust of Reality

I have a certain distrust of reality. This comes, in part, from my experiences in Halberstadt. Because Halberstadt is in the provinces where one does not see the world exactly as it is. My father, who worked as the in-house doctor at the local theater, told far-fetched stories about the First World War. *I believe the sharpest ideology that exists is the one that considers reality to be real.* This expulsion and denial of feeling is something that troubles me. The value of experience tells us that when human beings look inside themselves they actually understand all their feelings quite well and that they are not wrong. Yet it is every Robinson Crusoe for himself. Human beings can easily unite when the weakest feelings are in play, but they have the hardest time doing so when the strongest ones dominate. Every stamp collector in the world and every physicist, too, can communicate objectively. Although people all over the world can agree on something as important as the laws of nature, there is no agreement on how I raise my children, whom I marry, or what I do with my property.

A community can be created if strong feelings, like those of ownership, were lateralized and laid out side by side so that human beings can come to an understanding about them. Were everyone to do this, we would end up with a society in which terror arises when everyday feelings are intensified. This can lead to wars, murder, religious wars, ostracism, and morality—evil is the other—but it could also lead to understanding. Experience tells us that understanding rarely develops, whereas aggression is far more prevalent. This is a life experience people have acquired in the last 400 to 600 years. *The suppression of feelings develops when the emancipatory path of feelings cannot be pursued.*

Pax Romana

The Roman Empire—Pax Romana: everyone is equally oppressed. This is the moment when the powers of reason emerge. What surfaces from this necessity are administrations, institutions, urbs, the city, control, self-control, unshakable calm, the philosophical mind, and the division of labor. Otherwise civil war will break out. This is experience improperly handled because the emancipation of feelings was never attempted.

The Romans Are Crazy

When Asterix wants to defeat the Romans, he sometimes takes a bow and arrow, sometimes a lance, and sometimes a rock. He always feasts on roasted wild boar and has weapons suitable for the Romans, ones they do not have. Feelings are not just civil. They are also completely attuned to doing battle. *Feelings do not believe in the reality principle.* To a certain degree, they perceive reality, produce it, and do battle in it, but simultaneously they believe in something that goes one step beyond reality. Marx quite clearly calls this a "subjective-objective relation." He means that people cannot be objects or instruments. It is a fantasy of rulers that a soldier or worker is an instrument. Wherever there are living beings, a subjective interest resonates.

People behave peacefully in large majorities. But when a community or its will is *strained*—i.e., redirected toward something new, as was the case, for example, in 1933—then we wish not to repeat all the past's mistakes along with the Treaty of Versailles. We want to do everything anew. This entails the exclusion and constant persecution of the other. This means that we will suffer injuries if we form a new community. Were one to go back in time when the agrarian revolution in the Fertile Crescent, the region we call Babylonia, occurred, one would see cities form in which a castle and a shrine stood. A two-headed community developed: a priesthood and royalty. Both repress the people enclosed within the city walls whom they rule. This system isolates itself against everything outside that appears barbaric. This is how the first communities came to be. On the institutional side—this organizational side has nothing to do with submissive individuals—the buildup of aggression is preprogrammed and also prevalent in victims. It expresses itself outwardly. In the case of the Carthaginians, it is obvious that Hannibal is expected to sacrifice his child in order to appease the gods. This is a highly organized process that has nothing to do with the relationship between two people or those in a group or community. *The founding of communities has long suffered from a deficiency caused when they shut something out.* This exclusionary mechanism consists in the French Revolution, which wanted to turn people into brothers, in the guillotine, in the immediate eruption of civil war, and in the attendant system of property ownership that distinguished between the propertied class and the have-nots. Such institutional foundations have failed up till now.

Moral Cannibalism

There is a moral cannibalism we have learned throughout the course of history. We have spent the last 500 years in groups practicing ostracism aimed at not only Jews, but rather everything we imagine to be strange and foreign. We are massive factories that produce a faulty capacity for differentiation. To dismantle this, we must work at decomposing it just like our gastric juices break down something difficult to digest. When this happens in a story, we can laugh about it. If we can laugh about how fanatically moral someone is, then we have achieved another small bit of this decomposition. With the category of relationality, one can break down something that has become one-sided, ideological, or fanatical.

Imagine someone like Girolamo Savonarola, a Florentine religious fanatic. He is in the middle of his sermon. Suddenly, it starts pouring rain and becomes extremely cold—this happens in the Mediterranean climate—a winter storm that cools the fanatic down. He is still in the middle of his penitential sermon, but everyone runs away because of the storm. He, too, starts to freeze. The fact that he can freeze makes him human. A fanatic who is freezing is already a little less a fanatic.

All I just did is place a simple feeling next to a complex one. We have to do this all the time: *These petrified things must be made to dance by singing to them their own melody.*[4] Karl Marx wrote this sentence. It means that within every poison there is also an antidote. I can hardly maintain a prejudice while moving. If I use my ear to examine something that overwhelms my eyes and notice a wrong pitch, then the graven image is of less value than before. *Interaction is the natural remedy against prejudice.* This is more easily said than done, but it is still rudimentary. In Celtic speech and storytelling lies the antithesis: polyphony. There are many kinds of *alliance systems* that do not function like a uniformed parade. They are *formed among partisans.* Translated literally, a partisan is someone with a bias. Whoever is biased is ready for a fight and interrelates with others. They have opinions. The words "partisan" and "author" can actually be interchanged.

We Are Not Turning Roman

Imagine Asterix: his people sit around eating roasted wild boar. There exists a relation of trust. They have their own land, their own sensations, their own capacities for differentiation, and they keep the Romans from capturing them. Today, the Romans are, in a manner of speaking, big globalized companies that wish to confiscate responsibility by showering our daily routine with advertising and soothing design. The Gauls say: No, we do that ourselves. We have reservations. We are not turning Roman.

This Is How Siegfried Theurisch Administered His Poison

Siegfried Theurisch made his approach from the moral majority created and consumed in random quantities. If a group blabbered on in a good-natured way, a question raised ensnared it; THIS IS HOW SIEGFRIED THEURISCH ADMINISTERED HIS POISON. He disturbed speeches neither intensive nor strenuous enough for his taste or those that appeared to drift far from the concept at hand. He wanted to see dams created, a concentration. There is no mood, group, or flow not disturbed by this.

He monopolized in a very short span of time the attainable (or definable) morality in the group, or in other words the free-floating goodwill, and bit into it until the group fell apart. He was considered to be a troublemaker, but it was difficult for friends to guard themselves against this glutton, whose head and belly stockpiled goodwill, since they failed to banish him from the group without divorcing themselves from something of their own, namely, the GOODWILL they produced previously. In this respect, he was soon the leader of a hardly flourishing group that vegetated in his presence. The sole advantage of his irrepressible appetite consisted in the fact that he had an insect-like tendency, once fully bloated to twice the size of his mental capacity, to run into the *next* group in order to suck it dry.

—I have an appointment, Siegfried said.
—Oh well, retorted the weary ones.

Successful Feelings

There are strokes of luck throughout history where you can observe that feelings can also organize themselves. I can only tell stories about successful feelings in which one notices at the most unexpected moments that feelings between people can create a community.

426 *Difference and Orientation*

Figure 22. At a time when unemployment was high, Mirko Wischke drove his truck blind for a half a year with the help of his son. The trust that binds them can be called love.
© Alexander Kluge Archive

What Brings Voluntary Actions Together?

This is my favorite image to look at. As a metaphor. You see a blind truck driver who has been driving his truck without any eyesight for six months. He is afraid of being unemployed and for this reason he continues to drive. His nine-year-old son sits next to him and tells him what to do. That is a relation of trust. It works only if neither person gets ambitious. If the son were to say, "Let us try showing off a little. Try driving faster," it would go awry. This is equilibration, essentially *a circus-like achievement performed by two people*. This kind of thing is also possible for more than just two persons. Consider the Russian Revolution of 1905. At a single historical moment when revolutionaries had little power but plenty of reason to protest, they were able to communicate faster than if by telegraph. This means that a telegram from Kiev to St. Petersburg took longer than it did for people to spread the news themselves. There were no telephones, just *the capacity for intuition*.

Asterix's Strengths

There is, for example, a point in time when the Swiss drove the Austrians from their country, defeated Charles the Bold and the French, and the cities fought one another. There was a soldier named Nicholas of Flüe who isolated himself to become a monk and philosopher. Cities approached him to ask for advice. This man, well-informed in matters of war, gave them rules for how Switzerland can definitively stay out of wars: inwardly conservative, outwardly liberal. Switzerland prevailed with his advice for a good 300 to 400 years. It is an obvious building block. Yet it truly is an accomplishment to bring something so diverse as Switzerland's Italian, French, and German speakers, the rather stubborn mountain farmers in Graubünden, the city dwellers in Zurich and Bern (something as diverse as the Balkans) together with the banks in order to create according to the cantonal constitution a public sphere capable of both discussing and bargaining. Lessons can be learned from these steps taken in the laboratory where human societies form. Yet we need to secure the seventeenth-century paths that we can still ascribe to emancipation from the palaver of the eighteenth-century Enlightenment and its rhetoricians who again introduce as much egocentrism as in the times of the French

Revolution when one person sent another person to the guillotine to be executed. That surely did not amount to a communicative custom.

Basic Trust and Basic Fear

I do not trust basic fear because it is, so to speak, a twisted, disenchanted form of basic trust. Fear is a very bad counselor for emancipation and self-consciousness. There exists a certain balance politics of self-consciousness. For example, Siegfried destroys everything on account of his excessive self-consciousness. He possesses no equilibrium; he does not listen except to forest birds; he makes a mess of the Burgundian court; and contributes to its downfall: this is self-consciousness going it alone. I would be far more inclined to place trust in more muted forms in which one self-consciousness can unite with another in an almost musical way, or when both halves of our brains can correspond with one another. Fear is something paralyzing. Coincidently, I do believe there is such a thing as basic fear; it is not originary. It is always a matter of experience.

If I know I sprained my arm when I flew down the stairs as a child, I can still fly down whichever stairs in my remaining life in the metaphorical sense. Fear can be translated. There is, for example, hysterical fear necessary in every case of nervousness. Without a certain quantum of hysteria, we are simply not attentive. There is certainly deep fear, which the Romans called "*numen*" that can also lead to godliness. People require a quantum of it like an immunization. It is like a cloak, an armor. It protects in some circumstances, but it is neither motivating nor productive. In order to live, a motive stronger than fear is necessary.

We now arrive at an extremely complex alchemy because people require everything. A command in Napolean's army was "*faccia feroce!*" and the soldiers had to make a ferocious face. No superior or partisan leader can command soldiers not to be afraid. Fear must be able to live. In other words, all of our sensations must be identified as part of our capacity to differentiate. The French proponents of the Enlightenment were called "amis d'analyse," friends of analysis, friends of the capacity for differentiation. This is an original standpoint of the Enlightenment. The mass production of this capacity for differentiation is what links us with other people. The whole sphere of fear also belongs to it. It is satisfying when a story is told, when one converses in confidence, and when fears are exchanged. Fears are mitigated this way; shared fears are less dangerous; and a relation of trust develops. To admit one's fears is proof of trust. To tell someone of one's weaknesses—in this sense, fear is often a weakness—and not be punished, for it creates trust. The motive is trust not fear. What sets everything into motion is the motive; a stockpile that functions like fuel.

Stalingrad as Metaphor

Humans are inclined to produce trust. This is a dowry, an ability. We would rather be mistaken than not trust. This is measurable as a gravitational force among human beings. *Where trust expands, human beings can work magic.* Where trust is lost, particularly when a felony is committed (meaning top-down betrayal), we arrive at the phenomenon of Stalingrad: a highly industrialized army forgets all of their skills. They no longer believe they can even tighten a screw. They regress to the level of one of Frederick the Great's armies or even to that of an older army, and then they perish.

Sealed Time

Three hundred thousand German soldiers were affected by Stalingrad. The majority perished, and only 5,000 returned home. When they arrived there, no one wanted to know what happened. After 1945, people had very different worries. The reason why they were deployed is completely devalued. Unlike Odysseus, who could tell whole stories after his homecoming, nothing was told in this case. In 1918, stories were told after World War I. Storytelling was discontinued in 1945. Furthermore, it is one of the instances when a historical turn transpired in the matter of just a few days: the Battle of

Kursk, the fall of Army Group Center, or the Battle of Berlin was much more momentous, but never did a German army flounder so swiftly from pride to an inferiority complex as in Stalingrad. Not even the Romans did so at the Battle of Cannae. There are few historical experiences in which such a rapid shift to the subjective side can be detected. Carl von Clausewitz describes in his book *On War* that the subjective landscape in a person, what a soldier acts out, is just as important as the external events atop the command post or in the artillery. *Battle decisions happen in the will of people.* To grasp this and also apply it to other scenarios is extremely important.

Take, for example, *The Song of Roland*: the proud emperor Charlemagne and his Frankish army cannot save their rearguard man they sent out to the enemy. Or the Schleyer kidnapping: this man out on a limb could not be saved.[5] In these cases, a community loses its authority. The side I trust is the source of my community. There exists a drawing of a cannon on which the following words appear: "protego ergo sum," I protect, therefore I am. The state says this, but a community says this, too, when there is no state.

A Soviet citizen is sent up to the Mir space station. He travels through space. A considerable self-consciousness is bound up in the space vehicle up there; it still runs even though its cord is no longer intact. Compared to the Kursk disaster, it is virtually a triumph. But then the man returns to earth and is told: The Soviet Union that sent you into space no longer exists. What sort of citizenship do you have? One cannot switch passports while in space.

Actually, the man who returned does not exist. If one takes the word "homecomer" seriously—and I take it seriously when I think of Odysseus and all the many other returnees in the world up till now—then one must dress these stories in metaphors to be grasped like houses of experience where one can reside and verify whether what one thinks and feels is right. Stalingrad is one such house.

The Dragonfly

In a basin located in the alpine mountains 4,000 meters above Graubünden, there grow unspoiled plants in the depths of a lake green in color. Ever since the evolution of these mountains, i.e., 200,000 years ago, this place has remained practically unchanged, says geologist Schweickart.

On this sunny day, dragonflies zip around the water's surface. It is impossible that they could have ever flown around the mountain's ridges. Measured in human steps, the next body of water was a day's journey away.

An exceptional kind of dragonfly evolved here that has a hairy, dark-brown growth between its seventh and eighth segments. An unmistakable characteristic of these local dragonflies' parentage. They would have mauled every nonnative dragonfly.

My father caught one of these 200,000-year-old noble creatures in the year 1938 and released it in his garden pond. Driven from its home, it lived there seven years and perished when the garden was consumed by the firestorm. With the outbreak of the fire, the pond's concrete basin cracked and its water vanished entirely.

Although winter at 4,000 meters is severe, the dragonflies nest in tiny anomalies that allow for their element—water—at the edge of the ice.

Stranger, Speak!

In old texts like the *Odyssey*, every newcomer starts telling stories about where they are from and where they want to go. But above all, they recount where they are from. "Stranger, speak!" When people are interested in one another, they first tell something about themselves. I find that love stories start this way as well. Before the first touch, a story is told about oneself. That is not all that unusual as it first appears. Yet we are quite objective when it comes to this custom, meaning our societies are objectivistic and so hardened that they give priority to a person's achievements, their credentials, and their administrative references over everything else. On the other hand, that too is just the surface, for *people always behave intimately*.

People should show what they are, otherwise their mistakes are no longer distinguishable from what makes them right. It is a lovely thing to contemplate a person together with their subjective side. But one is far from ever being able to see through them. This is naturally because every stage in a person's life is present alongside every other. When I speak with someone, I speak with the six-year-old child in me who sits across from the forty-year-old in me, or I speak with both in my sixty-year-old self when I speak with someone older. *Every person is like a Russian doll.* In them is nested every age, experience, and form of speech. It is better to reveal this fact instead of concealing it.

Our ancestors the Celts knew this. Instead of a Roman *urbs*, they had *oppida* containing a headquarters and a civil service surrounded by a wall. An *oppidum* is actually a warehouse of commodities, a big repository for commerce. In front of these repositories, people congregated in bars and on benches and ate roasted wild boar of course and told stories over and over again, exaggerating repeatedly, backward and forward. In so doing, they warmed everything up to their body temperature. Just as our bodies maintain a temperature of 98.6 degrees Fahrenheit—without it we feel neither well nor can we go on living—this storytelling forms something like another social body that generates a moderate temperature neither too hot nor too cold for human beings. It does so by assembling as much of a mixture as possible out of both improbable and probable stuff such that it is right for people. This is storytelling.

Translated by Emma Woelk

Notes

These miniatures were originally published in German as Alexander Kluge, *Die Kunst, Unterschiede zu machen* (Frankfurt am Main: Suhrkamp, 2003), 9, 11–12, 18–19, 24, 27, 30, 37, 40, 44, 49–50, 54, 57, 59, 66, 79, 83–84, 87–88, 96.

The translated portions chosen are from Kluge's dialogue with journalist Reinhard Kahl entitled "Die Lücke, die der Teufel läßt," which was held in conjunction with the latter's Philosophisches Café, organized at the Literaturhaus Hamburg in June 2003. In the German original, the philosophical texts selected here for translation appear alongside stories taken from Kluge's two-volume omnibus *Chronik der Gefühle*, published in 2000.

The one image that appears in the original is included in the translated excerpts.

1. [Translator's note: Harry F. Harlow, "The Nature of Love," *American Psychologist* 13.12 (December 1958): 677. See also Alexander Kluge and Oskar Negt, *History and Obstinacy*, ed. Devin Fore, trans. Richard Langston et al. (New York: Zone Books, 2014), 153.]

2. [Translator's note: The source of this paraphrase in Nietzsche's work is unclear. Kluge uses this exact formulation in Alexander Kluge, *Die Lücke, die der Teufel läßt: Im Umfeld des neuen Jahrhunderts* (Frankfurt am Main: Suhrkamp, 2003), 269 and is presumably quoting himself here.]

3. [Translator's note: The Asterix in question is a French comic book character, a Gaul, who resists Roman occupation.]

4. [Translator's citation and note: Karl Marx, *Early Political Writings*, ed. Joseph O'Malley (New York: Cambridge University Press, 1994), 60. Kluge uses the word *Dinge* (things) in place of Marx's *Verhältnisse* (relations).]

5. [Translator's note: Hans-Martin Schleyer (1915–77) was a West German business leader assassinated by members of the Red Army Faction in October 1977.]

25

CRITIQUE, UP CLOSE AND PERSONAL

JOSEPH VOGL: *You once said that critique has much in common with the work of an undercover investigator. Where is this undercover investigator to be found, what does he see, how does he operate?*

ALEXANDER KLUGE: I cannot tell you that exactly, but I can say where critique comes from. This critical capacity—the capacity to differentiate practically at the crucial moment—this is an undercover characteristic that we know nothing about. If I exert just my consciousness, it is never critical enough. I mean, it may be critical, but it can neither carry out nor prevent anything.

JV: *Two aspects form the heart of both critique and* krinein: *on the one hand, there is the question of the capacity for differentiation. Ultimately, a person attuned to difference stands behind this*

	capacity; the person who lives of off making differentiations and lessons in perception, and perfecting the arts of differentiation . . .
AK:	. . . I am someone, but that is not enough . . .
JV:	*. . . not really . . .*
AK:	. . . to be good. At the same time, I am also something else. I am good by accident. The probability if I include this, then it has something useful, social, and human; it commands a majority.
JV:	*And what about the other side of* krinein, *which not only means "to differentiate" but also, in cases of doubt, "to decide"? Is there a connection between critique and decision—in a very direct sense?*
AK:	That is very difficult to say. We do know that a kind of impulse arises in our brains a few billionths of second before a decision is reached. Whether or not we can trust our decisions is something we do not exactly know. Yet what we can do is say what we are actually against when we take a break and when we refrain from doing something. This is where freedom resides. Freedom is not meant to be active and I am sure that we all—from the hero Siegfried to the *élan vital*—can completely mistrust our own impulses.
JV:	*Early twentieth-century psychology poses the question: According to what principles of circuitry does insanity function? One of the great psychiatrists of the day, Eugen Bleuler, has a very surprising theory on the relation between action and cessation. He says that it is quite easy to set circuits, circuit devices, and neuronal mechanisms in motion, and that freedom and ultimately reason consist in stopping these circuits set in motion. So freedom is less about acting spontaneously than it is about interrupting chains of action and functional sequences that have been initiated. Turning off.*

AK: ... at the right moment. This is actually what is called lateralization. Impulses are processed by our wonderful apparatus, where the blind Homers, our brain cells, sit and begin to interpret and puzzle out the world; they break the impulses down into action potentials lying parallel to each other—using this process, I can avoid something.

JV: *Are there certain areas of the body, body parts, that are somehow responsible for this, that somehow operate critically in different ways?*

AK: First of all, there are always two people in one. Sigmund Freud speaks of the two-staged development in humans. This is something no animal experiences. First, an entire being, along with its sexuality and capacity for differentiation, is formed between infancy and the age of six or seven. This is then followed by a latency period when the creature can learn—humans have a genuine period of learning—until puberty upends everything again and a second being, equally sexual, develops. This is the adult. I personally have always really liked these children or childhoods that are, as it were, independent beings, as if we were larvae and then later mutated beings. But this is not how it really is. Instead, it is always the same person, the same nerves, and the same experience. Whether I am a thirty-year-old or a seventy-year-old, I certainly still have my six-year-old self inside me. Thus, our control over the parallel circuits, the ability to stop, is based in the fact that we are two people. It is a luxury that we were either created to lead two lives or were made this way by evolution.

JV: *What kind of critical approach to the world would this child have? Can this perspective on the world be made visible as a critical perspective? Which operations would that involve?*

AK: That is for you to say! Which operations would that involve? This is something Jean Piaget has described in detail. Something is suddenly triggered in children—for a long time they experience the same experiment and outcome without learning anything. Then suddenly they learned something. It crystallizes, and this process of crystallization is the first form of the capacity for differentiation. It is never something acquired in isolation: I burn my finger and then never touch anything hot again. My mother punishes me, and therefore I will not do that ever again. These are assertions, and then suddenly an entire moral system is formed, and it is cumulative because it is learned from our forefathers through stories. This is the first form, and one cannot distinguish between what about it is conscious or unconscious, socially unconscious or personally and psychologically unconscious. I hear sixty fairy tales and suddenly know how to process them. This is one of the most wonderful ways to learn, and this is the only one I find to be active in human life. Everything else is reflections and responses based on hesitation and—as you put it—pauses.

JV: *But this seems to me to be a very basic act of critique: the exploration of points where chains of judgments and actions can be interrupted. I am thinking, for example, of . . .*

AK: I hesitate . . .

JV: *I hesitate, I waver, the impulse to act is curtailed . . .*

AK: . . . something in me hesitates, something in me fails. I get diarrhea and therefore cannot commit murder. In the case of Othello, for example, this would have saved Desdemona, if he had really had diarrhea, which can happen to a general like him.

JV:	*Or, for example, Orestes, at the moment when he kills his mother, suddenly he hesitates and almost lets his arm fall . . .*
AK:	. . . if only his arm had been paralyzed! If only he had experienced the kind of psychic paralysis that probably arises later out of feelings of guilt and is treated carefully by Freud behind his folding screen. If only it had happened in time.
JV:	*So critique as a pause, as the desire for a pause. In the* Oresteia *by Aeschylus, this is all the more trenchant at the moment when Orestes's hesitation indicates that even gods waver. At the end, even Athena hesitates and does not know what is right. When Orestes is accused by the Fury, who will not give up, his lot must ultimately be cast. It is a tie, a stalemate, an undecidable case. At this point, the entire cosmos hesitates in a way, including the gods, just as Orestes's muscles hesitated in the moment before he struck his mother dead.*
AK:	The slow development of a counter-fate as fates are pursued is a very wonderful thing and is something practical, as opposed to the purely mental activity that we understand critique to be in the twentieth century, which in a way did not save that many lives during the Russian Campaign. This critique, which confronts real relations like a court of reason, is actually overestimated. It has the status of a praetorian official . . .
JV:	*Forensic.*
AK:	One can confront evil neither forensically nor as a praetor.
JV:	*Meaning that there is judgmental critique, critique that only sees phenomena through the lens of their subsumption, their classification, their disqualification . . .*
AK:	There you have on the one side something real and a rational activity on the other—and that is not commensurable.

JV: *Could critique also be a fantastic activity?*
AK: Definitely. Could you paint an image for me of what you are thinking?
JV: *I am thinking of various experiments having to do with the question of the power of judgment that Robert Musil lays out, for example. Musil's* The Man without Qualities *makes a clear distinction between two forms of precision, assuming precision truly is a part of the capacity for differentiation. On one side, there is pedantic precision, a subsuming activity: I take an individual case, and it is subsumed under a principle. The background behind this whole story is the Moosbrugger case, i.e., the question of an insane perpetrator who, in an ecstatic fit, killed a prostitute. Pedantic precision looks at the act, the circumstances surrounding it, seeks out the relevant law, and comes to a judgment. On the other side, there is a fantastic precision, for which the object itself can never be close enough. This means that the thing is taken apart and various motifs are divided into submotifs, which are then infinitely divided into nerve impulses and beyond. The endless process of fantastic precision leads to an endpoint where judgment can no longer occur. Essentially, a space is created where judgment no longer exists and the act itself is suspended in a paradiscial existence. An act held in suspension, one brought to its own potential at the moment of its complete and total analysis: an act that is at once real and unrealized. It is difficult to judge when one gets too close.*
AK: You translated "fantastic" first into part of the imagination and then into a point of contact. Here the precision of concretion prevents judgment, meaning that too much contact with real relations and simultaneously with the imagination, which does not resist this contact, creates a space where I can understand something that

has been excluded because it cannot actually be understood. You have named one of the most difficult problems not just in Musil, but also in the world for that matter, since one's understanding hesitates when confronted by crime. This is one of the most difficult questions for critique.

JV: *It must not be forgotten that the criminal can also be traced back to differentiation, to discrimen. The criminal is someone who differentiates himself through his actions, whose actions to a certain extent bring onto the scene discrimination, meaning a disqualifying distinction or decision. In this sense, the criminal is a "critical object," someone who provokes a critical capacity with his entire energetic efforts. This is why Musil's case is so well known: each bizarre action provokes the capacity for differentiation, the art of distinctions, the artistry of decision.*

AK: Classical writers use the word "critique" much differently, even the Romantics use it differently. Neither the *Critique of the Power of Judgment* nor the *Critique of Pure Reason* means that one criticizes judgment, but rather that one expresses it. Critique is the positive capacity to differentiate between something new and an old falsehood. In literature by Ludwig Tieck and August Wilhelm von Schlegel critique is a positive concept. The idea of tearing something apart, as Marcel Reich-Ranicki would, would be totally absurd to them: Why would one waste time writing about something bad?

JV: *What would it look like—if we reflect on this together—if, through the capacity for differentiation, through critique in this totally emphatic sense, something were to emerge or be brought into being? What would that be? What objects could be used to demonstrate this? What could be produced through this productive capacity for differentiation that would not be condemnation or discrimination?*

AK: Let us consider the word "critique" itself. A Sonderkommando, an SS unit, is active in the East. They killed Jewish parents or those whom they considered Jews, but they forgot to kill the children. Then they get back to killing them, too. Two Wehrmacht chaplains intervene. Having been made aware by the chaplains, officers and soldiers also intervene. A high-ranking officer starts telephoning the unit's leadership and tries to save the children. This works for just one night. But because it created bad blood among his superiors that the intermediate authorities had not been alerted, a decision is made the next day against this officer. Now the children will also be exterminated, and he is confronted with a very practical question: "Make a suggestion about what should be done with the children. We have a suggestion: kill them, this is only logical. Do you have a suggestion? Do you want to charge your kitchen staff with raising the children? Do you want to bring them to the front with your unit?" He has no recommendation, and the children are killed. From this I can now learn that the critical must also be practical. If I cannot translate a critical idea or a correct moral position into real relations, then it is not critical enough. We can thus refine the word "critique" by adding back in something positive and practical, as you did previously when you said that the ability to stop is itself critical. Now if you use the example of Hamlet to illustrate cessation and hesitation: he brings it home with him from Wittenberg, where he studied.

JV: *Hamlet is perhaps not so succinct an example to describe . . .*

AK: Because he does nothing good!

JV: *Because he ultimately does nothing good and because this form of inaction is actually presented as a permanent crisis. I would rather ask where the firm interruption in the chain of actions, perhaps also of forms of judgment, can help to make relationalities and global situations visible.*

AK: Or to remedy them. To create the improbable rescue.

JV: *Or to present the state of things as if in a photographic developer bath. Just as montage, for example, or false connections can do that. Just as false connections in a chain of command bring a command into focus, in its drama, in its wickedness, in its malice. A false telephone connection can bring into focus an execution order for a firing squad that ends up going to the kitchen staff instead. It makes a relationality visible. I am also thinking here of literary, aesthetic experiments, for example, of the structure of the nonspecific refusal. The best-known example I can think of comes from Herman Melville, his story "Bartleby, the Scrivener," in which one character—a writer, a secretary—is presented, a character who ultimately does nothing but serve as a depot for the written word and commands, he is an organ in a legal office for implementing orders. But all of the sudden he says, "I would prefer not to." To not carry out any strange intents and not harbor any of his own. The simple refusal that does not even refer to a specific object, but rather indicates nothing other than an intensified passivity, suddenly and fundamentally calls into question a habitat, the space of action for a lawyer, a legal system. It therefore operates as a developer of these relations.*

AK: This is excellent. If you apply that to an attack on a location in Iraq where terrorists are

Chapter 25   443

	presumed to be hiding, but is actually a wedding party. And the attack is then prevented by a misdirected order, by a hesitation, or by mistake, then good has been done. Whether this happens intentionally or by accident is irrelevant for critique.
JV:	*I actually think that it is a crucial point to look for critical activity at this threshold between the intentional and the unintentional.*
AK:	. . . the disruption of automatism.
JV:	*. . . if automatism also means logicality and consequence. This is not an automatism in the sense of unconscious perpetuation, but rather an automatism of deduction. Like in Georg Büchner's* Danton's Death, *where it first says: We are the law, and then: We want no law, ergo: Kill. Deductions of this kind. This also means that logic is an automatism; even syllogism is an automatism. I could well imagine that there is an eminent critical moment in this undifferentiability between intentional and unintentional action. To give an example, again from literature: Maria Stuart is sentenced by Queen Elizabeth. The death sentence is signed and the death sentence is supposed to be carried out. At this point, Elizabeth hesitates and does not give the verdict to the executioner, but rather to a subaltern officer, who asks what he is supposed to do with it. She says, "Do with it what you will." At this point, a fundamental hesitation is introduced, a small blockade, about which one cannot say if it occurs intentionally or not . . .*
AK:	That is in Schiller?
JV:	*It is how Schiller did it. At this point, the order is issued, the decision, the path toward a decision furnished with an interruption half-voluntary and half-involuntary that once again holds fate in abeyance.*
AK:	And hope develops in the audience that this beautiful woman will not have to die. If she

JV: does not have to die, then her children and ultimately Ludwig XVI would also not have to die. *I believe that this means that critical activity, as the capacity for differentiation or interruption, offers an incisive perspective on actions always divided up among multiple agents. There is never a single commander entirely in control, but rather every commander is responsible for eliminating those who would interfere with an order or a decision being carried out. These interferers are always already there. They are probably there before the order is. Before the order can be conveyed, the channels that must convey the order are already there. Guaranteeing the reliability of these orders is a much larger problem for the commander than making the decision. Every decision that is still sovereign decays into a mass of potential obstacles, disturbers, and middlemen.*

AK: This, I believe, is a very therapeutic process for the development of history, since the channels, because they are uncontrollable, explain the whole. They usually do not indicate anything evil. The child is not killed by the hunter, but rather is set out in the forest and returns. This is an age-old fairy tale.

JV: *The fairy tale goes back even further. As an example, Oedipus's abandonment, in all its complexity, is quite telling.*

AK: But it goes wrong. Had Laius killed, something I would not hold against him, then he would still be alive. He thus actually preemptively assured that he would die.

JV: *On the other hand, this is of course tied to eminent cunning, possibly critical cunning, perhaps not for Laius or Oedipus, but rather for the spectators. Because as horrible as Laius's fate is, and as horrible as Oedipus's subsequent fate then is, something is still so broken by the*

Chapter 25   445

	end of the Oedipus *drama, also in Sophocles's version, namely, the curse, the oracle's prophecy, the spell, the automat. It took some effort to accomplish this, but it worked: interfering in the powers of precisely this fate by preventing a prophecy—at least* Oedipus *accomplishes this.*
AK:	There is the idea that this Oedipus travels home by land and encounters a wagon blocking his path. Laius's servants are very disrespectful, provoke him, and he is beaten up. And then he kills his father. If he—acknowledging the prophecy—basically took an alternate route when faced with resistance, then he would not have had to kill his father.
JV:	*The solutions are always in plain sight, right in the middle of the street. You could say—as a very open question—that it is even a principle of the tragedy, that it always has a traffic problem at these kinds of constellations. Two roads that cross, an evasive turn at just the right moment. The border of confrontation and action?*
AK:	If they open up the borders of action, then something results that cannot be called tragedy or comedy, but instead offers a way out. This drama of salvation—rescue at the last moment—is actually the highest form according to Aristotle, namely, tragic recognition, the way to escape fate laterally by a hair's breadth. This is something that captivates me; it is at the heart of the undercover investigation, so to speak. Aristotle describes a scene in which a woman wants to kill her son's murderer and when she raises the knife, she recognizes her son in the man she wants to kill. This is a recognition, a greeting. Another death by murder is not necessary now. At the same time, she is rewarded by getting her child back. This is what the Athenians cry about the most, he says. This the highest form of the tragic. But this

neither alleviates anything nor does it contain any redemption. At any moment, things can go wrong in a neighboring case. Making salvation possible for this right-at-the-edge-of-the-abyss on the level of the improbable; exploring these paths; mapping them; and keeping them recognizable, this is critique.

JV: *Could one speak with genre poetics and say that there is a comedic and a tragic critique?*

AK: There are healing, helping, and condemning forms of critique. Here I would prefer the job of a doctor to that of a judge.

JV: *Then critique is not only an art of differentiation, but also an art of finding ways out and paths of escape.*

AK: Assisting escapees is a typical profession in this context. Take Beethoven's *Fidelio*: the feeling that this woman who successfully gets her husband out of the revolutionary prison and keeps him safe until the commissar arrives from Paris and frees all of the prisoners—this small operation is based on the ability to love. This made the practical value of marriage apparent to me for the first time. I would even say that all romantic relations could be critically tested to determine whether they preserve something of the other in this form.

JV: *That would be a critical test of romantic relations. Now you could turn the question around and ask if romantic relations themselves perform critical tests and when they operate critically.*

AK: They are actually inaccessible to the court of reason. Because if I say that I love this other person, and someone then says to me: "But you cannot do that, she is ugly, or she has this and that unpleasant characteristic and they will resurface again and again. Or in five years you will not love her anymore"—these are all arguments that have no effect on love. This skin will not err in such an instance. It reacts critically like an allergy, or critically with approval in the form of a hug. The eye errs more readily in matters of love. But the ear, on the other hand, can accurately judge trustworthiness from childhood on. The ear can tell when the tone is right or wrong. The sharpest critics in the world say this, and not only because of music.

JV: *Senses and reflexes that operate critically . . .*

AK: It is always about differentiation. And the origin of the critical is always astonishment. This comes from Aristotle. I believe this is directly applicable and that every sense can do this in its own way.

JV: *Would that be a sense in the way that it is also used by Friedrich Nietzsche, who says that after the agony of listening to all of Wagner's operas, in which the nebulous and the dank are always at the forefront, a music for open, bright, southern skies must be created.*

AK: He says this with reference to *Carmen* and in doing so promotes an additional misunderstanding I consider highly uncritical. I find it uncritical in every respect that two lovers are condemned to kill each other. Because Don José, provoked by Carmen who lusts after the toreador, kills her, he must die himself. In the original story by Prosper Mérimée, this takes place in José's prison cell. Why do lovers always kill themselves? I do not understand this in this context or with Tristan and Isolde! This cannot be a fundamental part of real development because problematic lovers like this would have brought evolution to a stop. Humanity would have died out if no one had offspring. What we ascribe to lovers in novels and operas is an uncritical form of love. We can find completely undramatic, critical abilities for survival in every mother-child relationship, in many sibling

	relationships, and in many romantic relationships that do not end like *Tristan and Isolde* and thus refrain from dramatization.
JV:	*In this respect, the critical sense—just as Nietzsche speaks of the "historical sense"—would also be a critical sensory organ.*
AK:	A peacemaking sense. If I put my parents' marriage back together—I love them both and as a child I chose neither one over the other—if I bring Anna Karenina and her husband back together when Anna Karenina's four-year-old son has authority over his mother, an authority fundamentally greater and longer-lasting than this dumb captain who just breaks horses' backs; in other words, if love were recast, so to speak, not into something more practical, but rather something more discerning, then there are still ample instances of catastrophe, crises, and chasms; many people still leave someone, but it must not always be the case that they split up acrimoniously. It must not be that a person has no control over the one thing that he is able to test himself with his senses, namely, matters of love.
JV:	*That would mean the critical sense would be one of immediate proximity, of inconspicuous, forgotten, and overlooked options.*
AK:	. . . a sense that generates self-consciousness. I can generate self-consciousness most easily using what I deal with, and that is the human capacity to love.
JV:	*The other side would then be that the critical sense creates an eminent relation to the world at a certain point, namely, where it relates to needs. The critical sense would be one . . .*
AK:	. . . that recognizes need, but sharply scrutinizes what actually qualifies as a need.

Translated by Emma Woelk

Notes

A transcription of the German original was originally published as Alexander Kluge and Joseph Vogl, "Kritik aus nächster Nähe: Interview mit Alexander Kluge," in *Ästhetik der Kritik oder Verdeckte Ermittlung*, ed. Jörg Huber et al. (Zurich: Edition Voldemeer, 2007), 191–201.

It is reprinted in Alexander Kluge and Joseph Vogl, "Kritik aus nächster Nähe," *Soll und Haben: Fernsehgespräche* (Zurich: Diaphanes, 2009), 7–23.

This interview was recorded on camera on July 6, 2006, but never broadcast on German television.

26

The Actuality of Adorno

Dear Mayor,
Dear Friedrich Kittler,
Dear guests,
You can imagine that receiving this prize named for Theodor W. Adorno is emotional for me. I met Adorno when I was twenty-four years old and working as an attorney in Frankfurt. Previous recipients of this prize, Jürgen Habermas, Michael Gielen, Györgi Ligeti, Jacques Derrida, and—in my opinion the master of filmmakers—Jean-Luc Godard, also reflect parts of my own life and work.

At the beginning of the book I wrote together with Oskar Negt, *Public Sphere and Experience*, we include the somewhat convoluted dedication "September 11, 1903–August 6, 1969." The former date is Adorno's birthday, which we celebrate today, the latter the day of this death. Adorno would have turned 106 today. He died forty years ago. Because he lives on in his writings, compositions, and in the hearts of those who knew him, I would like to try to summon him here in St. Paul's Church. I would like to say a few words about Adorno's actuality by calling upon some of his own thoughts and emulating his way of creating linkages and networks.

It would have stunned Adorno to know that the day of his birth is connected in the public consciousness to news of a great tragedy in New York.

How would he deal with this perception? He is not a fan of calamity. He speaks instead of the antirealism of feeling that we humans possess and that primarily defends itself against the perception of disaster. Our fantasy is essentially an escape. Only when it has been ideologized or strong-armed, says Adorno, does it seek out sensation. I suspect that amid the flood of news, something singular in nature would stand out to him: the cell phone. Under the ruins of the towers, there were supposedly caverns and caves similar to those in Herculaneum and Pompeii, in which people survived for a short time while attempting to make radio contact with the outside world. A question arises: Could there have been ways out, escape routes amid the catastrophe? Cranes and excavators that were suddenly on call could not surmount the mountain of rubble. They could not have dug out those trapped, for their weight would have crushed possible caves below.

There was, however—I am trying to follow Adorno's possible associations here—a large steel company in the United States, Bechtel International Instruments Inc., based in San Francisco. They had a type of vaulted metal bridge available that was large enough to span the field of rubble. Using this bridge, it would have been possible to dig. This offer was made, but no authorized official was there to make a decision. This bridge has since been sold to Ukraine, paid for by donations, and now spans the so-called sarcophagus of the Chernobyl nuclear power plant, a crumbling grave made of cement created in the first hours of the terrible disaster there.

On account of this connection as well as his motivation triggered by the horrific impression (the recognition of this date that completely changed his own birthday, the birthday of a lucky man), Adorno would have made associative connections between two different disasters and would again have not hesitated to connect the Chernobyl disaster to the financial crisis that occupies us now in 2009 as events with a similar particularity. You see how he brings together singularity, particularity, and the universal, but also adjustments guided by subjective feeling. The universal connecting Chernobyl, the financial crisis, and presumably the terrorist attacks of 9/11 as well lies in the fact that before these catastrophes this reality had been abandoned. Something remained unacknowledged. This is a question of so-called exclusionary mechanisms.

Something lingers outside like the thirteenth fairy in the Brothers Grimm's tale "Sleeping Beauty," and returns to exact revenge. Therefore, Adorno would continue, it would be more accurate to compare the misfortunate of the financial crisis not only to the crash of 1929, but also to a nuclear disaster like the one at Chernobyl. In both cases, we are dealing with misfortunes many considered to be improbable that had extreme consequences. When one perceives a catastrophe, then the first question for Adorno is what had previously gone unnoticed. This is how Adorno's mind works; it relies on his sensuousness, and while he perceives he begins to philosophize. This is how a seismograph works. Such a person, Adorno would claim and I am following him in his footsteps, is practical in their observations.

It seems that a theory, which discusses the dialectic of enlightenment and diagnoses the disease of reason extending from its ancient beginnings to modernity, neither constitutes a system of doomsaying nor does it call for one. Upon closer examination, we can always find redemptive elements—either before the catastrophe occurs, or as it is unfolding, or by learning from it and then reversing it after the misfortune. But these elements lie scattered far from each other. Our historical experience tells us that they rarely, if ever, have found their way back to each other just in time.

The work of creating linkages (when a weaver creates a web, it is called a text) is necessary for perceiving the juxtaposition of redemption and catastrophe; this is heterotopia. One has to twist and turn the universal, the particular, and the treacherous singular just as the spider Arachne does with her webs in Ovid's poem.

One has to combine the facts into a story. Redeem the facts from human indifference! Arachne weaves texts into her garments worn by humans and gods; they are their second skin, a doubling of reality: empathy and ways out.

In this sense, Bechtel's metal scaffolding belongs to no system. It is available unexpectedly. A repair mechanism, a fragment of reality. In order for redemptive elements to find each other, one must allow hope to intensify that there could be survivors, that at least some part of the misfortune did not occur. Critique for Adorno is therefore no mere written document, no bookish record of being right compared to other books, but rather active and consequential repair work. Critique presumes counterproduction against false production. It does not solely happen in the annals of intellectual history.

What does Adorno look like? In 1956, I sat in the inaugural lecture held by the classics scholar Prof. Dr. Harald Patzer (you can see him in my film *Yesterday Girl*). In the row in front of me sits a short man with almost no hair. He has a fierce attentiveness and unusually large eyes. I did not know him. I just stared at him till he looked back and asked me who I was. I answered: You must be Adorno. All I knew of him was what Thomas Mann had written.

Adorno was a friendly and communicative man of his day. But when it came to his work, he was a man of extreme incorruptibility and strict earnestness. You must try to imagine how still his hands were when he spoke or presented. In a two-hour presentation, he would not make a single hand gesture to make his point. They stayed perfectly still while thoughts passed through his mind and turned toward us, his audience. His facial expressions are also completely calm. Only his eyes speak. No extraneous movement of any of the more than 200 facial muscles that a human being has at their disposal. I am familiar with images of Babylonians, middle-class people from 4,000 years ago. They are similar to him. He comes to us from a distant place.

In order to describe him more accurately, I would like to cite a central point in his thinking. You are familiar with Immanuel Kant's Categorical Imperative: every moral individual should plan his actions such that they could provide maxims for a universal system of laws. Friedrich Nietzsche radicalized this principle: always act such that you could live with your behavior knowing that you would have to repeat your actions for all eternity. This is meant entirely practically. Freud expounded on the same idea: the only thing that protects us from disaster, the continuation of the curse—evil—within ourselves, is allergies; we can trust not only the moral mind's critique but also that of the skin.

Adorno would presumably find Nietzsche's idea more lively and practical than Kant's formulation, but Nietzsche's phrasing would have been too existential for him, meaning irrelevant compared to the practical experiences of the 1940s. Adorno thus presents a more practical and decisive standard. Public expression (including poetry), learning and education, in fact every expression of life, he says, exists under the postulate that Auschwitz not repeat itself. Dear guests, you can see in this imperative of Adorno's a sentence that repeats itself: There is no praxis without theory. Disaster—the wrong life—is the motor of counter-operations in theory, which includes the power of judgment. On the other hand, altered praxis orients itself spontaneously toward theory (even when this is not the drive in and of itself) when the former discovers the latter.

With his legendary sentence "Wrong life cannot be lived rightly," Adorno does not mean we intend to wait until the right life arrives.[1] Instead, it means there is no life at all if we cannot break through the disaster that is Auschwitz (and everything that now and in the future takes on a different form but repeats Auschwitz). The wrong life is powerful and hermetic, and at the same time—when measured against our human features acquired from history—unreal and porous as a sponge. Adorno formulates it thus:

The almost insoluble task
is to let neither the power of others,
nor our own powerlessness,
stupefy us.[2]

What does it mean to "de-stupefy"? In Latin, the word that describes the education process is *eruditio*: to create something fully formed out of raw wood. This concept contains a bit of pathos in northwestern Europe. The scholar Alcuin developed schools at Charlemagne's court according to this principle. In the eleventh century, the splendid universities of Paris, Bologna, and Oxford were founded. At this time, there existed a theory of three powers, which theologians and legal scholars justified, according to which the church, the armed forces (knights), and the sciences were equals: *sacerdotium, regnum, studium.* Accordingly, the French royal crest, the fleur-de-lis, has three leaves.

This early, self-conscious awakening in Europe based on education does not last long. In our country, it reappears for a short time around 1800 in the era of classicism. We must keep in mind that barbarism makes up the majority of history. For the longest period of human history, slavery is the norm. Only very late and at first just in Europe's northwestern cities, a concept of freedom emerges that stands in opposition to legally recognized slavery. Adorno never ceases to emphasize that the foundation of our modern civilization is thin and shaky.

We must, Adorno would say were he here standing next to me, reevaluate the concept of *eruditio*. The natural state, the warped wood, from which humans are formed, is not dumb. The relation of educated teachers to those they are meant to educate or, better yet, those in whom something yearns for education, needs to be corrected. Max Horkheimer once demanded that the Institute for Social Research, the institution in charge of the Frankfurt School, take on not just social researchers and philosophers but also doctors and midwives. The art of midwifery, obstetrics, knows that newborns contribute spontaneously to their own births. It is not a matter of molding but rather providing assistance, *eruditio*. Nothing about an embryo is like raw wood. It is all potential; it is life.

In the *Dialectic of Enlightenment* there is a hidden text (attached to the appendix): "In the Genesis of Stupidity." Here intelligence, alert curiosity, the heart of philosophy, is compared to a snail's feeler. This is a characteristic everyone has, not only humans, but also animals. This alert spirit "timidly ventures forth."[3] If it is injured, meaning if it is threatened by fear or terror, it retracts into his shell. From the outside, this looks like stupidity. It also appears like lethargy, passivity, as something stupid, but at its core it is actually just a different aggregate phase of life.

I cannot think of any better metaphor for the guiding principle of the Enlightenment than *sapere aude*! Have the courage to draw on your own sensuous certainty, as in this image of the sensitive snail, the image of the defensive character of intelligence. This character is always present, even in places where we do not see it. Education means to harness it and to strengthen its courage. A magical art, a seductive art, an *ars amatoria*, as Ovid calls it. This is the essential core of my new book, released today, which I formally dedicate to Adorno (and Niklas Luhmann as well).[4]

This leads to a challenging question that lies at the heart of all of Adorno's work: The ability to love has its own way of accessing enlightenment. If reason is sick, which human capacities contain the antidote?

In reference to reason, Immanuel Kant speaks of the "lavishly cared-for germ" that nature has implanted in us.[5] We should therefore use this resource, this characteristic, to search for authentic vitality and tend to the construction of lively gardens. He speaks of a "lavishly cared-for" germ, rather than a "delicate" germ. Like Adam Smith and David Hume, he means empathy. All of Adorno's texts deal, either directly or indirectly, with this trace, THE LAVISHLY CARED-FOR GERM, though we cannot judge whether he pursues this out of an erotic desire or a desire for truth.

There is no enlightenment without the promise of happiness. The process of enlightenment must be founded upon something that answers the inborn search for happiness we humans possess. The claim that we could replace sick, instrumental reason with vital fragments, germlings, seeds, and buds containing the excluded other—you will notice that the expressions miss their mark but are still intelligible—is not aimed at something impossible. Our only option is to follow this trace if we want to survive.

How can this be done practically? It clearly has something to do with the way our experience is constructed. Every person has experience, but whether or not they can connect this experience to self-consciousness depends on whether they share this experience with others and recalibrate it. This is a question of the public sphere. The public sphere, according to Adorno—and Kant, too, in his preface to the second *Critique*—is a space like apartments and cities that our experience needs to live.

For Adorno, this has to do with one of his main themes, the entanglement of form and content, the competency required to adequately articulate any state of affairs. Form, he says, creates the thing itself. The thing controls the form. Diversity, polyphony, and the category of relationality (the whole is the untrue, but the singular is also nothing in the absence of the whole) is not a style, but rather a condition for emancipation, participation, and coherence.

Adorno consistently emphasizes the autonomy of different forms of expressions that have been passed down to us throughout history. They act as monads, blind to each other, but in their depths they push toward the other forms of expression and appear unexpectedly in them. The book in the opera, the emotions of opera in the "opera of the twentieth century": film.

For about 6,000 years, the book has thus contained an autonomous mnemonic world of forms. All reliable authors, even those whose books were lost in the fire at the Library of Alexandria, form a constellation, a collective score, a planetary bridge through time.

I can hear Adorno whispering to me saying that we cannot stop reading. It is also a matter of listening. An ancient author like Ovid, whose *Metamorphoses* effortlessly surpasses the networks of modern Internet systems, primarily recited his poetry aloud. The reliability of the ear is something distinct from reading. In modernity, we find this reliability in the only authentic invention for radio, the radio play.

The 400-year-old history of opera has the same reliability as the ear. The 80,000 operas written since 1600 form their own score, says Adorno. As a totality, they are not exactly monadic, but rather polyphonic.

Film history is particularly short: only 120 years. My maternal grandmother, born in 1872, is older than it. For a time, Adorno did not consider film to be an original art form. This was partially because of the culture industry's hegemony, which has a particular pull within the film industry, but also because he mistrusted Walter Benjamin's overestimation of film. In the end, I believe I convinced him to reconsider his position. He would not have contradicted me that since the Stone Age (or at least the invention of language) moving images and the art of montage existed within the human mind, regardless of whether it is awake or dreaming. He would have agreed that the language of the moving image has its own autonomy that simply does not obey words or music notes. He would have agreed when I say that the art of film is an echo of this.

Each of these traditions (reading, listening, and following moving images) appropriates a certain state of affairs differently and through its specific mode of expression it changes the thing itself. If I respect the autonomy of form and content, a polyphonic world of forms is created: a diversity, authentic expression.

Connections for understanding run subcutaneously; they act like underwater animals or partisans. Subjectivity is the anchor of the objective. For me, Adorno's modernity is found in positions like this.

One can understand Adorno only by tracing (1) the decisive partisan battle against the systems of lies surrounding us, and (2) the unflinching hope that fragments or pebbles of true vitality will at some point arrive to our shores, if necessary, like a message in a bottle. Children, Adorno maintained, recognize such things spontaneously. What you will still hear today is a piano piece composed by Adorno from the year 1945.

In our day and age, the dominant medium is changing. Everywhere in the world, our public spheres show signs of decay and regeneration, and the medium of choice seems to be changing. To Adorno's dismay, television became the dominant medium of the previous century. A dominant medium is what I turn on when something extraordinary happens, for example, on September 11 in New York. That was eight years ago today. I neither open a book nor do I sit down at the piano in such a moment. I do not seek out the closest movie theater. Instead, I turn on CNN, for example.

Regardless of whether I am fond of this medium or not, it has the trust of millions of people who get their news about emergencies there and not elsewhere. This is a dominant medium.

Today, trust is migrating to a certain extent away from television and into the Internet, which is faster and involves more people in its web. It also often moves more quickly.

As with a stormy sea (and this is how Adorno should be understood), each change in the dominant medium involves anew every previous dominant medium along with the expressive forms of the heart and mind, which remain in the minority and therefore survive all the more tenaciously. Polyphony, says Adorno, is a characteristic inherent in all social relations. In other words: the dialectic is not a logical dimension, but rather one that connects periods of time.

And thus classical demands come to us anew from the future. We need to be more and more forcefully oriented toward the classical public sphere as it springs forth from big newspapers. We need the book and all the unalterable texts from antiquity more than ever before. The gravitational pull of harmonious music is emotionally capable of setting texts into motion; it recombines fictions and documentation anew. We need this because realities such as the financial crisis or asymmetrical war directly affect human life spans; they hurt people; and at the same time they appear as great works of fiction. In order to deal with this and to orient ourselves within these labyrinths, we do not need a single common thread, but rather the radical diversity of expression postulated by Adorno.

To conclude, I would like to tell a story illustrating how reality itself juxtaposes forms of diversity and how it is up to us as to whether this leads to cooperation or Robinsonism. During the 1968–69 winter semester here in Frankfurt, in the midst of the student protests, and in the year of Adorno's death, the sociologist Niklas Luhmann stands in for Adorno at the Johann Wolfgang Goethe Universität. Adorno needed a sabbatical; he wants to finish his aesthetic theory. You are all familiar with the themes of the student protests. Entirely divorced from that context, Luhmann offers a seminar with the title "Love as Passion" to replace Adorno's course. Four students enroll in the seminar. Outside, revolutionary plans occupy the Sociology Department and later the Institute for Social Research. At the same time, Adorno's lover left him. He went to Luhmann for personal advice, given the fact that Luhmann's seminar had such a promising title.

This is a snapshot from the arsenal of an exceedingly inventive author named reality. In a laboratory like this one, in which extreme opposites reside so close to one another, the first great philosophy developed during the Axial Age of antiquity (500 B.C.E.); Weimar Classicism developed around 1800; and in 1968 there almost could have emerged a Frankfurter Classicism. The great minds on hand, such as Hans Jürgen Krahl, Luhmann, Adorno, and Habermas, would only have had to work closely together. We cannot hope enough for this type of collaboration in our world.

You will now hear a short composition by Adorno written in 1945.

Thank you for your patience.

(Alexander Kluge gave this speech on September 11, 2009, Adorno's 106th birthday.)

Translated by Emma Woelk

Notes

The original 2009 speech delivered on the occasion of receiving the Adorno Prize was published in German as Alexander Kluge, "Die Aktualität Adornos Dankesrede zur Verleihung des Adorno Preises," *Der Freitag*, September 11, 2009, 32. This version of Kluge's speech is also available online at http://www.kluge-alexander.de/zur-person/reden/2009-adorno-preis.html.

A revised version is reproduced in Alexander Kluge, "Die Aktualität Adornos: Rede zum Theodor-W.-Adorno Preis 2009," in *Personen und Reden* (Berlin: Klaus Wagenbach, 2012).

The present translation uses the original German version as it appeared in *Der Freitag* and on Kluge's website.

1. [Translator's citation: Theodor Adorno, *Minima Moralia*, trans. E. F. N. Jephcott (New York: Verso, 2005), 39.]

2. [Translator's citation: Adorno, *Minima Moralia*, 57.]

3. [Translator's citation: Max Horkheimer and Theodor Adorno, *Dialectic of Enlightenment*, ed. Gunzelin Schmid Noerr, trans. Edmund Jephcott (Stanford, CA: Stanford University Press, 2002), 213.]

4. [Translator's note: Kluge is referring to Alexander Kluge: *Das Labyrinth der zärtlichen Kraft: 166 Liebesgeschichten* (Frankfurt am Main: Suhrkamp, 2009).]

5. [Translator's note: Kluge uses "dem 'zärtlichen Keim'" (the tender germ]) to refer to Kant's phrase in *Was ist Aufklärung?* "[der] Keim, für den [Natur] am zärtlichsten sorgt." The English translation here has been modified from Nisbet's, which reads: "the germ on which nature has lavished most care." See Immanuel Kant, "An Answer to the Question: What Is Enlightenment?," in *Kant's Political Writings*, ed. H. Reiss, trans. H. B. Nisbet (Cambridge: Cambridge University Press, 1970), 59.]

27

INVENTORY OF A CENTURY

On Walter Benjamin's *Arcades Project*

Could There Be a Version of Walter Benjamin's *Arcades Project* for the Twenty-First Century?

Prof. Dr. Burkhardt Lindner, editor of the *Benjamin Handbook*, comments....[1]

PROF. DR. BURKHARDT LINDNER: *[According to his exposé of 1939, Walter Benjamin] divided his [Arcades Project] into six parts and called the first "Arcades," the second "Panoramas," and the next "World Expositions."*[2] *And then came "Interiors," "Streets," and then finally "Barricades." He wrote [his exposé] incidentally in the present tense such that it did not appear like a story from the past but rather as if he were an eyewitness of something taking place now. He*

ALEXANDER KLUGE: *then assigned a figure to each of these six keywords. Charles Fourier was linked to the arcades, Louis Daguerre to panoramas, Louis Philippe to interiors . . .*
...Philippe, Charles Baudelaire was associated with the streets of Paris, and Haussmann . . .
BL: *Exactly. Georges-Eugéne Haussmann for the barricades . . .*
AK: . . . such that there was within Benjamin's imagination one person who did, planned, or achieved something, on the one hand, and an object world naturally far more powerful, on the other. The whole of reconstructed Paris is certainly something different than Haussmann's plans, right?
BL: *Absolutely!*
AK: And in so doing, Benjamin puts into operation a microscope that is at once also a telescope.
BL: *Above all, he creates a tension between humans and things. Louis Philippe does not appear all that much—Benjamin hardly made notes about him—but he was important for a certain epoch or, shall I say, a certain way of life in Paris. This whole aspect of the* Arcades Project *can be best described as Benjamin's anthropological materialism. He did not use this keyword much. He deploys it programmatically at the close of his surrealism essay and then, in a curious move, names as witnesses or informants for this concept the writers Hebel, Büchner, and . . .*[3]
AK: Johann Peter Hebel?
BL: *Yes, Hebel, Georg Bücher, and Arthur Rimbaud. He names these three in that essay and then in the keyword is picked up again in several passages in the* Arcades Project.
AK: What exactly is anthropological materialism?
BL: *It refers primarily to an analysis that takes the sensory organs and human perception as*

its point of departure instead of an idea of humanity wedded to progress, as is the case with Kant and Hegel and even later with Marx.

AK: ... individual elements like the soles of one's feet, the diaphragm, parts of the multifaceted human eye. We do not just have five senses, but rather twenty-four, if not more. The sense of having then grew and changed all these senses.

BL: *Yes, Benjamin was quite interested in this bit he found in Marx.*

AK: This emanates, as it were, from this center as if it were the eye of Pater Seraphicus in the fifth act of Goethe's *Faust II* where the unborn see through his chest. We look at things similarly, and the things look back at us.

BL: *And that is of course an experience that every generation makes anew, because every newborn must go to great pains in order to take hold of the world for itself. So throughout the generations this ability is renewed again and again regardless of everything else happening in the world. This stage is unique to us humans. It is interesting that Benjamin already makes this distinction in* One-Way Street, *once in the planetarium piece where he says that as species people are unchangeable—they have existed for thousands of years—but humanity as species could become something new.*[4]

AK: And it changes!

BL: *Indeed, it changes.*

AK: On the one hand, evolution takes place at the level of the individual senses—sensory activities—that are changed ever so slightly as they move from farms to cities and then onward to factories where they then escape by emigrating to the United States, etc. In other words, it transpires on an ad hoc basis that never allows an ego to develop, a basis that all humans together produce and in so doing

	produce themselves much like an aura that is always shifting.
BL:	*And they experience this collectively, this notion of an image and body space that all humans share like language. Normally we usually say that we share thought or language, but for Benjamin there exists an image and body space that we share as well. And this is a notion that distances him from Marxism and that might sound completely far-fetched now, especially since he then connects it to dreams, because this humanity that is in the process of becoming is at the same time still dreaming, it does not know yet where it is headed.*
AK:	Each epoch dreams about the one to follow.
BL:	*That is exactly what he writes in the exposé to the* Arcades Project. *But these dreams are ambivalent. They are pipe dreams . . .*
AK:	It is possible that he does not mean dream in the sense of how we dream at night, how humans dream, but rather like something that exists between humans, something in the gap between subject and object. There is a seam there, and at this seam, at this border, something is dreaming, because people are doing something, but they do not know that they are doing it.
BL:	*Not at all, and in this respect there is a very central keyword that plays a significant role in the exposé—he uses it all the time—namely, the concept phantasmagoria. You could say phantasmagoria is a concept unique to Benjamin that he sets against ideology. Most intellectuals of his time, especially those who tended toward Marxism or were inspired by Marx—even Theodor W. Adorno and Siegfried Kracauer—always cared deeply about social consciousness. What do the people think? What kind of views do they have? How deluded are they? That did not interest*

>   Benjamin as much, even in his artwork essay. He first assumes the idea of phantasmagorias in the Arcades Project and says that the new—inventions, ways of life, buildings, and so on—is illuminated in the immediacy of its presence.[5] This is not about a heightened consciousness, though of course thought is involved. It is just like Freud when he says that when we dream, we also think. Of course we are thinking, what else are we supposed to do, right? But this immediate sensory illumination is what interested him, and not for the purpose of destroying it through ideological critique, but rather as a way of perceiving it at all. He was a pioneer in this respect, too.

AK: Because it is an unbelievable mirror that the subject answers phantasmagorically. After all, humans cannot be objective.

BL: *Yes, or they can only be objective under certain circumstances.*

AK: Under certain circumstances, yes, and then only partially objective. But in reality thought is condensed emotions, and emotions reveal things that humans cannot bear.

BL: *Of course, yet another work that emerged from the* Arcades Project *must be taken into account, one that is very important for Benjamin's persona, namely,* Berlin Childhood. *In the Berlin archives, he writes something like, "I was a child at this time, at the threshold to the year 1900." This present-past perspective on his childhood played a big role. And then he writes, "I need to excavate everything that is related to my childhood." This is why, when you look through these two thick volumes, it is so astounding that there are so few entries about present-day Paris. There is next to nothing about the Parisian world fairs from the thirties.*

AK: But 1851, the year of the Great Exhibition in London—that you will find.
BL: *That you will find. For Benjamin, photography is the basis of film. Photography is—at one point he quotes a very nice expression from the nineteenth century—"un miroir qui se souvient," a mirror that remembers—as a definition for photography. There is this moment when life becomes recordable, meaning that perception of the experiential world becomes recordable first in the immobilized image and then in film, which manages to do more. We must always keep in mind that Benjamin examines film as a medium, as we would say nowadays. This means he does not talk about individual films, genres, or particular directors. He does not do any of that. He even writes something to the effect, "I must wrest the contemplation about film from the specialists." He wants nothing to do with them. At the same time, he says that everything we assert about the current state of art today must be able to be tested and verified using film. Film is ranked highly as a medium, and it constitutes the standard for art, because film—let us put photography aside for the moment—is actually the first means of production that is grounded in reproducibility. This means that film . . .*
AK: . . . creates a third reality. I have nature and my biology—like when I am sitting on the toilet—and at the same time I am a cognitive human being and I am connected to everyone else—that is the second nature. I am interconnected. I am social. But I am a third thing, too. I have created a mirror and sit in front of this mirror. It is, of course, very valuable, as Eisenstein sees it, and it is misused when the consumer public goes to see bad plays. I think that is how he would see it.

BL: Perhaps.
AK: But Franz Kafka spends every afternoon at a matinee in Prague at the movie theater. It is a work of magic . . .
BL: There is that famous entry, "Was at the cinema. Cried."[6]
AK: . . . insofar as I am together with myself.
BL: Benjamin went to the movies more than people think. He just did not write anything about it. It was not an important source for him for understanding Berlin.
AK: But this basic fact of acquiring a new reality at the edge of the cinematic image's frame where the suggestion of what I am not showing is the true expression—where the invisible image outside the film and the image the film shows converge together into a single flowing action—is new.
BL: Yes. Above all, there is the idea that a certain closed totality in the artwork—as is the case with painting and theater—now ceases to exist, first on account of its reproducibility; the nature of film is that it can be simultaneously shown everywhere. It is constitutive. Were someone to sign a film and say it is finished, that does not work for film at all. And the other reason Benjamin describes is the explosive power of film. Incidentally, he already starts doing this in a short text on Battleship Potemkin where he actually polemicizes above all this tendentious concept against another critic.[7] There is the image of apartments, offices, and streets of the big city that hopelessly hem us in and then comes along the film that explodes this prison with its dynamite of a tenth of a second. What happens then? Nature opens itself up. Not just social reality— it is obvious that film could show what was utterly indiscernible, what not even paintings could show—but rather a new structural

formation of matter becomes visible. It does not pertain solely to the world of humans or social reality but rather to actual matter.

AK: Matter that can suddenly become both magical and spiritual for a moment.

BL: *Of course, because Benjamin always conceived matter in cosmic dimensions. From our standpoint, he had a perhaps somewhat startling and deficiently problematized concept of the cosmos, one in which the human stands, as it were, in correspondence with the cosmos that never wanes . . .*

AK: . . . such that the cosmos has fundamental rights just as we have human rights. This is a new kind of thinking.

BL: *Yes, I would say that as well.*

AK: That is in the epistemo-critical chapter from the *Arcades Project* and the prologue to his book on tragic drama.

BL: *Yes, the prologue to Benjamin's book on tragic drama actually describes his way of researching and his method of writing. The epistemo-critical prologue is where he rebuffs certain models, like the subject-object among others, in order to say, "I am taking this path and do so in the form of a treatise." The treatise unifies beautifully assembled fragments. Benjamin's concept, which any large study must produce in the form of a discrete theory of knowledge, is that just one theory is inadequate. To have just one presumes it is complete, that you can go out into the world and have it fit like a glove and thereby catch everything.*

AK: His concept travels neither from the bottom up (thereby allowing anyone to assert that "they produce") nor from the top down. Instead, it travels outward from the center like gravitation.

BL: *Yes.*

AK: How big was the *Arcades Project* at that point when Benjamin moved from Paris to Marseilles?

BL: *We know that in Marseilles he no longer worked on it. There was also nothing in his briefcase. He had a heart condition. He wrote the theses there.*

AK: The *Arcades Project* was left behind in Paris.

BL: *One portion remained in his apartment. The Gestapo confiscated it and then it turned up in Moscow before it was later returned via Potsdam to the Benjamin Archive where there is still a lot to be researched. Georges Batailles hid another portion. Because Benjamin left behind no record of his hiding places, other parts turned up much later thanks to Giorgio Agamben. The biggest portion in his sister's possession initially traveled with her to Switzerland and then somehow Pierre Missac entrusted it to Martin Domke who then took it to America after 1945. Max Horkheimer and Adorno then received the two boxes. Adorno wanted to know more than anything what became of the* Arcades Project, *Benjamin's magnum opus. Leo Löwenthal then searched through everything. Adorno was absolutely miserable when they found no such text. Benjamin once wrote to Gershom Scholem, "Not a syllable of the actual text exists."*[8]

AK: A compulsory labor that he delivered to the Institute for Social Research to earn his livelihood?

BL: *No, he wanted to write it. When it was finished, the Baudelaire essay was really supposed to be an entire book. He imagined there would be perhaps three or four books that together would represent the* Arcades Project.

AK: It was planned like an iceberg. All the material he collected was its underside and above are the several spires.

BL: *If you look at the Baudelaire texts, there are many quotations but nowhere as many as in the Baudelaire convolute. Its 100 or more pages are excessive.*

AK: But this convolute—open on all sides, held together solely by the gravity of Benjamin's interest, and irrespective of the actual theme—represents the invention of a new literary method, one that Balzac would have achieved at best in the form of a novel at some point in time, or one that formed the basis of Proust's collected works. It is a method respectful of the material at hand, the self-regulation of things, and description.

BL: *And a method that ignores the history of events. When you look at Benjamin's keywords, you might think that war never took place. Where exactly are the great politicians? He does not even account for the history of the labor movement. None of that interested him. An intermediate world he called phantasmagoria emerged between people's immediate lived realities and those in power. Partially inhabited by the bourgeoisie and partially factored in by the consuming masses, this world was of great interest to Benjamin.*

AK: What if one were to apply Benjamin's method—just like medieval monks transcribed by continuing another's work—laid out in his prologue to describe the twenty-first century, which, in this sense, has yet to be described?

BL: *There are at least conditions that one has to look at and ask whether they still exist. The first condition was that Benjamin was able to set a stage, namely, Paris . . .*

AK: . . . capital of the nineteenth century . . .

BL: *. . . as a space. History becomes spatialized. He is always talking about immobilizing history. Dialectical images can only arise when the space of history is a space into which the* *past enters, but is, in the beginning at least, immobilized time. Finding such a space for the twentieth century, which we are now trying to remember, will not be so easy.*

AK: Because a capital of the twenty-first century cannot be named.

BL: *The twenty-first century is out of the question. What Benjamin conducted is of course a form of memory work, so we would really first need to say something about the twentieth century. And there you would not find this space, unless . . .*

AK: There are still many cities, many capital cities.

BL: *. . . you were to say Europe. Europe is, after all, a small continent.*

AK: Or could you say the Internet?

BL: *No.*

AK: It is not a city.

BL: *I would not go in that direction. I would ask myself, "Is there something from the twentieth century that has not yet been dealt with, that we of the twenty-first century need to remember in order to understand the twenty-first century?" That is what Benjamin is doing. He takes as his starting point the belief that the nineteenth century was forgotten far too quickly. Everything is destroyed after World War I. New technologies and media show up. It is no coincidence that we have books by critical intellectuals like Ernst Bloch's* Heritage of Our Times, *Dolf Sternberger's* Panorama of the 19th Century, *and Benjamin's* Arcades Project *that begin to think, "There was something there from the nineteenth century."*

AK: The study of ruins as a mirror of the present.

BL: *There was a bourgeoisie back then that no longer exists. There was a proletariat back then that no longer exists. We must become more observant in this regard. To transfer this* way of looking onto the twentieth century is not so easy. I would just say that it would have to be Europe. We cannot forget that Benjamin was a European intellectual. Before his exile he wrote frequently about France and translated and critiqued foreign-language books. He traveled to and wrote about Moscow. He never saw himself as having been restricted to just being German and he never was afflicted by nationalist pride. This European consciousness has more or less disappeared today. All we have left of Europe is the financial crisis. We have almost nothing else left, just the Euro and the crisis.

AK: Take, for example, Lagos, an urban agglomeration, that is quite inventive, where new inventions, says Richard Sennett, keep city planners and architects on their toes. Or take a phenomenon like Shanghai, which is very young, or Mexico City, which is, on the other hand, very old. If we consider places like that, they would get his attention.

BL: Yes, but for me this is something we would have to look at using the perspective adopted in the artwork essay. The Arcades Project is for me a work that turns to the past archaeologically with a certain way of looking and the notion that we must wake up from the nineteenth century—we have not done so yet. We have to wake up from the twentieth century in spite of all the Holocaust research.

AK: A clean slate must be . . .

BL: . . . we have not done it yet. The artwork essay emanates from the present. Its thesis: the medium of film is the first work of art created with reproducibility in mind. Everything derives from that. What transpires in film is a radical change in the way the masses perceive things. It would be extremely interesting to study changes in twenty-first-century *perception according to the perspective in the artwork essay. The Internet would have to be consulted. But one should not make the mistake of understanding Benjamin as merely a media theorist. That is a big mistake because he poses the question in an essay about the artwork. The essay is not entitled "The Age of Technological Reproducibility," but rather "The Work of Art in the Age of Its Technological Reproducibility." Today, everything is art...*

AK: Take something else, a different work of art from bourgeoisie society, namely, the individual researcher, the collector, or even Benjamin himself that reappears again and again in a thousand, if not million different forms. You will even find him in China, too. Since the era of Michel de Montaigne up to today, this individual is a big error, in a certain sense, and a great achievement. How is it that this individual lives at a time when earth's 7-billionth inhabitant is born? This inflation, if you will, represents 7 billion ways out as well as 7 billion problems. At the same time, it entails a change in representation. After all, you cannot establish an Athenian polis with 7 billion people. You are essentially farther away from many things and much closer to others. And this question would have probably captivated him.

BL: *That would have captivated him, especially as it relates to the idea of the masses. The idea of the masses plays an especially important role in the* Arcades Project *where actual Parisian crowds are mentioned. Poe describes them nicely as does Baudelaire as throngs, riding in horse-drawn carriages, and so forth. Then there are the masses in the artwork essay that go to the movies. There Benjamin says what he also states more or less in his short text on the poverty of experience, namely, that the intellectual should not rely on his false wealth, on education, and so forth. He must surrender something to these masses, and he must learn something from them as well. But what he learns is not class consciousness. This is not the issue for him. Instead, he learns this new form of perception, whereby the human adapts to the machine. He talks about the shock of film, by which he does not mean the Eisensteinian montage. He means the change in light that often penetrates me when the pictures appear in rapid sequence. This shock persists. We adapt to it and experience it again and again on a daily basis. That is the radical change, what is revolutionary about film. If this then brings us to the demands of politics—namely, the politicization of art—then we must have first understood this first part. If we do not understand the radical change in the forms of perception and sensuousness, then we cannot even begin to talk about politics and art.*

AK: Considering this basic fact would bring him to the conclusion that film is the only medium—this sets it apart from television—that has a dark phase.

BL: *That is true, the Geneva drive.*

AK: This dark phase means that the brain possesses physiologically a break of 1/48 of a second, in which it actively creates associations. The magic of cinema is not that it creates any aura, but rather the spectator fills in a moment of rest, a gap.

BL: *That is an interesting thought . . .*

AK: Were films not simply plays adapted for the screen, but rather if they genuinely consisted of just light and dark—in other words, light effects—then this magic would work. A pause in my daily routine, a third reality, would come into being, in which I furnish a relationship to the cosmos, to society, and to everything else. This pause is called cinema. It just has not yet become reality.

BL: *That is exactly the point of the* Arcades Project. *Benjamin has another central idea I have not mentioned yet and that is the idea of the "now of knowability."*[9] *The now of knowability does not mean that my knowledge is relativistic—now I perceive one thing, in the next instant another, and in the third something else entirely different—but rather a moment has arisen now when a certain historical instant freezes and becomes spatialized, when it confronts me as a signature. He also made use of it in the artwork essay. That is why it makes complete sense to ask whether what Benjamin describes is now right or wrong, or whether it has become obsolete. Benjamin saw something that no one else had seen in this form. And he expressed it in terms of a tension between the Great War and an impending new war as well as in the tearing apart of the masses between Stalinism and fascism.*

AK: And Auschwitz, which he sensed was coming.

BL: *It is a dialectical image. The entire artwork essay is a dialectical image. No one else picked up on that.*

AK: The dialectical image develops what poetics had achieved since time immemorial. It makes metaphors, vessels of experience. This experience consists of both visible and invisible matter; the epiphany is not visible. What is missing is invisible, the missing letter in the alphabet that we are looking for. Benjamin takes this just as seriously as everyday experience.

BL: *Amazingly, the dialectical image allows him to affirm his messianic impulses. There are*

	texts like the Theses *where it is obvious that he thinks this way. There are only a few places in the* Arcades Project *where he talks about theology, but his basic thought is that universal history is a messianic idea. We humans cannot do it. Perhaps on Judgment Day . . .*
AK:	Universal history tells itself.
BL:	*That would be a great book in which everything, both big and small, is catalogued. It is a nice thought, but we are not capable of it . . .*
AK:	The Milky Way is in and of itself, for example, one such catalogue. It can be read backward 13 billion years. It is a good text.
BL:	*That is right. If we then allocated more Internet storage for things and living creatures, which is possible . . .*
AK:	Who invented the Internet? The CERN team. That would have immediately gotten Benjamin's attention. About 10,000 scientists working on the biggest machine in the world to investigate the Planck length and the origins of the world say more about the cosmos than any other machine to date by investigating something small. It is both a telescope and a microscope. And they, of all people, invented the Internet. That would have gotten his attention.
BL:	*That would have certainly grabbed his attention.*
AK:	Along with the fact it happened more or less by accident.
BL:	*I think Benjamin would have been more interested in that. I noticed that he gave up using a typewriter; he always wrote by hand. In terms of writing, I do not know how he would have reacted to computers, but the possibility of organizing the* Arcades *material in a new way by linking it together or adding new material and creating accordingly three-dimensional*

	text spaces, that would have fascinated him tremendously.
AK:	Prismatic perception, like crystalline structures.
BL:	*Before film, before the modern sciences, before Einstein, reality was simple, rigid, and fixed. It could be explained using the simple principles of cause and effect. All of a sudden, three-dimensional space appears that even alters time.*
AK:	. . . and which becomes multidimensional, and those crystalline prisms . . .
BL:	*There is that nice passage he writes to Scholem, in which he quotes from a book penned by a once popular physicist.*[10] *He writes how the act of crossing a threshold looks from an atomic perspective. It is an enormous human achievement to pass through a doorway given all the resistance there is.*
AK:	The resistance against atoms?
BL:	*No, the human being is in the final instance made of atoms and elements.*
AK:	Humans are porous, largely empty spaces. An empty space crosses a threshold.
BL:	*He says, "What is described there is a text by Kafka."*
AK:	Indeed. Nature wrote the text. Niels Bohr wrote texts of equal stature with Kafka's, but he wrote his from nature just as Kafka wrote his from . . .
BL:	*The decisive point for Benjamin would be that this knowledge of nature is not without echoes. It is depressing that today's researchers listen and look far and wide and then start searching for God particles, which is anything but comprehensible. There is no echo. These great researchers are a tad blind, insofar as they lack any sensitivity toward what they receive. They merely wish to confirm their supposed measurements. That is a one-sidedness that Benjamin would not have shared. In this*

respect, he is really anthropocentric in his thinking. That sounds today like someone from the hinterlands.

AK: Benjamin would say, however, that every human being who is born and who makes eye contact with his mother in the first three days after birth; who feels a primal trust, as Freud describes it; who harbors the illusion that others mean well for him (Freud, too, lived off this discovery until his death in 1940); if all this is indeed the case, then the world is anthropocentric and can be understood neither with nor without a subject because it needs this subjective-objective seam, this separatrix where errors accumulate.

BL: *I would say, too, that the constant effects we draw from the world in order to make our existence possible are in many cases unconscious or unnoticed.*

AK: A crystal lattice of collected fallacies would be something, be it a piece of information or a mirror image of the real. We could work with that.

BL: *Yes, I would accept that. We could work with that.*

AK: Such that an interesting form of our subjective spirit, its distraction, which he talks about . . .

BL: *Distraction is a central category in his artwork essay.*

AK: . . . creates attentiveness, such that the people who are supposedly the masses are at the same time . . .

BL: *He says, "The audience [in the cinema] is an examiner, but a distracted one."*[11]

AK: That is a wonderful observation that does not underestimate the reserves hidden in people who inhabit our planet.

BL: *He does not go into the theater thinking that he wants to examine something; he just wants to be entertained. And yet he still looks closely. He also talks about how devices perform tests, that man is tested—by which he does not mean those primitive test procedures like multiple choice or whatever, but rather a totally materialistic . . .*

AK: With YouTube something suddenly emerges that none of the critics or TV directors took into account. And when that is the case—and it does not happen very often—then that is this attentiveness in distraction.

BL: *It is also a more intuitive ability to conduct yourself in a situation in which a device is testing you. I cannot be 100 percent in control of that. I cannot pull it off by meticulously preparing myself. I have to abandon myself somewhat, but at the same time I am responding.*

AK: I have to direct my expectations toward those horizons that contain improbabilities, that right now, for example, as we are talking, an Einstein is born in Bangladesh who is brought by his mother to New York and who, at the base of a skyscraper, gets an opportunity to embark on his education because he serves yuppies. You could not rule out a globalized career like that according to Benjamin.

BL: *I would not want to rule that out. That really exists. You could even name names. Only I am still clinging somewhat to the notion that with the* Arcades Project *Benjamin was conducting a European project and that this Europe, as a result of globalization, which after all does not have much to do with Europe and does not particularly have Europe in its sights, is always forgetting itself more and more. Europe is after all the continent most steeped in history. And that, too, is an inheritance and something we bring with us. I very much regret that today these questions really only appear to be financial questions.*

AK: This is also the connection with all the other countries. Meaning that when, for example, the intestinal tracts of children in Saxony are poisoned by strawberries that were brought in from China but probably grown using European methods because the greenhouse is a European idea, then Benjamin would pick up on these sorts of connections.

BL: *Yes, and if he were planning on doing what you are getting at, namely, looking directly at the twenty-first century today instead of twentieth-century European history, which as I said the artwork essay does, then in that case he would definitely observe something like that. I am sure of that.*

AK: But I can assure you that I am just as interested in that other perspective. The study of ruins will tell us more than mirrors, more than if we attempt to do something that we ourselves cannot do within our means, namely, to define the present age.

BL: *One thing must be said. All the talk about the complexity of today's world is misleading. When you take a look at the past you see that things were much more complex, chaotic, and colorful. It is just that we always perceive the complexity as connected to a message of powerlessness. All the news reports tell us, "You are powerless." And this leads to us thinking that we will never find our way. Globalization is a simplification of the world, a terrible simplification, but a simplification nevertheless.*

AK: An abstraction.

BL: *Not just that. For the first time in history, the human is taking on planetary responsibilities. That is taking place, but, of course, in a disguised way. Humankind does not comprehend it.*

Translated by Andreas Freytag Hill

Notes

This dialogue was originally broadcast in German as Alexander Kluge, dir., "Inventar des Jahrhunderts," *News and Stories*, RTL, April 7, 2013.

A transcription of the German original appears in "*Inventar eines Jahrhunderts*: Über Walter Benjamin und die Passagenarbeit—Burkhardt Lindner im Gespräch mit Alexander Kluge," in *Burkhardt Lindner: Studien zu Benjamin*, ed. Jessica Nitsche and Nadine Werner (Berlin: Kulturverlag Kadmos, 2016), 490–506.

The dialogue was transcribed and translated entirely anew for the present translation.

1. [Translator's citation: Burkhardt Linder, ed., *Benjamin-Handbuch: Leben, Werk, Wirkung* (Stuttgart: Metzler, 2006).]

2. [Translator's citation: Cf. Walter Benjamin, "Paris, Capital of the Nineteenth Century: Exposé 'of 1939,'" in *The Arcades Project*, trans. Howard Eiland and Kevin McLaughlin (Cambridge, MA: The Belknap Press, 1999), 3–26.]

3. [Translator's citation: See Walter Benjamin, "Surrealism: The Last Snapshot of the European Intelligentsia," trans. Edmund Jephcott, in *Selected Writings*, ed. Michael W. Jennings, Howard Howard Eiland, and Gary Smith, vol. 2, *1927–1934* (Cambridge, MA: The Belknap Press, 1999), 217: "metaphysical materialism, of the brand of Vogt and Bukharin—as is attested by the experience of the Surrealists, and earlier by that of Hebel, Georg Büchner, Nietzsche, and Rimbaud—cannot lead without a rupture to anthropological materialism."]

4. [Translator's note: Lindner's paraphrases here Benjamin's *One-Way Street*. The original reads thusly: "Men as a species completed their development thousands of years ago; but mankind as a species is just beginning this." (Walter Benjamin, *One-Way Street and Other Writings*, trans. Edmund Jephcott and Kingsley Shorter (London: Harcourt, 1978), 104.]

5. [Translator's note: Lindner loosely paraphrases here the following portion from Benjamin's exposé: "Our investigation proposes to show how, as a consequence of this reifying representation of civilization, the new forms of behavior and the new economically and technologically based creations undergo this 'illumination' not only in a theoretical manner, by an ideological transposition, but also in the immediacy of their presence." See Benjamin, "Paris," 14.]

6. [Translator's citation: Frank Kafka, *The Diaries of Franz Kafka*, ed. Max Brod, trans. Joseph Kresh (New York: Schocken Books, 1988), 238 (translation slightly modified to reflect the German original). Cf. Franz Kafka, *Tagebücher, 1910–1923*, ed. Max Brod (Frankfurt am Main: Fischer Taschenbuch, 1976), 242.]

7. [Translator's citation: Walter Benjamin, "Reply to Oscar A. H. Schmitz," trans. Rodney Livingstone, in *Selected Writings*, ed. Michael W. Jennings, Howard Howard Eiland, and Gary Smith, vol. 2, *1927–1934* (Cambridge, MA: The Belknap Press, 1999), 16–19.]

8. [Translator's citation: Walter Benjamin, *The Correspondence of Walter Benjamin*, ed. Gershom Scholem and Theodor W. Adorno, trans. Manfred R. Jacobson and Evelyn M. Jacobson (Chicago: University of Chicago Press, 1994), 527.]

9. [Translator's note and citation: The German "Jetzt der Erkennbarkeit" is translated variously in Benjamin's translated works as either "now of knowability" or "now of recognizability," the latter being especially prevalent in convolute

N on the theory of knowledge in the English translation of his *Arcades Project*. Here, the former is used in order to complement Lindner's emphasis on epistemological concerns. Cf. Walter Benjamin, "Theory of Knowledge," trans. Rodney Livingstone, in *Selected Writings*, ed. Marcus Bullock and Michael W. Jennings, vol 1, *1913–1926* (Cambridge, MA: The Belknap Press, 1996), 276-77.]

10. [Translator's note: Benjamin, *The Correspondence of Walter Benjamin*, 563.]

11. [Translator's citation: Walter Benjamin, "The Work of Art in the Age of Its Technological Reproducibility," trans. Harry Zohn and Edmund Jephcott, in *Selected Writings*, ed. Howard Eiland and Michael W. Jennings, vol 4, *1938–1940* (Cambridge, MA: The Belknap Press, 2003), 269. The English translation is slightly modified to accommodate Lindner's modification.]

28

AN INSTANCE OF INTERNET TELEPHONY OVER THE HIMALAYAS

WANG GE: Good evening, ladies and gentlemen. Welcome to our roundtable discussion following the film screening.[1] In the age of reproducibility and telecommunication it is technologically possible for us to converse face-to-face over such a long distance. I think I do not need to do much introducing. Many of you came specifically because of Mr. Alexander Kluge and Professor Wang Hui. They are both public intellectuals, so to speak, not only in their own countries, but worldwide. To begin this discussion, I would like to pose a question to Mr. Kluge: Today we watched your long film. It is so specific and headstrong that it explodes the boundaries of conventional film genres. I would therefore like to ask you: Why do you work? Why does your work assemble *different images, quotations, aphorisms, and interviews into a universal work?*

ALEXANDER KLUGE: This is laid out in the history of film. You can actually say that all twentieth-century films make up *one* musical score, just as you could say that all operas from the 400-year history of that form, from 1600 until today, are one musical score that has accompanied and described bourgeois history and the bourgeois revolution like a distorting mirror. These operas are also thorough and, in the case of Richard Wagner, four evenings of three and a half hours each is so much longer than what you just saw. A film that wants to be thorough, that wants to engage the patience of real relations, so to speak, that wants to express its respect for Sergei Eisenstein—as well as James Joyce, because Joyce should have been the screenwriter for Eisenstein's film *Capital*—this commands respect for the fact that it is as thorough as possible. Eisenstein's film would have been even longer, had he made it.

WG: *But Richard Wagner's score always has a common thread running through it, a plot, and we have the impression that you strongly emphasize the fragmentary. You are probably trying to bring the breaks in narration to the fore in your film. What is behind this fragmentation?*

AK: I have two different reasons: everything authentic is fragmentary. You should respect fragmented reality. I did not invent fragmentary storytelling. The fragmentary is already present in Tacitus, in his Roman historical writing. The fragmentary is what Walter Benjamin and Theodor W. Adorno teach us: we should use it. We should not falsify or patch things together. The expression of a single moment is autonomous. People should be autonomous, but things that are represented are also autonomous, and the element that the camera is able to capture is the

	blink of an eye, a snapshot. These moments can now be brought together. A relationality of moments is thereby created and this RELATIONALITY, this is the category of film. Film is a very young art form.
WG:	*You mean . . .*
AK:	My maternal grandmother was born in 1872 before film was invented.
WG:	*This means that as you see it new possibilities remain open for film. Film is not a fixed category or genre, but instead it can always be expanded by further possibilities, and this can be experimented with. Is this what you mean?*
AK:	What I mean is that the reality of film is not sealed off. But I also mean that reality itself, history, is also not complete; it is rich. Our forefathers and the cells in our bodies that we carry with us all day are 500 million years old. That is real time. Our common history is also quite old—we were separated on Earth, developed modernity twice: once in 500 B.C.E. in China and again around the same time in Europe. With Heraclitus in Greece and Confucius in China. These are all tremendous mountains of time. We do not have just the mountains of debt and the financial crisis, but also the ways out that history teaches us. History is rich; it is a mountain of experiences.
WG:	*You see yourself as a chronicler of our time. What is a chronicler? Does this mean that you have a particular method for following and documenting history or actuality?*
AK:	It is not that I am a chronicler, but that history tells itself. I am a collector just as the Brothers Grimm heard fairy tales from the women who told them. This is how I collect, so to speak. This produces a chronicle, in that respect you are correct. But there are two types of time. One is called *CHRONOS*; this is mechanical time. She eats her children. The other is called *KAIROS*;

he is a Greek god. He is a small, bald gnome, the god of happy moments. If I arrive too late, my hand will slide off the back of his head. In the front, he has a tuft of hair I can grab onto. This is the god of the camera, if you will.

WG: *This is also etymologically related to the word* crisis, *correct? At the critical moment, when things could develop positively or negatively. SHISHI is also an important concept of Wang Hui's. Wang Laoshi . . .*

WANG HUI: Mr. Kluge has just addressed two points. The first point addresses the question of how the development and transformation of history can be documented. He very modestly said that he is only a documentarian. But this documentation itself is an intervention. It is an intervention of the documentary into history in which a key moment is used as an entry point. For example, the fact that we have the opportunity to watch and discuss this film today is one such intervention. Human reflection, allowing history to rise again through people, is itself part of history. If we refer to the definitions from Marx cited by Kluge in the film, then the most profound conception of history is not materialism or idealism, but rather naturalism and humanism: the history of nature. Seen this way, all human actions are a part of the history of nature. . . . In ancient China there was the concept of SHISHI: reality; fact; originally: a MATURED THING. I really like this concept because this reality differentiates itself from TIME. It is not a teleological, organized time that linearly progresses along set tracks, but rather a natural process brought about through the intervention of the individual and the interactions of countless actions. Marx actually used this concept of "natural history." We can view human history as the history of nature. This very special conceptualization of "nature" has an internal connection to the concept of Shishi and has led to many discussions about Marx because many believe Marx to be a teleologist. It seems that Marx would describe history as a process oriented toward a temporal goal. But Marx's theory and his observation of history, his assertion that though he is describing the history of capitalism, he also wants to simultaneously intervene in history, this is itself a part of the history of nature. If we view history this way, then concepts like Shishi, naturalism, and humanism are thoroughly compatible with one another.

AK: I can only agree with this. It must also be said that it is a great privilege to speak with you from 8,000 kilometers away. This really is a new "age of technological reproducibility" and it even has an aura, unlike what Benjamin describes. So once again: I bid welcome to the audience and, above all, you. This is an important day for me. It is daytime here and already late where you are. I completely agree with you, Professor Wang Hui: when I say "to collect," then it is not with indifference. If I have a store's leftover goods that can no longer be sold, and human labor power is embedded within them, then I am sad. A requiem can be written about this. But there are also cases in which the sadness, an emotion, a form of empathy for facts, is added. My guiding principle and that of my coworkers is "Redeem the facts of human indifference. Redeem the news from human indifference."

I would like to tell a story. We find ourselves in the year 2012, and your huge country became a republic in 1912. What a remarkable year. It is the year, for example, of the Balkan War, factors that make the outbreak of world war necessary in 1914. But it is also the year of the Titanic where a spirit of competitiveness emerged. We must conquer the "blue ribbon of the North Atlantic," then crash into an iceberg, and lose people. Now in 2012 we suddenly have a similar event. We see a ship off the Italian coast and instead of an iceberg the captain, who navigates just as incompetently as the captain of the Titanic, wants to prove himself along a rock.[2] It is very interesting how little chronos learns here—this is not kairos; not the small god, but the huge one that eats his children. At the same time, the history of lifeboats, the training of captains, and shipwrecks show no signs of improvement. We are thus able to say: Why do we hope that our twenty-first century will not be derailed again like in 1914?

This is what makes Marx, observation, and mourning so important.

Now I shall tell a very short story that I dedicate to Professor Wang Hui. As I was driving here, I asked myself what story I could tell you. This is the story of the waiters on the Titanic.[3] There were seventy-two waiters. A majority of them came from Abruzzo, Italy. They had brides there to whom they had promised their hands in marriage. According to local customs, every one of these women was not allowed to take the next man as their husband, but rather had to remain permanently alone—this is worthy of a requiem. An opera composer, Luigi Nono, thus wrote a LAMENT FOR TWELVE STRINGS AND TWELVE SOPRANOS in 1966, when your Cultural Revolution began. I just wanted to illustrate what you just said using different words: that lived time, labor, human essential powers, as Marx calls them, write a story and contain a tenacious economy that never relents and keeps tunneling onward—as a mole does.

And now a Marxian story.[4] There were pension funds that travel around the world, so to speak. In the early days when the Chinese economy was expanding, they invested money in an economic zone where they built factories and high-rises. Then they took the money away, sent it to India, and now the factories and the high-rises stand around without any capitalist purpose. The governor who supported this was sent to prison and committed suicide. His son became the chief auditor for the People's Republic of China. He now says: First we learned Marx, then we developed a particular form of production capitalism, and now we have to help the stockbrokers of New York understand their own actions in the form of adult education. We have to send our experts to New York and teach the capitalists how classical capitalism functions. The central theme: the distinction between a robber economy and the use value of capital.

WG: *I read an essay of yours in which you pointed this out in very broad terms. You described the rise of capitalism in different countries as a type of vagrancy. There was the Ruhr region, Detroit, of course the industry in Great Britain earlier, and then also in Tokyo, in the South of China, and now this migratory process to India and Bangladesh, etc. That is perhaps also the reason why you introduce Ovid's* Metamorphoses, Oedipus, *or* Ulysses *as metaphors for capital.*

AK: That is correct.

WG: *But how are we to understand future trends, or how would you go about predicting how this morphing capitalism will further develop? Will it travel further onward to India, Africa, and South America? Or are there other ways for realizing other possibilities for coexistence and economic life? What do you and Professor Wang Hui think?*

WH: I would also like to tell a story, since Mr. Kluge mentioned the Chinese special economic zone and the changes in India. I just returned from India. My story is this: about ten years ago, India began copying the Chinese special economic zones, but both India's system of property ownership and its political system are completely different from those in China. The plan to take on this system of special economic zones was thus met with great resistance. It led to bitter clashes between a huge number of farmers and the government, principally with governments led by leftist and communist parties. There are Maoist movements in underdeveloped regions. Since we were just talking about the founders: you could say that Maoism is a distorted version of Marxism. Speaking of Kluge's film, which discusses Marxism's many transformations, for example, into Leninism, Maoism is one of these transformations. I was once in Nepal and visited the headquarters of the Nepali Liberation Army. Its members follow a path of Marxism-Leninism in Maoist thought as well as the path of Pushpa Kamal Dahal.[5] In today's India, farmers have given rise to movements that carry out acts of violent resistance in the name of the Maoist party. But what relationship actually exists between these resistance movements and Maoism? There has been a distortion, there is no direct lineage. Similarly, during the Chinese Revolution, many issues were addressed that could be traced back to Marxism, but had also undergone a massive transformation. If we look at the different variations of capitalism, then we simultaneously discover its opposite, meaning that internal resistance also gives rise to movements that constantly allow for the creation of new variants. It is worth studying more closely movements based on these kinds of variants.

As I watched Kluge's film, there were a few sequences especially important to me because they contained lots of dialogue. This film not only consist of interviews with philosophers, thinkers, and artists and allows them to speak for themselves, but is clearly also in dialogue with Marx and Eisenstein. We could say that it refers to antiquity and the present, as well as the revolutions of the sixties, Kluge's generation, and those following the Cold War. The changes that took place between these space times—which intercede within these interventions in the transformation of capitalism—this is, in my opinion, a question we should explore today. We find ourselves in the middle of a financial crisis. If we look at the media and newspapers, people are constantly quoted who suggest possible solutions to the financial crisis, but the way in which culture, cinema, film, and thinking intervene in this crisis is a question intimately linked to our discussion today. Looking at it in this light, I get the impression that film, understood as archaeology, has a political and cultural significance today.

AK: I would like to analyze our own situation, the way we are sitting here today. That we can talk with one another separated by over 8,000 kilometers, even though we did not know each other beforehand, this can be traced back to a small group of scientists. Scientists are also farmers. They till the land of knowledge. They have ground beneath their feet. They were working at CERN in Geneva and they research the smallest particles with the largest machine in the world. By looking at this smallest element, they learn something new about the beginnings of the world and what happens in the galaxies. They are now researching dark matter and dark energy, the most powerful agents in our universe that Isaac Newton never knew. The people at CERN invented the INTERNET—initially for scholarly communication among only 5,000 people in the world. From this dead labor, as Marx would say (meaning from something far-flung that had long been invented already), they pieced the Internet together, and that is what we are using today to meet each other.

This can be characterized as an element that no one predicted. Lenin did not predict it. Marx did not predict the Internet, but it is composed of human labor power, a summation of lived time from people who invented something—and then these scientists pieced it together. It consists of cooperation that cannot be bought with money, by the way, because these scientists cannot be bought with money. Our modern world is composed of such elements, our second nature.

We once made a film in Shanghai with Richard Sennett. There was an architecture conference taking place around the city.[6] The film crew captured a family from Xinjiang. They were doing something in the big city similar to what they had done previously in their hometown in the country: like gleaners collecting the remaining grains from the field following the harvest, they were now, in SECOND NATURE, pulling apart scraps of cable for the copper. The family supported itself selling junk. This is a field from the second nature, so to speak. They were very happy to be together. Just as happy as they had been together at home, but now in a big city that is not their own. But the ground they sat and worked on had already been sold. This was part of a compound that was to be torn down a week later. They hoped, in a way, theirs would also be torn down and they would get in return replacement apartments in one of the suburbs.

WG: *I would like to continue with the question I just posed. Professor Wang Hui was just talking about classes and I am wondering if this term, the concept of class warfare, is even relevant anymore. You said earlier that class itself does not mean that there exists a kind of natural cohesion of people with similar interests, but instead is associated with a consciousness. I wondered whether this cohesive consciousness is even still possible today. Can solidarity be created and articulated, either through the Internet or in some other way? Because I get the impression that there are many scattered interest groups, but no longer classes.*

AK: If I may pass the question on to you, Professor Wang Hui? Who is the subject of history today? This is actually your question. And this subject, I would also like to ask, can it also be history itself? Because history contains all people as well as certain elements from every natural revolution involving bacteria, animals, and every other possible life form, we are older than our consciousness. This would interest me, were we to research it closely, whether it is actually history itself that can be the subject—and merely at certain fortuitous moments. Yet we must be careful: rationality and consciousness alone will not suffice, since dead labor, everything that our predecessors did, and everything of theirs that works in us must be added to the mix. We cannot ask, as Maximilien Robespierre did: Who is thinking correctly? Those who do not, they will have their heads chopped off. Rather, we say: What is more valuable than mistakes? Make more mistakes and you will become navigators. How else will you learn, if not through mistakes? There is a nice Dada quote; this is not a serious science, but the Dadaists lived in Zurich on Spiegelgasse just as Lenin did in 1916. The Dadaist said, "Wander through the Harz region of Germany while blindly following the directions of a map of London."[7] The Harz Mountains are a wild mountain range in Germany where accidents are inevitable if you hike through them with a London street map. You will have a direct experience breaking your arm. You will not break it a second time. We must drive the question to the point of exhaustion: What is the subject? What is cooperation? What can we do? It is possible that there is something in us that protects or helps us. I would like to tell another story.[8] There was an American fighter pilot in Iraq—his machine fires automatically—and he wanted to destroy a building in which enemy activity was suspected. But it was actually the site of a wedding party, and it would have caused a huge scandal and disaster. At the moment he wanted to fire, his bowels acted up and he soiled his pants. I do not know how to translate that into Chinese. It is entirely impossible for a pilot to change his pants in the plane and now he is filled with shame. The simplest type of moral outbreak is when I feel ashamed for soiling my pants. Because of this, he yanks on the controls of his plane, the missile falls into a swamp, and the family is saved. In this case, the villi of the lining of his intestine— his bowels—were smarter than his head. If we take these elements into account then, we must not feel powerless. Adorno said it is crucial that we not allow ourselves to be stupefied by the power of others or by our own powerlessness. We must therefore collect elements in keeping with this idea, and in this instance the fortuitous element was KAIROS IN THE BOWELS OF THE PILOT.

WG: *You just mentioned your mentor Adorno and often, as either student or soulmate, one plays a double role. One thinks both collaboratively, and at the same time as a continuation of and even in opposition to one's mentor.*

AK: One does this out of respect.

WG: *So what have you acquired from the Frankfurt School or Adorno? You are acquainted with the works of Bertolt Brecht and Walter Benjamin. Which variations or possibilities have you drawn from the intellectual tradition of the Frankfurt School?*

AK: I have already mentioned one principle: that we should not be afraid. First of all, the idea of cooperation plays a larger role in my work than in that of my teachers. Each of us sitting here today—both there and here—has sixteen great-grandparents who reside within our bodies and in theory should be waging civil war given how different they are. Yet they do not. They tolerate each other. We thus carry in us an example of a cooperative community all the time. This is how Gottfried Wilhelm Leibniz would describe it. And Johann Wolfgang von Goethe, who was said to be Chinese—he wanted to emigrate to China at the end of his life—would also see it this way. On this subject, he says that modernity has less to do with HOMO SAPIENS than with HOMO COMPENSATOR, the balancers. We have ears elaborately developed from the sides of fish. This ear can listen to music and is, at the same time, the organ that enables us to have balance. Without ears, we would be unable to walk upright, und we would not have two cerebral hemispheres—it is the organ that understands music. I think Adorno would find this just as beautiful as I do, and hopefully you do as well. We are balancers—*homines compensators*. This is our ability.

WH: I would like to return to the issue Dr. Kluge brought up about the American pilot. Why is thinking in the belly "truer"? I believe it has to do, to a certain extent, with Marx's theory: we all know that there was a line of thought in early German ideology that assumed that ideology was false consciousness. Marx observed the relationship between reality and ideology and tried to determine its relationship to a person's behavior. This was no simple observation. Assuming you are a socialist, but in your actions it matters not if you discuss socialist concepts, but rather what you actually do. This is a question of method. The originary truth can be found in this small example.

Kluge just emphasized cooperation. I would like to go back to the aforementioned question of class because the entire political struggle of the nineteenth and twentieth centuries was framed as class conflict. Yet Marx describes this in two completely different ways. On the one hand, he never defines the boundaries clearly. We know that there is an unfinished chapter on class at the end of *Capital* that does not give a definitive answer to the question of how a class should be defined.

If you, on the other hand, read "The Eighteenth Brumaire of Louis Napoleon," in which he describes the political and social struggles in France at this time, you will discover that countless and vastly different groups took part in these historical movements of the Napoleonic era. These people cannot be definitively divided up into those class categories that the concepts describing existing modes of production attempted to define. There were also alliances that developed out of the class conflict, and the dynamics of politics or people expanded far beyond the political, which had developed against the backdrop of so-called commodity logic and in reality served as the prerequisite for certain coalitions.

There were, of course, other conditions at play at that time, and we can also put ourselves in this situation and observe what happens. We find ourselves, for example, having a discussion today on *Capital*; we are performing a kind of archaeological research on *Capital* carried out across a distance of 8,000 kilometers. This scenario makes me wonder: Kluge is 8,000 kilometers away in Germany, but is nevertheless present here in Beijing, and in the conference room of the Central Academy of Art, and participates in a discussion here in Beijing. What does this actually mean?

Kluge brought up Confucius, Marx, and also Eisenstein. I sometimes have the feeling that our situation today represents a completely novel phenomenon, something historically completely new. If we look back at history, then this scenario contains something completely new. Part of this is due to the state of technology: without it, this conversation could not take place. Each new coalition requires certain technological conditions. This is a part of the reality to which this technological change and certain developmental conditions belong. This is the decisive factor. The second decisive factor is China. Under the conditions of global capitalism and globalization, China's position has undergone a massive shift. We previously talked about China against a European backdrop; we also mentioned the Enlightenment, the image of China in Leibniz and Voltaire; we sought the intellectual resources of the European Enlightenment. This is one approach, but it assumes a FAR East, observers from afar enter into our history and shape politics. To a certain extent, this is an alliance, an attempt to connect China, from afar, to European politics of the eighteenth century. It is a special alliance formed by observation and phenomenological intrusion, but it is a "Far East," a civilization, a nonreal existence. During its revolutionary period in the twentieth century until 1968, China was to a certain extent the point of origin for all revolutionary movements. At the same time, China was also the place that served European intellectuals as inspiration and projection surface; a dialogue existed between the two. There were also many people who came to China while many Chinese went to Europe. It did not create the kind of common "stage" we have today, but rather back then there existed two separate stages. When we discuss the capitalist movement and new politics today, China, when seen globally, has, to a certain extent, become an inner part of the market. Strictly speaking, it is almost impossible to understand what this capitalist world actually is without taking this stage into account. This is a completely new, special reality for this relationship. When we talk about this connection, this link, this alliance, or coalition, or when we say that a special connection is created through a new dynamic, or that countless possibilities open up, then the importance of this scenario, of this reality, becomes a precondition for a new understanding of *Capital*.

Let us assume that this condition were not met; how would we then interpret *Capital*? How would we view this film? We implicitly assume that a change takes place. When I watch the movie—regardless of whether we are talking about Marx, *Ulysses*, or anything else—I do not imagine a distant Europe, but rather what is happening around me. In other words, in this moment, a new political possibility arises. This is why, in my opinion, the concept of the multitude as developed by the Italian political theorist Antonio Negri, which describes the hybridizations of movements and the hybrid character of various aspects of modern politics, does not build on the old concept of class, but instead includes the idea of the hybridity of the stage or scenario. This is an issue when it comes to the development of new political possibilities.

WG: *You both talked about working together, about cooperation. Are there obstacles to this cooperation? There are of course moments, constellations, in which people want to avoid cooperation on a common project or toward a common goal. How do you see these barriers or unease, the lack of willingness to cooperate?*

AK: I would like to start with the obstacles. I would first say that there is a political economy of capital—this capital cannot say "I"; it is not a subject. It lacks an element necessary for subjectivity that people have. In this respect, the logic of capital and the political economy of labor power stand in opposition to one another. These are human essential powers. Simply put: the collected lived time of all people stands in opposition to capital. Let us take the Internet as a huge mass of information that no one, even if they lived for 300 years, could assimilate in its entirety. Here you see how disproportional the relationship between the economy and vitality is. I see this as a positive example and as a counterpoint to "capital gone crazy." But even the Internet has too much of everything. Like the desert has too much sand and the jungle too much vegetation. We need something like a field or garden. The field for its use value and the garden because we are human. How do we collaboratively create this from the POLITICAL ECONOMY OF PEOPLE? It really moved me that Professor Wang Hui brought up how we are sitting here today and that people made an effort to watch a nine-hour film. An audience, a professor, and a PhD who has dedicated her life to scholarship. I am also dedicating myself to a cause and my interpreter here does so, too. We dedicate a portion of our lives to knowledge. This is labor power, and it lasts as long as we live.

WG: *And our audience's attention is also labored time, correct?*

AK: That is labored time. It is labored time that cannot be bought. In ancient Athens, people received money and meals in exchange for political activity. We receive no money for knowledge, satisfied curiosity, or effort and interest, and yet these are elements out of which the world can be reconstructed at any point of time day or night. When a crisis develops, we experience the ways people

Chapter 28   501

cultivate these powers. Germany, for example, was very hungry following its defeat in 1945. There was no state or banks. An economy did not exist in the technical sense, there was only occupying power. And what did the women back then do to feed their families and children! How people spontaneously exercise solidarity, this was really a far more interesting form of humanity in my country than what exists here today. So we have to put up signs pointing toward this second economy, the economy of lived time.

I was also moved by the fact that the vice president of your country, the future presumed leader, honored only Ireland, out of all the European countries, with a visit. Crippled by the debt crisis, Ireland is one of the poorest countries in Europe. The Irish are moving overseas again, as they did in the nineteenth century. It is simultaneously the most spiritual country we have in Europe. It is not only the country of Joyce, Eisenstein's screenwriter, but also the country whose monks brought antiquity from the periphery back into Europe's barbaric Middle Ages. In the cloisters of Ireland, the best stories of the Occident were preserved at the periphery. It is a happy accident or good instinct on the part of your future party chairman that he visited this country. Something like this is definitely worthy of political attention.

WH: I would like to respond to that quickly. When you mentioned just now that Xi Jinping visited Ireland, something suddenly occurred to me: when I was in Africa, I became aware for the first time that, except in special cases, the Chinese leaders paid for their first state visit each year to Africa. This is the legacy of twentieth-century politics that lives on today in China. This does not require an in-depth archaeological investigation, but I did want to say that this has a certain significance.

Secondly, we were talking about obstacles. I get the feeling that these obstacles are quite large. One obstacle, in my opinion, has to do with public space, the public sphere, and the media. We, of course, know that the last philosopher of the Frankfurt School, Jürgen Habermas, wrote a standard work on the public sphere, but there is a very close connection between public space and the media. Today, media are more commercial than before; they follow the logic of capital; and are infiltrated by special interest groups. The expansion of the media does not necessarily signal an expansion of the public sphere or the expansion of exchange. For this reason, it requires, in a certain sense, a counter-media.

I personally believe that, in this sense, a film like this and our forum can be seen as a counter-medium, in which a public sphere can be created. The public sphere is not something that arises naturally; it is connected to mediality. Today, media are controlled by capital and they control the entire political field. This leads to the continual disappearance of the political subject under the control of this logic. We therefore desperately need the logic of counter-media that seeks out possibilities. This point is, in my opinion, obvious to the entire world, and we have the responsibility to reveal the question regarding the political and the public anew. This is our world today.

You brought up the question of depoliticization earlier. The topic of depoliticization has to be seen in historical context, of course. To see it within the historical whole principally means that it is seen within the context of historical change. The original impetus for politics has changed; a few representative bodies, ostensibly expressing the political, have changed. Although they still exist, a constant change is occurring. For example, during the twentieth century, the political parties and the avant-garde constituted the most important mechanisms driving politics. But because of these changes, even their roles have changed. New mechanisms must be found.

On the other hand, media and the public sphere played a very important role at the time of the French Revolution in the eighteenth century. These spaces are also subject to big changes today. What we need to investigate is the question regarding which new spaces and possibilities are actually opening up today. But these new spaces and possibilities are not just lying around; we have to create them. In my opinion, it is exactly these COUNTER-MEDIA that allow us to hold a discussion face-to-face and to simultaneously make visible our similarities, differences, and debates. Technically speaking, this space is a counter-medial space. Even if it draws on advanced media technologies, what it produces is a theoretical space that has nothing in common with the logic of media today. The fact that I am watching this film and know that it was also broadcast by a German television station is quite significant in my opinion.

On the one hand, the film has penetrated into the media and uses its technologies, but on the other hand, it uncompromisingly resists the cultural logic that dominates today's media. This internal resistance produces a space for possibilities; it is not only a film, but also something that poses many new political questions.

At this point, I would like to ask Mr. Kluge a question that has to do with the explanation provided in your film of Marx's concept of commodities. On your second DVD, it says that commodities are "enchanted people." You describe a process in the course of which commodities estrange people, people become commodities, and commodities become people. But in Chinese thought there is a further differentiation when it comes to things: on the one hand, things are dominated by a certain human logic, but on the other, this human logic is not the logic of your average person today. The logic of things is a commodity logic, a logic of exchange. It is a logic of use and exchange value.

Because exchange value outranks use value today, things themselves have undergone a massive change. Every thing is "enchanted" in a double sense. Notwithstanding the world of things, almost everything that we encounter in the world today is bound up in a relationship of this kind. If we want to understand the dynamic among people, then we have to set free the dynamic of things, meaning their estrangement, because the thing itself is fascinated by commodity logic. It is an obsession that has been loaned to it by people. But is this kind of dynamic inherent to the world of things? We are discussing the dynamic and the initiative of people, but we rarely speak about whether or not things themselves have a dynamic. If we do not dynamize the world of things to a certain extent, then we also will not understand whether or not the possibility of such a dynamic even still exists within the world of people. Because man is completely objectified and the politics of things consists of deobjectification and things themselves are also being deobjectified, the question arises as to whether this logic is even still valid.

AK: I am totally astounded by how much—we do not really know each other that well—I agree with what you said, because I also think that the most important thing here in this film is that all things are enchanted people. This is really true. It is a saying from Marx. He observes that the lived time of actual people, who exert themselves and work, goes into these objects, these commodities. Like my wristwatch and like the glass that you are drinking out of now. It is a metaphor when Marx says that if you cut into a machine with a pocket knife, blood will come out. But in reality, these things are actually reflections, mirror images of us people. If people do not organize or act autonomously, then things will become crooked, askew, and disturbing. They can be our tyrants. It is not only things that are thing-like, but also laws and institutions. All dead labor is in this sense man-made and boomerangs back at people when they fail to approach things with enough care. So the recognition of nature by humans and the recognition of humans by nature have to be extended to things and the produced society. What you said about the counter-public sphere, Professor Wang Hui, this is so right! This counter-public sphere rests in our hands. Sometimes it is like this: you can work wonders right in the middle of the media public sphere. For example, there is a terrible televised talent show in England. It is commercialist to the core and an unbearable scam on the audience. The jury is biased and has to settle on some pop singer. But then there was an accountant, an ordinary man. He had horrible teeth and sings the tenor aria from *Turanot*, which at first does not fit on the show. But the audience eats the Puccini piece up, virtually lives for the contestant, and forces the jury with its spontaneous applause to reward him. Unfortunately, this is only just a moment. It is a tiny moment of a counter-public sphere, because not long thereafter he gets his teeth fixed, started singing bad pop, and assimilated himself. But there was a moment when the media's thin web, its curtain, was ripped open. There are many of these instances, and it is in our hands, in the hands of people, to always create this counter-public sphere anew.

WG: *We were just talking about things as enchanted people, and Professor Wang Hui quoted Zhuang Zhou, who said, "equality of all things." There*

	is not only the order of things imposed by people, but there is also the way of things. These are probably different perspectives, meaning one is more Western, assuming a subjectivity, while the concept "equality of all things" has a traditional Chinese connotation. Which new dimension could this concept of the "equality of all things" illuminate?
WH:	As I mentioned at the beginning, this film also emphasizes that the human being is part of "natural history." This means that the human is returned to natural history and history is seen as this process. It also means that humans were separated from nature, which is why we developed a self-consciousness and live in the opposition of self and other. But we also recognize by reflecting on things that we are part of the world of things. We ourselves are also a part of this nature. Yet this idea of equality is not the same as believing that there is no difference.

I get this impression that this idea of equality is rooted both in European and in Chinese thought. This question is now how differences and diversity, even across time, can be understood as a fundamental element of equality. This equality does not mean that differences are eliminated. On a level of knowledge it means: How can humans begin again to understand themselves as part of natural history? Here we have to be proactive. We all have to ask ourselves this question.

There is another question in the film: Can a thing ask whether or not it has an ego? Conversely, we can, of course, also ask: What relationship does a person have to things? To the world of nature? There are many variations: you can assume an ecological standpoint and view things from this perspective. But there is also an impulse that works against reification, a mechanism of self-protection against the estrangement that leads us to lose our personal uniqueness. I think this can even be found within classical thought. We only have to use our archaeological tools to bring it to light. This would, first and foremost, signify a revolution in recognition, a change at the epistemological level. In so doing, we could reconceive ourselves and nature.

I would like to say a few things about politics. In general, when we talk about politics, the common opinion prevails that politics is a process in which different special interest groups play their games having to do with certain power relations. But politics has yet another side: we are always located within a specific environment; we express ourselves within a particular context; but we have to realize that our politics moves within history and that political events sometimes, as you just said, appear out of place. There are special historical relationships at play. We are talking, for example, about the fact that a huge revolution took place in China. This revolution is called the "Revolution of the Proletariat," even though the working class hardly existed back then, and the revolution was primarily carried out by farmers. Included in this proletarian class were many intellectuals, most of whom came from petit bourgeois backgrounds, some from landowning families. They were the true revolutionaries.

This variation, this being-out-of-place, is not determined directly by the historical circumstances. In this sense, it is a performance, but not a negative one. It shows the relationship between people, politics, and subjectivity. This means that a certain transcendence is always immanent to the political. If it were not for this transcendence, meaning if certain preexisting circumstances were not transcended, then the construct of politics would always be heteronomous; it would always function within the pure

WG:	logic of things. I regard this to be an important point: at different times—not just at different historical points in time, but also at particular points in our daily lives (Mr. Kluge perhaps had this experience in 1968)—we have experienced how a certain moment can possess political relevance.
WG:	*Mr. Kluge, on the cover of your new book,* Das fünfte Buch: Neue Lebensläufe [The Fifth Book: New Case Studies], *I see a photo by the famous Chinese photographer Liu Zheng.*[9] *We see a male model in a cellar and next to him are classical sculptures.*
AK:	Of all the many things I saw in the last year, this image had the greatest impression on me. In this photo a model stands on a newspaper (so that his feet do not freeze) and is photographed by a Chinese master of photography. Next to him are the Venus de Milo and a statue of Voltaire. Everything is in one place that would otherwise never have come together. Something I found really unsettling was the Fukushima catastrophe. In the year 869 C.E., the exact same type of tremor emerged out of the Marianas Trench and the exact same type of tsunami took place. Geologists predicted it, and it happened! This is not being dealt with. Geologists in Europe say that Istanbul faces a risk similar to Japan. Over the last thousand years, a similar pattern of earthquakes along the Anatolian Plate has struck the huge metropolis. Scientists say there is a 60 percent chance of an earthquake and tidal wave hitting the city. The nearest atomic power plant is only 200 kilometers away, just beyond the Bulgarian border—an old heap of junk much more ill-equipped than Chernobyl. It is already there, ready for a repeat of Fukushima. I will not even mention the American West Coast. This is how we deal with periods of time on our planet. We deal with them quite naively.

Something else really spoke to me. You mentioned the revolution earlier. To be more cautious, let us speak of social change. It demands a tremendous amount of time. It is actually a production process. From Galileo to today, bourgeois society needed 400 years to develop. In order to develop solidarity—only this concept can fill in the word "socialism"—we surely need at least 600 years. This is the more complex system. No one can say that it cannot exist. We can always find it on life's underbelly, and it emerges in times of need. This time requirement is crucial. We have to understand this as an overarching production process, rather than as a distribution or consumption process. Revolution is not a luxury liner. It is production. We are reflected in our products. Your work and my work are two lovely mirrors. This is also the case when a German worker and Chinese worker tighten a screw. They need no language for this, only their fingertips. They could express themselves and do so precisely, more precisely than any computer. These are all the things we must collect. The sum of all of them requires time; it, too, is a production process with which we produce self-consciousness. At first, we produce a counter-public sphere, and in the end people. This has already been happening incidentally in millions of families for quite some time. Of this process, we have a vessel, the house, the site of industry; these are life spans. This is the title and the subject of my new book. I rewrote my 1962 book *Case Histories* [*Lebensläufe*] this year because our central European life spans ripped apart in the year 1945 today no longer have the same significance for the world as I thought back then. Secondly, very different things also have their own life spans today, for example, industrial landscapes in northeastern China or in the German Ruhr region or in the English Midlands, which was once the center of the world's industry. These landscapes are being restructured, much like Detroit is. If you consider the ruins of Detroit's industrial steppe, you also have to recognize that Jeff Mills, a hero of techno—a music relevant in Shanghai, Moscow, Berlin, France, and beyond—comes from Detroit. What I am talking about are the "life spans of the industrial landscapes." Nothing about them remains unchanged, but neither is anything in decline in the sense of Oswald Spengler. There is a phoenix-like quality to life, real labor power, and resistance. This reminds me of the Gracchi who fought in Rome for this phoenix-like quality of history. The political remains in this respect a key means of expression.

WG: *I think we have had a really sharp conversation that has raised many questions and produced many insights. This corresponds to the gradual production of thoughts while speaking.*[10] *This is the wonderful part of any conversation. As Mr. Kluge just suggested, we look forward to further, ongoing discourse and conversations with each other and hope that today is only the beginning. Thanks to everyone.*

Translated by Emma Woelk

Notes

This interview was originally published in German as Rainer Stollmann and Alexander Kluge, "Ein Fall von Internet-Telefonie über den Himalaya hinweg: Alexander Kluge im Gespräch mit dem Soziologen Wang Hui, der Literatin Wang Ge und dem Publikum in Peking," *Ferngespräche: Über Eisenstein, Marx, das Kapital, die Liebe und die Macht der zärtlichen Kraft* (Berlin: Vorwerk 8, 2016), 35–52.

This two and a half hour Skype conversation was held on the morning of March 3, 2012, at the Central Academy of Fine Arts Art Museum in Beijing, China.

The three images included in the original German publication are not included in the present translation.

1. [Translator's note: The screening in question was a Chinese-language version of Kluge's 2008 film *News from Ideological Antiquity: Marx-Eisenstein-Capital* co-organized in March 2012 by the Goethe Institute and the Iberia Center for Contemporary Art in Beijing. Six hundred audience members attended the teleconference with Kluge that immediately followed. In attendance are Kluge (via Skype), the author and moderator Wang Ge, and Professor Wang Hui, professor of Chinese literature at Tsinghua University and author of *China's New Order: Society, Politics, and Economy in Transition* (2003), among other titles.]

2. [Translator's note: Kluge is referencing the cruise ship *Costa Concordia*, which wrecked off the Tuscan coast of Italy in January 2012.]

3. [Translator's citation: Cf. Alexander Kluge, "'Take the violinist on the sinking liner / The tone is painfully rich and mellow,'" in *Temple of the Scapegoat: Opera Stories*, trans. Isabel Fargo Cole (New York: New Directions, 2018), 141–42. This story originally appeared in *Kongs große Stunde: Chronik des Zusammenhangs* (2015).]

4. [Translator's citation: Cf. Alexander Kluge, "Adult Education for the Finance Industry," in Alexander Kluge and Oskar Negt, *History and Obstinacy*, ed. Devin Fore, trans. Richard Langston et al. (New York: Zone Books, 2014), 421–22. This story originally appeared in *Das fünfte Buch: Neue Lebensläufe* (2012).]

5. [Translator's note: Pushpa Kamal Dahal was the prime minister of Nepal from 2008 to 2009 and from 2016 to 2017, and the chairman of the Communist Party of Nepal.]

6. [Translator's citation: This sequence can be see in Kluge's follow-up film to *News from Ideological Antiquity*, *Früchte des Vertrauens [Grapes of Trust]* (2009).]

7. [Translator's note: For the correct provenance of this quotation, see note 3 in chapter 3 in this volume.]

8. [Translator's citation: Alexander Kluge, "An Unintentional Stroke of Good Fortune: A Story of Displacement," in Kluge and Negt, *History and Obstinacy* 203–4. This story originally appeared in *Die Lücke, die der Teufel läßt* (2003) and in translation in *The Devil's Blind Spot: Tales from the New Century* (2004).]

9. [Translator's note and citation: Ge Wang is referring to a photograph included on the slipcase for the hardcover edition of *Das fünfte Buch*. The photo, a self-portrait of the artist Liu Zheng, is also reproduced in: Alexander Kluge, *Das fünfte Buch: Neue Lebensläufe* (Berlin: Suhrkamp, 2012), 331.]

10. [Translator's note: For the provenance of this quotation, which is central for Kluge's thinking, see note 3 in chapter 1 in this volume.]

INDEX

Page numbers in *italics* indicate illustrations. Works of literature will be found under the author's name (under the title, if anonymous). Operas and films are indexed by title. Kluge's essays, films, and literature are indexed under his name, and the essays and films also separately by title.

Abich, Hans, 220
activism, 189–90
actors and acting, 143–50
"The Actuality of Adorno" (Kluge, 2009), 450–60
Adenauer, Konrad, 346
Adorno, Theodor W.: "The Actuality of Adorno" (Kluge, 2009), 450–60; aesthetic theory of, 353–63, 370, 373–75; Benjamin's *Arcades Project* and, 470; Bloch and, 45; on the fragmentary, 485; importance for Kluge, 4, 13, 16, 45, 46, 58, 59, 92, 101, 151, 359–63, 495–96; Kluge compared, 5, 8–9; Kluge on feeling(s) and, 416; Kluge on film and, 124, 148, 151, 211, 220, 221–22, 361–64, 377n3, 457–58; Kluge on literature and, 73, 74, 78, 79, 93, 102; Kluge on opera and, 306, 308, 313–15, 457; Kluge on theory and, 16, 353–60, 362–63, 370, 373–75; Kluge's first meeting with, 359–60, 450, 453; Marx and, 465; on music, 354, 355, 357, 361, 362, 370, 377n5, 458; translation of Kluge and, 18
Adorno, Theodor W., works: *Authority and the Family* (with Horkheimer), 402; *Dialectic of*

Adorno, Theodor W., works *(continued)* *Enlightenment* (with Horkheimer), 47–48, 50, 60, 140n4, 354, 361, 376, 455–56; "The Essay as Form," 7–8, 15; *Minima Moralia*, 359; "Transparencies on Film," 225n3, 362–64, 377n3
Adorno Prize, 450, 460
Aeschylus, *Oresteia*, 438
aesthetic theory, 353–76; of Adorno, 353–63, 370, 373–75; authenticity and experience in, 368–73; of Benjamin, 354–57, 359, 369, 372; of film, 362–76; mass culture and, 367–68; public sphere and, 373–76; Romanticism and, 357, 358
Agamben, Giorgio, 470
Aida (Verdi opera), 229–36, *233*, 242–44, 247
Alceste (opera), 232
Alcuin (Anglo-Saxon scholar), 455
Alemann, Claudia von, *192*
Alexander the Great, 416
Alexandria, library of, 298, 410, 457
alienation, 381–82
aliens from Sirius, Kluge's visitor from, 312–13, 415–16
allegory, 73, 332, 356
angels, 108, 229–37, *233*, 239, 241, 246, 356, 372, 404
Angermeyer, Heinz, 220
"An Answer to Two Opera Quotations" (Kluge, 1983/84), 229–47
Antigone (opera), 232
Antonioni, Michelangelo, 135, 322
Arachne, 111–12, 452–53
Arbeitsgemeinschaft Neuer Deutscher Spielfilmproduzenten (Association of New German Feature Film Producers), 222–23
Arcades Project (Walter Benjamin): aesthetic theory and, 354–55; anthropological materialism of, 463–65, 478–79, 482n3; Baudelaire section, 463, 470–71; *Berlin Childhood* and, 466; dialectical image and, 476–77; on distraction, 479; European consciousness of, 473, 480–81; fate of, in WWII, 470; intended structure of, 462–63; "Inventory of a Century: On Walter Benjamin's *Arcades Project*" (Kluge, 2013), 462–81; Kluge on film and, 204–5nn6–9, 204n2, 204n4, 205n14, 205nn16–17, 206n20, 206n28, 467–69, 475–76; "now of knowability" in, 476, 482–83n9; phantasmagoria, concept of, 465–66, 471; photography, importance of, 467; "primitive diversity" and, 74; for twenty-first century, 471–75, 477–78, 480
Aristotle and Aristotelianism, 101, 364, 416, 447
The Arrival of a Train at La Ciotat (film), 274, 325
artiste démolisseur (demolition artist), filmmaker as, 179, 180, 298, 366
Artists under the Big Top: Perplexed (Kluge film, 1968), 15, 224, 361
"The Art of Drawing Distinctions" (Kluge, 2003), 21n24, 407–32
The Assault of the Present on the Rest of Time/The Blind Director (Kluge film, 1985), 5–6, 15
Asterix, 418, 422, 424
Augsburg Concordat, 102
Augustus (Roman emperor), 275, 276, 391n6
Auschwitz, 44, 73, 153n3, 454, 476
Autobahn, 189, 205–6n18
Autopsy (TV show), 317n1
Averty, Jean-Christophe, 186
L'Avventura (film), 135

Baecker, Dirk, 332
Balzac, Honoré de, 333–34, 471
Barbey d'Aurevilly, Jules Amédée, *The She-Devils*, 126, 128
Batailles, Georges, 470
Battleship Potemkin (film), 468
Baucis and Philemon, 56
Baudelaire, Charles, 463, 470–71, 474

Bauer, Fritz, 143, 147, 153n3
Bauhaus, 95, 298
Bazin, André, 364
Becker, Hellmut, 13
Beckett, Samuel, 132
Beethoven, Ludwig von, 113, 446
belles lettres tradition, 93
Benjamin, Walter: aesthetic theory of, 354–57, 359, 369, 372; on the fragmentary, 485; *Gesamtkunstwerk* (total work of art) and, 140n6; history, theory of, 59, 60, 354; importance for Kluge, 5, 92, 495; on Klee's angel of history, 108, 372; Kluge on film and, 74, 124, 211, 216, 254, 322, 458; Kluge on literature and, 59–60, 74, 92, 94, 108, 109n1; on transitoriness and repeatability, 255; translation of Kluge and, 18
Benjamin, Walter, works: *Berlin Childhood*, 466; *One Way Street*, 464; *The Origin of German Tragic Drama*, 469; "The Storyteller," 109n1; "Unpacking My Library," 14; "The Work of Art in the Age of Its Technological Reproducibility," 474, 488. See also *Arcades Project*
Berg, Alban, 60, 79, 308, 416
Berlin: Symphony of a Great City (film), 212
Berlin Olympic Games (1936), television transmission of, 188
Berlin Wall, 65
Binding, Rudolk, *Opfergang*, 97
Bismarck, Otto von, 35, 81, 244, 295, 301
bits and binary notation, 254
"Bits of Conversation" (Kluge, 1966), 21n36, 142–53
"The Black Forest Clinic" (German TV show), 39, 42n22
Bleuler, Eugen, 435
blindness, 62, 95, 129, 135, 208, 215, 216, 426, 426–27, 436, 457, 478
blind spots, 51, 61, 71–73

Bloch, Ernst, *The Heritage of Our Times*, 45, 472
Bohm, Hark, 219
Bohr, Niels, 478
Bohrer, Karl Heinz, 5
Böll, Heinrich, 5, 220
books, 84–87, 98
boredom, 76–79, 167–69, 303
bourgeois society, 74, 126, 170, 231, 242–47, 276, 294, 300, 307, 310, 312, 344, 345, 374, 376, 380, 412, 471, 472, 474, 485, 507, 509
Brandt, Willy, 64, 223, 346
Brecht, Bertolt, 41n2, 69n12, 73, 91, 92, 95, 131, 140n3, 206n26, 211, 391n8, 495; *Baal*, 65; *Mahogany*, 65; *Stories of Mr. Keuner*, 147; *The Threepenny Opera*, 77, 83n8, 157
Bresson, Robert, 280
Brest-Litovsk, Treaty of (1917), 401
Brook, Peter, 134
Die Brücke (film, 1959), 152, 154n6
Brutality in Stone (Kluge film, 1960), 3, 20n4, 151
Büchner, Georg, 463; *Danton's Death*, 443; *Lenz*, 80
Bulgakova, Oksana, 209
Bülow, Fürst von, 210
bumblebee bat, 198, *199*
Buttgereit, Jörg, 219

Caesarius of Heisterbach, 81, 335
Camus, Albert, 132
Cannae, Battle of, 397, 399, 430
Capital (proposed Eisenstein film): *News from Ideological Antiquity: Marx-Eisenstein-"Capital"* (Kluge film, 2008), 5, 14, 16, 111–18, 216, 484–510, 511n1; "A Plan with the Force of a Battleship" (Kluge, 2008), on filming of, 208–16
capitalism, 65–67, 89, 111–12, 490, 492, 500
Capriccio (Richard Strauss opera), 312
Carmen (film), 35–36
Carmen (opera), 36, 40, 447
Casablanca (film), 276

catastrophe, 73, 181–83, 292, 295, 306, 321, 448, 451–52
Categorical Imperative, 405n6, 453–54
Celts/Gauls, 44, 178, 179, 413, 418, 424, 432
censorship in film, 316, 320–21
centuries, seams between, 26–28, 29–31, 35, 39, 41
Chaplin, Charlie, 124, 127, 184, 340
Charlemagne, 430, 455
Charles the Bold (king of France), 427
Chernobyl, 73, 77, 451–52, 508
The Children of Paradise (film), 276
China: competing computer systems in, 195; Cultural Revolution in, 312, 489; global capitalism and globalization affecting, 498–99; industrialization in, 113, 114; Ireland and Africa, state visits to, 501; Republican Revolution in (1912), 488, 491, 507; special economic zone, 489–91
chronicles and chroniclers, 43–44, 67–68, 486–88
chronos versus *kairos*, 10, 271, 486, 489
cinema: actors and acting, 143–50; Adorno, Kluge on cinema and, 124, 148, 151, 211, 220, 221–22, 361–64, 377n3, 457–58; advanced media technologies, use of, 503; aesthetic theory of, 362–76; American industry, 170, 185–86, 188; *Arcades Project* (Walter Benjamin) and, 204–5nn6–9, 204n2, 204n4, 205n14, 205nn16–17, 206n20, 206n28, 467–69, 475–76; *artiste démolisseur* (demolition artist), filmmaker as, 179, 180, 298, 366; boredom and, 167–69; censorship in, 316, 320–21; in classical public sphere, 254–55; close-ups in, 176; decline/obsolescence, discussions of, 169–70, 187–90, 224; destruction and creation in, 180–82; dialogue in, 131–33; documentary, 6, 133, 136, 140n7, 152, 156–58, 322, 368, 369–70, 487; dreaming in movie theaters, 413; elementalization in, 176; as episode between architecture and television, 172–73; as fantasy commodities, 275–78; "foot" of, 416; forms and, 173–78, *174*; French New Wave, 315; the gambler, the *flâneur*, and the one who waits, 166–67; German film industry, 185, 188; happy endings in, 102, 182–83; history of, 485; Indian film industry, 175; Kluge as cinema *auteur* (*see* Kluge, Alexander, films); Kluge essays on, 14, 123–224; Kluge on future of, 98; Kluge's notes for development of, 414–15; language and, 123–39, 163n1; literature compared, 125–31; minute films, 319, 321–25, 330n3, 334; montage in, 124, 161, 170, 209, 364–65, 367; as movement, 251; movie theaters, *193*, 274–75, 313–15; musealization of film, 299; music in, 149–50, 153–54n4, 362, 485; New German Cinema, 3, 14, 218–24, 315, 361, 362; new media/new technologies and, 187–90, 194–204, 275; opera compared, 172, 313–16; "primitive diversity" in early short films from American East Coast, 318–29; public sphere and, 186–87; reality/realism and, 132, 152–53, 155–63, 172, 183–86, 189, 486; relationality in, 156, 486; short focal lengths in, 176; suspense in, 168–69, 172, 205nn12–13, 316; symbolism in, *177*, 178–82; television and, 172–73, 188–89, 202; theory of, 484–87; time and, 166–67, 202, 257, 272, 273–75; transition from silence to sound in, 124–25, 170, *171*, 215; voice-over commentary in, 133–34. *See also specific titles and filmmakers*
the circus, 13, 14–15, 92, 142–53, 291n9, 359, 361

Citizen Kane (film), 137–38
city planning, segregation in, 281–82
class warfare and class consciousness, 475, 493–95, 497
Clausewitz, Carl von, *On War*, 34, 36, 394, 395, 397, 401, 430
close-ups, 176
Clouzot, Henri-Georges, 36
Club 2 (TV show), 256, 291n7
Cold War, end of, 65, 102, 492
collaboration/cooperation, 67–68, 102, 106, 492–93, 496, 497, 499–502
commodities and commodification, 275–78, 503–5
communism, 35, 65, 106, 349, 356, 491, 511n5
computers: China, competing computer systems in, 195; ENIAC Computer, 259, 260; microcomputers, 260; programs, viruses and computers organized as, 257, 259–61, 263
Conan the Barbarian (film), 177, 178–79
Confucius, 117, 486, 498
The Conquest of Mexico (Rihm opera), 310–11
constructivism, 95
The Coronation of Poppea (Monteverdi opera), 311
Corrigan, Timothy, 20n4
Cortés, Hernán, 311, 415
Costa Concordia (ship), 489, 511
Costard, Hellmuth, 219
Critical Theory, 18, 58–59, 100–103, 367, 374
critique: as activity, 438–44; for Adorno, 453; differentiation, as capacity for, 434–35, 440–41, 444, 446, 447; feeling(s) and, 446–48; intentional and unintentional, critical activity at junction of, 442–46; judgmental, 438; origins of, 332
"Critique, Up Close and Personal" (Kluge, 2007), 21n20, 21n24, 21n27, 434–48

cultural majority, 186
Cultural Revolution, 312, 489

Dadaism and Dadaists, 72, 82n3, 268, 494
Dafne (Schütz opera), 312
Daguerre, Louis, 463
Day of German Art (1936), 306
DCTP (Development Company for Television Program), 4, 330n5
Debord, Guy, 82n3
deconstruction, 130, 167, 298, 316
DeLillo, Don, *Underworld*, 65
Della Volpe, Galvano, 161
democratic process, 381
demolition artist *(artiste démolisseur)*, filmmaker as, 179, 180, 298, 366
Derrida, Jacques, 97, 450
Descartes, René, 160
Development Company for Television Program (DCTP), 4, 330n5
dialectics, 8–9, 48, 129, 391n7, 459. *See also* multidimensionality
dialogue in cinema, 131–33
dialogues. *See* Kluge, Alexander, essays and dialogues
diaphragm, as zone of resistance, 412–13
diarrhea, 75, 437, 442–43, 495
"The Difference: Heinrich von Kleist" (Kluge, 1985), 20n17, 25–41
difference/differentiation: Adorno versus Kluge on, 8–9; "The Art of Drawing Distinctions" (Kluge, 2003), 21n24, 407–32; authenticity in aesthetic theory and, 369; centuries, seams between, 26–28, 29–31, 35, 39, 41; child's acquisition of, 250; critique as capacity for, 434–35, 440–41, 444, 446, 447; essays, differentiatedness as medium of, 8–10; experience, testing, 411–12; eye's capacity for, 413; feeling(s) and, 91, 412–31; human capacity for, 90, 271–72, 407–9; human communication and, 257; invisible forces, power of, 407, 409–11;

difference/differentiation *(continued)*
  Kant on, 332; "the new obscurity" and, 264; populism and, 379, 384; storytelling and, 43–68, 90, 91, 94; time and, 271–73; war, modern human separation from, 37–38; yearning for what is lost, 407
Döblin, Alfred, *Berlin Alexanderplatz*, 160, 334, 383
Doetichem, Dagmar von, 163
Domke, Martin, 470
Don Carlos (opera), 232
Dorfmeister, Gregor, 154n6
Dos Passos, John, 334
Dovzhenko, Alexander, 280
dragonflies of Graubünden, 430–31
dramaturgy, 14, 33, 132, 153, 161, 163, 176, 185, 211, 234, 243, 280, 321, 333–34
dreaming/day-dreaming, 161, 183–85, 231, 232, 342, 347, 357, 394, 413, 458, 465–66
Dreyer, Theodor, 274
Dr. Mabuse, der Spieler (film), 213, 217n5
Duras, Marguerite, 134, 136

ears and hearing, 9, 85, 150, 171, 243, 245, 264, 408, 417, 424, 447, 457, 496
Easy (film), *192*
Ebbinghaus, Uwe, 331–36
Eblé, Jean Baptiste, 32
Eden family, 181–82
Eder, Klaus, 223
Edison, Thomas, 318, 321
"The Eiffel Tower, King Kong, and the White Woman" (Kluge, TV program, 1988), 321, 325–29, 330n2
Einstein, Albert, 394
Eisenstein, Sergei: *Capital*, efforts to film, 208–16; montage, theory of, 364, 367; *News from Ideological Antiquity: Marx-Eisenstein-"Capital"* (Kluge film, 2008), 5, 14, 16, 111–18, 216, 484–510, 511n1

Eisler, Hanns, 362
Eisner, Lotte, 220
elementalization in film, 176
Elisofon, Eliot, 173
Elizabeth I (queen of England), 443
Emergency Acts (Germany, 1968), 362, 376–77n2
emotion. *See* feeling(s)
Encyclopédie (of Diderot and d'Alembert), 395, 403, 405n1
Ende, Michael, *The Never Ending Story*, 238
ENIAC computer, *259*, 260
Enlightenment, 30, 295, 335, 383, 405, 412, 427–29, 456, 498
enlightenment, concept of, 61, 71, 77, 90–91, 132, 376, 396, 401–3, 412, 416, 452, 456
Enzensberger, Hans Magnus, 5
epiphany, 215, 273, 363, 365, 476
equality of all things, 505–6
eruditio, concept of, 454–56
essays: on classical and new media, 14–15, 229–336; on film, 14, 123–224; as genre, 7–11; images, use of, 19; Kluge as essayist, 4–7; on literature, 13–14, 25–118; reading and translating, 16–19; selection and classification of, 11–16; on theory, 15–16, 339–510. *See also* Kluge, Alexander, essays and dialogues, *for a complete alphabetical list*
Esterson, Aaron, 181, 206n22
Ethiopia and Eritrea, civil war between, 394
Etruscan shrew, *198*
experience: aesthetic theory, authenticity and experience in, 368–73; Benjamin on poverty of, 474–75; direct versus indirect (through media), 265–69, 284; *Erfahrung*, 12, 18, 22n42, 251, 255, 267, 294; *Erlebnis*, 18, 22n42, 168, 251, 272; *Public Sphere and Experience* (Kluge and Negt, 1972), 16, 22n40, 85, 109n5, 291n18, 391n7, 450–51; remembering,

forgetting, and reconstruction, 269–71; testing, 411–12; value of, 421; of war, 398–99. See also sensory experience

eyes, 9, 36, 40, 103, 149, 158, 171, 216, 230, 243, 245, 273, 276, 314–15, 359–60, 366, 386, 408, 413, 424, 426–27, 447, 453, 464, 479. See also blindness

Falklands War, 42n19
false consciousness, 187, 418, 496
families, emotions within, 305–7
fantasy, 339–52; appropriation of, 349–52; context and development of, 346–49; critique as fantastic activity, 439–46; domination and, 342–46; fantasy commodities, 275–78; imaginative capacity and organization of, 341–43, 347; labor, concept of, 339–41; phantasmagoria, concept of, in Benjamin's *Arcades Project*, 465–66, 471
Färber, Helmut, 165n12
fascism, 45, 73, 115, 140n6, 189–90, 349–51, 367, 390n1, 402, 412, 421, 476
Fassbinder, Rainer Werner, 219, 220
fear, basic, 428–29
feeling(s): antirealism/antirealism of feeling, 9, 21n25, 72, 88, 89, 103–4, 388, 420–21, 451; of basic trust and basic fear, 46, 417–19, 428–29; critique and romantic relations, 446–48; defined, 408; difference/differentiation and, 91, 412–31; families, emotions within, 305–7; incorruptibility of, 412; Kleist and, 27, 29, 30, 35, 36, 38–39, 42n21; Kluge on literature and, 77–78, 89–90; in Kluge's *Chronik der Gefühle* (2000), 43–68, 432; Kluge's film *The Power of Emotion* (1983) on opera, 6, 15, 305–9; Kluge's *Die Lücke, die der Teufel läßt* and, 77–78, 432; Kluge's mother,

emotional influence of, 81; Kluge's theory of, 16, 412–31; laughter and diaphragm, as zone of resistance, 412–13; about the other and otherness, 422–24; poetry as concentrated emotion, 77; "primitive diversity" in early short films from American East Coast, 318–29; property, viewed as, 412; robots as form of emotional intelligence, 417; sensations versus, 408; Sirius, explained to Kluge's visitor from, 415–16; successful feelings, 425–28, 426; in television and radio, 185–86
Fellini, Federico, 220
Fidelio (Beethoven opera), 60–61, 113, 446
film. See cinema
"Film: A Utopia" (Kluge, 1983), 12, 14, 15, 21n35, 166–204
fin de siècle, as phenomenon, 26–28
Flaubert, Gustave, 67, 81; *Madame Bovary*, 309
Die Fledermaus (Johann Strauss operetta), 210
Florence, as metaphor, 282, 298
The Flying Dutchman (Wagner opera), 236–42, 244–46
Fontane, Theodor, *Effi Briest*, 309
Fore, Devin, 22n42
Forrest, Tara, ed., *Alexander Kluge: Raw Materials for the Imagination*, 13, 20n3, 21n38
Forster, Georg, 374
Foucault, Michel, 47
Fourier, Charles, 463
fragmentation, 7, 8, 17, 26, 59, 202, 211, 213, 215, 221, 245, 269, 270, 271, 340, 348, 355, 357, 370, 377n5, 383, 384, 451, 456, 458, 469, 485–86
Frankfurt Lectures on Poetics, 7, 9, 10, 14, 100, 109
Frankfurt School, 4, 18, 102, 140n6, 455, 460, 495–96, 502
Frederick the Great, 392, 393, 429
French New Wave, 315

French Revolution, 30–32, 59–60, 101, 295, 299–300, 312–13, 375, 380, 393, 423, 503
Freud, Sigmund, 9, 184, 206n21, 206n24, 341, 358, 383–84, 387, 394, 403, 436, 438, 454, 466, 479; *The Ego and the Id*, 280–81
Frisch, Max, 67, 220
Früchte des Vertrauens (Grapes of Trust, Kluge film, 2009), 493, 511n6
Fukushima catastrophe, Japan, 508 353–76
functional dimension, 187, 206n26, 391n8
"The Function of the Distorted Angle in the Destructive Intention" (Kluge, 1989), 21n24

Ganseforth, Kersting and Agnes, 219
Gauls. *See* Celts/Gauls
Gaus, Günter, 222
Genscher, Hans-Dietrich, 63–64
geographers of Aristotle/Alexander the Great, 289, 416
Gesamtkunstwerk (total work of art), 129, 140n6, 165n12, 316, 468
Gielen, Michael, 450
The Glass House (film), 209
Gleim, Johann Wilhelm Ludwig, and Gleim House, Halberstadt, 28–29, 41
global financial crisis (2008), 105, 452, 473, 486, 492, 501
globalization, 480–81, 497–99
Gluck, Willibald, 312
Godard, Jean-Luc, 132–33, 134, 148, 220, 274, 322, 450
gods/God, Kluge on, 56, 62, 71, 76, 264, 308, 310, 418, 423, 438, 453
Goethe, Johann Wolfgang von, 105; *Elective Affinities*, 80, 265–66; *Faust II*, 160, 464; *Poems of the West and East*, 207n35; *Wilhelm Meister*, 52, 159–60, 164n7, 383
Golden Fleece myth, 336
Gone with the Wind (film), 276
Gorbachev, Mikhail, 61–62, 64

Gordon, A., 173
GPS, 336
Gracchi, 380, 510
Grafe, Frieda, 14, 205n13
Grandville, J. J., 94
Greek world, 47, 104, 251, 271, 282, 289, 307
Greiner, Ulrich, 7, 10
Greno, Franz, 86
Griffith, D. W., 318, 320, 414
Grimm, Jacob and Wilhelm (Brothers Grimm), 107, 225n2, 287, 299, 452, 486
Grotius, Hugo, *On the Law of War and Peace*, 397
Grünbein, Durs, 67, 81, 405n5
Gulf War, 394
Gutenberg, Johannes, 332

Habermas, Jürgen, 102, 264, 290n1, 294n10, 450, 460, 502; *The Structural Transformation of the Public Sphere*, 374
Hagemann, Walter, 123, 140n1
Haiti, slave revolt/war of, 404
Halberstadt, air raid on (1945), 28–29, 54, 68n5, 86, 234–35, 419–21
Hall, Benn M., 172
Handke, Peter, 164n7, 366
Hannibal of Carthage, 423
Hansen, Miriam, 12, 22n42, 313, 377n3
happy endings, 12, 75, 76, 78, 102, 182–83, 414
Harlan, Veit, 97
Harris, Sir Arthur "Bomber," 50, 68n5
Hartlieb, Horst von, 220
Hartung, Klaus, 163
Haussmann, Georges-Eugéne, Baron, 180, 463
Hebel, Johann Peter, 463
Hegel, Georg Wilhelm Friedrich, 35, 118n1, 464
Heidegger, Martin, 359, 367; *Being and Time*, 326–28
Heißenbüttel, Helmut, 100, 109n2, 126

Helms, Hans G., 1345
Hemingway, Ernest, 146–47
Henry IV (king of France), 388, 411
Heraclitus, 328, 486
Herder, Johann Gottfried, 257
Herzog, Werner, 164n5, 219
heterotopia, 102, 335, 452
Himmler, Heinrich, 344
Hindenburg, Paul von, 346
Hiroshima, mon amour (film), 134, 136
history: books, centuries connected by, 86; centuries, seams between, 26–28, 29–31, 35, 39, 41; chronicles and chroniclers of, 43–44, 67–68, 486–88; feelings, historical events as expressions of, 43–68; of film, 485; future/past controlling present, 295–97; of individual life spans, 102–3, 108, 432–33; Klee's angel of, 108, 372; now-time, 78, 86, 379; pessimism, historical, 89–90; populism and, 379–82, 387; primitive accumulation in, 90, 111–15; storytelling and, 73, 94–95, 108–9; universal history, as messianic idea, 476–77; of war, 392–96; weather, as historical actor, 64–65
Hitchcock, Alfred, 205nn11–13, 278–79, 280, 316
Hitler, Adolf, 48, 62–63, 97, 205–6n18, 344
Hoffmann, Heinrich, 330n4
Hoffmann, Hilmar, 218
Holbrooke, Richard, 63
Hölderlin, Friedrich, 31
Holocaust, 44, 46, 69n11, 73, 153n3, 454, 473, 476
Holy Alliance, 30
homeopathy, 409–10
Homer, 104; *Iliad*, 52, 59, 271; *Odyssey*, 47–49, 60, 61, 234, 245–46, 429, 431
Homo compensator, 108, 496
hope, 10, 30, 45–46, 49–50, 53, 57, 66, 75, 76, 104, 108, 219, 239, 311, 313, 379, 382, 403, 415, 421, 443–44, 453, 458, 460, 468, 489, 493, 496, 510
Hope, Bob, 329
Hopf, Florian, 206n28, 223
Horkheimer, Max, 8, 92, 101, 125, 211, 306, 328, 412, 455, 470; *Authority and the Family* (with Adorno), 402; *Dialectic of Enlightenment* (with Adorno), 47–48, 50, 60, 140n4, 354, 361, 376, 455–56
Hörmann, Günther, 346–47
Hugenberg, Alfred, 188
Humboldt, Wilhelm von, 374
Hume, David, 456
humor: laughter and diaphragm as zone of resistance, 413; National Socialism treated with, 97–98

Il trovatore (opera), 236
images, Kluge's use of, 19, 85–86
imaginative capacity, 341–43, 347. *See also* fantasy
India: film industry in, 175; special economic zone, 490–91
"An Instance of Internet Telephony over the Himalayas" (Kluge, 2016), 484–510
Institute for Film Design (Ulm School of Design), 377n4
Institute for Social Research, 375, 455, 470
Internet, 58, 98, 112, 331–36, 472, 474, 477–78, 480, 492–93, 497, 500
Intolerance (film), 318, 320, 414–15
Intrigue and Love (Schiller opera), 309
"Inventory of a Century: On Walter Benjamin's *Arcades Project*" (Kluge, 2013), 462–81
Ionesco, Eugene, 132
Iphigenie (opera), 60
Ireland, Xi Jinping's visit to, 501
isomorphism, 285–86

Jaucourt, Louis de, "Guerre *(Droit naturel & Politique)*," 392, 393, 396
Les jeux sont faits (film), 131
John XXIII (pope), 317n1
Joyce, James, 96, 208–9, 485; *Ulysses*, 208–9, 234, 490, 499
Jugert, Rudolf, 132

Kafka, Franz, 274, 468, 478; "A Report to An Academy," 50
Kahl, Reinhard, 432
kairos, 19, 20n4, 62–63, 271, 302, 304, 486, 489
Kant, Immanuel, 10, 32, 75, 101, 117, 129, 285, 332, 334, 358, 398, 401, 453–54, 456, 461n5, 464; *Critique of Practical Reason*, 457; *Critique of Pure Reason*, 30, 215, 297–98, 440; *Critique of the Power of Judgment*, 440
Karmakar, Romuald, 219
Kaufman, Mikhail, 209
Käutner, Helmut, 220
Kennedy, John F., 324
Khittl, Ferdinand, 134, 136, 219
Kiev, Soviet firefighters in, 55
Kissinger, Henry, 393
Kittler, Friedrich, 450
Klee, Paul, 108
Kleist, Heinrich von, 25–41; analytic writing of, 40; death of, 25; eighteenth century, as part of, 29; feeling in work of, 52; France, reactions to events in, 32–34; at Gleim House, 29; Kluge, "The Difference: Heinrich von Kleist" (1985), 20n17, 25–41; on oral tradition, 255–56
Kleist, Heinrich von, works: *The Battle of Hermann*, 42n23; *Berliner Abendblätter* (newspaper), 33–34; "Betrothal in San Domingo," 42n10, 42n12, 42n15; *The Broken Jug*, 31–32; "The Duel," 31, 34, 36, 38–39; "Improbable Veracities," 326, 330n7, 406n10; "Michael Kohlhaas," 31, 396; "On the Gradual Production of Thoughts whilst Speaking," 27, 34, 255–56, 291n4; *Penthesilea*, 42n8; "The Puppet Theater," 34, 39; *Schoffrenstein (The Feud of the Schoffrensteins)*, 31, 33
Kleist Prize, 8, 13, 25–26, 41n2
Klejman, Naum, 209
Kluge, Alexander, 3–19; biographical information, 3–4, 27–28, 46, 76–77, 81, 86, 96, 142, 150–51; as essayist, 4–7; essays as genre and, 7–11; images, use of, 19, 85–86; media, position statement on (1979), 11–12; montage, as principle in work of, 6; reading and translating, 16–19; texts, selection and classification of, 11–16
Kluge, Alexander, and Oskar Negt: *Geschichte und Eigensinn* (1981), 207n33, 290n1; *History and Obstinacy* (2014), 16, 17, 18, 85, 118n1, 206n26, 391n8, 511n4, 511n8; *Maßverhältnisse des Politischen* (Measured Relations of the Political, 1992), 16, 119n4, 390n2; *Public Sphere and Experience* (1972), 16, 22n40, 85, 109n5, 291n18, 374, 391n7, 450–51
Kluge, Alexander, parents of: coming to grief for reasons of love, mother on, 240–42; divorce of, 76–77, 96, 102; emotional influence of mother, 81; as storytellers, 105–6, 421; wine, father's ability to differentiate, 271
Kluge, Alexander, essay anthologies: *Gelegenheitsarbeit einer Sklavin: Zur realistischen Methode* (Part-Time Work of a Female Slave: On the Realistic Method, 1975), 5, 9, 14; *Personen und Reden* (People and Speeches, 2012), 5; *Theodor Fontane, Heinrich von Kleist und Anna Wilde: Zur Grammatik der Zeit* (Theodor Fontane, Heinrich

von Kleist, and Anna Wilde: On the Grammar of Time, 1987), 5
Kluge, Alexander, essays and dialogues: "The Actuality of Adorno" (2009), 450–60; "An Answer to Two Opera Quotations" (1983/84), 229–47; "The Art of Drawing Distinctions" (2003), 21n24, 407–32; "The Assault of the Present on the Rest of Time" (1990), 20n5; "Bits of Conversation" (1966), 21n36, 142–53; "Companions in Now-Time" (2007), 21n37, 84–87; "Critique, Up Close and Personal" (2007), 21n20, 21n24, 21n27, 434–48; "The Difference: Heinrich von Kleist" (1985), 20n17, 25–41; "Film: A Utopia" (1983), 12, 14, 15, 21n35, 166–204; "The Function of the Distorted Angle in the Destructive Intention" (1989), 21n24, 353–76; "An Instance of Internet Telephony over the Himalayas" (2016), 484–510; "Inventory of a Century: On Walter Benjamin's *Arcades Project*" (2013), 462–81; "Medialization—Musealization" (1990), 293–304; "Die Medien stehen auf dem Kopf" (1979), 21n34; "No Farewell to Yesterday: New German Cinema from 1962 to 1981, as Seen from 2011" (2012), 218–24; "On Film and the Public Sphere," 20n7; "On the Expressions 'Media' and 'New Media'" (1984), 21n19, 21n31, 249–89; "The Opera Machine" (2001), 305–16; "The Peacemaker" (2003), 20n11, 21n29, 71–82; "A Plan with the Force of a Battleship" (2008), 208–16; "Planting Gardens in the Data Tsunami" (2010), 331–36; "The Political without Its Despair: On the Concept of 'Populism'" (1992), 378–89; "Primitive Diversity" (2002), 318–29; "The Realistic Method and the 'Filmic'" (1975), 6, 20n6, 155–63; "The Role of Fantasy" (1974), 339–52; "The Sharpest Ideology: That Reality Appeals to Its Realistic Character," 21n25; "Storytelling Is the Representation of Differences" (2001), 43–68; "Storytelling Means Dissolving Relations" (2008), 88–98; "Theory of Storytelling: Lecture One" (2013), 20n12, 21n25, 21n26, 21n28, 21n30, 100–109; "War" (2001), 392–405; "What Is a Metaphor?" (2016), 111–18; "Word and Film" (by Reitz, Kluge, and Reinke; 1965), 12, 14, 20n18, 123–39

Kluge, Alexander, films: *Artists under the Big Top: Perplexed* (1968), 15, 224, 361; *The Assault of the Present on the Rest of Time/The Blind Director* (1985), 5–6, 15; *Brutality in Stone* (1960), 3, 20n4, 151; *Früchte des Vertrauens* (Grapes of Trust, 2009), 493, 511n6; *Miscellaneous News* (1986), 3; *News from Ideological Antiquity: Marx-Eisenstein-"Capital"* (2008), 5, 14, 16, 111–18, 216, 484–510, 511n1; *Part-Time Work of a Female Slave* (1973), 5; *The Patriot* (1979), 6, 89; *The Power of Emotion* (1983), 6, 15, 305–9; *Yesterday Girl* (1966), 13, 14, 142–53, 291n9, 359, 361, 453

Kluge, Alexander, literature: *Air Raid* (2014), 68n1, 68n5; "Anita G." (1962), 13; *Attendance List for a Funeral* (first published as *Lebensläufe* [Case Histories], 1962/1988), 3, 13, 43, 46, 68n1, 85, 102, 110n8, 151, 509; *Chronik der Gefühle* (Chronicle of Feelings, 2000), 3, 13, 43–68, 68n1, 73, 328, 432; *Cinema Stories* (2007), 97; "Clumsiness with a Deadly Result" (2000), 40; "The Final Film Screening in the Reich Chancellery"

Kluge, Alexander, literature *(continued)* (2007), 97–98; *Das fünfte Buch* (2012), 109, 110n6, 110n9, 508, 511n4, 511n9; "Heidegger in Crimea" (2000), 56–57, 68n4; "Historische Sekunde" (2000), 62–63, 70n20; "How Can I Protect Myself? What Holds Voluntary Actions Together?" (picture story, 2000), 53–54; *Das Labyrinth der zärtlichen Kraft* (The Labyrinth of Tender Love, 2009), 456, 461n4; *Lernprozesse mit tödlichem Ausgang* (Learning Processes with a Deadly Outcome, 1973), 68n1, 353–54; "The Luck of the Devil" (2004), 75, 82n5; *Die Lücke, die der Teufel läßt* (The Devil's Blind Spot: Tales from the New Century, 2004), 13, 71–82, 432, 511n8; "Man without a Head" (2000), 72; "Maxwells Tod" (2004), 79, 83n11; "Die mißglückte Scheidung" (2004), 77, 83n10; *Neue Geschichten* (1977), 58, 68n1; "Outward Signs of Power's Decline" (2000), 61–62; "Qualification for Judicial Office" (2000), 51–52; "Rumblings of the Swallowed World" (2012), 107, 110n9; *Schlachtbeschreibung* (The Battle, 1964 and later editions), 3–4, 16, 43, 56–58, 68n1, 73, 82n4; *Temple of the Scapegoat: Opera Stories* (2018), 511n3; *Tür an Tür mit einem anderen Leben* (Next Door to Another Life, 2006), 13–14, 92, 94, 95; "Übergabe des Kindes" (Handing Over the Child, 2000), 50–51; "Undoing a Crime through Cooperation" (2000), 55–56; *Die Unheimlichkeit der Zeit* (The Uncanniness of Time, 2000), 76, 85; "Unintentional Stroke of Luck" (2004), 75, 82n7; "We Fortunate Children of the First Globalization" (2006), 94

Kluge, Alexander, television: "The Eiffel Tower, King Kong, and the White Woman" (1988), 321, 325–29, 330n2; *Minute Films* (from 1996), 98, 322, 330n3
Knight, Arthur, 172–73
Koch, Gertrud, 353–76
Koolhaas, Rem, 115, 330n3
Korsch, Karl, 92, 211
Kosovo, war in, 394
Kracauer, Siegfried, 5, 465
Krahl, Hans-Jürgen, 102, 110n6, 460
Kristl, Vlado, 164n5, 219
Kückelmann, Norbert, 219
Kuratorium junger deutscher Film (Board for Young German Film), 219
Kurnitzky, Horst, 156
Kursk, Battle of, 429–30
Kutusov, Mikhail, 39, 302

labor, concept of, 339–41
La Fayette, Madame de, 268; *The Princess of Cleves*, 95–96, 131
Laing, R. D., 181, 206n22
Land of Smiles (opera), 244
Lang, Fritz, 13, 151, 209, 217n5, 220, 361
Lang, Jack, 286
Langston, Richard, 22n42
language: Benjamin on, 465; film and, 123–39, 163n1; origins of, 413
laughter. *See* humor
Launch of an Ocean Steamer (film), 321
Leibniz, Gottfried Wilhelm, 95, 283, 298, 358–59, 496, 498; monads, 72, 95, 216, 275, 457
Lemke, Klaus, 219
Lenin, Vladimir Ilich, 493, 494
Leninism, 491
Lequeu, Jean-Jacques, 101
Lessing, Gotthold Ephraim, 234
libraries, 84–87, 98, 298, 410, 457
Ligeti, Györgi, 450
Lindner, Burkhardt, 462–81

literature: Adorno on, 73;
    antiliterature, 73–74; books and
    libraries, 84–87; collaboration,
    Kluge on, 67–68; collaboration/
    cooperation in, 67–68, 102,
    106; film compared, 125–31;
    by Kluge (*see* Kluge, Alexander,
    literature); Kluge's essays on, 13–14,
    25–118 (*see also specific essays*);
    Romanticism and, 80–81; short
    story form, Kluge's preference for,
    67. *See also* stories and storytelling;
    *and specific titles, under specific
    authors*
Liu Zheng, 508, 511n9
Louis Napoleon, "The Eighteenth
    Brumaire of Louis Napoleon," 497
Löwenthal, Leo, 470
Lubitsch, Ernst, 35
Ludwig (Louis) XVI (king of France),
    444
Luhmann, Niklas, 102, 110n6, 456,
    459–60
Lukács, Georg, 155–56
Lulu (Berg opera), 308
Lumet, Sidney, 131
Lumière brothers, 153, 156, 274, 321,
    322, 325
Luxemburg, Rosa, 35, 404

Madrid Conference, 62
Magic Flute (Mozart opera), 309,
    317n2
Malle, Louis, 127, 132, 135
Mann, Thomas, 5, 8, 81, 359, 453;
    Buddenbrooks, 44, 67
Mao Tse-tung and Maoism, 117, 312,
    491
Marne, Battle of, 106
The Marriage of Figaro (opera), 370
Marshall Plan, 401
Marx, Karl, 60, 89, 94, 164n8,
    339–41, 348, 356, 418, 422, 424,
    464, 465, 487–90, 493, 496–99,
    503–5; *Das Capital*, 173, 210, 497,
    499; *Economic and Philosophical
    Manuscripts*, 390n5; Eisenstein's
    Capital (proposed film), Kluge essay
    on, 208–16; *News from Ideological
    Antiquity: Marx-Eisenstein-
    "Capital"* (Kluge film, 2008), 5, 14,
    16, 111–18, 216, 484–510, 511n1
Marxism, 16, 66, 104, 111–18, 349,
    465, 491
Marxism-Leninism, 491
Mary Queen of Scots, 443
materialism, 44, 190, 214, 245, 344,
    348, 349, 354, 463, 480, 482n3, 487
Max Planck Institute, 102
McKinley, William, assassination of,
    318
McLuhan, Marshall, 321
Mead, George Herbert, 290nn1–2
media: in classical public sphere,
    254–55, 503; as concept, 11–12;
    concept of, 249–54; counter-media,
    502, 503; counterproduction
    and, 10, 270, 286–89, 453; direct
    versus indirect experience and,
    265–69, 284; division of labor,
    communication not based on, 265;
    dominance in, 458–59; as fantasy
    commodities, 275–78; human
    nervous system compared to viruses
    and computers, 257, 259–61, 263;
    interfaces, seams, and joints in,
    281–85, 292n24; isomorphism as
    category of relationality and,
    285–86; "On the Expressions
    'Media' and 'New Media'" (Kluge,
    1984), 21n19, 21n31, 249–89;
    radio, 185–86, 252, 258; reality, loss
    of, 267–68; remembering, forgetting,
    and reconstruction via, 269–71;
    suspense in, 278–80; telephone, as
    medium, 252; time and, 257,
    272–75. *See also* cinema; new
    media; television
media corporations, 194, 201, 256,
    345
"Medialization—Musealization"
    (Kluge, 1990), 293–304

Méhul, Étienne, 313
Meier, Christian, 380, 390n4
Meinecke, Eva Maria, 147, 153n3
The Meistersinger (opera), 60
Méliès, Georges, 156, 321, 322, 324
Melville, Herman, "Bartleby the Scrivener," 442
Mérimée, Prosper, *Carmen*, 447
metamorphosis, 67, 363, 365
metaphor: aesthetic theory and, 353, 354; antirealism of feeling and, 10; Kluge on film and, 126, 127, 129, 163n1, 303; Kluge on literature and, 32, 34, 36, 58, 64, 77, 92, 101, 106; Kluge on media and, 292n23, 296, 298; Kluge on theory and, 353, 354, 379, 416, 426, 428, 429, 430, 456, 476, 490, 504–5; "What Is a Metaphor?" (Kluge, 2016), 111–18
Metropolis (film), 209
microcomputers, 260
Mills, Jeff, 510
minute films, 319, 321–25, 330n3, 334
Minute Films (Kluge TV programs, from 1996), 98, 322, 330n3
Mir space station, 430
Miscellaneous News (Kluge film, 1986), 3
Missac, Pierre, 470
Moderato Cantabile (film), 134
modernity/modernism, 72, 79, 115, 209, 319, 334, 358, 370–71, 373, 383, 452, 457, 458, 486, 496
Modern Times (film), 184
monads, 72, 95, 216, 275, 457
montage: Eisenstein's theory of, 364, 367; in film, 124, 161, 170, 209, 364–65, 367; as principle in Kluge's work, 6
Montaigne, Michel de, 47, 81, 92, 132, 400, 411–12, 419, 474
Monteverdi, Claudio, 310–11
Montezuma, 311, 415
Mörike, Eduard, 204n3
"Moses and Aron" (Schoenberg opera fragment), 354, 377n5

movies. *See* cinema
Mozart, Wolfgang Amadeus, 60, 309, 317n2
Müller, Heiner, 81, 86, 327, 405n5, 419; "Mommsen's Block," 66–67
multidimensionality, 9, 106, 124, 131, 245, 478; multiple universes/parallel worlds, 62, 96. *See also* dialectics
multimedia systems, 263–64
musealization, 293–304
music: Adorno on, 354, 355, 357, 361, 362, 370, 377n5, 458; fantasy commodities in, 277; in film, 149–50, 153–54n4, 362, 485; "nobility of musical language" in opera, 242, 243–44
Musil, Robert: analytic writing of, 40; death of, 26, 28; feeling in work of, 52; on *fin de siècle*, 26–28; "The German as Symptom," 199–200; importance for Kluge, 5, 18; as Kleist Prize winner, 26, 41n2; *The Man without Qualities*, 26, 34–35, 52, 64, 68, 300, 323, 386, 439, 440; on miscommunication between intellect and soul, 37

Nagel, Ivan, *Autonomy and Mercy*, 388
Napoleon, 32, 39, 57, 62, 94, 106, 302, 393, 413, 428
National Socialism/Nazis, 41n2, 45, 48, 53, 69n11, 97–98, 156, 188, 190, 343–44, 346, 377n2
Negri, Antonio, 499
Negri, Pola, 25
Negt, Oskar, 12, 15, 16, 18, 348, 374. *See also* Kluge, Alexander, and Oskar Negt, *for specific coauthored texts*
Nekes, Werner, 219
Nepali Liberation Army, 491
Neumann, Franz, 190
New German Cinema, 3, 14, 218–24, 315, 361, 362
new media: classical public sphere versus, 254–55; concept of, 249–54;

concreteness of, 202; direct versus indirect experience and, 266, 284; Internet, 58, 98, 112, 331–36, 472, 474, 477–78, 480, 492–93, 497, 500; Kluge essays on, 14–15; movie theater attendance affected by, 275; multimedia systems, 263–64; "On the Expressions 'Media' and 'New Media'" (Kluge, 1984), 21n19, 21n31, 249–89; YouTube, 334, 480. *See also* television

"the new obscurity," 264–65, 284, 291n10

News from Ideological Antiquity: Marx-Eisenstein-"Capital" (Kluge film, 2008), 5, 14, 16, 111–18, 216, 484–510, 511n1

Niagara Falls (film), 321

Nicholas of Flüe, 427

Nietzsche, Friedrich, 64, 388, 418, 447, 448, 454

9/11, 73, 329, 451, 452, 458

"No Farewell to Yesterday: New German Cinema from 1962 to 1981, as Seen from 2011" (Kluge, 2012), 218–24

Nono, Luigi, 311, 489

No Shooting Time for Foxes (film), 223

now-time, 78, 86, 379

Oberhausen movement, 218–23, 362, 377n4

objectivity, 7, 37–38, 44–45, 88–91, 96, 103, 109, 115, 128, 134, 159–60, 173, 195, 205n18, 212, 221, 335–36, 351, 382, 384, 389, 408, 411, 422, 458, 466, 479. *See also* subjectivity

October (Eisenstein film), 208, 213

Odysseus/Ulysses, 47, 48, 60–61, 234, 245–46, 310, 429, 430; Homer's *Odyssey*, 47–49, 60, 61, 234, 245–46, 429, 431; Joyce's *Ulysses*, 208–9, 234, 490, 499

Oedipus, 232, 444–45, 490

Olympic Games (Berlin, 1936), television transmission of, 188

"On the Expressions 'Media' and 'New Media'" (Kluge, 1984), 21n19, 21n31, 249–89

opera: angel of death, in Verdi's *Aida*, 229–36, *233*; "An Answer to Two Opera Quotations" (Kluge, 1983/84), 229–47; counter-stories, as twentieth-century mission, 234, 245–47; curses in, 240; essays on, 14–15; film compared, 172, 313–16; "higher artistic truth" in, 242–43; Kluge's film *The Power of Emotion* (1983) on, 6, 15, 305–9; "local color," concept of, 242, 244; "nobility of musical language" in, 242, 243–44; Senta, in Wagner's *Flying Dutchman*, 236–42, *238, 241*; as storytelling, 60–61, 79; "summit of achievement" in, 242, 243; *Le vaisseau fantôme* (the phantom ship) as French title of Wagner's *Flying Dutchman*, 244–45; victim logic in, 309–13. *See also specific opera titles and operatic composers*

"The Opera Machine" (Kluge, 2001), 305–16

Opfergang (film), 97

orientation, 10–11, 16, 17, 30, 33, 45, 78–79, 96, 101–2, 155, 186, 266, 273, 278, 298, 332, 380, 383, 391n7, 454, 459, 488. *See also* experience

Orwell, George, 117

Osama bin Laden, 107

the other and otherness, 290n1, 422–24

Ovid: *Ars amatoria*, 456; *Metamorphoses*, 48, 52, 59, 81, 86, 96, 111–12, 333, 334, 411, 418–19, 452, 457, 490

pacifism, 403–4

Paracelsus, 409

The Parallel Street (*Parallelstrasse*, film), 134, 136–37

Paramount-Palace, Broadway, New York, *193*

Part-Time Work of a Female Slave (Kluge film, 1973), 5
Pascal, Blaise, 44
passions. *See* feeling(s)
Patalas, Enno, 14, 142–53, 205n13
The Patriot (Kluge film, 1979), 6, 89
Patzer, Harald, 359, 453
Pauli, Siegfried, 419–20
Pax Romana, 422
peace, 395–96, 400–404, 422. *See also* war
"The Peacemaker" (Kluge, 2003), 20n11, 21n29, 71–82
Peasants' War, 47, 102, 116, 297
perestroika, 301
Philippe, Louis, 463
Philoctetes, 90
photography, 187–88, 467
Piaget, Jean, 269–70, 285, 437
Piccinni, Nicolo, 312
"Planting Gardens in the Data Tsunami" (Kluge, 2010), 331–36
"A Plan with the Force of a Battleship" (Kluge, 2008), 208–16
Poe, Edgar Allan, 40, 474
Polanski, Roman, 135
the political, Wang Hui and Kluge on, 507–10
"The Political without Its Despair: On the Concept of 'Populism'" (Kluge, 1992), 378–89
polyphony, 106, 127, 136, 363, 365, 424, 457–59
Poor, Sara, 12
populism, 378–89
postmodernism, 281, 291n10, 372, 373
postsurrealism, 82n3
Pound, Ezra, 395, 405n5
The Power of Emotion (Kluge film, 1983), 6, 15, 305–9
prejudice, interaction as natural remedy against, 423–24
primitive accumulation, 90, 111–15
primitive diversity: in Benjamin's *Arcades Project*, 74; "Primitive Diversity" (Kluge, 2002, on early short films from American East Coast), 318–29
printing press, invention of, 187, 332
production, 8, 15, 16, 90, 98, 113, 114, 125, 127, 132, 138–39, 159, 160–62, 170, 173, 178–80, 184–86, 188, 195–97, 201, 206n26, 221, 265, 268, 272, 275–76, 280, 283, 290n1, 294, 295, 298–300, 303, 340, 345, 357, 367, 375, 381, 385, 387, 389, 402, 414, 415, 429, 467, 490, 497, 509; counterproduction, 10, 270, 286–89, 453; overproduction, 189; symbolic production, 180, 182, 195
programs, viruses and computers organized as, 257, 259–61, 263
progress, 90–91
Prokop, Dieter, 185
Proust, Marcel, *À la recherche du temps perdu*, 68, 78, 79, 81, 96–97, 128, 202, 274, 277, 364, 471
Prussian State Library, 30
public spheres, 15, 186–87, 254–55, 256, 265, 345–46, 373–76, 396, 459, 502, 503
Pückler-Muskau, Hermann Ludwig Heinrich von, 293–94, 304n1, 334
pulse lasers, 194–95
Punic Wars, 399, 401
Pushpa Kamal Dahal, 491, 511n5

QWERTY keyboards, 409

Rabelais, François, 96
Racine, Jean, *Mithridate*, 393
Rack, Jochen, 43–68
radio, 185–86, 252, 258
Radisch, Iris, 7, 10
railways and trains, 172–75, 174, 206n19, 274, 325
Rambo I–VI (films), 368
Reagan, Ronald, 64
"The Realistic Method and the 'Filmic'" (Kluge, 1975), 6, 20n6, 155–63
reality principle, 9, 356, 367, 373, 400, 422

reality/realism: antirealism/antirealism of feeling, 9, 21n25, 72, 88, 89, 103–4, 388, 420–21, 451; cinema and, 132, 152–53, 155–63, 172, 183–86, 189, 486; concepts of time and, 30; Critical Theory and, 103; juxtaposing forms of diversity, 459–60; Kluge's mistrust of, 421; Kluge's theory of, 9–10; media and loss of, 267–68; populism and, 379; "The Realistic Method and the 'Filmic'" (Kluge, 1975), 6, 20n6; "The Sharpest Ideology: That Reality Appeals to Its Realistic Character" (Kluge), 21n25; storytelling and multiplicities of, 103–7; translation of *(Wirklichkeit, Realität)*, 18, 109n4; way out from prison of, 9–10, 76

Regenstein, young woman imprisoned by count of, 236

Reich-Ranicki, Marcel, 320, 323, 330n1, 440

reification, 148, 157, 506

Reinke, Wilfried, 8; "Word and Film" (with Reitz and Kluge, 1965), 12, 14, 20n18, 123–39

Reitz, Edgar, 8, 219, 377n4; "Word and Film" (with Kluge and Reinke, 1965), 12, 14, 20n18, 123–39

relationality: Adorno on, 457; counterproduction and, 286–87; between events across time, 75–76; fantasy commodities and, 277; in film, 156, 486; "higher artistic truth" and, 243; interruption in chain of actions making relationalities visible, 442; isomorphism and, 285–86; Kleist and, 33; prejudice, as natural remedy against, 423–24; sound levels and, 39; storytelling and, 72–73, 78–79, 88–98; "Storytelling Means Dissolving Relations" (Kluge, 2008), 88–98; *Zusammenhangs* (relationality/context), 9, 18, 176, 190, 243, 291n18

Rentschler, Eric, 21n38

republican process, 381

Resnais, Alain, 134, 136

Return of Ulysses (Monteverdi opera), 310

Reykjavik Summit (1985), 64

Richardson, L. F., 399–400

Richter, Hans Werner, 220

Rihm, Wolfgang, 310–11

Rimbaud, Arthur, 463

The River Line (Kennwort: Reiher, film), 132

Robespierre, Maximilien, 494

Robinson Crusoe and Robinsonism, 27, 250, 267, 269, 283, 308, 421, 459

robots as form of emotional intelligence, 417

Roehler, Oskar, 219

Roehm, Ernst, 344

"The Role of Fantasy" (Kluge, 1974), 339–52

Roman antiquity, 33, 58, 59–60, 283, 288, 380, 387, 390n3, 391n6, 392, 418, 422, 424, 428, 430, 433n3, 485

Romantics and Romanticism, 80–81, 357, 358, 440

Rommel, Erwin, 188, 344

Rose, Reginald, 131

Rossbach, Battle of, 393

Rossellini, Roberto, 315, 322

Roth, Max, 344

Russia, Napoleonic invasion of/retreat from, 32, 39, 57, 62, 106, 302, 413

Russian Revolution, 35, 276, 427

Rutschley, Michael, 5

Ruttmann, Walter, 212

Salabè, Piero, 88–98

Saroyan, William, 131

Sartre, Jean-Paul, 131

Savonarola, Girolamo, 424

Schamoni, Peter, 3, 223

Schikaneder, Emanuel, 309, 317n2

Schiller, Friedrich, 309, 443

Schleef, Einar, 81

Schlegel, August Wilhelm von, 440
Schleiermacher, Detten, 377n4
Schleyer, Hans-Martin, 430, 433n5
Schlingensief, Christoph, 67, 219
Schlöndorff, Volker, 219, 221, 223
Schmidt, Arno, 164n7, 234
Schmidt, Helmut, 223
Schmitt, Carl, 390n2
Schoenberg, Arnold, 311, 354, 377n5, 416
Scholem, Gershom, 470, 478
Schulte, Christian: dialogues between Kluge and, 305–16, 318–29; ed., *In Gefahr und größter Not bringt der Mittelweg den Tod*, 13, 20n3; on Kluge as film essayist, 20n4
Schütz, Heinrich, 312
Schwaiger, Reinholz, 194
Schwarz-Schilling, Federal Minister, 187, 189, 204
Scorsese, Martin, 315
Sebald, W. G., 86
segregation in urban development, 281–82
Seitz, Franz, 220
Sennett, Richard, 115, 183, 473, 493
sensations versus feeling(s), 408
sensory experience, 9, 64, 159, 161, 167, 217, 243–44, 270, 273, 342, 351, 386, 448, 463–64, 466. *See also specific sensory organs and senses*
September 11, 2001, 73, 329, 451, 452, 458
Seven Years' War, 392
Shakespeare, William, 66, 86, 182; *Hamlet*, 164n7, 441–42; *Othello*, 437
Sharp, Dennis, 172
Sheldrake, Rupert, 409, 410
Shishi, concept of, 487–88
Shub, Esther, 216–17n5
Simone Bocanegra (opera), 243
skin, as sensory organ, 9, 91, 137, 190, 407–8, 446–47, 453, 454
Sleeping Beauty (fairy tale), 240, 270, 452

Sloterdijk, Peter, 418
smells and smelling, 137, 408
Smith, Adam, 395, 405n5, 456
socialism, 35, 349–51, 404, 496, 509
Socrates, 284
Soldaten (Zimmermann opera), 79
Solferino, Battle of, 396
Song of Roland, 57, 430
Sophocles, 445
Soviet avant-garde film, 14. *See also* Eisenstein, Sergei; Vertov, Dziga
Spanish Civil War, 302
Spartacists/Spartacus League, 35, 404
Spengler, Oswald, 510
Der Spiegel (film), 323
Spiegel Crisis/Affair (1962), 43, 68n2
Sprenger, Ulrike, 317n1
Springer Verlag, 345, 352n1
Stalin, Joseph, and Stalinism, 112, 476
Stalingrad, Battle of (in Kluge's *The Battle*), 3–4, 16, 43, 56–58, 68n1, 73, 82n4, 429–30
Star Wars/SDI, 37, 395
the Stasi, 117, 323
Staudte, Wolfgang, 220
St. Bartholomew's Day massacre, 411, 414
Stein, Karl vom, 30
Sternberger, Dolf, *Panorama of the 19th Century*, 472
stock market crash (Black Friday; 1929), 210–11, 395
Stollmann, Rainer, 111–18, 413
stories and storytelling: Adorno on, 78, 79; autobiographical elements in Kluge's stories, 93–94; *belles lettres* tradition, 93; books/libraries and, 85; collaboration/cooperation in, 67–68, 102, 106; compression in, 79–80; cooperation, role of, 102, 106; counter-stories, 234; facts and fakes in, 418; heterogeneous stories, juxtaposition of, 92–93, 95–97; history and, 73, 94–95; influences on Kluge, 81, 92; reality, multiplicities of, 103–7; relationality and, 72–73, 78–79, 88–98; social body formed

by, 431–32; "Storytelling Is the Representation of Differences" (Kluge, 2001), 43–68; "Storytelling Means Dissolving Relations" (Kluge, 2008), 88–98; "Theory of Storytelling: Lecture One" (Kluge, 2013), 20n12, 21n25, 21n26, 21n28, 21n30, 100–109
Störtebecker, Klaus, 55
Stranger Than Paradise (film), 274
Straschek, Günter Peter, 157, 161
Straub, Jean-Marie, 164n5, 219
Strauß, Botho, 5
Strauss, Johann, 210
Strauss, Richard, 311, 312
Strobel, Hans-Rolf, 219
Strousberg, Barthel Heinrich, 175, 206n19
subjectivity, 31, 44, 164n7, 169, 211, 212, 307, 315, 382, 387, 458, 500, 506, 507. *See also* objectivity
surrealism and surrealists, 365, 369, 463, 482n3
suspense, 168–69, 172, 205nn12–13, 278–80, 316
Swimming Contest on Horses (film), 321
symbols and symbolism: direct experience and symbolic sequences, 267; in film, 177, 178–82, 195; in opera, 244–45
Systems Theory, 102. *See also* Luhmann, Niklas

Tacitus, 81, 485
Talmud, 58, 211
Tarkovsky, Andrei, 274, 280; *Sculpting in Time*, 274
telephone, as medium, 252
television: aesthetic theory and, 367; auteurism in, 14, 15; DCTP (Development Company for Television Program), 4, 330n5; as dominant medium, 458–59; essays on, 15; external pluralism, 196–97; feeling(s) in, 185–86; film and, 172–73, 188–89, 202; Kluge's work in, 4, 13, 15 (*see also* Kluge, Alexander, television, *for specific shows*); in "Medialization— Musealization" (Kluge, 1990), 293–94, 303; media/new media, concept of, 249–55; oral tradition and, 255–57; programming, 15, 183, 252–53, 255–56, 274, 275, 283, 325; Star Wars (SDI) commercial, 37; terrestrial reconnection of, 297; time and, 272, 273–74; "Word and Film" (Kluge, Reitz, and Reinke, 1965) on, 8, 139. *See also specific shows by title*
terrorism: September 11, 2001, attacks, 73, 329, 451, 452, 458; wedding party mistaken for terrorists, pilot's diarrhea preventing bombing of, 75, 442–43, 495
theory: Critical Theory, 18, 58–59, 100–103, 367, 374; of critique, 434–48; of feeling(s), 16, 412–31; history, Benjamin on, 59, 60, 354; Kluge essays on, 15–16, 339–510; of populism, 378–89; on reality/realism, 9–10; Systems Theory, 102; of war, 392–405. *See also* aesthetic theory; difference/differentiation; fantasy
"Theory of Storytelling: Lecture One" (Kluge, 2013), 20n12, 21n25, 21n26, 21n28, 21n30, 100–109
Theurisch, Siegfried, 425
Thirty Years' War, 393
The Threepenny Opera (Brecht), 77, 83n8, 157
Tichawsky, Heinz, 219
Tieck, Ludwig, 440
The Tiger of Eschnapur (film, 1959), 13
Tillich, Paul, 101
time: concepts of, 30–31; deceleration principle and gaining, 257, 262, 272; differentiation and, 271–73; film and, 166–67, 202, 257, 272, 273–75; losing, 272–73; now-time, 78, 86, 379; television and, 272, 273–74

Titanic (ship), 321, 488–89
Tolstoy, Leo, 81; *Anna Karenina*, 78, 91, 95, 309, 370, 448
Traffic in Front of the Opera House in Paris (film), 321
trains and railways, 172–75, *174*, 206n19, 274, 325
translation, 112–13, 176–78, 184, 195, 250, 253, 264–66, 274, 285, 300, 355, 382, 385, 441; Kluge essays, reading and translating, 16–19
Tristan and Isolde, 54, 447–48
Truffaut, François, 124, 205nn11–13, 278–79, 322
trust, basic, 46, 417–19, 428–29
Turandot (opera), 244
Turgot, Anne Robert Jacques, 187
Twelve Angry Men (film), 131
Tykwer, Tom, 219

urban development, segregation in, 281–82
utopia, Kluge's sense of, 74–75, 143, 365, 367

Le vaisseau fantôme (the phantom ship) as French title of Wagner's *Flying Dutchman*, 244–45
The Valkyrie (Wagner opera), 231, 232
vampire, Dutchman as, in Wagner's *Flying Dutchman*, 237–39, *238*
van der Waal forces, 410
Venice Film Festival, 14, 98
Verdi, Giuseppe, 229–36, *233*, 242–44, 247, 311, 370
Verdun, Battle of, 35, 46, 73, 75, 89, 335, 397, 398
Verhoeven, Paul, 219
Verne, Jules, 156
Versailles, Treaty of (1919), 401, 422
Vertov, Dziga, 209, 216
victim logic in opera, 309–13
video games, 170
Vienna, Congress of, 30, 393, 395, 400
Vietnam War, 395
viruses and computers organized as programs, 257, *259–61*, 263

Vivre sa vie (film), 132, 134
Vogl, Joseph, 434–48
Volksempfänger (1942), *258*
Voltaire, 508; *Candide*, 335

The Wages of Fear (film), 36–37
Wagner, Richard, 50, 60, 78, 140n6, 206n18, 209, 221, 225n2, 231, 232, 236–42, 244–46, 279, 311, 343, 447, 485
Waldleitner, Ludwig, 220
Wallmann, Walter, 303
Wang Ge, 484–510, 511n1, 511n9
Wang Hui, 16, 484–510, 511n1
Wang Laoshi, 487
war: achievements and limitations due to, 396–97; causes of, 399–400; defined, 392, 394; deserters, 405; experience of, 398–99; historical evolution of, 392–96; the other and otherness, 422–24; peace/disbelief in necessity of, 395–96, 400–404, 422; "War" (Kluge, 2001), 392–405; war crimes, 397–98. *See also specific wars and battles*
"War" (Kluge, 2001), 392–405
Waterloo, Battle of, 33
weather, as historical actor, 64–65
Weimann, Martin, 86
Weimar Republic, 41n2, 119n4, 343, 346, 376–77n2, 385
Weiss, Peter, 67
Welles, Orson, 137
Wenders, Wim, 164n7, 219, 221, 366
Wendtlandt, Horst, 220
"What Is a Metaphor?" (Kluge, 2016), 111–18
Wicki, Bernhard, 152, 154n6, 220
Wieland, Christoph Martin, 29
Wilhelm II (Kaiser), 301
Wings of Desire (film), 366
Wischke, Mirko, *426*, 426–27
Wolf, Friedrich August, 374
"Word and Film" (by Kluge, Reitz, and Reinke; 1965), 12, 14, 20n18, 123–39

Workers Leaving the Factory (film), 325
World War I, 26, 35, 44, 46, 65, 88–89, 106, 116, 244, 399–400, 401, 429, 472, 476, 488. *See also specific battles and events*
World War II, 26–27, 28, 44, 93, 142, 306, 328, 343–44, 394, 398–99, 401, 476. *See also specific battles, events, and groups, e.g.*, National Socialism
Wozzek (Berg opera), 79
Wrong Move (film), 164n7

Xi Jinping, 501

Yesterday Girl (Kluge film, 1966), 13, 14, 142–53, 291n9, 359, 361, 453
Young Törless (film), 223
YouTube, 334, 480

Zazie dans le métro (film), 132, 134
Zeit der Schuldlosen (*The Time of Your Life*, film), 131
Zhuang Zhou, 505
Zimmermann, Friedrich, 79, 220
Zola, Emil, 213

www.ingramcontent.com/pod-product-compliance
Lightning Source LLC
Chambersburg PA
CBHW020216240426
43672CB00006B/333